HISTORICAL DICTIONARY

The historical dictionaries present essential information on a broad range of subjects, including American and world history, art, business, cities, countries, cultures, customs, film, global conflicts, international relations, literature, music, philosophy, religion, sports, and theater. Written by experts, all contain highly informative introductory essays on the topic and detailed chronologies that, in some cases, cover vast historical time periods but still manage to heavily feature more recent events.

Brief A–Z entries describe the main people, events, politics, social issues, institutions, and policies that make the topic unique, and entries are cross-referenced for ease of browsing. Extensive bibliographies are divided into several general subject areas, providing excellent access points for students, researchers, and anyone wanting to know more. Additionally, maps, photographs, and appendixes of supplemental information aid high school and college students doing term papers or introductory research projects. In short, the historical dictionaries are the perfect starting point for anyone looking to research in these fields.

HISTORICAL DICTIONARIES OF PEOPLES AND CULTURES

Jon Woronoff, Series Editor

Southeast Asian Massif, by Jean Michaud, 2006.
Berbers (Imazighen), by Hsain Ilahiane, 2006.
Tamils, by Vijaya Ramaswamy, 2007.
Gypsies, 2nd ed., by Donald Kenrick, 2007.
Kurds, 2nd ed., by Michael M. Gunter, 2011.
Jews, by Alan Unterman, 2011.
Catalans, by Helena Buffery and Elisenda Marcer, 2011.
Australian Aboriginals, by Mitchell Rolls and Murray Johnson, 2011.
Ismailis, by Farhad Daftary, 2012.
Bengalis, by Kunal Chakrabarti and Shubhra Chakrabarti, 2013.
Inuit, 2nd ed., by Pamela R. Stern, 2013.
Druzes, 2nd ed., by Samy Swayd, 2015.
Bedouins, by Muhammad Suwaed, 2015.

Historical Dictionary of the Bedouins

Muhammad Suwaed

ROWMAN & LITTLEFIELD
Lanham • Boulder • New York • London

Published by Rowman & Littlefield
A wholly owned subsidiary of The Rowman & Littlefield Publishing Group, Inc.
4501 Forbes Boulevard, Suite 200, Lanham, Maryland 20706
www.rowman.com

Unit A, Whitacre Mews, 26-34 Stannary Street, London SE11 4AB

British Library Cataloguing in Publication Information Available

Library of Congress Cataloging-in-Publication Data

Suwaed, Muhammad
Historical dictionary of the Bedouins / Muhammad Suwaed.
pages cm. — (Historical dictionaries of peoples and cultures)
Includes bibliographical references.
ISBN 978-1-4422-5450-3 (hardcover : alk. paper) — ISBN 978-1-4422-5451-0 (ebook)
1. Bedouins—History—Dictionaries. I. Title.
DS36.9.B4S86 2015
305.892'72003—dc23
2015024415

∞™ The paper used in this publication meets the minimum requirements of American National Standard for Information Sciences Permanence of Paper for Printed Library Materials, ANSI/NISO Z39.48-1992.

Printed in the United States of America

Contents

Editor's Foreword

The Bedouins have traditionally been people of the desert. For centuries they were strongly rooted there, migrating to find water or food for their herds, and this wandering is largely what distinguished them from other Arabs living in the region. Migrations have become less frequent, and many Bedouins have settled down to farm or have moved to towns or cities. They are still culturally different, however, due in part to their attachment to tribes and clans. There are only 25 million or so Bedouins, but they continue to play a role in two dozen different countries spread over the Middle East and Northern Africa. They are an "international" and "tribal" people whose reality is quite different than the romantic perception of popular culture.

This *Historical Dictionary of the Bedouins* focuses on the reality, describing those who still ride camels and migrate periodically but also those who are part of mainstream populations. Dictionary entries address life, food, clothing, and homes; tribe, clan, and family; loyalty and revenge (the vendetta); education, culture, and religion; migration, sedentarization, and urbanization; significant people; warfare against the Byzantine and Ottoman Empires; Western colonizers; events during the recent Arab Spring; and the many countries that have large Bedouin populations. The bibliography provides sources for further reading.

This book was written by Muhammad Suwaed, a leading scholar on the Bedouins and of Bedouin origin. He is a senior lecturer in the Department of Social Sciences in Western Galilee College and Kinneret College in Israel. His field of specialization is the society, culture, and politics of the Middle East, but his primary focus has long been the Bedouins. In 1994 he was distinguished by the prime minister of Israel for his work on the Bedouins. Obviously, he is a close observer of the Bedouins in Israel, which helps him understand the intriguing situation there. Over the past few decades he has written substantially on related topics, including two books on the Bedouins in Palestine.

Jon Woronoff
Series Editor

Acknowledgments

It gives me great pleasure to thank the many people and institutions that assisted me in writing this book. Firstly, I would like to thank Jon Woronoff for his suggestion to write this historical dictionary on the Bedouins and for his instruction and guidance during the writing. He was involved and showed interest in every detail and article.

I would especially like to express appreciation for the research fund from Western Galilee College and Kinneret College, whose support helped me to reduce the financial burden that was involved in writing the book.

I would like to express my feelings of esteem and thanks to the staff working in the library at Western Galilee College and Kinneret College for the patience and support they showed me during the many hours I spent writing the book there.

Finally, I would like to thank my family members for their willingness to support me throughout the long period of time I was occupied with this study despite the difficulty this caused them.

Reader's Notes

When writing Arabic names using English transliteration, there are no clear and precise rules. Sometimes a name has a number of written forms, for example, *Mhmd* to Mohammad or Muhammad, Quran to Koran or Qur'an, and Mecca to Makka or Mekkah. There are usually two forms of transliteration, for literal writing and phonetic transcription. The first form is writing the source in English letters, and the second method is copying the phonology, namely the pronunciation of the source, to a word parallel to it in English without being restricted by letters. For example, *Ahmd* in the first method is written as Ahmd, while in the second method is Ahmad. In addition, the more common name is written using the second method.

As languages have different phonological characteristics, in many cases it is impossible to execute a "perfect" transliteration that will enable a reader in the target language to express the transliterated word in the source language. Therefore, in transliteration I was forced to "compromise" every so often and renounce linguistic precision. Sometimes I use the accepted name in English, as transliteration is not possible. Thus I use Egypt instead of Masr and Jordan instead of El-Ourdun.

Acronyms and Abbreviations

AD	Anno Domini (in the Christian Era)
AP	Arabian Peninsula
ARAMCO	Arabian American Oil Company
BC	Before Christ
BM	British Mandate
CBS	Central Bureau of Statistics
CE	Christian Era
FAO	Food and Agriculture Organization
FIS	Islamic Salvation Front
FLN	Front de Libération Nationale
IAF	Israeli Air Force
ICC	International Criminal Court
IDF	Israel Defense Forces
JEM	Justice and Equality Movement
LIFG	Libyan Islamic Fighting Group
NTC	National Transitional Council
PKK	Kurdish Workers' Party
PLO	Palestine Liberation Organization
SA	Saudi Arabia
SLA	Sudan Liberation Army
SPLA	Sudan People's Liberation Army
UAE	United Arab Emirates
UAL	United Arab List
UAR	United Arab Republic
UN	United Nations
UNRWA	United Nations Relief and Works Agency

Map

ATLANTIC OCEAN
STRAIT OF GIBRALTAR
SPAIN
MOROCCO
WESTERN SAHARA
MAURITANIA
SENEGAL
MALI
ALGERIA
SAHARA DESERT
TUNISIA
MALTA
MEDITERRANEAN SEA
LIBYA
NIGER
CHAD
GREECE
CRETE
EGYPT
SUDAN
CYPRUS
LEBANON
ISRAEL
Suez canal
TURKEY
BLACK SEA
SYRIA
JORDAN
RED SEA
ERITREA
ETHIOPIA
DJIBOUTI
SOMALIA
IRAQ
SAUDI ARABIA
YEMEN
KUWAIT
BAHRAIN
QATAR
PERSIAN GULF
U.A.E.
OMAN
ARABIAN SEA
INDIAN OCEAN
IRAN
RUSSIA
GEORGIA
ARMENIA
AZERBAIJAN
CASPIAN SEA
KAZAKHSTAN
UZBEKISTAN
TURKMENISTAN
AFGHANISTAN
0
1000 KM.
©A. Orgad Maps

Chronology

3000–200 BC Thamud kingdom in Yemen.

1200–275 BC Yemenite kingdom of Saba.

722 BC Destruction of Kingdom of Israel by Sennacherib, king of Assyria.

400–300 BC Nabateans enter Palestine.

300 BC–AD 200 Minaean Kingdom in Arabia.

241–238 BC First Punic War between Rome and Carthage.

148 BC Death of Massinissa, King of Numidia.

146 BC Destruction of Carthage.

115 BC Foundation of Himyar Kingdom in Yemen.

112–106 BC Jugurthine War between Rome and Numidia.

103–76 BC Rule of Alexander Yannai.

100 BC Expulsion of the Nabateans from the Negev.

37–4 BC Rule of Herod the Great.

AD 105 Annexation of Nabatean Kingdom to Roman Empire.

106 Death of last Nabatean King Rabbel II.

220–638 Rule of Ghassanid tribe in Arabia.

268–633 Rule of Muntherids in the kingdom of Al-Hira in southwest Iraq.

400–480 Qusai ibn Kilab, leader of the Quraysh tribe, who rehabilitated the el-Kaabah.

464–497 Hashim ibn ‘Abd Manaf, great-grandfather of Muhammad, made Mecca a center of commerce.

494–524 Basus War in Arabia between Taghlib and Bakr tribes.

523 Massacre of Himyar Christians in the town of Najran.

531 Foundation of Arab-Roman kingdom in Arabia under kings of Ghassan.

570 Collapse of Marib dam in Yemen.

610 Appearance of the Islamic religion.

622 Muhammad immigrates to Medina. Start of Hijra.

624 Battle of Badr, deportation from Arabia of Jews members of the Qainuqa tribe after Muhammad failed to convert them.

625 Siege of Medina and deportation of the Banu Nadir tribe.

627 Siege of the Jewish tribe Banu Qurayza in Medina by the Quraysh tribe of Muhammad, their surrender to the Muslims, and their decapitation.

630 Conquest of Mecca by Muhammad. Conversion of Oman to Islam.

632 Delegation of Tayy tribes from Palestine reaches Mecca. Death of Muhammad.

634–644 Rule of Umar.

637 Fall of Jerusalem to Caliph Umar. Battle of Qadisiyah and fall of jazira, Iraq.

638 Muslims defeat the Ghassanids in the battle of Yarmoukh. Annexation of the Himyar Kingdom by Persian king Khorsau I to the Sassanian Empire.

644–656 Rule of Uthman.

656–661 Rule of Ali.

661–680 Rule of Mu'awiyah, first Umayyad caliph.

661–750 Umayyad dynasty.

661–714 Al-Hajjaj ibn Yussuf, minister of defense of Umayyad Kingdom.

684–685 Marwan Umayyad, caliph, founds Marwanid dynasty.

744–750 Rule of Marwan II, last Umayyad caliph. Start of Abbasid caliphate.

751 Downfall of Umayyad dynasty.

896 First Zaydi Imam in Yemen.

968–1171 Fatimid caliphate in Egypt.

1052 Bani Hilal defeat of Zirids in a battle at Haidaran.

1057 Conquest of Kairouan by Bani Hilal.

1071 Seljuks win battle of Manzikert in eastern Turkey.

1171–1250 Ayyubid dynasty in Egypt.

1244 Beginning of Marinid dynasty rule of Morocco.

1250–1517 Mameluke dynasty in Egypt.

1258 End of the Abbasid caliphate.

1268 Yemeni tribesmen attack Sada.

1332 Birth of philosopher of history Ibn Khaldun.

1389 Battle of Kosovo and Ottoman conquest of Serbia.

1402 Tamerlane defeats Ottomans in battle of Ankara.

1406 Death of Ibn Khaldun.

1453 Ottomans capture Constantinople and end of Byzantine Empire.

1465 Murder of heir to Marinid dynasty in Morocco and end of the dynasty.

1501–1722 Rule of Safavid dynasty in Iran.

1507–1650 Portuguese rule of Oman.

1516 Ottoman conquest of Palestine.

1534 Ottoman conquest of Tunisia.

1543 Conquest of Iraq by Ottoman Empire.

1620 Death of Yemenite imam Qasim ibn Muhammad, founder of Qasimite dynasty.

1702 Birth of Abdul-Wahab.

1735 Battle in Yizrael Valley and defeat of House of Madi by Daher el-Omar.

1744–1822 First Saudi state.

1749 Rise of Al Said to power in Oman; his family still rules today.

1752 Utub tribe build a mud wall around Kuwait City.

1762 Ascent of Al-Sabah family to dominance in Kuwait.

1775 Death of Daher el-Omar in Acre.

1783 Penetration into Bahrain of Utub tribes from Arabian Peninsula, end of Iranian domination.

1796–1925 Reign of Qajar dynasty in Iran.

1799 Napoleon's siege of Acre.

1804 Death of Ahmed Jazzar.

1805–1819 Ottoman Suleiman Pasha is governor of Palestine.

1812 Visit to Palestine and Eastern Transjordan by Johann Ludwig Burckhardt.

1819–1831 Ottoman Abdullah Pasha is governor of Palestine.

1820 Britain gives control over Bahrain to Al-Khalifa family.

1823–1891 Second Saudi state.

1830 French invasion of Algeria.

1831 Egyptian conquest of Palestine and Syria.

1832 Tanzimat reforms in Ottoman Empire. Choice of Manama as home by British political agent, Bahrain becomes British protectorate.

1834 Revolt in Palestine against the Egyptians by the House of Madi. Death of the Madi family's leader, Sheikh Massoud, who is killed by the Egyptians. Aqil Aga also took part in the revolt.

1836 Foundation of Emirate of Al-Rasheed in Nejd, Arabia.

1840 Departure of Egyptians from Palestine.

1858 Ottoman law of lands in Palestine.

1859 Death of Muhammad al-Sanusi, founder of Sanusi Lodges in Libya.

1860 Conflict between Druze and Christians in Lebanon, massacre of Muslims in Lebanon and Damascus.

1861 Ottoman tabu law in Palestine.

1865 Conquest of Riyadh by Al-Rasheed, forcing the House of Saud into exile.

1870 Death of Al-Hasi Aqil Aga.

1880 Birth of Ibn Saud. Revolt of Iranian Kurds. Start of Bahrain as a British protectorate.

1881 Establishment of French protectorate in Tunisia.

1902 Conquest of Riyadh by Ibn Saud.

1906–1911 Constitutional revolution in Iran.

1911 Italy declares war on Turkey and attacks Libya.

1912 Italy is granted control of Libya in the Treaty of Lausanne.

1914 Sanusi revolt against Italy in Libya.

1915 Death of emir of Kuwait Mubarak al-Sabah, suspected by the British of supporting Turkey.

1916 Sykes-Picot agreement on division of the Ottoman Empire between Great Britain and France.

1916–1917 Arab revolt against the Turks under Lawrence of Arabia.

1917 Balfour Declaration on Jewish national home in Palestine. British conquest of Palestine and Iraq from Ottoman Empire.

1918 Emir Faisal and T. E. Lawrence enter Damascus in order to establish the Kingdom of Syria.

1918–1948 Rule of Zaydi imam Yahya in North Yemen.

1919 Foundation of municipality of Manama.

1919 War of Arab el-Fadal tribe under Emir Mahmoud Faour against the French in south Lebanon.

1919–1920 Hashemite Kingdom of Syria.

1920 King Abdullah proclaimed emir of Transjordan. Defeat of Emir Faisal by French troops and foundation of French Mandate in Syria. Also foundation of Contrôle Bédouin corps in Syria.

1921 Annexation of Kurdish areas in Caucasus to Turkey. Coronation of King Faisal as first king of Iraq.

1922 Winston Churchill announces separation between Palestine and Transjordan and separate management in both territories.

1923 Balka tribe revolt in Transjordan.

1923–1932 Second war between Sanusis and Italians in Libya.

1925–1927 Druze revolt against the French in Syria.

1925–1944 Reign of Reza Pahlavi in Iran.

1926 Foundation of the Republic of Lebanon.

1927 Ikhwan revolt in Saudi Arabia.

1931 Foundation of Desert Patrol by Glubb Pasha in Jordan.

1932 Establishment of the kingdom of Saudi Arabia. National census in Lebanon.

1936–1939 Arab revolt against the British in Palestine.

1940 Legislation of French Mandate Law of Tribes in Syria.

1943 End of French rule in Syria and Lebanon.

1944–1979 Reign of Mohammad Reza Pahlavi in Iran.

1947 United Nations decision on partition of Palestine.

1948 Israeli War of Independence.

1951 UN declares Libya independent. King Idris the First is proclaimed ruler.

1953 Abolition of French Mandate Law of Tribes by Syrian government.

1954 Israel grants the Bedouins Israeli citizenship. Murder of 11 Israelis in Scorpions' Pass by Azazme tribesmen.

1956 Independence of Morocco and Tunisia.

1958 Dismissal of King Faisal II of Iraq and his prime minister and their murder by General Abd al-Karim Qasim and his "Free Officers." Foundation of United Arab Republic unites Egypt and Syria.

1961 Breakup of United Arab Republic.

1962 Algerian independence from France through Treaty of Evian. Last Zaydi Imam in Yemen. Abu Dhabi first emirate to export oil.

1962–1970 Civil War between North and South Yemen.

1967 Six-Day War between Israel and Arabs and Israeli conquest of Golan, Sinai, Judea, and Samaria.

1968 Baath Party takeover of power in Iraq.

1969 Colonel Muammar Gadhafi overthrows King Idris in military coup.

1970 Fighting between Jordan army and Palestinian fighters in Jordan: Black September.

1971 Withdrawal of British protection from Arab Trucial Sheikhdoms and foundation of United Arab Emirates.

1973 October (Yom Kippur) War between Israel, Syria, and Egypt.

1974 At Arab summit in Rabat, Morocco, the Palestinian Liberation Organization is declared the sole legitimate representative of the Palestinian people.

1976 Outbreak of Lebanese Civil War between Christians, Muslims, and Druze.

1979 Islamic revolution in Iran led by Ayatollah R. Khomeini. Peace Treaty between Egypt and Israel. Return of Sinai to Egypt.

1980–1988 Iran-Iraq War.

1981 Assassination of Egyptian president Anwar Sadat. Foundation of Gulf Cooperation Council.

1982 Massacre in Hama by Syrian troops of Hafez al-Assad. "Peace for Galilee" Operation by Israel in Lebanon. Assassination of Lebanese president Bashir Jemayel. Sabra and Shatilla massacre by Phalange Christians of Palestinians and departure of Arafat and his PLO leadership to Tunis.

1987 Foundation of Desert Rangers unit in IDF.

1990 Unification of North and South Yemen.

1991 First Gulf War after invasion of Kuwait by Iraq under Saddam Hussein. Shiite Intifada in Iraq. Death of Amos Yarkoni, senior Bedouin tracker in the IDF.

1992 Civil war in Algeria.

1994 Signature of Oslo Accords between Jordan under King Hussein, PLO under Yasser Arafat, and Israel under leadership of Rabin and Peres: foundation of Palestinian Authority, withdrawal of Israeli troops from West Bank and Gaza.

1999 Ascent of King Abdullah II to Jordanian throne.

2000 Death of Hafez al-Assad and rise to power of his son, Bashar al-Assad.

2003 Fall of Saddam Hussein from power in Iraq after American invasion.

2010 Outbreak of riots in Tunisia, which led to Arab Spring revolt in the whole of the Middle East.

2011 Outbreak of Syrian Civil War and revolution against Bashar al-Assad. Civil war breaks out in Libya. Tribes help to overthrow Colonel Muammar Gadhafi in Libya by Islamic revolutionaries. Arab Spring revolt also breaks out in Yemen against rule of President Abdullah Ali Salieh.

2012 Salieh is dismissed in Yemen.

2013 President Mohamed Morsi is deposed from office by coup in Egypt. He is placed on trial.

2014 Israel starts Protective Edge Operation in Gaza Strip in an effort to eradicate Hamas rocket launchers and all terrorists operating there. More than 2,000 Palestinians and 72 Israelis are killed.

Introduction

The term *Bedouins* was given to nomads who came from or lived in the desert and consisted of a sedentary population (from the *badia*, or desert). However, in time, it came to define their socioeconomic essence as people who raised grazing animals and were compelled to conduct a nomadic life, to live in tents that could be dismantled, carried, and re-erected easily, and to move with their livelihood and living accommodation, according to the environmental conditions—those that provided water and grass.

The Arabian peninsula was the original land of the genuine Bedouin tribes of the Middle East and the Arab tribes of North Africa, as tribal migrations occurred throughout history. In geographical regions like the Middle East, where in vast areas water was the most determinative commodity of population density and means of survival and prosperity, migration waves occurred more often than in other parts of the globe.

Migration could be triggered by climate change, population increase, wars, occupation, religious differences, natural calamity, and resource-related conflicts. It could also occur due to technological innovations and economic development that offered new opportunities or turned previous income resources into irrelevant ones.

However, more often than not, migration occurred due to different circumstances: Wars and catastrophes of nature created pressure. On the one hand, too many people had to survive in areas of dwindling resources, and some were forced to move on and find a new place and a new means of existence; on the other hand, similar events in other places could affect local people who left or were forced to abandon their territory, and a vacancy was created. And, as always happens, vacant areas attract newcomers whether from the adjacent area or from afar.

The size of a migratory wave as well as its duration, direction, and social impact vary according to the time and circumstances. Sometimes migrating people simply move through; sometimes they settle or establish their presence in other ways, changing the ethnic, social, or religious fabric of a given society; and sometimes they take over and replace the previous society, forcing the earlier occupants of the area to migrate elsewhere.

In the area covered by this book, some migrating groups maintained their original tribal affiliation and lifestyle and preserved their traditional culture with either no or minimal adaptation to their new cultural environment. But in most cases these immigrants, especially original Arab tribes, merged with the local population and created new cultures.

As mentioned above, not all Bedouin tribes are of Arabic origin, as all Muslim nomadic groups in the area adopted the term *Bedouins*. There are Bedouin tribes of Turkmen, Kurdish Baluch, and Berberic origin, and there are "Arabized" African people and hybrid people who are categorized as Bedouins.

The tribal map in various countries was formed according to time, as nomadic tribes arrived in each country at different times, due to different historical circumstances and in some cases from different directions. In addition, some large tribes split up and moved to more than one country, while others followed regular seasonal migration routes until demarcation of the previous kingdom, empire, or state cut off parts of a given tribe from its main body.

Throughout history, there were several migratory waves from the Arabian Peninsula to other parts of the Fertile Crescent and beyond; some such migration waves had occurred in the ancient pre-Islamic era. Long before the emergence of Islam, there was a significant presence of Arabic-speaking tribes in Greater Syria; their presence there played a central role in the Arab conquest, especially when Arab forces clashed with those of the Byzantine Empire. When the Muslim army arrived in eastern Syria, the Arab Bedouin tribes accepted Islam and joined the military effort.

Some migrations occurred with or following the Muslim conquest, and several other migration waves occurred after this grand event. They were in response to political, economic, and climate changes; to colonization and borders, to Arab-Israeli wars, and to the creation of the state of Israel.

The Bedouins were also affected by the arbitrary drawing of borders by the colonial powers in the aftermath of the removal of the Ottomans from their imperial territories in the Middle East and North Africa during World War I, and even more so when the colonies were replaced by states after World War II and the frontiers became even more entrenched. Most serious for some was the creation of the state of Israel, which cut through the territory of some, and also resulted in a series of wars and continuous tensions.

The Bedouins constituted a problem in scope and essence over hundreds of years, as the various governments were not enabled to penetrate into the desert militarily and maintain there a constant presence sufficient for control over their lives and their movements.

Starting from the end of World War I that ancient pattern of relations, in whose framework the Bedouins could deal with a government on an equal basis, disappeared gradually. Until then the two sides depended on the camel or the horse for the purpose of mobility during battle, and their types of weapons were identical; against the sources of power and the organized, trained, and motorized units of the authorities, the Bedouins pitted their supreme familiarity with the desert, which usually assured them a possibility of escape and disappearance. But gradually the government started to enjoy an advantage over the Bedouins due to two new factors that remained in the Middle East after the war. The first was based on the technical innovations in types of weapons and in mobility in battle, which were introduced by the European governments that replaced the Ottoman government in the region. The Bedouins could not obtain modern equipment, and if they purchased it, they could not purchase everything and not in significant quantities. The second factor: the airplane and the motor vehicle enabled the government's army to reach every corner with relatively great speed, which brought the factor of surprise. On the other hand, the Bedouins stayed limited to their traditional war methods and could not cope with an army equipped with modern weapons. Henceforth the desert was no longer a place for Bedouins alone, and they ceased to enjoy it as a place of refuge. It was now in the capacity of the representatives of the government to penetrate into it and change the lifestyle of the Bedouins as they saw fit.

The first governments that coped with the Bedouin problem were the colonial mandate and authorities, which were founded in various states like the British mandates in Iraq, in Transjordan, and Palestine, and the French mandate in Syria. Although they had in their hands the means for suppression of the Bedouins, which was demonstrated a few times in the 1920s, the Bedouins continued to constitute a problem for the government for several reasons:

1. The Bedouins were scattered over extensive areas that were hard to access.
2. The Bedouins continued to live according to rules and customs of the desert; for example, during drought, the Bedouins who were struck would raid the herds of others in order to ensure their existence. Thus, there was imposition of big "protection taxes" by large and strong tribes on weak tribes and on remote villages.
3. The Bedouins dwelled sometimes in regions close to new borders that had just been created by the colonial authorities when they split up the former Ottoman Empire into smaller states. The Bedouins, who had not been accustomed to these borders, tended to cross them for grazing needs, or in order to carry out raids on tribes on the other side. These actions clashed with the basic principles of the colonial governments, as, according to the political concepts in the West, the government alone was permitted to keep law and order in the territories of its state; therefore, launching raids and imposing "protection taxes" by the Bedouins were forbidden. Thus, the behavior of the tribes compelled the colonial authorities to organize military systems and huge administrative bodies in their new areas of jurisdiction in order to supervise the unmarked borders, which stretched along thousands of kilometers.

The colonial states and especially Great Britain and France sought to rule with a minimum of expenses and manpower. Following World War I, there was public pressure in both states to significantly reduce the military organization. Therefore, the mandatory governments had to find a method that would be both efficient and cheap. The solution came from the experiences they had acquired in other places where tribal groups dwelled in their empires. The rulers used the system of "indirect rule" in these places. The British called this system "the Sandman system," as the governor of a district in India by the name of Robert Sandman was the first to operate it successfully, in an attempt to stop the raids the fanatical tribes carried out in the northwest border region between 1860 and 1870. Later a French governor in Morocco, Marshal Leotti, used this system when he dealt with the Berber tribes in the Atlas Mountains.

The principle of "indirect rule" was based on collective responsibility. The whole tribe bore responsibility for the activity of each one of its members; when a tribesman broke the laws of the government, the punishments fell on the whole tribe. The punishments were usually payment of a fine in livestock or refusal of the government to offer services to the Bedouins, who had been accustomed to them in the past. The tribe's head was responsible on behalf of the government for obedience of his tribesmen to the laws of the government. It is understood that the responsibility of the tribe's head clashed with the traditional format of behavior, which could arouse the tribesmen against their leader with the claim that he ceased to protect them and their interests. But against this the government took care to support the tribe's head and his post and also supplied benefits, which the tribe's head shared among the tribesmen in order to appease them.

In the relations between the colonial authorities and the Bedouins, the fact was emphasized that the tribe, as an independent political entity, no longer existed. Henceforth it would no longer manage relations with external parties according to conditions of its own and to the conditions of free play, which it had enjoyed previously. On the other hand, the "indirect rule" system maintained the internal autonomy of the tribe. Nomads far from the arm of government needed an arrangement that would enable them to manage their daily affairs and would ensure the life of the individual. Therefore, the colonial authorities found it suitable to leave the traditional customs in force. In their opinion, it was best to leave the legal organization in its traditional format, as it could treat all the matters that arose among the tribesmen, and the tribe desired this.

The system of "indirect rule" became the main system operated toward the Bedouins in the colonial states. This system made it much easier for the authorities, in that it ensured their rule in their region of authority with a minimum of expenses and manpower. The system also suited the Bedouins, as although their life changed in certain fields, the lifestyle that they knew and loved was not harmed in its basis and essence.

The colonial government required from the Bedouins law and order, without harming their traditional world and lifestyle. The colonial authorities did not think that they had to change this world excessively, so if the traditional Bedouin framework of life is what was keeping law and order, it was preferable to leave it in its existing state.

The damage to Bedouin tribes came as a result of fixing the borders between the colonial powers. After World War I a process started in which borders were outlined and the superpowers shared territories among themselves, mostly according to their needs and not according to the needs of the local populations. The harm to Bedouins was double: The first damage was that the free wandering of the tribes was limited as a result of the demarcation of borders, and the Bedouins could not move about freely as they had done in the past. The second damage was that in not a few cases the borders between the superpowers cut through tribal territories, and not a few tribes found themselves on both sides of the border. When the nation states were founded in the Middle East and North Africa mainly from World War I onward, they demanded from the Bedouin tribes not only that they keep the existing law and order but also that they be loyal to the state, that they recognize the right of the politicians to govern, and that they participate in the development of social life and the state.

However, as in every period, these demands did not go down well with the political traditions of the Bedouins. Firstly, the Bedouins were seldom loyal to the overall group, bigger than their tribe; secondly, it is possible that a Bedouin would recognize the fact that a certain tribal body controlled him to a certain extent, but he did not recognize its right to govern; thirdly, just as the Bedouins refrained from collaborating with groups that are not connected to them in blood ties, so it is also difficult to expect them to cooperate in development programs on behalf of a social framework like the state, which is so distant from them hierarchically.

Although from the point of view of the politicians the best way to cope with the Bedouins is elimination of the framework fixing their existence, namely the tribal structure, from a technological-military point of view it was possible to do this. Moreover, there were parties in the nation-states that rejected the necessity for liquidation of Bedouinism. Of these the Hashemite Royal House in Jordan was especially prominent. They believed that if they would keep the tribal framework, they could obtain the full political support of the whole nomadic population. While there were politicians who appreciated the existence of the tribal structure, the problem remained how to keep its existence at a time when the economic rationale for existence of the tribe was removed. The solution was not far from the "indirect rule" system of the colonial authorities. The politicians imposed a new role on the tribe that was necessary for the tribesmen no less than its traditional roles. Instead of a military unit, the tribe became an administrative unit, where all the contacts between the Bedouins and the authorities take place with the mediation of the chiefs of the tribes. Everything the tribesmen needed—licenses, employment, privileges—could be obtained by these means.

The government on its part strove to reinforce the chiefs of the tribes among the tribesmen. The government took actions designed to show it was standing behind the tribe's chief, for example, visits of government officials to the tents of the chiefs. Moreover, the politicians imposed special representation of the Bedouins in the chambers of deputies as in Jordan, Iraq, Yemen, and so on.

However, there were some politicians who opposed the tribal framework and keeping it in its traditional format; they were mainly those who saw in Bedouinism a threat to their political and ideological goals. So, for example, in Syria and in Iraq these were politicians from the socialist camp, members of the Baath Party, and in Jordan they were Palestinian opponents.

From a political point of view all the opponents viewed ominously the support the Bedouins gave to their enemies from the old regime. In Iraq and in Syria the socialists did not even try to acquire the support of the Bedouins, due to ideological reasons. They knew that tribalism was maintained by means of the heads of the tribes, who had at that time the largest estates in their countries. As socialists, anti-Bedouin politicians were devoted to the idea of agrarian reform as an ideological principle. Therefore, they knew that they had no basis for collaboration with the chiefs of the tribes, owners of the big estates.

These politicians did not rise to power in Iraq and in Syria until 1958, but until then they devoted their efforts to the struggle against the special status the Bedouins enjoyed. They hoped that if they would succeed in this struggle, they would undermine the Bedouin support for the politicians of the old regime and also the foundations of tribalism. They opposed, for example, the principle of Bedouin representation in the chamber of deputies and attacked it. The anti-Bedouin politicians tried to settle the Bedouin nomads by force, while those who favored the Bedouins, if they tried to adopt a policy of settlement of the Bedouin nomads, they did this peacefully and by encouragement, not by enforcement.

Nomad-state relations in countries and in regions in the world are very complex, but at the start it seemed that simple relations between ruler and ruled were concerned. The more the power of the modern state developed and the more centralized its regime became, the more the complexity and variety in the contrasting political trends in relations with the nomads and of the state and its enforcement institutions stood out.

In the Middle East and Africa (until the middle of the 20th century) the rule of governments in the marginal regions was only limited. This situation enabled nomads to threaten the stability of the state's regime and to eat into lands and property of the villages and the permanent settlers, and in practice to damage the state. But the modern state, by means of an infrastructure it had built in the border regions and with the help of its law enforcement machinery (police, army), managed to intensify its presence in the border regions, and thus the nomads turned from rulers to subjects.

The advantage of the nomads was canceled, and a policy of settlement of the border of the modern state squeezed them to the margins. Henceforth the nomads had to adapt themselves to a lifestyle coping with the dichotomy: On the one hand, the state enabled them to maintain the traditional framework, but on the other hand, it limited them to the grazing place, to the cultivation region, and to the subsistence region. Gradually a view was generated among representatives of the state, according to which the nomads were regarded as a nuisance, and therefore one should settle them permanently. The space therefore ceased to be an area in which the nomads could express their independence, and they started to improvise methods of survival whose principle was evasion from the restrictions the state imposed on them, without losing the tribal frameworks. It seems that this struggle expressed their power from a spatial and functional point of view. The tribalism and ethnicity, that is, the tribe and the cultural world it represents, became the important components in the identification of the nomad in any case, much more dominant than the identification with the state. The result was often clashes with the establishment. The issue of relations between the populations of Bedouins and the state in the Middle East and Africa is connected in fact to the question of the policy the governments should adopt. This issue assumed importance both regarding the development processes of the political-economic idea in states in these regions and also regarding the processes of cultural change that take place in the Bedouin societies.

The combination of the two processes creates a third process, in whose framework the connections and relations between the Bedouins and the state are tightened, many intensive planes of contact are created between them, and these hide within them potential foci of tension and conflict. These foci expose the societies of Bedouins to an additional dimension influencing the processes of change among them, a dimension whose influence on them in the past was relatively small. This is the political-spatial dimension in which two conflicting ideological trends are expressed: the centrifugal trend of the nomads, as part of their cultural structure, versus the centripetal trend of the state expressed in its policy toward them. These conflicting trends have varied spatial and functional expressions, and the tension generated between them stands as the basis of a process of shaping and production of the space in the nomadic subsistence regions. The central issue connected to the centrifugal-centripetal tension is the very settlement and sedentarization of the nomadic Bedouins and the character of this process. From the point of view of governments, the proper spatial use of the resources and supply of services in the traditional territories of the Bedouins will be accomplished only when the Bedouins give up their traditional lifestyle and increase their involvement in agricultural production in permanent settlements. In fact it is widely thought that governments take advantage of arguments like improved services, regular and safe food production and supply, and good salary conditions in commercial agriculture in order to sedentarize the Bedouins.

Tribalism, which can be explained by their Bedouin heritage, is still common in the modern societies of some Arab countries. The states of Saudi Arabia, Jordan, the Gulf Emirates, Libya, and Iraq were actually founded on a tribal basis or have a Bedouin heritage. Tribalism is also strongly present in Lebanon, Yemen, Mauritania, Sudan, and rural parts of Iran and Turkey.

The Bedouins do not call themselves Bedouins; they call themselves Arabs as a collective name. Muslim historians of certain periods also preferred to use the ethnic definition rather than include these tribes as part of a homogeneous social component of nomad herders and tribal warriors. The reason they used the name *Arabs* is mainly due to the fact that several semi-nomadic groups and sedentary people of Arabic origin preserved the traditional cultural characteristics, or chose to keep their traditional lifestyle for centuries in changing environmental conditions.

The nomadic lifestyle was a regular phenomenon in the vast region included in this volume. The main reason for the presence of nomad tribal societies of various ethnic origins in the Middle East, North Africa, and some neighboring countries was the natural environmental conditions of large parts of the region, endowed with desert and semi-arid lands, which dictated to people who grew grazing animals to follow the pastures.

As this region was for centuries crossed as a major trade route, the local inhabitants also developed the concept of transport animals and used their fast mounts to provide guides and security escorts to these large caravans, and eventually they were hired as guides and escorts by other civilian factors that traveled through these areas. Hence, in time, the Bedouins have excelled in tracking, water finding, and other skills required of guides, and were always ready to join military campaigns as warriors and service providers.

In general, the Bedouin tribes of Arab origin, or the "Arabized" groups, are far more common than the Bedouins of other ethnic origin, with the exception of certain specific mountainous areas, where the local rural population converted to Islam and joined the armies that conquered the area from the previous political actors.

In recent years the modern state has forced nomads to settle, and by so doing they interfere with the natural process adapted to the physical, economic, and social conditions of this population. In other states, such as Oman and Saudi Arabia, the Bedouin heritage is respected. Although some of the men are drawn to seek work in developing urban centers, the authorities aim to assist those who choose to maintain their lifestyle, by building roads and water systems along with regional schools and clinics, or a mobile version of these services.

At the beginning of the 20th century, one quarter of the Middle East population was nomadic. Today, only a small percent are still nomads or semi-nomads. Most of the tribes have settled in permanent settlements, but tribal culture is still dominant in the political culture of the Middle East.

The tribes exist everywhere. In many countries the regime is based on tribal loyalty. When studying the Middle East, ignoring the issue of tribes is a mistake, since understanding tribal structure is most crucial to understanding the politics in the region. The thesis that the modern states perceive that bringing progress will unify the tribes and eliminate tribal entities is incorrect: tribal entities have changed, but they have not disintegrated, and in some countries the regime is using them and relying on them.

Besides its political impact, the recent Arab Spring has had a tremendous cultural impact on several modern Arab societies, as people have become more aware of their ethnic and cultural heritage, and tend to take pride in their tribal affiliation and unique traditions. Thus, it is quite common today to see people dressed in traditional attire in the streets of several modern cities, or to hear an urban VIP refer to his tribal roots.

This volume will refer to the place of the Bedouins in the history of the Middle East throughout the ages from various angles: the nomadic phenomenon and its role in the history of the area, Bedouin-state relations, Bedouin relations with other components of the population, military history and intelligence, and processes of settling nomads. It will also refer to the cultural and folkloric aspects of the Bedouins, tribal law, religion, pilgrimage, and rituals at holy places, folk medicine, food and beverages, and status of women.

At present, tribes and tribalism at large present a serious challenge to the political elites of the independent Arab states. Today's Bedouins are no longer nomadic tribes wandering in the desert or camel riders. Camels, like thoroughbred horses, have become cherished possessions, and prestigious camel races are as popular as horse races.

Nevertheless, tribal identity still exists in the social and political consciousness of several million Arabs who live in modern cities. This phenomenon reflects the fact that tribalism in the Arab world is not a way of life, but rather an identity ingrained in the political culture and social psychology.

Relations between the regime (whether local or foreign) and the tribes are subject to change with regard to inner-state security: When the central administration is weak, the tribes strengthen, and vice versa. Although in some North African countries the central regime managed to weaken the major tribe, the impact on the social and political developments in other states, as in most Arab countries of the Middle East, and especially in Jordan, Saudi Arabia, the Gulf Emirates, Yemen, and Libya, has been such that the tribes remained central political players. Tribalism has an important role in political decisions and in the building of national identity.

States like Libya and Yemen could not otherwise exist as independent political entities and depended heavily on the tribes' acceptance and support. Thus, in both states, the army and the police were based on the tribes the regime relied on, reflecting the power of the given tribe, while the opposition was usually led by leaders of tribes whose interests clashed with those of the central regime, which led to unrest.

The persistence of tribal identity in the region is a result of the failure of the national project of modern states and the Arabic autocrats' clinging to political survival. Polarization of the tribal cultural identity is one of the most worrisome symptoms of the legitimacy crisis of the Arabic state. Although the nomadic way of life is restricted, some of the new Arab governments in the post–Arab Spring era must cope with the enormous problem of tribalism.

In the idealistic imaginery, the Bedouin resides in the desert, and gets his livelihood from his herds and camels. The word *Bedouin* raises in one's imagination a picture of black tents, camel caravans wandering in vast, endless plains, bearded men wearing flattering robes, and courageous robbers riding fast horses. The Bedouins living in the Middle East today do not really fit this romantic image. True, some of the old ways of life are still in evidence, but raids and robberies are a legacy of the past. Regular contact with the sedentary Arabic population has modified the Bedouins' way of life.

The tribe is the basic unit to which an individual belongs. It is a coalition of clans under the leadership of a sheikh. In the past the tribes were unified in confederations (*kabail*). These confederations were less organic, they did not obey one leader, and they did not necessarily live close by or move together. On the other hand, they were more stable and existed for several generations.

This means that it is becoming harder and harder to say with any precision just who a Bedouin is since some of them, an increasingly small contingent, live in a traditional Bedouin manner, actually herding cattle, engaging in migration, and sleeping under a tent, while more and more are sedentary and living off agriculture or increasingly urbanized and living like everybody else in the city. Most of them will self-identify as Bedouins, but for others this is something of the past, just a fading if tenacious memory.

This also makes it hard to determine with any precision just how many Bedouins there are today. A rough figure might be according to estimates 25 million inhabitants who are 8–10 percent of the population of the Middle East and North Africa. Most of them have already undergone a process of settlement and most of them live in permanent settlements: 10 million Bedouins in Sudan, 2 million in Algeria, 2 million in Saudi Arabia, 1.5 million in Iraq, 1.3 million in Jordan, 1 million in Libya, 1 million in Egypt, 800,000 in the United Arab Emirates, 700,000 in Syria, 500,000 in Yemen, 300,000 in Kuwait, 220,000 in Israel, 500,000 in Iran, 250,000 in Morocco, 200,000 in Lebanon, 180,000 in Tunisia, 100,000 in Mauritania, 70,000 in Bahrain, 50,000 in Qatar, 30,000 in the Palestinian Authority, and 30,000 Bedouins in Oman.

A

AAD. Aad was an ancient Bedouin tribe that lived in the south of the Arabian Peninsula, in contemporary **Yemen**. They founded an Arab kingdom that continued from the 10th century until the 3rd century BC. Their name is mentioned in the Koran, where they are described as a pagan people whom God punished when he liquidated their kingdom by means of a strong tempest that continued for eight days, resulting in the annihilation of the tribe. *See also* PRE-ISLAMIC PERIOD.

ABBASID REVOLUTION. The Abbasids used the Umayyad policy of exploiting disputes between the tribes in order to repress them and govern them. They adopted the traditions developed by Yazid ibn al-Muhallab during the revolt. He supported **Islamic** expansion when he was governor of Khurasan. He disowned the Umayyads and stated that a member of the **Banu Hashim** should be appointed as *Amir al-Mu'minin* (commander or prince of the faithful). He also claimed that he was a **Qahtan** and raised the black (the Abbasid color) flag as a sign of opposing the Umayyads, whose flag was white.

He was aware of the fact that the powerful **Yemenites** in Khurasan were hostile to the Umayyads and rivals of their Mudar supporters. After they rose to power, they relied on the people of Khurasan and secretly arranged for the support of some southern tribes like the Qahtan and other Yemenite tribes, exploiting the fact that the Umayyads mistreated the southern tribes. In addition they managed to maintain good relations with the Mawali (Persian) tribes and to draft some members of the Mudar confederation.

The Abbasids claimed legitimacy on two counts: they were descendants of the Prophet's family and they were followers of the political activism and customs of Shiite Zayd ibn Ali, the great grandson of "Ali and Fatimah," who led a rebellion against the Umayyads in 740. They managed to gain ample support and popularity and also used it to strengthen and establish their rule, after they seized power from the declining Umayyads and founded the second Muslim dynasty.

ABD-AL-QAYS. Abd-Al-Qays was an Arabian tribe of the Rabi'ah branch of the Adnanite tribes, who lived in the vicinity of **Bahrain** and its islands. This tribe was more sedentary than nomadic, and like some neighboring tribes, had already accepted and converted to **Christianity** before the advent of **Islam**. *See also* PRE-ISLAMIC PERIOD.

ABU BASMA REGIONAL COUNCIL. The Abu Basma Regional Council was formed in 2003, with the approval and support of the **Israeli** government, to find a concrete solution to unify a number of unrecognized Bedouin **settlements** in a given region ("Abu Basma Plan" Resolution 881), according to which a new regional council was formed to give them a municipal status that would enable them to receive the basic state services and infrastructure.

At present the Israeli government is in the process of building additional Bedouin towns in the **Negev** that will be fully equipped with relevant infrastructure, such as running **water**, electricity, and paved roads, along with schools, medical clinics, post offices, and so on, in the hope to resolve the situation. *See also* RAHAT.

ABU DHABI EMIRATE. The emirate is a political and economic coalition of tribes under the leadership of the **Bani Yas** tribe. The leading family of this tribe, Nahyan, came to the Abu Dhabi Island from the Liwa **Oasis**, in the 18th century, and forged ties that connected the economic factors and **pearling** between the coast and inland regions and maritime businesses, and created wealth that was invested inland. The Bani Yas tribe offered ships, pilots, and divers; some clans of this tribe adopted a lifestyle of fishing and pearling, while others adopted various aspects of **trade**. The Marar, Mahair, and Mahariba clans dealt chiefly with diving and piloting. The Hawamil and Qubaisat grew palm trees and raised **camels** in and around an inland oasis, while other clans shifted to maritime occupations. The desert Bedouin tribes Mazaria and Awamir were responsible for security and protection of trade between the coast and inland regions.

Originally, there were three independent tribal groups: the group in Abu Dhabi, including those settled in the inland villages of Liwa and Buraimi; those in the northeast Trucial States known as the Qasimi Empire; and the tribes of the western mountains, which have since become part of Oman. The tribes in the northeast Trucial States swore allegiance to different **sheikhs** and were granted a financial reward in return. The sheikhs relied on their support in case of a dispute. The most powerful tribe in the area, the Naim, lived in Ajman, later in the Buraimi district, and some of them also settled in Sharjah.

In 1937, the Sultan of Muscat signed an agreement with the Petroleum Concessions Company, and the Naim sheikhs agreed to be subject to **Oman** sovereignty. However, they changed their minds and were granted their own petroleum franchises, which led to a dispute and to Saudi intervention. Al Bu Shamis, which was the Bedouin section of the tribe, separated and formed its own identity. Some of them settled in coastal towns and oases, mainly in Hamriyah and Hirah.

At the turn of the century Balush of Dhahirah reached an alliance with the Bani Yas of Abu Dhabi and Al Bu Falah in the Buraimi district. However, after a redefinition of tribal loyalties a conflict broke out between the Balush and their former protector, Bani Kitab. The Balush turned to Zayed Bin Khalifah for help, while Bani Kitab asked for the protection of Rashid Bin Ahmad the lord of Umm Al Quwain. The allied states' leaders met in Khawanij, near Dubai, in 1906, and reached an agreement between the different tribes with regard to the areas of influence. *See also* SAUDI ARABIA; UNITED ARAB EMIRATES (UAE).

ABU RABIA, HAMAD (1929–1981). Hamad Abu Rabia was a politician of the Abu Rabia Bedouin tribe and the first Bedouin ever to serve in the **Israeli** *Knesset* (Parliament). Abu Rabia grew up in the **Negev** and reached the **sheikh** status at an early age. He was among the first Bedouins in Israel who sought higher **education** and consequently became active in politics, especially in social and educational matters. In 1973, he was elected to the Knesset as a delegate of the United Arab List party. When that party merged with the Communist Party, he was reelected in the 1977 elections, and served in the Knesset Committee for Public Services. In the elections of 1979, the United Arab List won only one seat in the Knesset, and the two candidates, Abu Rabia and Jabr Muadi, agreed to alternate. However, when the time to alternate came, Abu Rabia refused to vacate his seat, and after some bitter litigation, was assassinated by Muadi's sons.

ABU TAYI, AUDA (1875–1924). Auda Abu Tayi was **sheikh** (chief) of the Huwaytat Bedouin Arab tribe at the time of the Great **Arab Revolt** (during World War I) and played an important role in that revolt.

He was a descendant of several generations of Arab warriors from Arabia and was proud of his heritage. His love for freedom and independence and his open resentment of the Ottoman Empire attracted several warriors from his tribe. When Lawrence and Faisal bin Al Hussein looked for allies against the Turks, he was among the first to join them. He considered himself an Arab patriot and rode with Lawrence against the Turks. He and his tribesmen played an important role in the defeat of the Ottomans in Aqaba (July 1917) and Damascus (October 1918).

After the war was over and the demarcation lines were drawn in the area, Auda retired to the **desert** and built a modern palace at Al-Jafr east of Ma'an, in south **Jordan**. He died in 1924 of natural causes and was buried in Amman, the capital of modern Jordan.

ADNANITES. The Adnanites are Arabs who underwent Arabization, as they were descendants of Adnan. They occupied the northern, central, and western stretches of Arabia. Adnan is thought, according to tradition and according to many Arab genealogies, to be the father of a group of Ishmaelite Arabs who occupied these areas. Adnan's ancestry is unclear, as the number and names of ancestors between Ishmael and Adnan are unclear, but the names and number of those between Adnan and the Prophet Muhammad are clear. Adnan is believed to be a descendant of Kedar, Ishmael's son, but Ibn Ishaq claims that his forefather was Nebaioth, who had descended from Kedar.

He is mentioned in **pre-Islamic** poems written by poets like Lubayb Ibn Rabia and Abbas Ibn Mirdas. Pre-Islamic Arabs were proud of Adnan's family tree and used it against the **Qahtan**, who were a minority among them. Layla Bent Lukayz, a pre-Islamic poetess, was taken prisoner by a Persian king and forced to wed him, so she wrote a poem for other Arab tribes, asking them to rescue her as she and all of them belonged to Adnan. In poems written by the pre-Islamic poet Qummaa Ibn Ilias it is apparent that Arabs consider it an honor to be a descendant of Adnan.

Adnan's name was found in some **Thamudic** inscriptions, whereas in **Nabatean** inscriptions some of the Nabatean people are called "*Abd Adnan*" or the servants of Adnan, in order to honor him. Adnan died after Nebuchadnezzar II returned to Babylon, and then his son Ma'ad moved to central Hejaz after the Qedarite kingdom near Mesopotamia was destroyed and its Arab citizens were forced to live in the Al-Anbar province and along the Euphrates River, under the authority of the Neo-Babylonian Empire. *See also* IRAQ.

AGRICULTURE. The distribution of the population in the Middle East is mainly a consequence of the dependence of man on natural factors. Man settled in the place in which he found fertile land and **water** for irrigation: in **oases**, in river valleys, or in a place whose climate is rainy on the coastal plains and in hilly regions in which he could live from agriculture. An agricultural society developed in these places. In places in which the quantity of rain was insufficient or the land was unfit for agricultural cultivation, man found his subsistence as a **nomadic shepherd**.

Working the land is not important in Bedouin life. Beoduins hate work in the field and work in general. They even treated agricultural work with scorn, and therefore in the historical periods, they did not appreciate agriculture and would place their herds on cultivated fields. But from the end of the 19th century and the beginning of the 20th century, the Bedouins, in addition to income from raising animals, started to deal with field crops, mainly wheat and barley. At the start this was very limited and a secondary branch to raising animals. The method of tilling the land was simple. The Bedouin tilled small areas, as he still placed an emphasis on **wandering** with the flock. A cause for the **sedentarization** of the Bedouins—a strong central government, technological development, and development of means of transport—brought changes in the traditional economic practices of the Bedouins. In parallel, there was a decline in the importance of the livestock farm and the beasts of burden and riding of the Bedouins, and thereby the Bedouins lost their relative advantage, following the damage to their freedom of wandering.

Consequently, a process of sedentarization of the Bedouin tribes started. They started to look for alternative employment. They changed from shepherds and raisers of animals into farmers whose income was from field crops. Today the Bedouins not only are occupied with agriculture but also are integrated in other modern occupations, which reduced their dependence on the traditional farm but increased their dependence on the general labor market.

AHL SAHEL. Ahl Sahel, or Ait Sahel, was a mixed tribe formed from Arab and **Berber** components—the former came from the Sahara. It belonged to the "lef Taoggat" alliance. The tribe obeyed an "Amghar" chief, assisted by a council. Generally, they were independent and did not pay taxes. *See also* MOROCCO.

AHL SERIF. Ahl Serif was a tribe with a diverse background, composed of Arabized **Berber**s and families of the Andalusians of Chourfa origin. They were refugees who had fled the town of Fez in the 8th century, at the time of the persecution of the Idrissid dynasty by Moussa ben Abi El Afiya. *See also* MOROCCO.

AHMAR. Ahmar was an Arab tribe whose name came from Hamriyine, which was an Arabic Maaqilite tribe that came to settle in **Morocco** in the 13th century. Their presence in the current region close to Marrakesh dates from the Saadian epoch (16th century), when they were conscripted to confront the Portuguese, who took up positions all along the Moroccan coast.

AIT JMEL. This was an Arab tribe, going back in origin to the Bani Maqil, who had settled in the Sahara at the beginning of the 13th century. It was part of the big confederation of the **Tekna**. It was divided into four subgroups: Ait Jemal, Ould Bou Ata, Ait Lahcen, and Ait Moussa Ou Ali. *See also* MAURITANIA; MOROCCO.

AJMAN. Ajman was a Bedouin tribe of northeastern Arabia, a side branch of **Banu Yam**, the principal tribe of Najran (near Yemen), with member groups in **Saudi Arabia**, Qatar, and the **United Arab Emirates**. Sometime in the 18th century, the Ajman and another subtribe called **Al Murrah** separated from the Yam and moved eastward. Unlike the Yam, which was mostly composed of Ismaili Shiites, both these subtribes were Maliki Sunni.

The Ajman were known for their military skills and were a central player in politics during the 19th and early 20th centuries. Their leadership in Saudi Arabia was challenged by Faisal ibn Turki, the second imam of the State of Saudi, who later married into the tribe. A section of the Ajman joined the **Ikhwan** movement in 1912, and took part in the rebellion against **Ibn Saud** in 1929, in which the Ikhwan were defeated. Most of the Ajman tribe abandoned their nomadic life and settled in the United Arab Emirates and in the northeastern parts of Saudi Arabia, in the area of Wadi el-Ajman, which is on the road between Riyadh and Dammam.

AL-AWAKIR. Al-Awakir is a **Libyan** tribe. This tribe is the most common one in the town of Al-Bayda, the town in which the Sanussiyah order was founded, and which saw the start of the 2011 Arab Spring revolution against Muammar Gadhafi. This tribe is a veteran protagonist in the opposition of the Ottoman and Italian colonialism, has participated for a long period in Libyan politics, both during the monarchy and also during Muammar Gadhafi's presidency, and resides in the hometown of the National Transition Council (NTC) chairman, Mustafa Abdel Jalil.

AL-HASI, AQIL AGA (?–1870). Aqil Aga al-Hasi was born in **Egypt**, sometime in the early 19th century. He was a member of the Egyptian Nadi tribe. His father, Moussa al-Hasi, left Egypt in 1814, after he murdered one of his close associates. However, he settled near Acre in the **Palestine** province and served the Ottoman governor Suleiman Pasha (1805–1819) and his successor, Abdullah Pasha (1819–1831), as commander of the hired cavalry unit. He was killed in battle in 1830, leaving three sons, Ali, Aqil, and Salah.

Aqil Aga replaced his father in the service of the Ottomans and played an important part in the history of Palestine. He became the head of the Nadi tribe and commander of an irregular soldiers unit in the service of the Ottoman governor of Acre. His position enabled him to take part in almost everything that occurred among various ethnic and religious groups in northern Palestine. He did not necessarily represent the views of the authorities. Thus, he was dismissed and rehired repeatedly, and when he was dismissed he used his men to raid and plunder in order to force the authorities to understand that he was the key to order and security in the region. As there was no alternative, they were forced to rehire him for the job, but not for long, and he would be dismissed and rehired again, and yet again.

During times of bloody ethnic conflicts Aqil was known and respected for protecting the non-Muslim subjects in the region. When the situation deteriorated, several **Christian** dignitaries met Aqil, who gave them his word that he would protect them and strike anyone who attempted to attack and harm a Christian or a Jew.

His protection of the non-Muslim subjects in Safed district during the riots of 1860 brought his name to the attention of foreign consuls, who praised him and recommended European travelers to use his services as a guide and escort. He was honored by the British Consul in Jerusalem and by Napoleon III, the king of France, who visited the area and presented him with the French Legion of Honor and a gift of rifles.

However, as his unruly behavior returned during his participation in the riots of 1864–1865, the Ottomans had had enough of him, and were left with no choice but to go after him and his men. Looking at this large force, Aqil realized that it was invincible, and hence, escaped to El-Balkaa, leaving his assets and property to his assailants. Suddenly, the "Lord of the **Galilee**" found himself practically penniless. Therefore, he used his past contacts and approached Ismail Pasha, the governor of Egypt, for help and pardon. His intervention worked, and Aqil returned to Acre in 1866, where he was reappointed and served as protector of the Galilee roads until his demise in 1870.

AL-RASHEED EMIRATE. This state was founded in Jabal **Shammar** "the Mountain of Shammar" in Nejd in Arabia, in 1836, and its rulers feuded with the House of Saud for control of the inclusive area of Nejd. Its capital was Ha'il. The Rashidis removed the Saudis from Riyadh in 1891 after the Battle of Mulayda. Thus the Emirate of Nejd was abolished and its territory included in Jabal Shammar. The House of Rashid tried to forge amicable ties with the Ottoman Empire, but at the end of the 19th century the latter's star was waning.

The Saudis had been exiled to **Kuwait**, but in 1902 Abdulaziz **ibn Saud** reconquered Riyadh for the House of Saud, and this developed into a full-fledged war with the Rashidis for the region of Qassim, which the Rashidis lost, and their emir, Abdul Aziz ibn Mitaab al-Rashid, died.

Ibn Saud emerged as much stronger through his alliance with Great Britain after the Ottomans lost their status in the region at the end of World War I. At the end of 1921 the Saudis launched a campaign that led the Emirate of Jabal

Shammar to surrender to them, and it was then included in the Sultanate of Nejd. Many of the Jebalis of the Shammar were driven into exile by the Saudis and the British to **Syria** and **Iraq**, where they live today.

The rulers of the Emirate of Rasheed were successively as follows: Abdullah I bin Rasheed (1836–1848) became ruler after he led a revolt with his brother against the government of Ha'il. His son, Talal bin Abdullah (1848–1868), was a reformer and builder who initiated construction projects. He completed the Barzan Palace in Ha'il. During his reign, the inhabitants of Qassim, who were tired of **Wahabi** despotism, turned to him and at a favorable moment annexed themselves to the kingdom of Shammar. He made **trade** contacts with Iraq and tolerated Shiite dissident merchants.

In 1865 the Rasheed conquered Riyadh and forced the leadership of the House of Saud into exile. Talal died from gunshot wounds, maybe by suicide, and of his seven sons, the eldest, Bandar, was only 18 or 20 years old when he died. Talal's brother Mut'ib bin Abdullah (1868–1869) was killed in the Barzan Palace by his nephew Bandar (1869), who became the next emir, who was killed in turn by his uncle, Muhammed. The latter, Muhammed I bin Abdullah (1869–1897), ordered the execution of all Bandar's brothers (Talal's sons), his cousins (children of Talal's sister), and their servants and slaves. Despite this violent start, his reign was a period of prosperity and stability, and there was expansion of Jabal Shammar's territory to the north and west. In 1891 the Saudi leader and his family left Riyadh and went into exile in Kuwait. Abd al-Aziz bin Mutib (1897–1906), the son of the third emir Mutib, had been adopted by his uncle Muhammed, who died of natural causes. He was crowned unopposed, but their Ottoman allies were weakening. In 1904 the young Ibn Saud, the future founder of **Saudi Arabia**, recaptured Riyadh and defeated Abd al-Aziz in the battle of Rawdat, who died in it in 1906. Three emirs, Mutib II bin Abd al-Aziz (1906–1907), Sultan bin Hammud (1907–1908), and Saud I bin Hammud Al-Rasheed (1908–1910), were all killed by their own relatives. Saud I bin Abd al-Aziz (1910–1920) was only 10 years old on accession to the throne, his mother's family were regents for him, and in 1920 he was assassinated by his cousin. His successor, Abdullah II bin Mutib (1920–1921, died 1947) surrendered to Ibn Saud in 1921, when he was only 14 years old. The last emir was Muhammad II bin Talal (1921, died 1954), who also surrendered to Ibn Saud, and with this the dynasty ended.

AL SANA, TALEB (1960–). Taleb Al Sana is a Bedouin lawyer and graduate of the Hebrew University in Jerusalem. He was born in Tel Arad, a Bedouin village near the town of Arad. He is an active politician who has served in the **Israeli** Knesset for several years. He has been elected in the list of the Communist party and later as a representative of the United Arab List, until he lost his seat in the 2013 elections. He is still an active member in several voluntary organizations, especially those engaged in promoting the rights and welfare of the **Negev** Bedouins.

Al-Sana, who currently resides in the town of **Lakiya**, is known for his outspoken criticism of the Israeli government and is often criticized by Israeli right-wing spokesmen.

ALEIQAT. This tribe was one of the first to arrive in the area during the **Islamic** conquest of **Egypt**, and settled in **Sinai**. It was a relatively small tribe. Its descendants live today on the west coast of Sinai.

ALGERIA. Archeology reveals that people lived in this area since the Neanderthal and Paleolithic pre-historic eras. Neolithic cultures developed in the African coast of the Mediterranean from 6000 to about 2000 BC. The earliest foreign settlers in recorded history were the **Berbers**, who settled on the coast and immediately inland, but later spread to the mountainous areas. The Phoenician mariners settled on the coast during the last millennium BC. They built the city of Carthage, which became the dominant urban center in North Africa. Berbers from the interior traded and mixed with the Carthaginians and became skilled in manufacture, **agriculture**, and **trade**. Carthage fought the Romans for more than a century and were defeated in the third Punic War. The Romans decimated the city of Carthage in 146 BC. Rome ruled the territory of Algeria for many decades, and the Vandals briefly conquered it. In between foreign rulers, the Berbers established two kingdoms, Numidia and **Mauritania**.

Muslim Arabs invaded and conquered Algeria in the 7th century, and after the downfall of the Umayyad dynasty in 751, the area was ruled by the local Berber dynasties: the Almohads, Almoravids, and Fatimids, who also conquered **Egypt** and abandoned Algeria. However, when they were unhappy with the behavior and conduct of their successors, they sent over the Muslim Arab tribes of Banu Hilal and Banu Sulaym, who defeated the ruling dynasty and ravaged the country.

As a result of this invasion, the entire Maghreb disintegrated into a number of sheikhdoms, and the nomadic tribes, both the locals of the Berber origin and those of Arab descent, established their niche and moved from one sheikhdom to another, following their seasonal migration route. During the years that followed, the Algerian coast was under Spanish rule, Ottoman rule, and pirates' rule. Piracy led to a military naval attack by Great Britain and the United States on Algeria in the early 19th century.

In 1830, the French invaded and conquered Algeria. From this year onward, the tribes in Algeria were gradually eradicated by the colonial forces, and this process continued until and after the start of World War I. The government fought tribal resistance against the French authority, which also exacerbated intertribal and intratribal disputes.

In Western Algeria, the rebelling tribes were caught between the French army and the army of the Sultan of **Morocco**, who decimated the Bani Amr tribe, and the French army defeated Eli Mokrani. As a consequence of the human losses in these battles some tribes disappeared or were significantly weakened, while others were strengthened; however, they did not change their tribal organization, as they did not replace it with any other social organization. Nevertheless, changes in the laws defining land and property ownership, which deprived several people, especially those who abandoned them and were not present when government agents drafted ownership claims, influenced the continuation of the traditional tribal lifestyle that they had prior to the wars, due to the process of dispossession of land in Algeria. The government took additional measures to break tribal loyalty and force cultural change: it divided the tribes into several branches and included them in their new locations as members of foreign tribes.

According to historian scholars, before the French intervention, the lands that the nomadic tribes crossed jointly belonged to the tribes that grazed them, as a sort of collective property. Private property of assets and lands existed predominantly in the mountains where common lands were few. There were also some private lands in the plains. Some tribes had deeds of property. The new regime ruled that all collective property belonged to the state, and the state could reallocate it.

Historical records show that before the French colonization almost two-thirds of Algeria's population (67 percent) lived in **tents**, whereas a census conducted in the 1960s and 1970s showed that 500,000 people or 2.5 percent of the total Algerian population lived in tents. The impossibility to maintain their annual **migration** routes caused a collapse in the tribal economy, as the tribes who lived off agropastoralism were no longer capable of reproducing the material basis of their existence.

After an arduous war of independence from 1954 to 1962 the French were driven out. But the successive governments were unstable, and an exceptionally bitter civil war led by **Islamists** broke out in 1991 and only stabilized around 2002. In the last general elections in Algeria, which were held in April 2014, President Bouteflika was reelected for the fourth time with 82 percent of the vote.

AMUR. Amur was a **Moroccan** tribe. Before the colonization, the Amur as well as the Awlad Sid Ahmad Majdub lived under **tents**. Certain families had gardens and palm trees in the *ksour* (fortified **market** towns) of the region.

The development of the Amur was linked to their status and the riots linked to the tracing of the **Algerian**-Moroccan frontier, south of Taniet Sassi. Were they subjects of France or of the Moroccan monarchy? The treaty of 1845 resolved this issue. In 1847 a French column took possession of the ksour that had been declared French. In 1855 most of the Amur tribes submitted to France, and the French authorities gave them a regular organization in three *caidats*. These numbered approximately 520 tents in 1859.

Until 1848, they paid their taxes with their senior branch and camped with them. In 1849 they abandoned Si Hamza and rallied to Sidi Shaykh Ban Tayab, who refused French occupation. In 1863, the uprising of Awlad Sidi Shaykh put a halt to the French military expansion in the south, near Oran. Awlad Sidi Ahmad Majdub, having participated in this uprising, was given a pardon (*aman*) and placed in the circle of Sebdou, where he stayed until 1878. They formed an independent caidat from Awlad Sidi Shaykh. In 1881, Awlad Sidi Ahmad Majdub joined with the Amur in an insurrection led by Sid Abu Amama. The French authorities occupied Ain Sefra and created a military post there.

In 1882, the French authorities gave the Amur confederation a new organization in three tribes: Awlad Salim, Awlad Bubkar, and Swala. In 1905, the military territory of Ain Sefra was created. The caids of the tribes and the side *ksour* were placed under the authority of the Agha of the Amur and of the ksour of Ain Sefra, Si Moulay Ould Si Muammed ben Miloud. In 1914, the governor general of Algeria decided on the merger of the two subtribes of Awlad Sidi Muhammad and Awlad Sidi Abu al Anwar (dependent on Ain Sefra) with Awlad Sidi Ahmad Nadjub (dependent on Geryville). These reorganizations of the Amur and Awlad Sidi Ahmad Majdub gave a more formal character to the tribes, with a more coherent organization.

ANAZAH. Anazah is an ancient Arab tribe known from the **pre-Islamic era**, and unlike other such tribes, maintains autonomous tribal groups in several modern states, such as the Gulf states, **Iraq**, **Syria**, and **Lebanon**. Scholars place them as part of the large Rabi'a branch of the Adnani tribes.

Anazah has two main branches: one has been nomadic and wandered on the Arabian steppes, near the borders of Syria and Iraq, while the other branch, called Bani Hizzan, has been sedentary from an early age and has settled in the valleys of Al-Yamama in the eastern Nejd. Families of the Bani Hanifa, of the Bakr ibn Wa'il, who lived in the area of modern Riyadh and their modern descendants, trace their origin to 'Anazah (Anazah).

The Ottoman era recognized the Anazah as masters of the **oasis** towns of northwestern Arabia. The Anazah did not cultivate the land, but only spent the winter months in the area and taxed the local farmers. In the summers they used to move northward, to eastern Syria of today, and tax the crops of the locals who lived in the Hawran region. Other clans of the tribe moved across the Arabian steppes northward to the tributaries of the Euphrates River.

One branch of the 'Anazah tribe that migrated to **Jordan** and Syria became so large and powerful that it practically developed into an independent tribe, known as the **Ruwallah**, and fought for dominance with other tribes in the area. Another branch of the Anazah, the Amarat, moved to the Iraqi **deserts**.

Arab genealogists divide the modern Anazah into two main branches: Dhana Bishr ("children of Bishr")—which includes the 'Amarat of Iraq—and Dhana Maslam, which includes the Ruwallah of north Arabia.

All through history there was limited settling of Bedouins near towns and villages. Settled families of the Anazah were found in **Saudi Arabia**; however, smaller groups of tribes settled near towns in **Kuwait**, Jordan, Iraq, Syria, and the West Bank. The establishment of borders between the states in the Middle East forced the nomadic tribes to accept citizenship in different states, and in most cases, it compelled them to change their lifestyle and settle down, but many of them were proud of their heritage and clung to their own tradition.

ANJERA. Some historians support the existence of rural, sedentary, and Arabized tribes in the region of the Straits of Gibraltar before the arrival of the Bani Hilal tribes (9th century). The *Jebli* dialect spoken by this group is regarded as the spoken **Arabic** in the *Maghreb* (place where the sun sets or "the West"), before the arrival of the Bani Hilal and Bani Maqil (between the 11th and 13th centuries).

Being part of the Bled Siba, its superiority over the neighboring tribes is evident. *See also* MOROCCO.

ARAB REVOLT. In June 1916, the sheriff of Makkah, Sheriff Hussein ben Ali, declared a revolt against the Turks. This revolt was known as "the Arab revolt." Great Britain financed the revolt, supplied weapons, and also sent specialists for guerrilla warfare, and at their head was Colonel T. E. Lawrence. The sheriff's army constituted the right flank of General Edmund Allenby's armies, which conquered **Palestine** and **Syria**.

In the sheriff's army, which was composed mostly of **nomads**, the tribes from Hejaz including Ateibe, Hathil, and Wathkif participated, as well as the tribes from Transjordan, like the Bani Zaher, Rawala, Hawitat, tribes from Horan, and tribes from Palestine, chiefly from the **Negev** region: the Jabarat, Tiaha, **Tarabin**, and Azazme. The Bedouin tribes of the Negev deserted from the front, while they fought by the side of the Ottomans in the Suez Canal against the British, after an appeal to them from Sheriff Hussein to join his forces.

The Bedouin tribes participated in the war effort to expel the Turks from the region, and their main activity was to carry out sabotage actions on the Hejaz railway line and attack Turkish posts in various areas. Thus, for example, the Bedouin leader Uda Abu Taya from Arab al-Hawitat succeeded in conquering Aqaba from the Turks and defending it until the forces of Sheriff Hussein entered it in July 1917.

Seventy Bedouins from the Negev, under the command of Abed Allah el-Gair, participated with Amir Zaid, the son of Sheriff Hussein, in an attack on the "*bey*" of El-Kark (Gur el-Mazraa), on the shore of the Dead Sea, and destroyed the Turkish boats that transported commodities to the Turkish forces in Jericho.

ARABIC LANGUAGE AND DIALECT. The Arabic **language** belongs to the Semitic branch. The Arabic language originated in the Arabian Peninsula, where it spread until the 7th century AD. **Islamic** conquests helped spread the language to the Fertile Crescent and the other parts of the Middle East and North Africa.

Over centuries, Arabic displaced the Greek, Aramaic, and Coptic languages, which were spoken in **Egypt**, **Palestine**, **Iran**, **Turkey**, **Syria**, and **Iraq**. Arabic became the mother tongue among most of the inhabitants of the region. On the other hand, in Iran, Turkey, Kurdistan, and other Muslim parts of Central Asia, the local languages continued to predominate. They were subject to significant influence, in part, by the Arabic language, because Arabic was considered to be the Holy Language of the Islamic **religion**, as it was the language of the Koran. Likewise, in northwest Africa also, the local languages were widespread along with Arabic. Moreover, in the Arabian Peninsula, Arabic ramified into various dialects, but on the strength of its spread over a large world space, many more dialects were created from it, in a manner that was distinguishable, one from the other, and also from the classical literary layer of the language. Already in its past, it is possible that even before the spread of Islam, the distinction had sharpened between the two layers of the language—the literary and colloquial.

Before Islam, standard Arabic was used in **poetry**, speeches, and formal use, as in negotiations between the tribes, in commerce, in Haj, and also in every official communication. Today standard Arabic is the proper spoken language in the Arab world, but changes have taken place in it, chiefly in the vocabulary.

Arabic was composed of several dialects that fused into one language, but the existence of these did not liquidate them at all. Moreover, they existed and exist with their speakers in intra-tribal daily life. When the speakers needed a common language in their contacts with members of other tribes, they adopted the fused language, literary and official Arabic. Indeed, the various readings of the Koran, written in the fused language, reflect, among others, the dialectic differences in the Arabian Peninsula before Islam. The Koran notes that the tribes had special dialects. Therefore, it could be noted that the Arabic diglossia had already been created among the Arabs before Islam. Each tribe had its own special dialect, and in parallel, the common pan-tribal language that served everybody was formed from the various dialects that were in contact. Since then, to date, the Arabic diglossia is a sociolinguistic fact in the whole Arab world.

Immediately at the beginning of the Islamic conquests, that is, from the start of the 7th century AD until the start of the 20th century, Bedouin tribes wandered from place to place in the regions of the Islamic Empire, which stretched from the Pyrenees Mountains on the France–Spain border in the west to India in the east.

In the period of the Islamic conquests the language that was used was spoken Arabic, and it was close to the literary language; it served as a means of communication between the Muslims in the New Muslim society. When the conquests ceased and the Arab regime was weakened and the non-Arab elements started to take authority in Muslim society, literary Arabic started to gradually crack and the language spoken in daily life started to change for several reasons: mainly the contacts of the Bedouins with the population that spoke other languages, such as Persian and Aramaic in Iraq, Coptic and Greek in Egypt, **Berber** in **Morocco**, and Greek in the Syrian region, and the transition to a permanent residence, which was close to towns and within them, and so on.

The development of the Arabic dialects was accelerated after the weakening of the **Abbasid** government in the 10th century, at a time when the Arabic-speaking region was divided into independent districts, such as the Mamelukes in the Syrian region, the Fatimids in Egypt, and so on. As a result of the combination of dialects in every district, groups of dialects were created, such as Iraqi, Syrian, Egyptian, North African, and the like.

The partition of the Arabic-speaking region into districts and states from the 18th century onward, as a result of the political situation, caused a certain geographical separation between the speakers of Arabic, and consequently, internal linguistic processes started. After the Ottoman government started weakening, at the start of the 20th century, European states such as England and France controlled the Arabic-speaking population. The English ruled Palestine and contemporary **Jordan**, and the French ruled Syria, **Lebanon**, and **Algeria**. This stamped an imprint on the spoken Arabic language.

Each of the dialects spoken in various states has a special flavor as a result of the mixture of the language of the locals ruled by a foreign regime, with the language of the foreign rulers, and also as a result of the independent internal linguistic development in the Arab regions themselves.

The large number of dialects in the Arab world from the Middle Ages is derived from the mobility of the Arab tribes within the Islamic Empire, from a mixture of the language of the Arabs with the languages of the locals, from the weakening of the Arab regimes, and from the rule of regimes speaking different languages.

It is also possible to select the dialects according to the sociological differentiation: a Bedouin and a settler (villager and townsmen). Likewise, there is a distinction in dialect according to the distribution into states, such as the Arabic spoken in Egypt, Morocco, Algeria, Iraq, Lebanon, **Kuwait**, Saudi Arabia, and so on. In every type, similar to this, various dialects exist, developing in a certain direction for social and political reasons. For more than 300 million people, Arabic is their mother tongue, although they do not speak the same Arabic in every region. In Egypt, for example, they speak a different Arabic from that which is spoken in Syria, as in Egypt the Arabic has been influenced by the ancient Egyptian language, and in Syria the Arabic was influenced by the Phoenician, Aramaic, and French languages.

ARAMSHE. Aramshe is a Bedouin village in northern **Israel**, next to the border between Israel and **Lebanon**, belonging to the local council Mateh Asher. The **settlement** was founded as a permanent settlement for the Bedouin tribes that lived in the region. On 5 August 2006, during the Second Lebanon War, the settlement was bombarded with a burst of Katyusha missiles, and consequently three female members of the same family were killed.

From the 1980s, the village started to develop. Many of the inhabitants served in the **Israel Defense Forces** (IDF) and had liberal professions. Fine stone houses were built and a great deal of money was invested in the village's infrastructure. Some 2,000 inhabitants live in the village.

ARARAT A NAQAB. Ararat a Naqab is a Bedouin town located near the ruins of the archeological site of Biblical Aroer. It was an urban center founded in 1982, as part of the **Israeli** government's project to settle the **Negev** Bedouins. The town was declared a local municipality in 1996, and according to the data of the Central Bureau of Statistics (CBS), in 2011, its population was 13,623. *See also* RAHAT.

ASHQIB AL-SALAM. Ashqib Al-Salam is a Bedouin urban center and local municipality southeast of Beer Sheva, founded in 1979 as part of a government project to settle the **Negev** Bedouins. Its name refers in part to the Sagiv creek that flows nearby, and in part it is a reminder of the Camp David peace accord signed between **Egypt** and **Israel** at the time.

According to the Central Bureau of Statistics (CBS), in January 2011, the population of Shaqib was 7,739. *See also* RAHAT.

ASSAD, BASHAR AL- (1965–). Bashar al-Assad has been the president of **Syria** since the demise of his father, **Hafez al-Assad**, in June 2000. The current number of Bedouins in Syria is estimated to be around 2 million people. Accordingly they received 30 seats in the parliament, which is comprised of 250 seats.

The Arab Spring revolt in Syria broke out in March 2011. The Bedouins fought on both sides, depending on their geographic location and their ties with the Assad regime. A few months before the start of the armed conflict, the leaders of important tribes, the Hasana, who lived near Homs, the **Shammar** confederation, which is the largest and most important tribe in Syria, and the Anazah tribe from southern Syria, spoke about the need for more freedom, and about joining the Syrian National Council, the body representing the Syrian opposition.

Other tribes that joined the opposition were: the Agheidat—who, like other Syrian tribes, extended across central and eastern Syria; the Hadidiyin, who joined the resistance troops near Aleppo and Idlib; the Mawali near Hama, Aleppo, and Raqqa; and the Bani Khalid, who joined the ranks of the Free Syria Army near Homs. Members of the Mawali tribe were also fighting the Syrian Army near Ma'arat Nu'man.

However, tribes whose leadership had developed close links with the security services in Syria and **Lebanon**, like the **Baggara**—a group of tribes in the Jazira, east of the Euphrates River—fought both for and against the regime. Their fighters joined the Syrian army in its attacks against the opposition-run suburbs of Aleppo. Others gathered around the tribe's leader, Al Bashir, in exile in **Turkey**, where he became a leader of the Council of Arab Tribes of Syria and leader of the Jazira and Euphrates Front, to liberate Syria (al Safir, 2013). Leaders of tribes that fought against the regime claimed that the tribes supporting the regime were bought out by the Assad dynasty.

The revolt has enabled the Bedouins to reassert themselves as political and military protagonists on the national scene, as either opponents or bastions of the current regime. In the event that there is no solution, the Bedouins will remain divided and fight for both sides. If the revolution fails and Assad prevails, the tribal leaders and their armed men who fight him could seek shelter in Lebanon's Bekaa Valley or look for asylum in **Jordan** or **Saudi**

Arabia. The victorious regime, whichever it may be, will need the loyalty and cooperation of the Bedouin tribes to rebuild Syria's infrastructure and reunite the country's diverse population into one nation.

ASSAD, HAFEZ AL- (1930–2000). By 1970, the Syrian Ba'ath Party had divided into two factions—one emphasizing the achievements of the socialist reforms and the other, led by Assad, attempting to build a practical and credible force against **Israel**. He organized and commanded a successful coup d'état, assumed general command, removed most of his political rivals from the Ba'ath Party, and became the sole head of the state. Being an Alawite, he sought relations with other minorities like the Druze and Bedouins and managed to form good ties with many Syrian Bedouin leaders, and also invited the **sheikhs** in exile to return to Syria.

As head of the state he supported the Bedouins, recognized the unique authoritative status of the sheikhs, and gave them the opportunity to exercise it according to their customary tradition. He also gave the Bedouins the right to manage their land and was rewarded by their apparent loyalty. In 1982, when the Syrian army slaughtered thousands of people in Hama in response to an **Islamic** uprising led by the Muslim Brothers movement, it was claimed that the army was helped by intelligence reports on the movements around Hama and Aleppo, gathered by members of the Hadidiyin tribe.

Agents of the government also mediated when disputes among the Bedouin **tribes** ensued. Assad involved Bedouin dignitaries in his administration. In 2010, the governor of Deraa was the sheikh of the Agheidat tribe. Being a *Bedouin* (a true Arab) is considered an honor, and thus, there are Ba'ath members, including important officials of the Internal Security System in Syria, who are proud to claim that they are of Bedouin origin. This trend continued during the governance of his son and successor, **Bashar al-Assad**, who needed the support and cooperation of a tribal leader who still had considerable backing in the Badia.

AWLAD HIMAYD. This tribe belonged to the Sudanese **Baggara** fraternity, a collective name for a group of nomad, cattle-**herding** tribes of Arabic origin, from the Kordofan and **Darfur** regions in **Sudan**. The lands of the Awlad Himayd were in the eastern parts of South Kordofan. They were nomadic people who shared routes with other Baggara tribes. Their travels took them as far as the heights of the White Nile.

The majority of the Awlad Himayd were shepherds, and the rest were farmers, growing sesame, millets, okra, and groundnuts. They also grew gum arabic and collect gums and honey from the woods.

They were considered courageous, great hunters of elephants and big game like the giraffe, antelope, *tiang*, and ostrich. They were also known to be great fighters of wild beasts such as, lions, tigers, wolves, and hyena. All Baggara tribes were Sunni Muslims. *See also* ISLAM.

AWS. The Aws tribe, which lived in the region of the town of Yathrib (al-Madinah), in the north of the Arabian Peninsula, reached this place from the south of the Arabian Peninsula—contemporary Yemen. It is known from Muslim history that this tribe supported the Prophet Muhammad and the new **religion** of **Islam**, and they helped him while he migrated to the town of Yathrib in the year 622, following the opposition of the **Quraysh** tribe toward him and his new religion. They played a central role in the promulgation of the religion of Islam and the birth of the Muslim state. *See also* SAUDI ARABIA.

AZAZME. Azazme is a Bedouin tribe that lives in southern **Israel**. In the 19th century they were allies of the **Tarabin** tribe and enemies of the Tiyaha tribe, with whom they fought over territory. The conflict was resolved by the Ottoman authorities in the early 20th century. About the same time, some clans of the Azazme tribe settled and founded a village at al-Khalasa, on the site of an ancient **Nabatean settlement**.

In 1930, the tribe's population was estimated to be around 10,000. This was split into 10 subgroups. They became seminomadic, as some tribe members took to **agriculture** and grew wheat and barley, and sometimes millet and watermelons.

In 1948, the tribe's population was estimated to be 3,500. They had ongoing quarrels with the Israeli authorities, who did not recognize the right of the tribes to all the land they claimed was theirs. The Israeli army forced them away from parts of the disputed territory. Thus, when an Israeli bus was attacked and passengers had been murdered, the United Nations observers claimed that it was a retaliation act of the Azazme, although the Israeli Army thought that the assailants came from across the border.

In the late 1960s, the Israeli army transferred them to the hill area east of Beer Sheva. Other sections of the tribe crossed the border eastward to **Jordan**, but the Jordanian government blocked their passage, fearing that a mass exodus of **Negev** Bedouins would follow.

Today, as a result of the government's decision to settle the nomadic tribe, the Israeli section of the Azazme tribe comprises about 18,000 members, living in three large villages, two of which, Shaqib al-Salam with a population of 6,500 people and Bir Hadaj with a population of 5,000 people, are recognized by the government and get infrastructure and services. There is also Wadi al-Na'am, which is an unrecognized village with 5,000 inhabitants. Some tribe members live in tiny, illegal, and therefore unrecognized settlements.

AZD. Azd is an Arabian tribe. They were a subtribe of the Kahlan tribe, one of the two branches of **Qahtan**. In the ancient times, they lived in and around Ma'rib, the capital of the ancient **Saba** Kingdom, which is in present-day **Yemen**. Their lands were irrigated by the Ma'rib Dam, one of the greatest irrigation systems built in the ancient world. After the third collapse of the dam (in the 3rd century AD) most of the tribe left the area and moved to other parts of Arabia.

For a time, the Azd Uman were the dominant Arab tribe in the eastern realms of the caliphate of Oman and were also the chief merchant group of **Oman** and Al-Ubulla, and were involved in **trade** with India. **Bahrain** and Oman provided the ports for Muslim naval fleets headed to Fars and Hind. From AD 637, the conquering forces were dominated by the Azdi and allied tribes from Oman. The Azd Uman became prominent in Basra during the governance of Ziyad bin Abihi and his son Ubaidullah. When their wealth and influence increased, many Azd tribes settled in Makran and Sindh. Their power was reduced during the governance of Al-Hajjaj ibn Yusufas in **Iraq** but began to recover during the reign of Caliph Sulayman ibn Abd al-Malik in 715.

B

BAGGARA. Baggara is a collective name for Arab groups of over a million members who live in the Sahel in North Africa, mainly between Lake Chad and southern Kordofan. In Chad they are called Shuwa/Diffa Arabs, and in **Sudan** they are called Baggara, derived from the **Arabic** word that means "cowman."

All these groups used to be traditional nomadic cattle herders, although today, some of them have settled down. All these groups speak a common **Arabic** dialect called *Shuwa* Arabic or Chadian Arabic; however, they do not consider themselves one people, but rather a group of people with a similar, common culture. The bulk of the "Baggara Arabs" live in Chad; the rest live or seasonally migrate southeast to Niger or southwest to Sudan.

The origin of the Baggara is undetermined, although DNA tests indicate that they have a common lineage with the **Qahtanite** Arabs, a characteristic they share with other Arabic speaking tribes in the Sahara. The Sahel group traces its ancestry to the Juhaina Arab tribes, who migrated directly from the Arabian Peninsula to North Africa.

The Baggara of **Darfur** and Kordofan in Sudan were the backbone of the Mahdist revolt against the Ottoman-Egyptian rule in the 1880s. Under the British system of indirect rule, the major Baggara tribes received a semi-independent status. Today, most of them are loyal members of the Umma Party. Many of them have formed semiofficial militia groups—the infamous **Janjaweed** and the Murahleen (mounted raiders)—armed by the Sudan government, who attacked and captured the land and livestock of non-Arabic elements in Sudan. However, by the mid-1990s various Baggara groups made a local truce with the Sudan People's Liberation Army forces.

BAHRAIN. Bahrain, before the onset of the oil industry, was situated in a highly tribalized region, characterized by **sedentarization** of both the urban and rural populations. **Ibn Khaldun** stated that Hadara was incapable of absorbing **tribalism** and tribal solidarity. He saw these two concepts as complementary and that an urban **settlement** was necessary for the continued domination of the tribes. He distinguished between **nomadism** and urbanism, and viewed the two concepts as defining different factors in the life of the Bahraini islands.

Bahrain is a tiny state in the Persian Gulf whose population stands at a million and a half people, out of whom half a million are migrants without status and at the time 70 percent of its citizens are Shiite Moslems. The royal family that has ruled Bahrain since the end of the 18th century is Sunni Moslem, which has fostered deep connections with **Saudi Arabia** and the United States.

The tribes have influenced Bahrain down the centuries. In the 15th century, the Al-Jaber family from Najd, which had connections with the strong Kingdom of Hormuz under Portuguese control, ruled the islands. In the 18th century the area was ruled by the Al-Madkhur family from **Oman**, as a dependency of **Iran**. In 1783, the Utub tribes penetrated from the **Arabian Peninsula** and terminated the Iranian domination. In the 19th century the British government got involved, and the Al-Khalifa family from the Utub **clan** became significant. These two groups accompanied the state into the 20th century.

In the latter period, the socioeconomic processes under the tribal influence chiefly determined the urban expansion in Bahrain and the Persian Gulf. Tribal towns such as Muharraq, Budayya, and Hidd were founded and expanded following the growth of coastal commerce. This mainly resulted from the settlement of the Utub confederacy in Bahrain, **Kuwait**, and Zubara. These clans created increased activity in the **pearl**-fishing **trade**, and this was spurred on by a wave of **migration** from the Arabian Peninsula. Thus, following the settlement of tribes in growing towns, the pressure on **agricultural** land diminished.

Therefore, in the 19th century, the Bahraini tribes had become maritime merchants and lived in urban quarters, *suqs* (**marketplace**), and houses of wealthy traders. There was a sharp distinction between their stone buildings and the poor mud and reed huts of the local communities. The pearl trade was showing its progress in Bahrain. Owing to the expansion of maritime trade with India, the agricultural land occupied by the local nontribal groups was abandoned. The production of **food** for internal consumption remained large, but exports of agricultural goods, mainly dates, was replaced by pearl fishing, controlled by the tribal upper classes.

Muharraq, situated on an island in the northeast of the Bahrain archipelago, became the "capital" of the al-Khalifa rule and the Utub tribe, and provided a home for the royal family and those who arrived after 1783. There were signs of growing prosperity, such as stone buildings and splendid architecture, which were due to the progress of pearling and fishing.

Al-Khalifa tried to retain political authority by controlling the commercial economy of the state, and by the early 20th century, the nomadic tribes had mostly settled in the cities. In the urban communities a new "tribal/mercantile" ethos developed. Many neighborhoods in the big cities mentioned earlier had a tribal name, and their organization was based on kinship.

In 1832, a native British political agent in Bushehr chose Manama as his home, and it soon became a British protectorate. However, at the start of the 20th century, Manama was described as a backward swamp, without stone houses and proper sanitation, but its population of 25,000 already exceeded that of Muharraq, which was chiefly composed of nontribal Shiite Baharnas, Iranians, and Arabs from al-Hasa, Qatif, and Basra. The fragment of Sunni inhabitants included many coastal tribes, slaves, and only five hundred Utub members.

Great Britain intervened a lot more in Bahraini matters, and Manama became the political capital of the state after Muharraq declined in influence and the royal family moved inland to Sakhir in the 1920s. In 1919, the municipality of Manama was founded (*baladiya al-manama*), as also an *emir* (king) for the ruling family, who had administrative control over the territory. The socioeconomic life of the capital was transferred here, leading to the establishment of the state of Bahrain. The baladiya was entrusted with the supply of **water** and electricity, with the cleaning and repairing of roads, and security in markets, gardens, and cemeteries. It was also entrusted with hiring night guards and a standing police force to replace the emir's entourage. It was funded by taxes on water, houses, and commercial installations (*see* URBANIZATION).

In 1905, Britain gained legal authority over the foreign residents of the country—Indians, Iranians, and immigrants from the Arabian Peninsula—and acquired more influence over the country. The non-Bahrainis obtained formal representation on the city council, as opposed to the informal relations with the tribes in the previous century. The first *majlis al-baladiya* was composed of four foreign members out of a total of eight, and they were appointed by a British political agent.

Fay Lorimer described the exploitation of the Shiite villagers by the urban Sunni tribal groups and referred to the Shia as a "class" as opposed to the Sunni—a "tribe." He claimed that the Shia lacked the ideology of kinship and, therefore, did not achieve political leadership. Linguistic terminology described this schism as "Shia," who were called *Baharna* or native residents of "Bahrain," in contrast to "Sunnis" who were termed the *Arabs* or new tribal arrivals to the islands (*see* ISLAM).

The other schism, the rural/urban split, continued after the 1930s. It saw the development of the oil industry destroying the traditional economy. After urban development, there was a sharp erosion of the land available for agriculture, which resulted in the enlargement of the road and transport systems. In 1959, only 5 percent of the population was employed in agriculture.

There are still great socioeconomic inequalities between the sectors in the state. There is a sharp contrast between the backward impoverished rural villages and the modern residential areas situated around the historical towns. The poor villages have produced the greatest anti-establishment opposition, particularly since the **Iranian** Revolution of 1979.

Until the end of the 19th century the British interests in Bahrain were chiefly economic, but in 1880 and 1892, agreements were signed making Bahrain a British protectorate, thus increasing Britain's meddling in Bahraini affairs. Manama became a focus of the power struggle between the Al-Khalifa rulers and the British, which reshaped the politically and economically significant quarters of the city. Until the reforms of the 1920s, Kanu and Fadhil, the seats of mercantile and British authority, were the wealthiest neighborhoods in the city. They were named after prominent Arab families and were the oldest residential neighborhoods. They were called al-Fadhil, after a Sunni family, whereas Kanu was named after the family that belonged to the Hawala Arab tribes, which had emigrated from **Iran** in the latter part of the 19th century.

Until 1905, Shuyukh was the official home of Ali b. Ahmad Al-Khalifa, a member of the Al-Khalifa family, who lodged a garrison of 12 to control the marketplace (suq). In 1905, after a dispute between the employees of a German firm and his soldiers, Ahmad was exiled by the British to India and his house was auctioned, but the Al-Khalifa family still owned most of the Shuyukh district, which by that time had become an extension of the suq. The neighborhood also housed the first municipality, through which all the administration was done.

At the end of the 1920s, the house of Charles Belgrave, the British adviser to the ruler of Bahrain from 1926 to 1957, was built close to the agency. This house became an administrative and financial center. A building close to the Bahrain Gate (Bab al-Bahrain) gave direct communication from the port to the suq; it lodged the new police, customs, and mixed courts departments, and the post. As the government ministries were built, they stretched more outward, toward the coastal region, away from the inland rural region.

Hamad bin Isa Al-Khalifa, the present-day king of Bahrain, is a scion of the Sunni royal family. The relations of the Al-Khalifa family with the Shiite majority have been unstable since the first days of the dynasty, when, with its ascent, the family confiscated the lands of the Shiite natives of Bahrain and made them vassals. The protest in Bahrain, which broke out in 2011, was suppressed by a combined effort of the forces of the ruling Sunni Al-Khalifa family and a joint force of the Arab oil states in the Persian Gulf with Saudi Arabia at their head. Thirty demonstrators were killed during the protest, most of them Shiites, and more than three mosques were destroyed, again most of them of the Shiite community. The demonstrators, who were members of the Shiite families, required social justice, a joint demand for many societies in the Middle East. An additional demand was democratization of the political life, which was controlled by the Al-Khalifa family since 1783.

The Shiite demand, combining a demand for social justice with political reforms, has existed for almost one hundred years. The economic data of Bahrain has pointed to continuing prosperity, especially with the discovery of oil in Bahrain. In 1932, Bahrain became the first state in the Persian Gulf where oil was discovered. The production of oil brought far-reaching changes from the demographic and economic points of view on the small island. The state had seen economic prosperity following a rise in the prices of oil in the world from the 1970s, but this was the property of a few, mainly of the ruling family and its proxies from the members of the Sunni tribes. The Shiite opposition complained that many Shiite villages suffered from overcrowding and a severe lack of infrastructure, while close to them there were huge, magnificent estates, under the ownership of the various members of the ruling family. Besides this, the unemployment among the Shiite youngsters was several times greater than their Sunni counterparts.

The demographic problem in Bahrain lay in the Bahraini royal house. The Bahraini government, in recent years, adopted a policy that was designed to change the demography in the state; thousands of immigrants, from **Syria**, **Jordan**, and **Yemen**, all of them Sunnis, were recruited to the security forces. Besides the exaggerated economic benefits, they along with their families were also given full citizenship. Basically the anti-Shiite government policy was what put the Shiites onto the streets in February and March 2011, as part of the Arab Spring revolution. Apparently if the government had not summoned army forces from the neighboring states they would have achieved a large part of their demands.

Five months after the suppression of the protest the Bahraini king made efforts to hold a national dialog with the Shiites. However, his promises mainly concerned the economic aspects of the protest. He declared that he did not plan to change the government system, to give greater authority to the elected parliament. The result was that the members of the Shiite opposition announced that they would no longer take part in the dialog, which was empty of content from their point of view. Today peace is kept in Bahrain, but the reasons for protest have stayed unchanged. It is inevitable that a further round of violence will break out between the Shiite majority and the Sunni government; the question is only when. *See also* KUWAIT.

BAKHTIARI TRIBE. The Bakhtiari tribe is made up of **clans** dwelling in the mountainous areas between the Chaharmahal, Fars, Khuzestan (the Taftoon Field), and Lorestan provinces. The tribe is split into two separate branches: Haft Lang, with 55 clans, and Cahar Lang, with 24 clans. These are mixed with the Arab and Lor clans. It is also called the great Lor. Most scholarly opinions state that this tribe is of **Kurdish** origin. Their chiefs have been influential in politics since the Safavids and Nader Shah in the early 18th century. Some of their chiefs helped participants in the constitutional revolution to conquer Tehran during the Period of Minor Despotism, when the **Qajar** king Mohammad Ali Shah suspended parliament and the constitution in 1907.

The two big groups, the Haft Lang and the Cahar Lang, are called *boluk*, which are split into a number of tribes, like the Duraki, Behdarvand, and Babadi in the Haft Lang and the Mamivand, Mohammad Saleh, Muguyi, and Kianerti in the Cahar Lang. The Bakhtiari term for these tribes is *bab*, each of which is a confederacy comprising a number of *tayefas*, each one of which is composed of seasonal *tiras*. Each tira is composed of family type groups of various descents, called *tas* or *awlad*. During the seasonal **migrations**, these function as a **herding** unit (*mal*) and camping unit (*ordu*), with 2 to 12 **tent**s pitched next to each other.

The tas or awlad are descent groups, as is the *bonku*. The tira and tayefa are political and administrative subdivisions. *See also* IRAN.

BALQA REVOLT. The Balqa area in Transjordan was divided into two opposing tribal confederacies, one of which—the Balqa alliance—was comprised of numerous small tribes called al Balqawiyya. The group also included the Ajarma, the Daja, the Bani Hasan, and the **Bani Hamida** tribes in the north. This confederation was led by the Adwan tribes, and professed a semisedentary lifestyle. They had herds of livestock, but they also cultivated land. The eastern part of the Balqa including the **desert** that stretched east of the Hejaz railway was inhabited by the nomadic tribes of the **Bani Sakhr** confederation led by the Fayiz tribe, whose ruling family possessed a number of villages southeast of Amman. Their lands were tilled by migrant peasants from **Palestine** and Syria.

In the summer of 1920, a period of no central authority in the area, the Bani Sakhr tried to expand their territory, but they were stopped by the Ajarma tribes. Alliances switched, and the tribes changed their support according to the tribal interests. When the British decided to back the Hashemite emir, Abdullah Bin Hussein, as king of Transjordan, they backed the interests of the nomadic tribes in the Balqa region at the expense of the semisedentary tribes.

The Bani Sakhr were the chief beneficiary of these developments. Their leader, Mithqal, was favored by the Hashemite king, and the tribal territory became his power base, where he later established his capital, Amman. By the summer of 1922, with the help of the British, the central government tried to govern the sedentary population by means of tax collection, establishment of law and order, and provision of health and **education** services. Nevertheless, when there was a dispute, the ruling house always favored the Bedouin nomad tribes.

The urban population, especially professionals, the middle class, and members of the Istiklal Extreme Nationalist's Party, were against the monarchy and resented its policy of favoritism. As soon as government agents clashed with the local population, riots broke out, mostly due to excessive taxation. The Balqa unrest increased. Abdullah was seen to be imposing British oppression to replace Turkish oppression.

In late August 1922, Adwan and Ajarma refused to water the **camels** of the Bani Sakhr in their wells at Hisban, in the Balqa territory. The leaders of the two rival confederations jostled for power, while the urban population organized demonstrations and demanded a comprehensive reform, reduction of government salaries, and the establishment of a representative assembly. However, some important tribes swore loyalty to the emir. They later used his newly formed Arab Legion to fend off the threat of the opposition. In September, the Balqa alliance marched toward Amman. They took over Suwaylih and its police stations, severed telephone and telegraph lines, and obstructed traffic on the Jerusalem-Amman road. On the following day the Arab Legion defeated them, and the leaders of the opposition fled to Jabal Druze (Druze Mountain) in southern **Syria**.

The failure of the revolt was the end of the Balqa alliance. The Arab Legion carried out arrests in Hisban, and the Bani Sakhr looted the camps of Adwan and Ajarma. When the emir managed to establish a centralized ruling system, he pardoned the Adwani **sheikhs**. They came back to Balqa and made peace with Abdullah and the Bani Sakhr. Moreover, their wealth helped them to establish good relations with King Abdullah. The Bani Sakhr renounced some of their former privileges, and the British prompted the emir to reform his administration. *See also* JORDAN.

BALUCHIS. The Baluchis live mostly in Baluchistan, an arid area in the southeast part of the Iranian steppe. It stretches from the Kerman **Desert** to the rest of the Bam and Beshagard Mountains, and to the western frontier of the Sind and Punjab provinces of Pakistan. When the Seljuks attacked Kerman in the 11th century, the Baluchis moved to Makran. They were then nomads and had never been governed by a centralized government, but lived under a tribal regime. **Iran** and Pakistan divided Baluchistan between themselves, and there was a land dispute between them, leading to an agreement in 1959. The Iranian part is now a section of the Sistan and Baluchistan province. The main towns in it are Zahedan, Zabol, Iranshahr, Saravan, Chahbahar, and others.

Baluch is the name of several tribes, a few of which live in the Republic of Turkmenistan. They speak Baluchi, which is a West Iranian **language** of the Indo-European family of languages under the influence of eastern Iranian jargons. It is split into two groups—Sorhadi (northern) Baluchis and Makrani (southern) Baluchis. There are a number of clans in the group: the chief ones are the Bameri, Balideh, Bozorgzadeh, Riggi, Sardaar Zaie, Shahbakhsh, Lashari, Mobaraki, Mir Morad Zaie, Naroyee, Nooshsiravani, Barohooyee, Baram-Zehi, and Shir-Khanzayee. The faith of the group is mostly that of the Hanafi sect of Sunni **Islam**. Some tribes in the Sistan region are also considered as Baluch, but their language is Sistani, which is a remnant dialect of Persian. The main tribes are Sarbandi, Shaharaki, Sargazi, Zamir-Farsyoon, Mir-Arab, and Sanjarani.

The Baluch tribes in the Sarhadd district (south and southeast of Zahedan) are always moving, either to pick dates from palm groves in the Maskel lowland or to find pasture for their sheep in the Sarhadd highland. The first group of date pickers lives in a *bonend*, which is a set of mud or brick huts where they live during the date harvest, and the second in the *halk*, where several families own a herd camp together. Lineage and not neighborhood is the main factor for marriage, prayer, house building, seasonal **migration**, quarrels, and the like. The territorial groups are formed from groups of descent, which are strengthened by matrimonial ties.

There is a confederacy of five "leading" tribes in Iranian Baluchistan, namely the Barakzi, Mir Moradzi, Bozorgzada, Bolida'I, and Sirani, to which the Mobaraki belonged in 1963. With other tribes, the Riggi and Esma'ilzi clans were dominant in Iranian Baluchistan, and the other tribes clung to them.

BANI AHSEN. Bani Ahsen is an Arab tribe of Bani Maqil. These are nomads who came to **Morocco** from Arabia in the 12th century. In the 16th century, they **wandered** between Missour and Almis of Guigou. In the 17th century, they advanced toward the northwest to the region of Sefrou, in order to reach the forest of Mamoura and the Plain of Gherb. In the 18th century they were pushed more westward by the Zemmour tribe, which moved up from the south. They are located in the region of Rabat on the Atlantic Coast.

BANI HAMIDA. Bani Hamida used to be a nomadic **shepherding** clan that controlled a territory east of the Dead Sea in the era of the Ottoman Empire. Local land disputes led to the shattering of property, including important archeological discoveries, such as the Moabite stone stela, which contained one of the earliest Hebrew scripts.

At the end of the 19th century, the Bani Hamida became renowned for breeding superb Arabian **horses**. Literary accounts of travelers from that period reveal that tourists who wanted to see Petra and other attractions in the area soon learned from experience that to reach their goal they had to make arrangements with the **sheikh** of the Hameideh. *See also* JORDAN.

BANI HASSAN. Bani Hassan was a part of a group of nomadic warrior tribes of Arabian origin who immigrated to North Africa in the 11th century. Bani Hassan descended from Maqil, an ancient Arab tribe, whose exact origin is unknown, but most scholars believed it came from **Yemen**.

This particular tribe settled in **Morocco** but later moved to **Mauritania**. Several armed conflicts between the Arab and **Berber** tribes led to a war in which the Bani Hassan and other warrior Arab tribes won and managed to establish their dominance over the local Berber tribes. Thus, since the 17th century, the **Arabic language** and culture have dominated the area. The Arabic dialect of a vast area in North Africa is called Hassaniya, after the Bani Hassan tribe, who introduced it.

Several other Arabian tribes joined the Maqils and became part of the Bani Hassan tribe.

Many descendants of the Bani Hassan tribes today still adhere to their ancestors' perception of their hereditary supremacy. This view has led to oppression, discrimination, and even enslavement (*see* SLAVERY) of other groups in Mauritania. In addition to this North African tribe, there is a Bani Hassan Bedouin tribe, which lives in the heights of northern **Jordan**.

BANI HELBA. An Arab **Baggara** group that lives in **Sudan** and Chad. They had been granted a large *hakura* (land grant) in the southern **Darfur** region by the government. During the 1980s, recurring drought in Chad drove several **clans** of Bani Helba to migrate eastward and join their kin in Darfur. The Bani Helba had been highly influenced by the ideology of Arab supremacy and had been actively involved in attacks upon the *Fur* (non-Arab). Many of the Bani Helba joined the **Janjaweed** militia, who raided and terrorized villagers during the last Sudanese civil war in the 1980s and 1990s.

The Bani Helba includes 15 major clans, which are Wolad Wolad Ghanim, Ghieth, Wolad Ali, Wolad Furkha, Gumaan, Zanateet, Hathalil, Bani Monzoor, Isharia, Mosawiyaih, Bani Labid, Hazazra, Gimailat, Mistinan, and Alwanaih.

BANI KHIRANE. This is a Bedouin Arab tribe of Bani Hilal that passed from Arabia to **Egypt** in the 10th century and entered **Morocco** in the 11th century under the reign of the Almohads. They are farmers who have preserved a Bedouin character.

BANI MALIK. Bani Malik, or Banu Malik, is one of the major Arabic tribes in the Arabian Peninsula. They attribute their progeny to Malik al-Ashtar, a known warrior who fought for a nephew of the Prophet Mohammad. Through Malik, they considered themselves descendants of **Qahtan**, the great ancestor of the southern Arabs. The Bani Malik is a side branch of the bigger tribe Khuza'a (also named Haritha), after the **Arabic** name of the peninsula.

The Bani Malik lived in the past in Ahwaz, Qatif, **Bahrain**, and **Iraq**. In Iraq today, they are found in the area of Basrah, Nassyriah, and the Al-Diwaniyah district in Iraq's middle area, east of the Euphrates River. The territory of their major subtribe, Al Ali, is rather extensive, from Al-Diwaniyah in the north to Al-Rumaitha in the south. They are semi-settlers and cultivate their immediate area, but when a given **water** source dries up, they move to the area of the next river.

BANI MATHAR. Bani Mathar is a Maqil tribe originating from Oran in South **Algeria**. In 1754, a conflict erupted between two *beys* in Algeria, and the tribe was divided into two. Each side supported a protagonist, and the fraction supporting the loser had to seek refuge with the sultan of **Morocco** to evade the conqueror. The sultan settled them in Ras El-Ain, which would carry the name of Ras Bani Mathar. They had been loyal to their nomadic traditional lifestyle until the middle of the 20th century.

BANI RASHEED. Bani Rasheed, or **Rashaida**, one of the largest tribes living in the Arabian Peninsula, is counted as one of the Adnani tribes, as they are the descendants of Rasheed Al-Zaul of the **Banu Abs** tribe.

The tribal lands of Bani Rasheed stretch from western **Saudi Arabia** to the Najd and from its northern border to the holy city of Madinah. Rashaida **clans** also live in **Kuwait** and the Gulf states, and some of their groups are also found in **Sudan** and Eritrea.

BANI SAKHR. Bani Sakhr is a large Bedouin tribe in **Jordan** who lived mainly from **camel trade** and the protection they could provide for villages, travelers, and so on. In 1867, soldiers of Muammed Said, pasha of Nablus, on behalf of the Ottoman Empire army, defeated the Bani Sakhr and ended their practice of collecting protection money from local villages. A few years later, an official survey revealed that they began to raise sheep and cattle, while their camel stock had reduced. In the 19th century, the clans of the Bani Sakhr lived on both sides of the Jordan River, on the edges of the Jezreel and the Bait Shean valleys. In 1799, warriors of the tribe joined other local forces in an attempt that failed to stop the invading army of Napoleon. The Bani Sakhr always rejected the Turks. Thus, due to the ongoing disputes, they left their territories west of the Jordan and concentrated near Wadi Farrah, from where they spread to other parts of southern Jordan.

In June 1917, one of the military leaders of the Bani Sakhr met secretly with T. E. Lawrence to coordinate the efforts against the Turks.

Until 1920, the Bani Sakhr was an ally of the Al Rashid dynasty. The alliance ended when the **Ibn Saud** dynasty conquered the throne in **Saudi Arabia**.

On 8 April 1933, **Sheikh** Mithqal Pasha al-Faiz, who was chief of the Bani Sakhr, and a member of a delegation, met the Jewish Zionist leadership in King David Hotel in Jerusalem. During the British mandate, after some years of drought and famine, most of the Bani Sakhr gave up their nomadic lifestyle and settled. This tribe is loyal to the ruling dynasty of Jordan and, more often than not, cooperates with the Jordanian government.

BANI SNASSEN. This tribe, also called Bani Isnassen, is of Zenata tribal origin, but it also contains Arab elements. According to tradition, the current tribe settled more to the east, near Mascara in **Algeria**. They had to leave it toward the 19th century in order to confine themselves to the mountainous region, which bears their name today. The tribe is divided into four fractions: Bani Khaled, Bani Atike, Bani Ourimeche, and Bani Mangouche. One can add Triffa, who are of Arab race and dialect, and who are composed of the Ouled Sghir, Laatamna, Hawara, and Ouled Mansour.

BANI YAS. Bani Yas is a tribal confederation, originally from central Arabia, that today lives in the **United Arab Emirates** (UAE). The Bani Yas have a coalition with other tribes in the region from Dubai to Khawr al Udayd located southeast of Qatar. In the past, the tribe was led by their rulers, the Al Nahyan, predecessors of the modern city of **Abu Dhabi**, whose headquarters was in Al Dhafra. The ruling families of the UAE and Abu Dhabi are both from important subbranches of this tribe.

Bani Yas is the major leading tribe of the Abu Dhabi Emirate. The tribe is subdivided into 20 subsections. The present rulers, the Al Nahyan family, migrated from their center in the **oasis** of Liwa to the Island of Abu Dhabi in 1793. Many members of this tribe used to spend their winters with the **camels** in the **desert** and move near the coast and engage in **fishing** in the summer. In 1833, a big group of Bani Yas moved to Dubai under the leadership of Maktoum bin Buti al Maktoum, whose descendants rule Dubai to this day.

Tribesmen of Mazrui, the main Bedouin section of Bani Yas, lived in **settlements** close to Liwa, on **pearling**, camel trading, and date plantations. These Liwa villages had settlers mostly in the form of sedentary or semisedentary Hawamil section tribesmen, many of whom possessed goats and sheep. However, many of them also own boats and in the past had a share in the pearling industry. The Mahariba section was also nomadic and semisedentary. They were involved in pearl diving and owned a small fleet of 40 pearling boats.

These tribes formed a confederation, which was the basis for a nation state in a vast, varied territory. The subgroups of Bani Yas intermingled and married with each other and shared grazing areas and boats. They lived in the Liwa villages or in Abu Dhabi city, where intermarriage was easy. They were known for their generosity, **hospitality**, chivalry, and patronage of the arts.

BANU ABS. The Banu Abs tribe is an **Adnani** Bedouin tribe known in records since the time of Christ. It is a side branch of the powerful Ghatafan tribe of central Arabia. The tribe lives today in the Arabian Peninsula, and its neighboring Eritrea and **Jordan**. Branches of this tribe are found in **Egypt**, **Sudan**, **Israel**, and **Lebanon**. There are also communities of this tribe in Europe and the United States. This tribe is connected to one of the earliest popular war and love stories in **Arabic** literature, the story of Antar and Abla.

This tribe had been involved in wars in the past and was known among all Arabs for their independence and bravery. One of the Arabian rulers from this tribe, King Zuhair, was famous for ending the vicious continuous tribal wars in the Arabian Peninsula. King Zuhair had also predicted the arrival of the Prophet Muhammad and advised his people to follow him. The entire tribe converted to **Islam** before the **Hijra** of the Muslims to Medina. Its members participated in the Arab conquests and helped spread **Islam**. Several peoples today, throughout the Middle East and North Africa, claim ancestry to this legendary tribe. The Ottoman Empire recognized the special status of the Banu Abs and granted them autonomy.

The large and prestigious Rasheed tribe has descended from the Banu Abs. Today, many of the politically active members of the tribe are in the **Kuwaiti** Parliament. Other variations of the name are Al-Absy, Al-Absi, Absy, Absi, Abzi, and the like.

BANU BAKR. (*Banu bakr ibn wail.*) This tribe belonged to the **Adnanite** tribes of North Arabia and were from the large branch of the **Rabi'ah** confederation. The tribe is known for being engaged for 40 years of the **pre-Islamic era** with its relative tribe Taghlib. The pre-Islamic poet Tarafah was a member of Bakr tribe. The original lands of the Banu Bakr were in Negd, in central Arabia; however, its nomad sections moved northward in the pre-Islamic era. They settled in the plains of Al-Jazirah, on the upper Euphrates River. The region of Diyar Bakr and the city of Diyarbakır in southern **Turkey** are named after this tribe. Some segments of the tribe remained in their original land in al-Yamama. Their descendants lived in the area, mostly in and around Riyadh.

BANU HAMMAD. Banu Hammad is an Arabic tribe that had migrated from the Arabic side of the Persian Gulf to **Iran**. However, many members of the tribes have left Iran and returned to the Arab Gulf States. Today, people from the Banu Hammad live in the **United Arab Emirates**, Qatar, and **Bahrain**.

BANU HANIFA. The Banu Hanifa are an ancient Arab tribe that lived in Al Yamama, in central Arabia. According to legend, they came to Yamama from Hejaz. They belonged to the great **Rabi'ah** branch of the North Arabian tribes. In **pre-Islamic** times, the Banu Hanifa seemed to have been mostly sedentary. Historical sources attribute the building of Hadjr, the predecessor of today's Riyadh, to this tribe.

The Banu Hanifa played an important role in early Islamic history, being among the first tribe in Arabia to embrace **Islam** and renounce **Christianity**. However, after the death of Muhammad, one of their leaders, Musaylima, declared himself a prophet equal to Muhammad. This declaration, along with other apostasy movements that spread in Arabia, led to the Ridda Wars, in which the Muslims of Medina won but with heavy losses. After the wars, the Banu Hanifa made peace with the Muslims and rejoined the new Islamic state. For a while, the tribe members were banned from the early Muslim conquering forces, but eventually they joined the Muslim forces in **Iraq** and some of them settled there.

During the 9th century local difficulties with the regime drove many of the Banu Hanifa eastward to Iraq and westward to **Egypt**. Perhaps some of their descendants, who merged with other people, still live near and around Riyadh. *See also* SAUDI ARABIA.

BANU HARITH. The Banu Harith are an Arabic tribe that descended from the **Qahtanite** people, who converted to Judaism in **pre-Islamic** times. The **Christian** invasion forced them out of their place of origin. Some of them moved to Hejaz, while others moved southward to Sana'a.

The Harith who migrated to Hejaz were urged to convert to **Islam**, but those who wanted to remain Jewish were allowed to remain Jewish and had to pay a given token, but they were included in the constitution of Medina and were recognized as allies to the Muslims, and given the same rights of protection as Banu Awf.

A small fraction of the Banu Harith lived and thrived semiautonomously in the border city of Najran until the 1930s, when the city was conquered by the Saudis. In 1934, Governor Amir Turki bin Mahdi gave the local Jewish community one day to leave or convert. The remainder of the Banu Harith fled south to Sana'a and Aden. They migrated to **Israel** along with a majority of the Yemenite Jews.

BANU HASHIM. Banu Hashim was a **clan** in the **Quraysh** tribe. Hashim, the grandfather of the Prophet Muhammad, was a member of this clan; therefore, those who descend from him are called Hashemites.

The **pre-Islamic** Arab people classified themselves according to their clan and its roots. The two major lines were the Adnani, the descendants of **Adnan**, the traditional ancestor of the Arabs who lived in north, central, and west Arabia and the **Qahtani**, the descendants of Qahtan, the traditional ancestor of the Arabs who lived in the south and southeast Arabia.

The house of 'Abd al-Muttalib of Banu Hashim of Quraysh was considered nobility in pre-Islamic Makkah (Mecca of today) due to their hereditary duty to look after pilgrims coming to Makkah to worship the *Kaabah*. This was the sacred shrine that according to Islamic tradition was built by the patriarch Abraham and his son Ishmael.

The Muslim community of Makkah made ***hijrah*** (immigrated) to the town of Yathrib, the previous name of Medina.

Over the centuries there were many false lines of descendants that spread eastward and appeared in south India and Pakistan.

There have been many attempts to resolve the confusion surrounding the descendants of Muhammad, the most famous one being the *Kitab al-Ashraf*, a list produced by the Ottoman caliphs in the 19th century AD, which is kept in the Topkapi Palace in Istanbul. The clans that are considered the legitimate descendants of the Prophet's line are the Hashemites, former sharifs of Makkah, who rule the Kingdom of **Jordan**, and used to rule the **Iraqi** Hejaz and the Fatimi line, who were the caliphs of Egypt. *See also* SAUDI ARABIA.

BANU NADIR. The Banu Nadir tribe is one of the three Jewish tribes that lived close to the town of Yathrib (today al-Madinah), in Hijaz, in the Arabian Peninsula, in the 7th century. The other two main tribes were the Bani Qainuqa and the Bani Qurayza.

Similar to the rest of the Jews of Yathrib, the tribal members bore Arab names but spoke **Arabic** in a separate dialect. The tribe's members were farmers and dealt with the growth of dates and also loaned money and **traded** in jewels. The tribe lived near wells on parts of the most fertile lands in the region.

Starting from the year 622, the year of emigration of Muhammad from Makkah to al-Madinah (Yathrib) until 624, Muhammad tried to spread his new **religion** among the Jews of al-Madinah. His attempts did not succeed, and in the year 624, a month after the battle of Badr, the Jewish members of the Qainuqa tribe were deported from al-Madinah to Al-Kura, and thence to Edrai (southern Syria, not far from the Kinneret). However, the Banu Nadir tribe did not intervene in the events, as they saw the deportation in the framework of struggles between the tribes.

One of the members of the Banu Nadir tribe was the poet Ka'b ibn al-Ashraf, a son of an Arab father and a Jewish mother, who was numbered with its leaders. Al-Ashraf was hostile to Muhammad and wrote poems that expressed this hostility, and more poems that were perceived by Muslims as insulting. On account of this al-Ashraf was murdered by Muslim Arabs. After al-Ashraf's murder, the relations between the tribe and Muhammad escalated. The Muslim sources ascribed to the Banu Nadir a conspiracy to murder Muhammad, which was revealed to him only when he waited to receive a financial contribution and imposed a deportation order on the tribe's members.

The tribe decided to oppose the deportation order, out of belief that other tribes would support them. However, after a siege of 14 days, during which the Muslims burned their date orchards, contrary to the practices of war in the Arabian Peninsula, and when help was late in coming, the tribe surrendered. After the defeat of the tribe in the year 625, the sons were permitted to go into exile and to bring with them a load on a single **camel** for all three people, while the rest of their assets and belongings were seized. The tribe members wandered northward with 600 camels accompanying them.

Members of the tribe who were deported linked up with other Jewish tribes, most of them in Khaybar, and with the enemies of Muhammad and the Arab tribes of Makkah. After a battle that took place between the two sides, the Muslims won. Their leader, Hai ben Ahitov, was executed with his son, as also were all the members of the tribe of **Banu Qurayza**. The struggle that the Muslims launched against the Jewish tribes weakened their power greatly. *See also* SAUDI ARABIA.

BANU QAINUQA. The Banu Qainuqa tribe was one of the three **Jewish** tribes that lived close to the town of Yathrib (today Al-Madinah) in Hijaz (northeast of **Saudi Arabia**) on the Arabian Peninsula in the 7th century. The other two main tribes were the **Banu Qurayza** and the **Banu Nadir**. The Muslims deported them from the city in the year 624 after they joined their opponents.

BANU QURAYZA. Banu Qurayza is a Jewish tribe that lived in the north of the Arabian Peninsula until the seventh century, close to the town of Yathrib (subsequently, the town of Al-Madinah).

In the year 622, the Prophet Muhammad reached Yathrib from Makkah. After his arrival, tension between the flourishing Muslim population and the Jewish population grew. In the year 627, Muhammad's tribe, Quraysh, imposed a siege against the city together with their allies, in a battle called "the Battle of the Trench." Members of the Banu Qurayza tribe held negotiations with the besiegers but to no benefit, and finally they were forced to surrender to the Muslims. The Muslims, under the command of Muhammad, killed almost all the men by decapitation, apart from a few of the men who converted to **Islam**.

BANU SHAYBAN. Banu Shayban was an Arab Bedouin tribe known since **pre-Islamic** times that lived in the area of Al-Jazira and moved with its herds according to the seasons. They used to spend their winters in Negd in central Arabia and wander to the fertile plains around the Euphrates River in the summer, from Al-Jazira in the north down to the Persian Gulf in the southeast. Their main territorial disputes were with the **Banu Taghlib** and **Banu Tamim** tribes. The tribe was famous for the remarkable quality of its poets (*see* POETRY), its use of a pure form of **Arabic language**, and its fighting ardor.

In the early **Islamic** era, the Shayban were allies of Muhammad's clan, the **Banu Hashim**. The Shayban played a leading role in the conquest of **Iraq** during the campaign against Persia. In Umayyad times, the Shayban remained powerful in Jazira and were involved in local revolts. During the period of the 8th to 11th centuries, members of this tribe filled high-ranking positions in the caliphate. Members of the tribe are mentioned in the historical records in Iraq and **Syria** in the late 10th and 11th centuries. As the tribe has fragmented and dispersed, it is not clear which of the modern **clans** and subgroups can trace their ancestry to the Shayban.

BANU TAGHLIB. Banu Taghlib was a large and powerful Arabian tribe in Mesopotamia and eastern Arabia that traced its lineage to the large branch of North Arabian tribes (**Adnanites**) known as **Rabi'ah**. Their ancestral homelands were the region of Nejd, from which they moved northward to the Jazirah plain in northern **Iraq** during the 6th century. At that time, the tribe was **Christian**, but they converted to **Islam**. Its formidable size and strength led a known classical Arab genealogist to state, "Had they not converted to Islam the Taghlib would have devoured the Arabs."

The tribe was engaged in a 40-year war with their related tribe, **Banu Bakr**, in the late **pre-Islamic era** (494–534), and their **migration** to Al-Jazirah is sometimes attributed to that war. One of the most famous classical Arab poets (*see* POETRY), Amr ibn Kulthum, comes from this tribe. The Taghlib were one of the few Arab tribes that did not accept Islam during Muhammad's time or during the rule of his immediate successor.

The most famous Taghlib in the Umayyad era was the Christian poet Al-Akhtal, who is even today regarded as one of the finest Arab poets of the classical era. He was said to have been a close companion of the Caliph Yazid I.

Around 750, sections of the tribe began to convert to Islam in the hope of obtaining more political power within the Muslim realm. Gradually, since then, the tribe has settled and melted into the populations of northern Mesopotamia, where some families claim a Taghlibi descent even today.

BANU TAMIM. The Banu Tamim or the Bani Tamim tribe is one of the major Arab tribes whose history goes back to the **pre-Islamic era**.

Today, people of the Tamim tribe live in **Saudi Arabia** and all its neighboring countries, except **Yemen**. They can be found in all the Gulf States, **Kuwait**, **Iraq**, **Jordan**, **Syria**, **Lebanon**, and the **Palestinian authority**, while some groups have migrated to **Egypt** and Tunisia. Banu Tamim are proud of their heritage, and they record all births and important family data.

BANU YAM. Banu Yam is the principal tribe of the Najran Province in **Saudi Arabia**, and they belong to the Arab tribe of Qantanite origin, which makes them natives of southern Arabia. The Arabian **Desert** plains formed their surroundings, which suited their **nomadic** lifestyle. Today most of them have settled in small villages. Most of the Yam belong to the Isma'ili branch of Shi'a **Islam**. In recent centuries, groups of Yam migrated to other parts of Saudi Arabia, especially to the area of Jeddah and Dammam. In the past, Yam raiding was feared and considered a menace, a practice they abandoned only in the beginning of the 20th century.

BARA'SA. Bara'sa was a **Libyan** tribe. Muammar Gadhafi's second wife was a member of this tribe, and many of his sons and daughters are thought to have supported it. Some of its members were appointed to intermediate-level bureaucratic positions. Even as numerous members moved to the opposition in 2011, the tribal leaders did not make overt statements as to their allegiance.

BARASA UBAIDAT WAR. The Barasa Ubaidat War was a 30-year armed conflict between two rival tribes for the domination and control of northern Cyrenaica, in **Libya**. The war started in 1860, when the Ubaidat refused to accept the Ottoman government's appointment of Abubakr Haddouth as the leader of **Barasa**. The war lasted until 1890, and the Ubaidat won it. During the Ottoman regime, there were several previous tribal wars in the area. These wars ended during the Italian invasion of Libya in 1911, which unified all the tribes against the invaders under the leadership of the Senussi tribe leader.

BASUS WAR (HARB AL-BASUS). This war was a 40-year conflict between two rival clans, the Taghlib and the Bakr, in Arabia, in the medieval period (494–534). This war lasted very long and its ramifications were incorporated into an Arab aphorism that warned people against **vendettas**.

BEDOUIN ARAB ORGANIZATION. The Bedouin Arab Organization (*Jama'yat Al-Budo Al A'rabia*) was founded in **Negev** in 1934, to form a united body and generate a plan for a national struggle against the Zionist enterprise, as part of the Palestinian national struggle against the Jewish population in **Palestine**. They planned to organize attacks on the Jewish traffic and **settlements**. Furthermore, in order to achieve it, they had to recruit the Bedouin tribes for the cause. As the Bedouins were scattered over vast spaces, sheikhs' assemblies seemed to be an effective instrument for organization and information exchange. At some point they tried to distribute letters and leaflets, but as most of the population was illiterate, they needed to pass along instruction and information verbally.

On 17 September 1947, the tribal leaders participated in a large convention to decide the best policy guidelines that the Arab states should adopt in the forthcoming United Nations General Assembly regarding the future of Palestine. They all wanted the British out and demanded that the UN declare Palestine an independent democratic state, with a right to self-determination, to express opposition to the partition of Palestine, and to establish social, **educational**, and health services for the Bedouin tribes in the Negev, and allocate resources for economic development in the area.

In a later meeting, attended by the sheikhs of the **Tarabin**, the Azazme, and the Tiaha tribes, they raised the idea of forming a national guard in every tribe, to keep order and discipline subject to instructions from the Supreme Arab Committee, headed by Haj Amin el-Husseini, the mufti of Jerusalem. The society was the central body that led and represented the Bedouins in southern Palestine at the time. *See also* ISRAEL.

BERBERS. The Berber people (or Imazighen, singular Azamigh, meaning "free people" or "free and noble men") have lived in the region between the Atlantic Ocean in the west, the Mediterranean Sea in the north, the Siwa **Oasis** in **Egypt** in the east, and the Niger River in the south since approximately 10,000 BC. Numidia was an ancient Berber kingdom that became a Roman province and client state. Massinissa, its great king (238–138 BC), ruled a territory that stretched from **Mauritania** to the borders of Carthage and included Cyrenaica in modern-day **Libya**. Between 112 and 106 BC the Romans fought with King Jugurtha of Numidia, in the Jugurthine War, which the Romans won.

In the 7th century AD, Muslim Arabs invaded this region and pushed the Berbers back to the Maghreb region, which included **Morocco**, Mauritania, **Algeria**, and Tunisia. The Muslims who invaded Spain in 711 were mostly Berbers and their leader, Tariq ibn Ziyad, was a Berber. The invasion of the Arab Muslim tribe Banu Hilal from Hejaz and Najd in the Arabian Peninsula, which the Fatimid Empire instigated in the 11th century AD, made deep inroads into the Zirid Berber domains and authority. There were several Berber dynasties in the Middle Ages, notably the Zirids, Hammadids, Almoravids, Almohads, and **Marinids**.

The Arabs spread their **Islamic** faith far and wide in the Maghreb, and the process of Arabization and Islamization greatly influenced the Berbers from a cultural, linguistic, political, and ethnic point of view. The Berbers had dark skin and mixed in with the Arab invaders but retained their independent **language** and ethnic identity. However, some studies claim that the DNA of Berbers was not influenced much by the Arab invasions and that they only changed the local population from a religious point of view. There was also a phenomenon of Berber piracy in the Renaissance era and Berber **slavery** in the modern era. The Ottoman Empire failed to make any great impact on Berber history, but the French in the European colonial era did make inroads into the population. Their settlers (*pieds-noirs*) intermingled with them and changed their racial character slightly. A famous contemporary Berber is the Franco-Tunisian football player Zinedine **Zidane**, who captained the victorious French team in the World Cup Final in Paris in 1998. Also many Libyan Berbers joined the insurgents in the Libyan Civil War against Muammar Gadhafi in 2011.

There are 25 to 30 million Berber speakers in North Africa today, speaking approximately 300 dialects of the language. Today there are approximately 9.5 million Berbers in Morocco, 4.3 million in Algeria, and smaller numbers in nearby countries. The Berbers are divided into groups speaking different dialects: the largest of these are Rif, Kabyle, Shawia, Touareg, Haratin, Shluh, and Beraber.

Although most Berbers are sedentary farmers, some of them cultivate crops in the lowland in the winter and graze their flocks of sheep in the summer in the mountains. Others are pastoral **nomads** throughout the whole year. The principal Berber crops are wheat, barley, fruits, vegetables, nuts, and olives. They herd together sheep, cattle, and goats, and also grow **camels**, oxen, mules, and **horses** for transport. They live in single-floor houses made of stone, build strongholds for defense and storage out of mud, and live in goat-hair **tents** when they graze their flock. Many Berbers are migrants in Spain and France, and many migrant laborers have moved to big cities both in Europe and in North Africa. *See also* AGRICULTURE; HERDING.

BIR AL-MAKSUR. Bir Al-Maksur is a Bedouin village, with a status of local council, in the northern district in **Israel**. The **settlement** lies in the Lower **Galilee** southeast of Shfaram and was recognized as a local council in the year 1990. The settlement was founded for members of the Hujirat tribe. The number of inhabitants in the village stands at nine thousand people today.

BISHA'A. This is a ritual practiced by the Bedouin tribes in **Jordan**, south **Israel** (**Negev**) and **Sinai**, and also in certain **desert** tribes of **Saudi Arabia**. It is part of the Sharal, the honor code of the desert tribes. The purpose of this ritual is to detect lies.

The *Bisha'a* is performed only when there are no witnesses to an offense or misdeed and there are doubts regarding the truth. It is supposed to be taken voluntarily, but naturally, honor decrees and people feel obliged. The ritual is usually a public affair, and **women** are allowed to participate. Declining from taking the test or running away is considered proof of guilt.

The right to perform *Bisha'a* is granted only to a public figure called *mubesha*, who is expected to conduct a hearing before he announces the need for the test. The right to act as mubesha is passed on from father to son throughout the generations.

Today, performance of the ritual and others like it is quite rare, as most Bedouins prefer to use the regular court systems for justice.

BUAINAIN. Buainain is an Arab Bedouin tribe, a subtribe of the large **Banu Tamim**. They live primarily on the western side of the Persian Gulf. At the end of the 18th century, after the island was conquered by Al Khalifa, many of them moved to **Bahrain**. **Clans** of this tribe also live in **Saudi Arabia** and Qatar. Unlike other Bedouin tribes, the Buainain did not live as nomads but used to depend on their diving skills and were part of the lucrative **pearl-diving** industry.

The tribe was highly influential in Qatar and built Al Wakrah, Qatar's former capital, toward the end of the 19th century. Several members of this tribe returned to their original village, Ainaim in Saudi Arabia, and eventually built the new city of Jubail, where they are the principal dwellers.

C

CAMEL. The Bedouins call the camel "the ship of the **desert**" (*sfinat el-sahara*). This appellation was given to the camel on account of its capacities to live in the hard conditions of the desert, and this is demonstrated in its various characteristics: its feet have "hooves" that are wide and are adapted to stepping easily over the desert sands without sinking; the camel has a pair of eyes and above them developed eyelids that serve as a shield for the eye from the sand grains borne in sandstorms; the body of the camel is covered with wool called "*waber*," which helps in the regulation of the temperature in a slow manner and gradually, which is beneficial, as it maintains the balance of **water** in the body in addition to balancing the body's temperature. The camel can live for 15 days without drinking water. The camel has helped the Bedouins in their survival in the desert, aiding them on their journeys, in carrying things, in wars, and in **agriculture**. The camel has enabled the development of ancient **trade** routes; the connection between East and West has been managed on the humps of the camel. The camel has made possible the fragile existence of the son of the desert. Therefore, it is not surprising that the camel has become an object of admiration among the Bedouin tribes and a part of their entire folklore.

The camel constituted the central means of transport in trade. The Bedouin tribes in their commercial journeys, similar to the rest of the societies in the ancient world and the old world, conducted this in trade caravans. This method was popular until the success of the transport revolution at the end of the 18th century, which was a derivative of the industrial revolution. From the time trains and cars started being used for transport of freight, the use of trade caravans decreased significantly, until it totally disappeared.

The trade caravans in the east used to encamp or unload their goods in castles called *khan*. The Bedouins used the fur of the camels as a mattress, ate its flesh, and drank the milk of the female camel. The camel earned a great deal of respect from the Bedouin. He sorted the camels into various breeds—every breed or type of camel was different in price and in form, as also in the quantity of milk that the female camel produced.

The camel together with the **horse** merited special treatment by the Bedouins. The camel constituted a measure of money, honor, and power. In the past, they would assess the wealth and power of the tribe by the number of camels under its ownership. In the past, the camel constituted the bride's price. The bride price was calculated by the number of camels that the bride's family would receive; the higher the class of the bride, the higher the number of camels. Likewise the camels constituted the price of ransom payments; the tribes paid in the form of camels to prevent bloodshed, and during quarrels, camels were offered as payment to prevent a **vendetta**. The camel was considered a loyal friend of the Bedouin under severe desert conditions; it was his desert ship. The camel constituted an example of patience. An emotional connection developed between the Bedouin and the camel; the Bedouin sang to the camels, and they answered with their shouts of joy. Arab poets composed verses of **poetry** in honor of the camel.

The honor of the camel was severely damaged with the appearance of off-road vehicles, capable of moving quickly and efficiently even in the hardest of territories. The Bedouins adapted themselves very quickly to the off-road vehicles and abandoned the camels—life became easier and quicker. The slow swinging of the camel's hump was replaced by the swiftness of Jeeps. The honor of the camel passed from the world and apparently did not come back.

A few places still use the camel as a beast of burden. The dominance of the camel today is found in the camel races, which are considered a hit, and here hundreds of thousands of dollars are poured out for a female camel or in memory of the winner of the race. *See also* HORSE.

CHAAMBA. This is a big Arab tribe based mainly in the north of the Algerian Sahara. They are descendants of Banu Sulaym, who migrated from Arabia following the Banu Hilal tribe, and settled in Cyrenaica and Tripolitania. They live in the **oases** of Ouargla and El-Oued. Their main towns are Metlili, El Meni'a, and Zelfana, located in the Gherdaia province. Groups affiliated with them live in the great western Erg (Bani Abbes and Timimoun), and a section of this tribe lives among the Toureg of South **Algeria** and the **Libyan** town of Ghdemes.

One part of the Chaamba lives as **nomadic shepherds** who roam on the fringes of the **desert** according to seasons, while the other part has adopted **agriculture** and become *fellahin* (farmers). The fellahin live in *ksour* or *ksars* (castles) on the fringes of the desert (Ksar Metlili, El Meni'a [Mneaha], Zelfana, etc.). They speak Badawi, the common Bedouin **language** in the Sahara, which is a dialect containing expressions drawn from the Makkahn dialect specifically as concerns **camel** breeding.

The tribe consists of three main groups: the Chaamba of Gherdaia, the Ourgla group, and the Chaamba Mouadi. The Chaamba are allied with the Banu Sulaym, the Achecha, and the Messaba tribes.

CHRISTIAN TRIBES. Christianity had entered the Arabian Peninsula by missionary actions or by the entry of monks, who wanted to live a modest life within the **desert** and far from the life of luxury. Christianity spread among many tribes from the **Syrian** region, **Iraq**, and within the Arabian Peninsula.

There is no unanimity among researchers as to an exact date of the arrival of Christianity to the Arabian Peninsula. Some state that this occurred immediately in the period of Jesus, after Bedouin tribes from Eastern Transjordan came to listen to the words of Jesus. Regardless, Christianity had already entered Arab countries by the 1st century AD. By the 4th century it had already spread among them. The first Arab Christians were those who started to preach Christianity among the Arabian people.

According to most of the fathers and historians of the church, the apostle Paul was the initiator of the Christian movement in Arabia, as in his Epistle to the Galatians, when he talks about the time following his conversion, he states: "Neither went I up to Jerusalem to them which were apostles before me; but I went to Arabia, and returned to Damascus" (Galatians 1:17). What his specific itinerary was, the duration of his stay, his motive, and what he executed there has not been specified. His journey is known to have lasted a year.

Persecution of early believers in Jesus by the Roman and Persian empires forced many of them to flee to Arabia. The propagation of Christianity among the Arabian tribes was done by churches, which were present in Iraq, Syria, and Abyssinia. This was executed in several ways by missionaries who came from various churches in the region and in different **languages**. This demonstrated the distribution of the various factions of Christianity in Arab countries, such as the Nestorian faction, which reached **Yemen** and Najran, and the Jacobin and Monophysite factions, which existed among the Christians at the center of the Arabian Peninsula. The writers belonging to these factions supplied more proliferate and credible information, as each of these sects had their own sphere of influence in the peninsula, especially in the northern kingdoms of Hira and Ghassan.

It is worth mentioning that the Arabs who accepted the Christian **religion** did not establish "an Arab church." Despite the existence of an Arab diocese, they did not use the **Arabic language** as a language of religious ceremonies, which were special to them. It is possible that this was an important factor for many tribes to leave Christianity and turn to the **Islamic** religion from the 7th century onward. The Arab tribes who accepted Christianity were those who adopted the Syrian (old Syrian) and Greek languages in their churches, despite the existence of ceremonies in the Arabic language at a later stage, so until today there is an influence of Syrian and Greek in churches in the Middle East. It is possible to explain this matter on account of the fact that while the Arabs accepted Christianity, the Arab language had not yet been adopted as a written language. Many Arab tribes, all over the Middle East, accepted the Christian religion. In the Syrian region, Christianity was accepted by the Quda'ah, Salim, Ghassan, Tai, Bharaa, Tenukh, Lahm, Kanda, Iyad, Taleb, and Ghassassna tribes. These were Syrian Arabs who came to Syria from Yemen and had connections with the Byzantine Empire since the 4th century. Subsequently, they played their part as a buffer state, which prevented the Bedouin tribes from attacking the Byzantine Empire.

The Kingdom of Ghassan consisted of a large tract of territory located in northwestern Arabia bordering on Syria in which a large number of Arab tribes lived. By the 3rd and 4th centuries AD, these tribes had already formed a confederation big enough to trouble the Roman Empire. The kings of Ghassan trace back their ancestry to the tribe of **Azd** in Yemen. Gafa Haha was their first king. The **Nabatean** Kingdom, which spread from the Gulf of Aqaba to Damascus and Hejaz, was annexed to the Roman Empire in AD 105, and with the increasing number of Arab tribes, in 531, under the Emperor Justinian, a real Arab-Roman kingdom was formed under the kings of Ghassan.

Christianity was introduced among the Syrian Arabs living in the Syro-Arabian desert, under the rule of a certain Arabian queen, Mavia or Maowvia (or Mu'awiyah), who agreed to make peace with the Romans she had fought if a certain monk, called Moses, would be appointed as the bishop of her tribe. This was under the reign of Valens (374), who had Arian heretical tendencies. Moses was brought to Alexandria to be ordained by its bishop, Lucius, who was also accused of Arian heresy, and Moses refused to be ordained by him for that reason.

However, Christian propaganda also relied on the many holy hermits and monks who had settled in the Syro-Arabian Desert, whom the Arabs respected. Jerome and Theodoret explain that St. Hilarion and Simeon the Stylite profoundly impressed the Bedouin Arabs. Many of the latter accepted Christianity and were baptized by the priests and bishops of Syria. During the 4th, 5th, and 6th centuries also, the Ghassan tribe embraced Christianity, and the proverb was spread: "They were lords in the days of ignorance [before Mohamed] and stars of Islam."

Also in Valens's time, an Arab prince called Zacome or Zocum, who had given birth to a son through the prayers of a Syrian hermit, converted to Christianity, with his whole tribe.

Banu Jafna was the most important among the Ghassassna, and they were also the royal family of the Ghassassna. The **Ghassanids** founded monasteries such as the Hind Monastery, the Hali Monastery, the Iyob Monastery in Azur, and Manadra, who founded the Manadra state. In the 3rd century the

Lahm tribes settled in southern Iraq and on the desert border, and they decided that Hira would be their center and they founded a state of their own. The Sassanian Persians recognized the independence of this state, and they gave their prince the title of king. Their king Nuaman Abu Qabus, in the 3rd century, accepted the religion of Christianity, and the tribesmen followed suit. In the north of the Arabian Peninsula (contemporary **Saudi Arabia**) the tribes that accepted Christianity were the Harbaa, Adrah, Katchaa, Bani Harth, Bani Shatiya, Us, Hajraj, Jorham, Assad, Tai, Sakon, Saksak, Banu Kalb, Taleb, Tenukh, and Kanda.

The first Arab **migration** into Hira occurred around AD 192, by the tribe of Tenukh under the leadership of its **sheikh**, Malik ibn Fahm. Other tribes like the Iyad, Azd, and Quda'ah soon followed suit, together with others who settled around Anbar and built the city of Hira, not far from the Euphrates River. It is known that even in the time of Alexander the Great, north and south Mesopotamia was populated by many Arab tribes, who constituted more than a third of the population and whose sheikhs and princes were subject to Persian control. During the reign of one of these princes, **Imru al Qais** I, Christianity was introduced in Hira. This was done after the persecution of Christian martyrs in the Sassanian Persian Empire and their migration as captives from Syria and other Roman provinces into Iraq, during the reign of Hormuz I (273–274). The Hira Christians were called *Ibad* or worshippers, as opposed to pagans.

Numan I, King of Hira, was a great builder of castles, and his kingdom rose to power and fame under him. These castles were celebrated in Arab **poetry**. The city of Hira was renamed "the Hira of Numan." In 410, St. Simeon the Stylite settled in the Syro-Arabian Desert, where he carried out miracles and became a target of pilgrims, who wanted to witness his sanctity. Numan was afraid that his Christian subjects would desert to the Roman Empire, and therefore banned pilgrimages to Simeon, but St. Simeon is said to have appeared before him in a dream in which he threatened him with death if he did not repeal the edict. Numan did just this and became a supporter of Christianity, and this change caused the Arabs of his kingdom to accept the new religion.

However, the Sassanian rulers detested the Christian religion and encouraged the princes of Hira to persecute their Christian inhabitants, and one of these princes, Mundhir ibn Imru al-Qais, massacred 400 Christian virgins at the altar of the goddess Ouzza, the Arabian Venus. However, his wife, who was a devout Christian by the name of Hind, from the royal family of Ghassan, established a famous monastery after her own name, in which Nestorian bishops and patriarchs were buried. "This church was built by Hind, the daughter of Harith ibn Amr ibn Hujr, the queen daughter of Kings . . . the servant of Christ. . . . May God, in whose honor she built this church, forgive her sins, and have mercy on her and on her son. May He accept him and admit him into His abode of peace and truth"—this was written during the reign of her son, Amr ibn Mundhir (554–569). He was succeeded by his brother, Numan ibn Qabus, who melted down a gold statue of Venus and distributed its pieces to the poor, and many Arabs converted to Christianity following his example. Later another member of the family, Mundhir ibn Numan, opposed Muhammad in battle at the head of a Christian army from **Bahrain** but fell in battle in 633.

Christianity spread among Arab tribes starting from the 1st century AD. The **Banu Tamim** tribe, one of the strong tribes of the Arabian Peninsula in the pre-Islamic period, was Christian. One of the important poets of the Arabian Peninsula in the pre-Islamic period, Tarfa ibn el-Abed, was Christian. One more tribe that accepted Christianity was the Manadra, and the first among its kings was Godima el-Abrash (233–268), who declared the city of el-Anbar the capital of his kingdom.

Christians were also found in and around the city of Mecca, as the Christian cemetery was outside the city on the road to Bar Anbasa; likewise, part of the families of the **Quraysh** tribes, such as Abdullah ben Jahash, Otman ben Hayarath, Raka ben Nofel and others, accepted the Christian religion.

Christianity entered Yemen in the 4th century, in the period of the second Himyar state (AD 300–525). Churches were built in Aden, Tafar, and Najran. There were some attempts of conversion among the Jews of Yemen. With regard to the Kingdom of Yemen or what was called Arabia Felix during the reign of Constantine the Great (312–337), a philosopher from Tyre named Meropius accompanied by his two sons and other disciples tried to spread Christianity in this **Himyarite** kingdom, between 320 and 325, but they were either slain or made captives. Two members of the group, called Aedesius and Frumentius, were taken before the king, who was impressed by them and made one his cup bearer and the other a custodian of his treasures. After the king's death, they resolved to return to their country, but the queen regent prevented them, asking them to stay and be guardians of her infant son until he reached maturity. They obeyed, and Frumentius made a search for the few Christians dispersed in the Himyarite kingdom. He treated them kindly and built churches and shrines for them. When the young king was crowned, Frumentius went to Alexandria; he was consecrated as a bishop and sent to Himyar, where he increased the number of Christians and made the church wealthy there.

The first ecclesiastical organization in southern Arabia appeared during the reign of the Emperor Anastasius (491–518). The Himyarites, who had been followers of Judaism since the time of the queen of Sheba or **Saba**, converted to Christianity. The first disciple of Christianity in Yemen was a poor Syrian mason called Phemion. One of this man's first converts, Abdallah ibn Thamir, became a miracle worker and converted the town of Najran to Christianity. He was identified with Harith or Arethas, the Christian prince and martyr of Najran, whose tribe's name was Harith of Arethas, but this is unlikely.

The Kingdom of Himyar became a province of Abyssinia in the early 6th century. Dhu Nuwas (517–527) was a Jew who revolted against Elesbaan the Abyssinian king and resolved to avenge himself on the Christians. He committed a general massacre of them in Najran, and those who refused to renounce their religion were burned to death along with the monastic virgins and matrons. Dhu Nuwas informed Kabad, the king of Persia, and Al-Mundhir, the prince of Hira, of the occurrence and urged them to follow him and exterminate their Christian population. However, Elesbaan decided to take revenge on Dhu Nuwas and descended on Himyar, where he massacred thousands of Jews. Dhu Nuwas was defeated and killed and his whole army trounced. Churches were rebuilt on the ruins.

Later Christianity in southern Arabia flourished under the leadership of Abramos, a Christian Abyssinian who became king of Himyar. In the second half of the 6th century Christianity in South Arabia seemed on the threshold of a golden age. His reign ended in 550. But during his reign, the temple of Kaaba in Mecca had become a shrine for thousands of Arabs, and Abramos mourned the large number of pilgrims to it. Its custodians were from Muhammad's tribe, the Quraysh. To counter this, he built a magnificent church in Sanaa. The Quraysh avenged themselves by hiring a person of the Kenanah tribe to defile the church by spreading dung on it. After doing this, he fled the scene and spread news all over Arabia of his desecration of the Christian church. Abramos resolved to destroy the Kenanah and Quraysh tribes, and destroy the Kaaba, and at the head of a strong army, invaded Hejaz, defeated the tribes, and approached Mecca.

The guardian of the Kaaba and chief of the Quraysh then was Abdul-Muttalib ibn Hashim, Muhammad's grandfather. He offered peace to Abramos, by offering him a third of the wealth of the Hejaz. However, the frightened inhabitants of Mecca took refuge in the mountains and poured rocks and stones from a narrow pass at Abramos's army, which did not know that the tribesmen were on the heights; Abramos's army was almost totally annihilated. He was defeated and retreated to Sanaa, where he died after a short time as much from the humiliation as from his wounds.

The Abramos kingdom had weakened to a great extent, and Saif dhu Yezen was appointed king of Himyar by the Sassanian kings, and he defeated and killed Masrouk Abramos's son with a two-thousand-man army composed of soldiers sent by Khosroes Noushirwan, the Persian king. As a result most of the Abyssinian residents, of whom many were Christians, were deported from Himyar. Saif was murdered by Abyssinian members of his own court. No more Himyarite princes were placed on the throne. Islam took over in the region.

There were traces of a following of Christianity under Islam and remnants of Christian influence in the Koran. Muhammad treated the Christians with more courtesy than he treated the Jews. He wrote to the Bishop of Najran: "There shall be guaranteed you the protection of God and His Apostles for the possession of your churches and your worship and your monasteries, and no bishop or priest, or monk, shall be molested . . . so long as you remain true and fulfill your obligations." Burt Omar, Muhammad's second successor, struck a death blow to Christianity in Arabia. Many Christians, impressed by Muslim arms, converted to Islam, and others immigrated to Syria.

In the 5th century, Bahrain became the main center for the Nestorian Christians and the Eastern Church. Bahrain remained a center for Christianity until its inhabitants accepted Islam in the year 629.

It is possible to conclude from everything mentioned above that Christianity penetrated into most of the Arab tribes; churches were built in the villages and towns of the Arabian Peninsula, although the Arabs generally did not have a religious sentiment and a religious culture was not rooted in them, especially not in the **nomad**s among them. The reduction of Christians in the Arabian Peninsula occurred due to Christian migration, which left the region. One part, from the 7th century onward, encountered two alternatives, either to accept the Islamic religion or to stay a protégé under the Muslim government and in exchange they would pay a poll tax.

As there are dozens of Christian tribes scattered all over the Middle East, it is worth noting some tribes as an example of the Christian tribes found in **Jordan**: Banu Samur, who live in the Ajloun region; Rabachiya, who live in the Ajloun region; Awisat, who live in the Ajloun district; Mazahara, who live in the Ajloun region and are descendants of the Ghassassna; and Maaiya, who live in the Madaba region and are descendants of the Ghassassna. The Maaiya are considered the most ancient Christian tribes in Jordan. The Maaiya had already reached the Syrian region from the Arabian Peninsula in the 3rd century AD as part of the Ghassassna, who accepted the Christian religion.

CLAN. A clan (*ashira*) is a union of families grazing their flock in common, tilling their land together, and even fighting together, in order to defend their land and their sources of **water**. Their common origin is one prehistoric man. His memory unites the tribe members, tending to make a pilgrimage to his grave in order to preserve the connections between the families. The most important person in the clan is the head of the clan—the **sheikh**.

COFFEE. Coffee has a unique place in Bedouin society and culture. Its entire preparation from grain roasting to pouring is performed in public. For the Bedouins, coffee is not just a drink, and its preparation is a type of ritual.

It is prepared in stages, using a number of vessels: (1) "*Al-Journ*"—the mortar, made of tree trunk, preferably terebinth or oak wood, with a wooden handle called "*id el-journ.*" (2) "*Mehmasa*"—an iron saucepan into which they put the green coffee grains for roasting; each saucepan is equipped with an iron handle used for turning the coffee grains, so as to roast them well from all sides. (3) "*Al-Bakareg*" (*Dlal*)—special copper kettles for boiling the coffee. (4) "*Al-Fanajin*"—special china cups for drinking coffee. (5) The "*Seniya*"—a copper serving tray.

The coffee ceremony constitutes a unique sign **language**, conveying messages that specify happiness and sadness. For example, expression of sadness or mourning will be conveyed by pouring the coffee, and leaving the *dllah* (the coffee kettle) in an upside down form, with its spout facing down, a custom parallel in a way to the custom of lowering the flag to half mast in other cultures.

Coffee is different from other drinks; it has the status of a noble drink offered to dignitaries and special guests. Serving coffee is a sign of nobility and **hospitality**, which is always performed slowly and ceremonially, before the exchange of gifts and talks.

To start with, the *Finjan al-Deif* (the guest's cup) is poured out as part of the welcome to the guest; next, the *Finjan al-Keif* (the cup of pleasure) follows, which is an expression of pleasure and joy; and finally the *Finjan el-Saif* (the sword's cup) follows, which expresses a military alliance between the guest and the host. Custom dictates that before offering coffee to a guest, the host drinks a cup to reassure the guest that the coffee is good and harmless.

There are other coffee-pouring ceremonies, like *Finjan al-Gaha* (the delegation cup), performed and consumed when a reconciliation meeting is held, *Finjan al-Khutouba* (the cup of betrothal), *Finjan al-Thar* (the revenge cup), *Finjan el-Farach* (the cup of joy), and *Finjan al-Taaziya* (the cup of condolence), poured during a funeral and time of mourning.

See also FOOD.

D

DABKA. Dabka is a dance of men in a line, accompanied with strong stamping of their feet and bouncing into the air, or a dance in a line or a circle, while waving hands or handkerchiefs. This dance is stormy, rhythmic, and very sweeping. The Dabka dancers are required to possess very high physical fitness. *See also* MUSIC AND DANCE.

DAHIYA. Dahiya is a Bedouin man's dance. It is a dance performed in a line. There are a line of men who dance according to the rhythm of their song, to the accompaniment of a drum or some other traditional Bedouin **musical** instruments, mainly moving right and left, forward and backward. The Dahiya is only danced at traditional events, mostly at weddings, and it also symbolizes the brotherhood of men. The dance is performed for a long time, even until the early morning hours.

DARFUR TRIBES. The region of Darfur in **Sudan** is the size of France, but its semi-**desert** nature only supports a population of about seven million people. This relatively small population is subdivided into several tribes, subtribes, and smaller groups of people. According to experts on the subject, most residents of Darfur, including those who consider themselves Arabs, are in fact indigenous, black, and African, and had been Arabized long ago. Others believe that some Arab tribes from the Guhayna Bedouin movement did settle in Sudan and brought their culture and **language** with them, but centuries of intermarrying have blurred the ethnic distinction. Thus, the main cause for ensuing conflicts is not ethnicity or **religion**, but the thousands of years of conflict between the farmer and the **wandering** herder. In fact, until very recently, conflict between these different groups was a matter of disputes over **camel** theft or grazing rights.

In the past, Darfur was an independent sultanate that prospered from human **slave trade**, but in 1916, it came under the Anglo-Egyptian rule with the rest of Sudan. However, due to a lack of interest it was left to fend for itself. In the past, Darfur enjoyed relative peace as all its fragments accepted **Islam**. **Migration** in and out of the area created an intricate mosaic society, wherein various ethnic and social groups coexisted. Therefore, many believe that distinctions between the Arab and African tribes stemmed more from lifestyle than racial identity.

Thus, when drought set in, and the desert began to consume the Sahel region, the balance was broken, as northern herders had no grazing land to go back to, and remained in the south, competing with the farmers for dwindling resources. The growth of both human and stock animal population worsened matters, and the tribes became enemies. The degrading conditions led to a huge upheaval in the region, and local conflicts were highly affected by the civil war in Sudan. As the Sudanese civil society was ethnically charged, the Darfur conflict reflected it by changing it into a "racial" tension, where Muslim fought Muslim; African farming tribes were driven out of Darfur at gunpoint by the **Janjaweed**, the black Arab nomads armed by the Arab-dominated government of Sudan.

In 2000 and 2002, portions of "The Black Book," written in part by members of the largely non-Arab, black African Western Justice and Equality Movement (JEM), appeared in Haltom and spread like wildfire, setting the stage for the rebellion against Khartoum in Darfur. In 2003, two rebel movements, the Sudan Liberation Army (SLA) and the JEM, launched an insurrection against the Sudanese government, as nomads had been attacking sedentary inhabitants. Janjaweed forces and Sudanese soldiers attacked hundreds of villages in the region, and four hundred of them were destroyed. Millions of people were dislodged from their homes. As of 2015, 400,000 people have been killed, and 2.5 million displaced from their homes. In June 2005 the International Criminal Court (ICC) started an investigation into human rights violations, and in March 2009 Omar al Bashir became the first incumbent president to be charged by the court for murder, rape, and plunder. *See also* AGRICULTURE; HERDING.

DAYS OF ARABIA. *Ayyam Al-Arab* (days of Arabia) is a term for wars that took place among the Arab tribes in the **pre-Islamic period** (Al-Jahiliyya).Without a central rule, the tribes competed for natural resources and regional hegemony, and this competition often led to wars, raids, robberies, and when there were fatalities, to revenge. The situation led to the evolution of customary laws and reconciliation norms aimed to stop the continuance of **vendetta**—blood revenge.

Those intertribal wars inspired storytellers and poets (*see* POETRY) to tell the generations to come about the bravery and chivalry of the heroes of their day. Some of these tales and poems have a place of honor in classic **Arabic** literature. However, not all the wars were about **water**, grazing land, or territory; some wars started for trivial reasons and lasted for many years because both sides were too proud to call it a day and put an end to the hostilities.

One example is the **Basus War** (*ḥarb al-basūs*), which was a 40-year (AD 494–534) conflict between two rival clans, the Taghlib and Bakr tribes, which started over nothing more than a dispute over a **camel**. It went down in history as an example of a redundant war that ensued for no real reason. Another "war for no real reason" was the Dahes and Ghabra War, which broke out between the Abbas and Dobian tribes and started over a dispute regarding the **horse** race results, and lasted for years.

DESERT. Most of the countries in the region of the Middle East are wildernesses or to a large extent deserts; that is, the states in the region are characterized by their barren landscape, and therefore, there is not much **agriculture** here, and a **nomadic settlement** has been the dominant one, at least until the start of the modern era.

The definition of a desert is "a region in which less than 200 mm. of rain falls in a year" (and if a quantity less than 200 mm. of precipitation falls, it is impossible to execute dry farming). There are states like **Kuwait** and **Egypt** where the barren territory occupies 100 percent of the land, and on the other hand there are states that are not deserts, such as **Lebanon** and extensive parts of **Iran** and **Turkey**. Among the deserts, these are worth noting:

(1) The Sahara Desert covers most of North Africa. It is the biggest desert in the world. The Arab name of the Sahara Desert is "*Zaharaa Kubra*," which literally means "the Great Desert." The huge desert is spread over a territory of nine million square kilometers. The Sahara Desert stretches from the Atlantic Ocean in the west to the Red Sea and the Suez Canal in the east. It is found in the territory of no less than 10 states: Egypt, **Libya**, **Tunisia**, **Algeria**, **Morocco**, **Mauritania**, Mali, Niger, Chad, and **Sudan**. It is hot and dry in the Sahara Desert. In the daytime the temperature reaches 45 degrees Celsius as a routine matter and often also climbs to extreme values of 50 degrees and more. The quantity of precipitation in most parts of the Sahara is less than 100 mm and there are regions where there is not a single drop of rain for years.

There are no big permanent settlements in the heart of the Sahara, and large towns are only found on the edges of the desert. Two percent of the territory, that is, approximately 200,000 square kilometers, is fertile **oases**, and small settlements or encampments and rest stations for the **camel** caravans crossing the desert are developed around them.

The population of the states in the territory of the Sahara Desert is concentrated on the coastal strip or along rivers. The inhabitants of the desert—nomads and **oasis** settlers alone—number 2.5 million.

(2) The Arabian Desert is a wide desert stretching over most of the **Arabian Peninsula** (most of it in **Saudi Arabia**). In the north it borders the Syrian Desert; in the east, the Persian Gulf and the Gulf of **Oman**; in the south, the Arabian Sea and the Gulf of Aden; and in the west, the Red Sea. Its area is 2,330,000 sq km.

Jordan, Kuwait, the Union of Arab Emirates, Qatar, **Bahrain**, **Iraq**, Saudi Arabia, Oman, and **Yemen** are located in the territory of the desert.

In the summer, the average temperature in the desert stands at 40–50 degrees Celsius, and in the winter the average temperature reaches 5–15 degrees Celsius and can even reach 0 degrees. The quantity of rain in the desert is 35 mm yearly.

The Bedouin lifestyle in the desert is considered to be the first social structure known to humanity. This was the first attempt to cope with natural conditions. The Bedouins were the first people who developed connections to the environment. The lack of **water** and **food** caused them to look for original solutions. The first solution that was found was a nomadic life. They adapted to an environment that was sometimes generous and sometimes contained a huge lack of necessities for subsistence. They knew how to obtain their needs from the local plants. Likewise, they knew how to domesticate plant-eating animals, which was of great help in their life of **wandering** from place to place in search for water, food, and pasture.

Despite the simplicity and difficulties in the living conditions in the desert, the desert has generous traits in that it is considered as the place of origin of the prophets and sages, and the shelters of saints. The desert also had an important role: it made the Bedouins independent, brave, respectful of others, and generous.

The conditions of nature in the desert, characterized mainly by lack of water, influenced the conduct of man in this space. The perpetual need to search for sources of water led to the formation of a tribal society, characterized by loyalty to the tribe and to the leader, by a solitary lifestyle, and by concentration on a nomadic lifestyle.

The desert dwellers wandered from place to place to look for sources of water and weeds for their flocks; likewise they lived in **tents** made of goat hair, which were easy to dismantle and rebuild, and easy to carry during their wanderings. Nomadic herders of livestock were found in the arid and the semiarid regions. Their economy was based on the growth of animals and a little agriculture for subsistence. The animals (**camel** or **horse**) helped in their movement and as freight transport. As for the camel, its flesh and milk constituted food, and its wool and leather was used for clothing and tents.

The nomadic tribes concentrated in big groups because of the need to organize their wanderings efficiently, the range of which could reach 2,000 km a year. The range of wanderings was fixed according to the animals. It was relatively limited, with **shepherd**s found on the edges of the settled regions, and also relatively wide, with grazers of camels found in very arid regions. The natural conditions influenced the customs of the inhabitants. They lived in tribes. Most of them were nomadic tribes, and a minority of them were permanent settlers in oases and towns. In addition to the climatic difficulties, many dangers lay in wait for the inhabitants of the desert—among them raids, attacks, and acts of robbery by members of hostile tribes.

The inhabitants of the desert needed protection, and without a state or courts, the family members defended one another. Thus, a custom developed among the tribesmen according to which the relatives of a murder victim had to avenge his death by injury to the murderer or to his family members. This custom was called **vendetta**. The fear of the tribesmen from vendetta deterred them from acts of killing, and on the strength of the custom it was possible to put an end to vengeance and to quarrel without violence by means of reconciliation ceremonies. Thanks to coping with many dangers, the tribesmen appreciated bravery and loyalty.

From the 1950s, the desert started to change its face, especially in oil-rich countries, where new concentrations of population arose around the oil sites. For example, in the Gulf States, since the 1950s, huge quantities of oil were found in the region. Until then the region was barren and totally unsettled. Since the 1950s, the region started to develop quickly, and rich, modern cities developed close to the concentrations of oil. The oil constituted a source of income from export, oil production, and the oil industry: for example, **Abu Dhabi** and the city of Kuwait in Kuwait, Jeddah in Saudi Arabia, and in general all the big towns in the oil states.

It must be emphasized that the states of the Persian Gulf have no natural sources of water. The states desalinate water. The states have an abundance of oil, wealth, a great deal of energy for electricity, and therefore, by desalination they replace the lack of water in the region. If in the past this and the lack of water were a factor preventing settlement, today the money and technology enable a foundation of air-conditioned cities, desalination of water, and development, despite the physical conditions.

DESERT RANGERS BATTALION (GADSAR). This is also called “the Bedouin Gadsar” or “the Desert Rangers.” It is an infantry regiment (Hir) in the **Israel Defense Forces** (IDF), where the Bedouin soldiers mostly serve. Israeli Arab soldiers who are not Bedouins also serve here. The battalion was founded in 1987. At the start, it was subordinated to the Southern Command rear headquarters (Maafad), but later it was subordinated to the southern brigade of the Gaza division.

At the start the regiment was founded as a small unit of platoon size. This was the first time Bedouin soldiers served as fighters and not as trackers. Over time the regiment grew, and today it counts two regular companies, a permanent company (the sole one in the IDF) and a headquarters company composed of Bedouin and Jewish soldiers. In the year 2011, a reserves company was founded in the framework of the regiment, which established two precedents: a combat company of Muslim fighters in the reserves and a reserves company that served in the framework of a regular battalion. *See also* ISRAEL.

DOUKKALA. Doukkala, also called Doukkala Al-Baida (Doukkala the white), is a mixture of Masmoudian **Berbers** (and also Sanhajians) and Arabs, introduced by the Almohads in the 12th century, after the former revolted against them. Leo Africanus estimated their population at 400,000 in the 16th century. Also the Doukkala were obliged very early to look for external resources notably in temporary emigration; they constituted a class of **wandering** merchants and artisans, well-known in **Morocco**.

DRESS. The clothes of a Bedouin **woman** are black. She wears a dark and decorated dress and covers her head and face with a black scarf or veil. In winter, she wears black clothes woven from wool and in summer from cotton. The Bedouin women love to decorate their dresses with fine and lovely embroidery and colors. In the past, women wove models of geometric forms, in addition to forms of plants and animals.

The Bedouin men wear a white *kefaya* on their head, and above it an *akal* of a black color. For their body, they wear a cloak of a brown color. Today, the traditional dress of the men and women is something for the adults; the young men and women do not wear traditional dress.

DULAIM. Dulaim is one of the largest tribes in the entire Middle East, comprised of more than seven million people. The tribe's history goes back to **pre-Islamic** times. Historians believe this tribe participated in the first Arab Conquest in the 7th century. It is the strongest tribe among the three tribes of Zubid. Originally, it was composed of four major **clans**, but later they absorbed additional clans that were large. Today, their descendants comprise the largest Sunni tribe in **Iraq**, living in the southern part of Al-Jazira. They can also be found in Iraq's neighboring countries, **Syria**, **Jordan**, and **Kuwait**. The traditional leaders of the Dulaim tribe are the Albu Assaf clan. However, several members of this tribe keep their surname as Al Dulaimi and its derivations.

The Dulaim played an important role in the establishment of modern Iraq. With their reputation as raiders who displayed good fighting skills, several tribe members joined the armed forces and contributed to the stability of the state's politics and economics.

About one quarter of the Dulaim live as nomadic **shepherds**, while the rest of them are settled or semi-settled. They serve in the army, in the police, and in all sorts of law enforcement units.

During the Saddam Hussein era the Dulaimis formed 10 to 20 percent of the Iraqi army (Iraqi Republican Guard). The events that followed the American invasion, specifically the bombing of Fallujah and the targeting of Sunni tribes, led to most of them fighting against the appointed Iraqi government and the U.S. forces in Iraq.

The tribe is centered near Anbar (western Iraq), but there is a massive presence of Dulaim all the way south to Babylon (Al Hillah) and west to Ramadi and also northward to Taji, Samarra, and Mosul, and in the capital, Baghdad, especially in its western quarters.

E

EDUCATION. Among the Bedouins there are two stages of education: The first stage is the stage before the national state; this is the education that existed in the period of **wandering** and is called traditional education. The second stage develops among the Bedouins from the period of the national state onward, and this is what is called modern education.

In traditional education, as there were no schools for formal education in the **desert**, the education was concentrated in the hands of many agents who belonged to one of the following social circles: the home, which included the father, the mother, and the siblings; the family, which included the uncles and cousins; the society, which included friends and acquaintances from the tribesmen, and later independent friends.

In traditional education one needs to distinguish between the education of boys and that of girls. The education of a Bedouin girl does not deviate from the borders of her encampment. Girls remain in the possession of the mother until the day of marriage. They learn the craft of cooking, weaving, growth of flock, the art of sewing, and the rules of medicine and hygiene from the mother. The Bedouin girl learns from the mother about the tribe to which she belongs, its size and strength, so she can boast about it before her future husband. There are Bedouin girls who know how to declaim *kassida* (Arab **poetry** with rhymes), or to tell stories and **fables** of the desert, which they learned from their mothers.

As for the boys, until the seventh year approximately, the children stay with their mother; they go after her wherever she goes and all their concern is for her. The attitude of the boys is an attitude of affection. The wandering Bedouins, known as fighters, induce the boys to ride on a horse, to hold a dagger, a sword, and even a rifle at an early age. When boys reach the age of 16, approximately, they involve them in raids. The education of boys starts from an early age. This is essential for the Bedouin tribe, as they can be attacked at any time.

The Bedouin children from an early age start to sit in the company of adults. From this meeting, which involves listening and looking at the ways of adults, the children learn the customs and tradition, the many fables, and also the roles of adults, which they will be in the near future.

Children at the age of 18 join the band of adults in the tribe.

The education of the boys is defined from generation to generation. Education is a matter of a process that matures.

Stage A—Infancy (0–5 years): At this stage the child is totally subject to the influence and immunity of the mother and the siblings. The child is close to the mother. The mother's concern in the first three years is the weaning, so that the child will be healthy. She believes that inasmuch as he will wean from the milk of her breasts, it will benefit him physically and mentally. At an age above four, when the child understands the **language** well and starts to understand the environment, his mother takes him for a visit with the neighbors, when she implores him to behave well. She says to him that if he does not behave well she will leave him at home the next time. To leave a child at home when the mother is not there means a severe punishment for the child in infancy. Often the host expresses her opinion on the quality of the education of her friend and if the children behaved well or misbehaved. The essence of the education for the child, at this stage, is to teach him the basic rules of behavior.

Stage B—The learning age (6–8 years): At this stage the transition period starts, where the child moves from the environment of females to an environment of men. Education at this stage is very intensive, as after this stage the child does not learn but mainly refines his knowledge, his behavior, and his absorption skill in the society. This is also the period in which the child is subject to an educating influence from four different directions: the continuation of the mother's education; the transition to the father's education, the influence of society by means of the father's friends, and also joining the peer groups of other children. All these, together with the mother, take care that the child moves away from the company of females and comes close to men. Coming closer to the father distances the child from the concentration place of girls—*mahram* (the women's room). This is because the father can be found in the *shick* (the guests' room) with the men or in any occupation close to the home, but not within it. Here a string of missions starts between the father and the mother, the goal of which is to disconnect the child gradually from the females. The father, sitting in the shick, imposes missions on the son directed to serve the guests, for example, to bring the kettle of tea and to pour it for the guests, to bring trees for the burner; the father casts remarks at his son, such as, "Do not be like the women." The father brings his son to his side and illustrates the order in which to prepare **coffee** and the manner in which to serve it. By doing all this, the father inculcates in his son the value of **hospitality** and getting used to the presence of men. On the other hand, guests, strangers, and friends of the father can serve as an important source of information and contribute as agents in the indirect education of the child. They can also inform him of things that he does not witness at home.

The father, sitting with the men and the guests, gives his son positive support when he thanks him for the service. At this stage bravery and self-confidence are instilled in the child, for example, if a goat or ewe disappears, he is sent to search for it. Usually, the animals will be found close to the encampment or they would have joined the neighbor's flock, and the child would go look for it there. This is, of course, the first step to more distant missions. In a task of this sort the child also develops appreciation of family property.

Stage C—Advanced socialization (9–12 years): In this period, the intensive training from the father continues, as also disconnection of the child from the mother and her authority. At the end of this period the child is supposed to be fit to become a member of the group. He is already capable of functioning authoritatively in the family but still under the father's name and not independently. He is qualified to hand out orders to siblings older than him and to siblings younger than him, but still to consider his mother's opinion. Of course the father provides authorities like these only if he is convinced that the child is fit for this. In the economic field, the child is already trained to be an independent **shepherd** and at the end of this period, that is, at age 12, he is already a shepherd.

In the framework of the economic contribution in the field of raising sheep, the child had already learned how to get to know more distant environments from the home and was also aware of the environmental dangers of predators or hostile parties. The boy who prepared coffee by himself, without the father's help, and served it to the guests, had gained the right to be present in their company. Moreover, when the father was not at home, the child took great responsibility, as he could decide and execute the preparation of carcasses for the guests. When the child sacrificed in honor of the guests, he proved his maturity and understanding; likewise this proved that the child had internalized education.

Stage D—Integration of society (from age 13 onward): This is the stage at which the boy reaches the group of men and becomes part of their company. The individual gains "the final" authorization to be called a man, but only if he is capable of carrying out the task of protecting the family or tribe. The authorization is given by riding on a **horse** and carrying weapons, which he will use only under supervision and at the hour of need alone.

The transition from traditional education to modern education started at the end of the Ottoman period, although it was for the estate of lone Bedouins, mainly the heads of tribes. The lifestyle of the Bedouins and their dispersal over extensive regions hampered the existence of traditional education. If schools such as these were established, it was done spontaneously; they were founded mostly under the initiative of the heads and notables of tribes. These schools were founded without planning. They suffered from a lack of an educational-instructional climate. There was no water or toilets in the schools, and only tribesmen or the male children came to these schools.

The big turning point came with the foundation of the national states, especially after the transition of the Bedouins from a **nomadic** life to permanent **settlements**. The establishment of schools started only after the **urbanization** process of the Bedouins and the foundation of the first settlements. In villages and settlements the governments founded various educational institutions in order to supply education to the Bedouin children.

The urbanization process and the construction of educational institutions increased the number of those joining the education system. The development of education systems and the legislation of both compulsory education and free-education laws in the various states not only increased the number of those joining the educational system but also caused the girls to throng into these educational institutions to learn. They acquired the basic high school education and often higher education as well.

In recent years, far-reaching changes have taken place in the Bedouin education system among the Bedouins who were settled in the permanent settlements, although this was not so for the Bedouins who still lived in the Arab deserts, for example, the Bedouins in the **Sinai** Desert in **Egypt**. The education institutions there are still primitive, and not all the Bedouin children throng to them. But the general picture is that the educational system among the Bedouins has developed in a major way in recent years and received a huge thrust. The educational system has become an accelerating factor in the process of modernization. Education contributes to social changes and serves as a lever for empowerment. Education leads to economic development. It creates equality of opportunities and serves as a tool for social, economic, and political mobility for the Bedouin population. Apparently, the thrust did not come on its own, although there were a number of chief motives:

1. Special attention from various governments was given to the Bedouin educational system and to the education of Bedouin children.
2. The traditional sources of income of the Bedouins changed, the lack of lands and traditional sources of subsistence increased the interest in education, and they saw in education an important factor—they could obtain alternative employment to the traditional one.
3. The influence of the young intellectual layer among the Bedouin children left its mark in the sympathetic attitude of the people to education, to a concern for their children to study and to be interested in activity in schools and in the education system.

EGYPT. The Bedouins in Egypt constitute 10 percent of the state's population, and they are found in all the state's districts and provinces. It is important to note that Egypt was a center of civilization and **trade** for thousands of years, attracting others for all sorts of reasons. Therefore, nomadic tribes of various origins were always present in Egypt.

Bedouins who live in Egypt today came via two different routes. There were tribes that came to Egypt from North Africa and others that came directly from the Arabian Peninsula. The Arab-Muslim conquest of Egypt, at the close of the 7th century AD, opened the door of tribal **migration** from the Arabian Peninsula into Egypt. In the first quarter of the 8th century, the Muslim governor of Egypt encouraged migration of tribes to Egypt for two reasons: to increase the share of Muslims in the population so as to help convert the locals, and several troops of his army were tribesmen and many of them did not wish to return to the Arabian Peninsula. Therefore, he encouraged them to bring over their families and their entire **clans**. He also promised to employ in his service new recruits to serve in his army and in various law-enforcement agencies he was about to employ. Other tribes were admitted to Egypt by special agreements and were granted specific grazing lands.

The peak of Bedouin penetration into Egypt was during the period of the Fatimid caliphate (968–1171). The Fatimids encouraged migration of tribes into Egypt, as they relied on the tribesmen to strengthen their regime and contribute warriors to their forces. Bedouin tribes from the Arabian Peninsula, Greater Syria, and **Iraq** migrated to Egypt and erected **tent** encampments on the banks of the Nile and in the **Sinai Desert**. This policy brought the Banu Hilal from northern Arabia and allowed them to settle in the Sharqiya district. They also transferred several members of the Sanabs and Tayy tribes from **Palestine** in 1051 to Egypt and settled them in a chosen district.

In the second half of the 12th century, the Ayyubid Dynasty (1171–1250) transferred tribes like the Bani Jarm tribe and other clans from the Gaza region and settled them in the Sharqiya district. The rise of the Mamluk (Mamelukes) dynasty in Egypt in the mid-13th century (1250–1517) neutralized the tribes and reduced their political influence. They were no longer an important element in the army and guards, and therefore, lost their privileged status. As a result, they no longer felt obliged to cooperate with the regime, and felt free to take part in a series of revolts, opposition movements, and attacks against the government targets.

Since the foundation of the state in the year 1250, the Arab tribes did not recognize the Mamelukes' right to rule, claiming that the Mamelukes were slaves and foreigners in Egypt. They held the opinion that the government had to be Arab and work for the Arabs. Thus, relations between the Mamelukes and the Arabs were characterized by hatred and quarrels, leading many tribes to leave Egypt. Some returned to the Arabian Peninsula, some moved westward to **Libya** and from there to other North African countries, and some moved far into the desert. Throughout the Mameluke period, the Bedouin tribes continued to oppose the government. Tribal revolts became a constant feature and continued even after the Ottoman conquest of Egypt in 1517.

During the entire Ottoman period (1517–1914) the Bedouins accumulated power and wealth; part of the Bedouin groups enjoyed significant incomes from taxes on the **agricultural** crops and from protection fees. The Ottoman governors chose to integrate the Bedouin leaders in the leasing method (*iltizam*) they introduced. Their economic importance grew, and they practically dominated the economic activity in several fields, like the trade caravans from the Nile and on land, supply of crops from Upper Egypt (*tzaid*), protection of the Haj convoys, and raising and breeding **camels** and **horses** and providing logistic supplies to the military forces. They controlled the land and naval trade routes, and dominated the sedentary population by raids and robbery of crops and livestock (or collecting high protection fees for not doing so).

In the middle of the 18th century, the Bedouins reached the peak of their power in Egypt. The Habaiba tribe ruled the Delta, under the leadership of **Sheikh** Habib and his sons. In Upper Egypt, a semiautonomous framework was organized and led by Sheikh Hamam, leader of the Hawara tribe. The district enjoyed a local nomadic surplus, stable economy, and control of the growth and trade of crops. The Bedouin elite accumulated wealth and property in the villages where they settled. It is important to note that such an independent semiautonomous district developed during a period when there was a weakening of governance in other parts of the declining Ottoman Empire.

Muhammad Ali, who ruled Egypt in the first half of the 19th century (1805–1849), introduced a strong, uncompromising governing regime that broke down the Bedouin power in upper Egypt in the first quarter of the 19th century. He managed to subdue the Bedouins in Egypt, and also the Bedouins in the Syrian region, who were under Egyptian rule for a time (1831–1840).

In the 20th century, the Egyptian Bedouin tribes participated in the Egyptian nationalist movements. They joined the revolt of Ahmed Orabi against the British in 1882. Some Bedouin tribes, those of the Red Sea area, joined the revolt of 1919 against the British. They were full of anger against the British, especially after the British forced them to settle and limited their freedom to roam.

Today, the Bedouins in Egypt are scattered all over the country. There is a concentration of Bedouins in Faiyum, Aswan, Bahira, the Sinai Peninsula, the Alexandria region, Matruh, the Western Desert, and so on. Most of them live in a low socioeconomic situation. President Muhammad Anwar Al Sadat

(1970–1981) and President Muhammad Hosni Mubarak (1981–2011) were interested in their Bedouin subjects; both of them met the leaders of the principal tribes, had good relations with them, and allocated resources to improve their social and economic situation. After the Arab Spring riots overthrew the Mubarak regime, and the people elected Mohamed Morsi in June 2012 as president supported by the Muslim Brotherhood, the Egyptian army was forced to start a military operation against terrorists in Sinai in summer/autumn 2012. This brought credit to the army, which staged a coup against Morsi in June 2013, overthrew him, and established its own government—later, under Abdel Fattah el-Sisi, the army chief in command, who was elected in March 2014 as president.

In October 2014 insurgents, mostly Bedouins from Sinai, killed 30 Egyptian soldiers and police in an attack, and the army retaliated by killing scores of the rebels. The army also was forced to seal off 120 tunnels used for smuggling goods and arms to Gaza. Some of the 300,000 Sinai Bedouins complain about mass arrests, shelling schools, road checkpoints, and other tactics similar to Israeli tactics in Gaza. But an economic downturn has come upon the Sinai Bedouins, who once built smart houses from profits even obtained from smuggling African migrants. Due to Sisi's crackdown on them, more than one thousand Bedouin families left the Rafah strip for Cairo, and of those who remain, many repeatedly attack the Egypt-Israel-Jordan gas pipeline. By being cruel to them, the government has made these Bedouins their enemies.

F

FABLE. The fable is a tool for transmission of messages. It transmits the messages when it relies on tradition and figures from tribal history. Usually, old sages and transmitters of tradition read out the fables and sayings. There is wisdom of life in them, guidance, and outlining of a system, and they concern relations between man and fellow man, between man and government, the attitude to the law, to the weak, and so on.

For example, when the Bedouins spoke about the need for keeping tradition and the link to the sources, they said: "*Eli ma endu Aada, wala endu Naaka walada, menin tejeh Al-Saada?*" [He who has no tradition of fathers and no female **camels** giving birth, from where will happiness come to him?]. Happiness lies in the opinion of the Bedouin elders in keeping the tradition and form of life, which the fathers instilled in the sons. *See also* FOLK STORY; POETRY.

FADIL. Fadil is a Bedouin tribe that wandered in the Golan Heights region until the **Israeli** conquest of the Golan Heights during the 1967 war. The origin of el-Fadil is from an ancient Bedouin tribe from **Iraq** that migrated to Golan in the 15th century. They wandered in the region between the Bnot Yaakov Bridge in the south, Kuneitra in the east, and Banias in the north. El-Fadil took control of most of the lands in Golan, mainly in the northwest region of fertile Kuneitra. In the winter they reached the Hula Lake in their **wanderings**, and sometimes even went as far as the Yizrael Valley. El-Fadil deals with the family of "sheriffs," the family of the Prophet Muhammad.

FAHS. Fahs is a **Moroccan** tribe of various **Sanhaja** fractions who followed Moulay Idriss I as *makhzen* (central power). They were settled in Tangier by Ahmed Pasha Rifi, until the town was reconquered by the English and placed under his authority in 1679. Their **language**, costume, and habitat are those of the Jebala. This is a tribe devoted to the *makhzen*; it supplies a large portion of the *makhznis* (auxiliary force) of Tangier.

FANATICISM, TRIBAL. Tribal fanaticism (*Al-Azbiya Al-Kabaliya*) is an ancient custom that means full loyalty to the tribe, loyalty in every situation and under every condition. This custom was very dominant in the **pre-Islamic period**—Al-Jahiliyya. The **Islamic religion** at the start of the 7th century called for cessation of this custom, and instead of loyalty to the tribe it called for loyalty to the Muslim state. Despite this, the custom did not disappear and it continues until this day.

FAOUR, MAHMOUD (1877–1927). Mahmoud Faour was the head of the **Fadil** tribe, a tribe that **wandered** in the Golan Heights region at the start of the 20th century. Faour together with his tribesmen played a central role in the Golan region, at the end of the Ottoman period. They participated in the Arab revolt against the Ottoman government in World War I. Likewise, he led a revolt against the French forces in the Golan region in the period between 1919 and 1921.

FOLK STORY. Folk stories are folklore stories. Their propagation was mainly by word of mouth. Usually, the writer was anonymous, and the place and time were undefined. The Bedouin folk stories constituted an inseparable part of the history of tribal culture.

They contain a combination of panhuman characteristics and features unique to Bedouin culture. The folk story is basically auditory and is conveyed from generation to generation by storytellers.

The story's plot is characterized by foundations of charm and magic. Every human society, including the Bedouin society, needs its own folk stories as tools to cope with hardships, fears, and anxieties, and even to receive confirmation for successes. The folk story organizes reality and gives it meaning. It transmits guidelines to a way of life by means of symbols and hints, thereby giving an opportunity to the audience of listeners to consolidate their worldview and their identity. Below is a folk story (the source is Yosef **Suwaed**—my father, the writer).

> Once, when the **desert** was still deserted of people and only the sound of the wind blowing in the sand was heard around, two neighboring brothers lived in it. Ali and his wife were hardworking and goodhearted, whereas Naïf and his wife were idlers and bad spirited. One day, a rustle of branches was heard around the encampment, and surprisingly a nomad appeared who had erred in his path and gone around for many days in the desert. The nomad collapsed on the threshold of Naif's **tent**, and he asked for **water** for his dry throat. Lazy Naif expelled him, without helping him, as he preferred to continue to sit on the mat and smoke.
>
> When Ali returned in the evening and saw what his brother had done, he was very ashamed. While his wife watered the whining goats, Ali put the stranger into his tent and poured him water and bitter and stimulating

coffee. When the guest recovered, Ali invited him to a rich meal and slaughtered a sheep for **food**. Naïf looked from the side and laughed at his brother, who had wasted a good sheep on a poor and strange nomad. After a number of days, the nomad went on his way, and life returned to its normal path.

As the years passed, Ali and Naif went out on their **camels** in a mission to the town but lost their way. Quiet reigned around, and only the rustle of branches and the steps of tired camels were heard. Suddenly they saw a big and magnificent encampment. With the remainder of their forces they approached the encampment, and then the same wretched nomad came out to them, but now he was a rich and honorable man. The nomad invited Ali to his tent and treated him, whereas Naif, who was ashamed of his deeds, continued to wander in the barren desert and died of thirst together with his camels.

The desert was full of steps of camels and voices of people and many generations passed, but a father always told his son the story of Ali and Naif, and explained that the desert was arid and dangerous, and assistance and respect for a guest can determine who will live and who will die.

FOOD. The sources of a Bedouin's food were those available in the region they lived in. They gathered or grew vegetables, ate dates and other fruits when they were available, and **traded** their products for grain, **coffee**, tea, and other basic necessities. Until the transition to a permanent **settlement**, their food was based on what their environment could provide.

As **shepherds**, they raised animals that provided wool and skins for clothing and other necessities and also provided meat and milk products. However, as milk got spoiled relatively quickly, the Bedouins, like all **nomadic** tribes, learned how to preserve it in the form of certain milk products, such as yoghurt, from which they produced *zubda* (butter) and *samna* (processed butter), which would keep for a very long time. They used to drink sour milk (*labaneh*), from which they learned to produce *labaneh* balls, which could be preserved in olive oil. They gathered wild plants, which provided green leaves, berries, edible roots, and wild herbs, to spice and enrich the food. They learned to make *rub* (carob honey), which is both food and a good medicine for gum pain.

The Bedouins prepared tea from herbs that they collected from nature, such as *marva* and *atar*. *Shanina* is a drink that the Bedouins prepare from yoghurt. They add **water** and salt to yoghurt to make this refreshing drink, which is especially good to drink on hot summer days.

In the past, the Bedouins lived mainly on natural food products, milk, and meat from the beasts that they raised. However, today, with the influence of globalization, the Bedouins are exposed to food recipes from other cultures: Indian, Chinese, Mexican, and so on, and they have started to add them to the family menu. In the past two decades, as men and **women** have started going out for "salaried work," snacks and fast food have been added to the Bedouin cuisine, especially among young couples. Traditional food has stayed mainly in the cuisine of adults among the Bedouins or it is presented at social events, for example, at weddings. *See also* MADFUNA; MANSAF.

G

GADDADFA. Gaddadfa is a **Libyan** tribe. Muammar Gadhafi was born into this tribe in a **desert** town 84 kilometers south of Sirte. The tribe is subdivided into six subtribes, which reside in Tripoli and Benghazi, but chiefly in the region extending from the Sirte to the Sabha area in Fezzan, where Gaddafi was educated in high school. They were not many in number and did not play an influential role in the struggle with the Italians and under the monarchy. They were chiefly grazers.

They were permitted to join the security forces and the police, and Muammar Gadhafi led the coup in 1969, from a position in the air force, which was the corps that played a leading part in the repression of the dissidents in the civil war against him in 2011. Not only did Gadhafi appoint members of his own tribe to protective security positions around him, but he also conscripted some members of other tribes like the **Warfallah** and the Magariha. The tribe is also said to have become rich under his rule, but the National Transitional Council (NTC) made contact with it in order to counter Gadhafi in its own uprising.

GALILEE. In the Galilee region in the north of **Israel**, more than a hundred Bedouin tribes lived until the foundation of the state of Israel. Most of them were seminomadic. These Bedouins had originated from the Syrian **Desert**, the Arabian Peninsula, and North Africa, and had reached Galilee chiefly in the period of the Ottoman Empire. At the time of Israel's War of Independence in 1948, part of them left for **Syria**, **Lebanon**, and **Jordan**.

The Bedouin population in Galilee today is 100,000 Bedouins. They live in dozens of villages there. With the increase of population in Galilee, as also an intensive cultivation of the land, an accelerated transition took place with the Bedouins of Galilee passing to permanent **settlement**. The government of Israel supported this and built permanent settlements, especially for Bedouins, on cheap land, and developed the public infrastructure—schools, Kupot Holim (health maintenance organizations), and the like. They also provided the infrastructure of **water**, sewage, and electricity.

GEBELAYA. Gebelaya, an Egyptian tribe, is a small non-Arab group/subtribe of approximately 1,500 people who live in the area of Mount **Sinai**. It is believed that they are descendants of the Macedonian people, who were sent by Emperor Justinian in the 6th century AD to build, serve, and protect the monastery.

GHARAIBEH. Gharaibeh is a semisedentary Bedouin tribe that lives in the northern parts of **Jordan** and cultivates the plains of Houran. The *fellahin* (peasants) of the area are generally called Houranies (not to be confused with Hawarneh), as the area, now divided between **Syria** and Jordan, used to be a single entity during the Ottoman regime. The ancestry of this tribe is undetermined, as there are no records or written documents of any kind, but according to tradition, this particular **clan** descends from an Arab Bedouin tribe called Bani Johma, who wandered from Northern Arabia. Other stories claim that they have no connection to Bedouins at all, but they are in fact descendants of Semitic tribes that lived in the area of Hebron and migrated northeast sometime during the Ottoman occupation of the Middle East.

Their name derives from the word *ghareeb* (foreigner), believed to be given to them when they had settled in northern Jordan, in a town called Huwwarah, located in the biblical Hawran plain, near Irbid, the major city of northern Jordan, and Ramtha, the town replacing the ancient Ramoth-Gilead. Members of the clan live in several other towns and cities in Jordan, including Irbid, Zarqa, and the capital, Amman.

GHASSANIDS. The Ghassanids (al-Ghasāsinah) are an Arab tribe whose origin was in the southern part of the Arabian Peninsula. In the 1st century AD (before the birth of Muhammad) the tribe migrated to the Fertile Crescent and settled in the region, which today is under **Syrian** control. They took to **Christianity** and maintained a local government under the Byzantine Empire.

The historical importance of this tribe lies in the fact that it constituted a connecting link between the Arab tribes of the Arabian Peninsula, before the rise of **Islam**, and the "Western" empires of that period—the Persians and the Byzantines. The Byzantines saw the Ghassanids as a strong ally whom they could possibly use in their struggle against the Sassanian Persians, who always threatened the eastern parts of the Byzantine Empire. The Byzantines supported the Sassanians, who helped them to find a strong buffer state. The rule of the Ghassanids continued for more than four centuries from 220 until 638.

The Ghassanids stayed loyal to the Byzantines until the 7th century, after the Muslims put an end to their rule following the battle of the Yarmoukh, in the year 636. The Ghassanids converted to Islam, joined the Muslim armies, and participated in the Islamic conquests in North Africa and Andalusia. The caliphs from the House of Umayya used them in the management of the state due to the managerial and financial experience that they had.

GHMAD. Ghmad is one of the largest among the Arab southern tribes (**Qahtan**) of the **Azd** confederation. The Ghmad are known since the **pre-Islamic era**. Several fighters of the Ghmad, like most other Azd tribes, joined the armies of the early Muslim empire. The tribe is subdivided into three major groups: the Al-Baha, who live in the central highland mountains (sarat); the Hejaz, who are nomadic Bedouins living in the **desert** region; and the Tohm, who live in the narrow Tihama valley on the coast of the Red Sea. All Ghmad are Sunni Muslims.

This tribe comes originally from the Al-Bahah region of southwestern **Saudi Arabia**. They are highly respected in Saudi Arabia as hard-working people. In the early 20th century, they started to grow and sell tobacco. The members of this tribe are proud of their heritage, and most of them add Al-Ghmadi to their surname. In recent years, many members of the Ghmad have moved to big metropolises like Riyadh, Jeddah, and Dammam, where they acquired **education** and became professionals and businessmen.

GHOUJDAMA. Ghoujdama or Rhoujdama is the Arabization of the word *ighoujdamn*, and a word derived from *aghoujdim*, which means "tree trunk" in **Berber**. The name Rhoujdama was mentioned for the first time by Al-Baydaq in the 12th century, taken up again by Ibn Khaldoun in the 14th century, and by Leo Africanus in the 16th century. Ibn Tomart (the Almohads) in 1126–1127 dispatched his disciple, Abou Muhammad Atia, as the governor of Rhoujdama, where he lived until he was killed. In response to this act, Ibn Tomart destroyed the town of Rhoujdama after a battle there called "Azallym."

In 1148, a second confrontation with the Almohads (caliph: Abdelmoumen) took place at "Aman Melloulnine." In the late 17th century (in 1680), the Alawite sultan Moulay al-Rashid confronted the inhabitants of Demnat, the political center of the big tribe, the Haskoura, of which the tribe is a part. Under the reign of Sultan Moulay Ismail (1672–1727), Demnat had for its governor Pasha Ghazi. Later, the tribe recognized the authority of Moulay Abdullah and after that his son, Sidi Ahmed ben Abdullah.

In 1893, Moulay Hassan I was attacked by inhabitants of the region. In reprisal, the sultan gave a gift of a cannon and a quantity of arms to Glawi El-Madani (head of the neighboring Glawa tribe) to impose his rule in the region. In 1896, the Rhoujdama removed Glawi from authority, thanks to a *dahir* (decree) of Moulay Abdelaziz, and this lasted until the end of the French protectorate in 1956. *See also* MOROCCO.

GOLDBERG COMMITTEE. The Goldberg committee was founded according to the decision of the government of **Israel**, Decision No. 2491, of 28 October 2007. The committee was chaired by the retired judge of the Supreme Court Eliezer Goldberg. The goal of the committee was to recommend to the government a policy for arrangement of a Bedouin **settlement** in the **Negev** and to suggest to the government a policy that would bring a solution to the dispute of the Bedouins with the state, since 1948.

The committee held 20 meetings and went on four tours in the field. It is worth noting that the meetings of the committee were open to the public, and an audience of citizens was indeed present in its meetings.

The committee chairman noted in the foreword to the report that time was of the essence: "The factor of time is not neutral, it is urgent and it has critical meaning. The more time passes the harder the solution is. An inclusive and speedy solution will arrange the settlement of the Bedouins in the Negev, it is the present need" (p. 5).

The committee noted in the report that the central issue from the point of view of the struggle between the Bedouins and the state is the issue of land. The report indicates that while the Bedouins do not cease to claim their right of possession of the lands in the Negev, the state refuses to recognize the demands of ownership, as they are not backed by sufficient proof with regard to the lands concerned, without which, according to their classification and essence, it is impossible to acquire ownership of them. The veterans' struggle on the Negev lands and the right to them spoiled relations between the Bedouins and the state, especially when it was another factor to their existing set of plights. According to the Goldberg Committee, it is no longer possible to bypass this issue and to leave it unsolved. Without a solution it will be impossible to establish the trust between the Bedouins and the state.

In the committee report the following was written (p. 20):

> The policy towards the Bedouins needs to be based on the need for recognition of the right of minority members in the Negev to live in the existing settlements within development of these settlements, and within preservation of the tribal structure, and all of it in coordination and consultation with the tribesmen and their institutions. . . . The problematics derive from the clash between the two legal systems, between the Israeli law and the internal laws of property of the Bedouins as they respected them for generations and according to which they live until the present day.

GOUNDAFA. Goundafa are natives of the south, of the Anti-Atlas Mountains. They settled alongside the Wadi Nfiss and gradually accumulated power and influence. The modern founder of the clan was a schoolmaster, "Si Ahmed N'Ait Lahssen." In 1875, he extended his family's control over part of the Nfiss Valley. The sultan got angry at this and sent soldiers to subdue the Goundafa. The problem was solved when Si Ahmed was named the local caid.

After Si Ahmed's death in 1885, his son, Si Tayyeb Goundafi, acquired considerable Goundafa lands. Supported by the French authorities, he controlled a territory extending over the whole Houaz Plain and Nfiss Valley, and also the High Valley of Souss. When he died in 1928, he was one of the three lords of the Atlas to stand behind the pasha of Marrakesh, Thami Glawi, whose shadow dominated that of the king on the international scene. *See also* MOROCCO.

GRAVES OF HOLY MEN. The religious conception of the Bedouin is not always compatible with the normative **religion** of **Islam**. Since the period of Al-Jahiliyya—the **pre-Islamic period**—the Bedouins did not change much; their religious conception was grounded in the experience of the **desert**.

The Bedouins were exposed to natural disasters and subject to nature's graces. In order to cope with this reality they formed a world of concepts and beliefs that gave them a feeling of security. Allah's presence was very important in their belief, but he was not the sole party. The inhabitants of the desert attributed mythical powers to holy men; they believed that their spirits hovered above their graves after their death, and as they always were and still would be closer to Allah, they could serve as advocates for them, if they visited a holy man's grave and followed the appropriate ceremonial rites. Not all graves of holy men served the same purpose; certain holy men were capable of curing diseases; others were blessed with the power of returning thefts and lost properties; there were those whose favor could ensure economic prosperity or the birth of sons. The place of the grave was immaterial to the power of the holy departed.

The ceremony of pilgrimage to the grave of the holy man is called *ziara* (visit). The *ziairbidra* can take place in a limited, family format, in the company of several escorts, or masses, in which the whole family or tribe holds the visit, with a great audience. Thus, the pilgrimage can bear a festive character—**tents** are erected around the grave of the **sheikh**, **horse** and **camel** races are held, and there could be **music** and **dance**. When the visitors reach the right level of spiritual elevation, the spirit of the holy man might grant their request and serve as a mediator between them and the Creator.

The right time for a visit is in the afternoon hours; the ceremony is performed at night, and the visitors sleep where they built their camp and leave the following morning.

Orthodox Muslims object to these customs, perceiving them as contrary to their monotheistic religion; thus in recent years and with the **Islamic** revival, the rite for holy men has lost its importance, although it still exists.

GWARINA. The Gwarina are various settlers who lived in the Hula region, in the north of **Palestine**, during the period of the British mandate. Their origin is from **Egypt**, and they reached Palestine in the 1930s. The Gwarina tribe settled in 2 to 10 villages, of which the central one was Haltza (Kiryat Shmona today), which became the place of residence of the head of the tribe. They ascribed their name to the fact that they dwelled in a *ghour* region, which in **Arabic** means the bottom of a low plain, and this means the Jordan Valley.

The Gwarina, as opposed to the rest of the tribes, lived in huts and not in **tents**. They repaired a number of houses in the ruins of the villages in their environment, in order to use them as granaries. They obtained their income in land work and in rearing buffaloes. Many of the Gwarina members are scattered today in a number of villages in **Israel**.

H

HAJIRAT. Hajirat is a Bedouin tribe that lives in the north of **Israel** (the **Galilee** region). The tribe's origin is **Syria**. They penetrated into **Palestine** apparently in the 18th century. Today most of the tribesmen live in the village of Bir El-Maksur.

HAMMAM, SHEIKH (1769–1709). He was Hammam ben Yosef, a leader of the Hawara tribe, called "**Sheikh** El-Arab" (the sheikh of the Arabs). He was considered one of the important people of upper **Egypt** in the Ottoman era. He founded a strong tribal state in upper Egypt (*el-Zaid*). The state stretched to the region between Mani and Aswan, and the capital was the city of Partosh. Sheikh Hammam founded an army that was composed mainly of members of the Hawara tribe. His state was destroyed by the Egyptian ruler Ali Bey Al-Kabir (1728–1773), in the year 1769, with the help of several members of Sheikh Hammam's family. After the conquest the sheikh fled to Nuba. He died on the way.

HAMS. *Hams* is a group of men within the tribe whose friends are blood relatives of one another. Blood relation means that there is one common father for all the group's members, up to five (*hams* in **Arabic**) generations backward. Every Bedouin in the *hams* is responsible for the security and honor of each member in his group. If one group member was murdered by a member of another group, each one of the members of the *hams* of the victim had to avenge his blood, that is, kill the murderer or one of his *hams* members. *See also* VENDETTA.

HAWAZINA. The Hawazina tribe is a Sudanese **Baggara**, a collective name for a group of nomad cattle-**herding** tribes of Arabic origin. This particular tribe roams the area around Kurdufan. Their annual travel covers a distance of about 300 kilometers. They know the ecosystems, climate, vegetation, risks of all sorts, and **water** resources better than any other inhabitants of the region. All Baggara tribes are Sunni Arabs, and they share similar physical characteristics, costumes, other cultural features, and the general way of life.

HEIB. The Heib is a Bedouin tribe that dwells in the north of **Israel** (the **Galilee** region). They live mainly in three central places: Kfar Tuba-Zangariya, Beit **Zarzir**, and Ramat Heib. The tribesmen apparently originated from Syria. They penetrated into **Palestine** in the 17th century. This tribe was very strong in the period of the Ottoman Empire. The tribesmen imposed their authority on the villages and tribes in the Safed and Hula region. In the period of the British mandate in Palestine, many of the tribesmen joined the Zionist camp; the peak was in the 1948 war, when most of the tribesmen participated in battles on the side of the Israeli forces. The tribesmen were considered a tribe loyal to the state of Israel, and many of its members were integrated into the Israeli security services. *See also* ISRAEL DEFENSE FORCES (IDF).

HERDING. Herding is one of the most ancient professions. The first man was the first **shepherd** as his son Abel also was. It is known that shepherds existed in the Middle East since the domestication of the goat and sheep at the start of the Neolithic period. Sheep were raised for the sake of their milk, their meat, and their wool. A man called a shepherd was employed for herding the flock, someone who looks after the flock and supervises it in the grazing areas. The job of the shepherd is to find **food**, **water**, and shelter for the herd, to protect it from carnivorous animals, natural hazards and robbers, and also to maintain its unity and integrity.

As the main source of income of the Bedouins throughout history was the growth of beasts, herding was the central profession in their life. They employed a significant number of shepherds; the number of shepherds depended on the size of the flock.

Today on the background of the permanent **settlement** of the Bedouins, herding is declining in value. The Bedouins undergo occupational change, separate from the herds, and pass to hired work: free professions and clerical work, etc. Today herding as a principal source of income exists only in regions that have not yet completed the processes of permanent settlement, as for example in the **Sinai Desert** in **Egypt**.

HIJRA SETTLEMENTS. Ertawia was the first *hijra* or agricultural **settlement** in Arabia, and was founded in 1912. It was situated on the caravan route between **Kuwait** and Riyadh. It was known for its great quantity of water and good grazing land. It was located within the territory of the Mutair Bedouins, a tribe disloyal to **Ibn Saud**, who tried to settle them. They decided to become sedentary, and sold their **camels** and started farming and learning the Koran, the hadith, and Wahhabi teachings from preachers, whom Ibn Saud had sent to Ertawia. The Utayba tribesmen next settled in Ghut-Ghut, and were followed by other tribes, who founded two hundred settlements in central Arabia or in Najd, until 1918.

In this period, Ibn Saud recruited 60,000 soldiers from the hijra colonies and created the force of the **Ikhwan** (brothers). Then Ibn Saud conquered Eastern Arabia, but Hejaz (Makkah, Jeddah, and Medina) only fell in 1926. When, in 1921, he defeated the Rashidis of the **Shammar** confederation, who had ruled northern Arabia since 1836, Wadi Sirhan and the territory of the **Shararat** tribe was conquered by him.

Their mud-brick houses consisted of one room for guests, one for dinners, a third for sleeping, and a fourth for storage. They worked at growing wheat and barley for family sustenance, and when not engaged in **agriculture** or commerce they prayed in the mosque. Thus, they had exchanged tilling the land and sowing fields for raiding. There were three types of settlers—the farmers, who were in the majority, preachers, and **tradesmen**: these groups were differentiated by tribal distinctions. Some of the farmers answered the call of the jihad as fighters, and some of the traders were blacksmiths, who were not fighters, nor tribesmen, but members of the lower class, who had joined it for protection. They made horseshoes and put them on **horses**, made javelins and swords, and repaired weapons and tools. Hundreds of preachers studied under the Wahhabi *ulama* in Riyadh and then went to the villages to spread the teachings of the Koran.

The hijras remained functional until 1926, when Ibn Saud completed his unification of **Saudi Arabia** and signed the Hadda and Kuwait s with the British in the Persian Gulf and with the Hashemites in Transjordan and **Iraq**. However, the Ikhwan wanted Ibn Saud to continue his expansionist policies, and therefore, split into a group that stayed loyal to Ibn Saud and another that was a fanatical opposition. These did not recognize international borders and under the direction of Faisal al-Dawish of the Mutair carried out a few raids into Transjordan, Kuwait, and southern Iraq in opposition to Ibn Saud. In 1929, they rebelled openly against him, but he overpowered them in the battle of Esbalah. Thus the Ikhwan and the hijras together with them were destroyed in this battle.

In 1932, Ibn Saud declared the foundation of the kingdom of Saudi Arabia and the formation of a National Guard and standing army. The Ikhwan fighters joined the National Guard, and the hijra settlers abandoned them and returned to pastoral nomadism or moved to urban areas.

HIMYARITE. Himyar (Mamlakat Himyar) was an ancient kingdom in the south **Arabian Peninsula**, the site of contemporary **Yemen**. The kingdom was founded in 115 BC and thrived until the early 3rd century AD. Its economy was based on **agriculture** and **trade**, mostly commodities that came from or through India (spices, sapphires) and Africa (ivory, furs) that were in high demand in the Roman Empire.

Since the 4th century AD, the kingdom was plagued with unrest. The decline in trade caused the Romans to conquer Aden and imposed a siege on Marib, but the adventure proved to be too costly and they left without completing the conquest of Himyar. In AD 340, the Abyssinians conquered Himyar and ruled it for 30 years, after which it gained independence for almost a century. In 450 AD, the great dam of *Marib* burst open and the flood that ensued ruined cities and cultivated fields and triggered a mass emigration to the neighboring kingdoms.

The last king of Himyar was Yūsuf Dhū Nuwās, who converted to Judaism with many of his immediate tribesmen. In AD 523 he fought the **Christians** who lived in the towns of Najran and Zafar, who were supported by the Christian Abyssinians. Eventually, the Byzantine emperor Justinian I notified Kaleb, the king of Aksum, about the anti-Christian actions of Dhu Nuwās. A joint action was undertaken by the Christian armies comprised of the Byzantine fleet and Abyssinian soldiers from Aksum, who invaded Himyar and defeated and killed King Yusuf Dhu Nuwas. Himyar was annexed by the kingdom of Aksum, and its nobility was forced to convert to Christianity.

One of its Abyssinian governors, Abraha, initiated military actions against the **Quraysh** tribe in Hejaz. He managed to conquer the town of Makkah but did not destroy the *Kaaba.* The discontented Himyar population rebelled against the Abyssinians and appointed their own king. The revolt spread all over the kingdom and was supported by forces of the Sassanian Empire. They managed to oust the Abyssinians, but Himyar was annexed by the Persian forces to the Sassanian Empire.

HORSE. The horse along with the **camel** has gained special treatment by the Bedouins. The Bedouin tribes in the ancient Arab world, in the entire Middle East in particular, lived mainly in the wilderness. They fought in bloody wars among themselves, some of which continued for decades. Arab horses were the main tools of war, which helped in the transport of warriors and their belongings. These horses were endowed with very high survival capacity, physical fitness, and tolerance, in comparison to the rest of the horses. The heroism that the Bedouin horsemen showed on the battlefield was also connected to the horse of the rider. The Bedouins were proud about the speed of their horses, their mobility, and stiff resistance on the battlefield.

The Arab horses were grown and nurtured for years for riding, tolerance, and effort, in severe climatic conditions in terms of view of temperature, arid conditions, poor grazing, and mobile sand. In addition to their doing the main task of carrying the rider and acting as a war tool, the Arab horse was a source of beauty, pride, power, sport, and excellence. It is believed that the

Bedouins of the Middle East have had a special relationship with their horses for thousands of years. Not only did the Bedouins treat the horse as a means for riding, but also their attitude toward the horse is mingled with love, friendship, and loyalty. The Bedouins took a great interest in the growth of their horses.

The Bedouin heritage is filled with examples that highlight the status of the horse in Bedouin societies in the **pre-Islamic period**. The horse has an important place in **poetry**. Arab poets have composed verses of poetry wherein they describe their speed, beauty, and endurance on the battlefield. Wars have broken out between tribes on account of horses and prestige; for example, the Bedouin heritage elucidates the intertribal war called *Dahas Wael-Gavraa*, which broke out in the pre-Islamic period between the tribes of Abbas and Dubian and continued for many years; the reason for it was the rivalry that existed around a horse race between the horse called *Dahas* and the mare called *El-Gavraa*.

The Bedouins were proud of the origin of their horses; they knew how to recite the family tree of the horse and took pride in the nobility of their horses.

Over the years, a very wide folklore and culture developed around the growth and use of the Arab horse, especially among the Bedouin population. Horses served as a fantasy (show exhibits with riders), and horse races were conducted, especially at weddings and on holidays.

HOSPITALITY. The Bedouins attribute a special and noble value to the guest, and hospitality is an expression of honoring the guest. The customs of generous hospitality evolved from the fact that the **desert** is a vast, barren area, where there are no accommodations or services, and a person **wandering** or traveling in this harsh land can find himself without shelter, **water**, or **food**. The awareness of this possibility led nomads, since ancient times, to offer these necessities to anyone in need, a friend, a foe, or a complete stranger. The Bedouins developed this custom further and developed a unique cultural tradition and set a procedure; they received the stranger as a messenger of God, "*Al-Deif Deif Allah*" (the guest, a guest of God), and treated him accordingly.

Tradition dictates that the host will fulfill the needs of the guest. He is not supposed to ask the guest what he wants or needs, but has to offer everything in his capacity. Thinking of or considering other options is perceived as a negative trait, a curse from the Lord.

The guest is described by three images: an *amir* (prince), an *asir* (prisoner), and a *shaaer* (poet). As a prince, the host supplies the guest with all he lacks to make him feel relaxed; as a prisoner, the guest cannot order or demand anything but must be grateful for all that the host does for him; and as a poet, the guest must praise his host and his house.

A guest is always protected, regardless of his status and prior relations. In fact, the host is obliged to protect him. Thus, the guest must show respect and is expected to behave according to social conventions. A host is expected to make the **coffee** himself and butcher a lamb in the guest's honor, although dignitaries and family elders can have younger servants do this.

HOWEITAT. Howeitat or Huwaytat is a large **tribal** confederation that lives in **Jordan** and **Saudi Arabia**. This tribal group has several branches including the Ibn Jazi, **Abu Tayi**, Sulaymanniyin, and several other associated tribes.

Unlike most Bedouin tribes, the Howeitat claim that they are all descendents of an Egyptian ancestor named Huwayt. However, it appears that their presence in the area dates back to the 18th century, when tribes of northern Arabia were pushed northward by expansion of the Wahhabite of central Arabia. By the late 18th century the Howeitat were already established around Aqaba and in regions northward, while some associated clans laid claim to land in **Egypt**.

They became semisedentary, combining **agriculture** in the fertile areas with nomadic **herding** in other parts. In the early 20th century many of them were engaged in raiding, collection of tribute, and **camel**-herding.

During the Arab revolt, the major subclans, Abu Tayi and Ibn Jazi, supported the Hashemite cause and mustered the Bedouin tribes to assist Prince Feisal bin Hussein. In later years, the Howeitat returned to farming; however, many of them served in the Jordanian armed forces, while the branches living in Saudi Arabia provided manpower to a significant portion of the Saudi Arabian National Guard.

HURA. Hura is a Bedouin village in the district of Beer Sheva, the major city in southern **Israel** that never developed into an urban center as planned. In 1996, it received the status of local municipality. Most of the residents of Hura are Bedouins from two major **clans**, Abu Alkian and Al-Atawneh. According to the Israel Central Bureau of Statistics (CBS), in January 2011 the population of Hura was 17,500. *See also* NEGEV BEDOUINS; RAHAT.

HUSSEIN, SADDAM (1937–2006). Saddam Hussein was one of the Ba'ath party leaders and became the sole leader of **Iraq** in 1968, and in time, turned into a notorious dictator. He never mixed with the local population and lived for a long time in his own compound, surrounded by soldiers of his own tribe, Jubbur, and the Ubayd. However, after the Iraqi troops were forced by the Iranian forces to retreat from Khorramshahr in 1982, he extended this policy and received men from other tribes into the army. As a repercussion, he drafted 50,000 young Republican Guards and assigned them to protect his person from the Jubbur (near Tikrit) alone, and rewarded the tribe by building roads, and installing electricity and **water** systems in their territory. Since the late 1980s, senior members in the Republican Command Council have revealed their tribal origins to the public. A Basra university professor claimed that instead of uniting the nation, the regime's support of tribal justice was "sowing the seeds of division, inciting one part of it against the other and depreciating legal justice."

Regardless of tribal loyalty, on January 1990, **Juburi** soldiers planned to assassinate Saddam Hussein at an Army Day parade. When the plot was discovered, several Juburi soldiers were executed, and hundreds of others were dismissed from the army. Later, Ubayd soldiers also were estranged from his rule. In 1992, Saddam Hussein survived and suppressed a Shi'ite **Intifada** (people's uprising) and in 1993, he changed his attitude toward the Basra tribes and asked them to bring with them their war banners and rifles, and dance their war dance in his honor, and asked their poets to write songs and eulogies praising and blessing him. (*See* MUSIC AND DANCE.)

Then, in 1995, he was compelled to suppress a rebellion of the Dulayim, a Sunni tribe that rebelled after the execution of the air force major general of the Dulayim. These events led Hussein to distrust these three major Sunni tribes, and he removed them from all key positions. Furthermore, he allied himself with lower-ranking **sheikhs** and made them assemble their entire tribe to swear loyalty and alliance to him.

During his presidency, the tribes that swore allegiance to him received financial support, weapons like RPG rockets, and cannons. This meant the chief could organize a private army composed of his tribesmen. Saddam used tribal law and conventions to his benefit; he justified the invasion of **Kuwait** of August 1990 in terms of tribal honor, claiming the Kuwaitis had injured Iraqi tribal honor. He used a similar excuse to justify fatalities that "occurred" to members of his family who deserted to Amman.

HYAYNA. Hyayna is an Arab tribe composed of three fractions, Ouled Amran, Ouled Alian, and Ouled Riab. Marmol, who traveled all over the country in the middle of the 16th century (1540), spoke of a tribe rich in **agriculture** that counted 25 families and supplied 4,000 fighters to the Makhzen. The Hyayna tribe were only spoken about and originated in the 17th century, under the Saadian dynasty. It seems they settled in the territory in the late 16th and start of the 17th centuries. They accompanied the Saadians of the south and conquered Fez in 1549. In order to close the Taza Straits to the Turks, the Saadians settled with the soldiers in this strategic military zone to defend Fez, their capital. *See also* MOROCCO.

I

IBN ABI WAQAS, SA'D (595–674). Sa'd Ibn Abi Waqas was an early convert to **Islam** in 610–611 and one of the important companions of the Islamic Prophet Muhammad. Sa'd was the 17th person to embrace Islam at the age of 17. He is mainly known for his command in the conquest of Persia in 636, governorship of it, and diplomatic journeys to China in 616 and 651. Sa'd was from the Banu Zuhrah **clan** of the **Quraysh** tribe, and was the cousin of Aminah bint Wahb, mother of the Prophet Muhammad.

Sa'd is considered to be the father of the **Suwaed** tribe, who live today in the **Galilee** region, in the north of the state of **Israel**. *See also* IRAN.

IBN SAUD, ABDULAZIZ (1880–1953). Ibn Saud was born during a tribal war that marked the end of the second Saudi state. He rose to attention when he led his men to reconquer the Rashidi-held Riyadh in 1902. He proved himself in handling foreign affairs.

In the early 20th century, **horse** and **camel trade** in the regions along the Gulf coast improved considerably, and their inhabitants looked for a better government and accepted Ibn-Saud when he invaded the area. In World War I, he was part of the alliance of the local leadership with the British, which led to a significant accrual of wealth and inspired the Arab Revolt (1916–1918) led by the Hashemites; with British support, the Ottomans were driven out of the Arabian Peninsula and, eventually, the entire Middle East.

Thus, the tribes became more autonomous and tried to live near the caravan paths and commercial centers. As the British backed different Arab leaders according to previous relations and their own interests, the Saudi rulers who befriended the tribes cemented the integration of territories and boosted commerce. Ibn Saud did his best to mediate intertribal skirmishes and calm traditional enmities, and managed to fend off those who threatened his authority. In a couple of decades he expanded his territory and repressed (sometimes brutally so) tribal unrest.

The ruling dynasty used intermarriage with tribal and urban families in order to consolidate their rule. Ibn Saud possessed an impressive appearance, but as a devout Muslim could marry only four wives at a time; thus, he divorced and married repeatedly and sired 45 sons, including the subsequent kings of **Saudi Arabia**. After he won out in military conflicts with the forces of his main opponent, Sharif Husayn, who was authoritarian toward the tribes after the rebellion, he gathered many tribesmen as supporters and became the sole leader of Saudi Arabia.

As a ruler, Ibn Saud chose to leave tribal social elements as they were, following the classic Islamic pattern of empire-building. Foreign and internal conflicts left him no time to bring about internal societal change. The worldwide economic depression of the early 1930s left its mark on the Saudi economy, as the number of pilgrims decreased and revenue slumped. However, when oil was discovered in 1938, things changed but slowly. Saud sought American assistance and managed to form the right contact and then established the Arabian American Oil Company (ARAMCO), whose input increased revenue considerably. However, ARAMCO's management was inefficient and, in building the railway line in 1946 to connect the interior with the Red Sea, the government got itself into debt.

Saudi Arabia was administered by means of a partially elected consultative council of notables in the Hejaz and a system of regional governors. However, the real power and authority lay with the king and his close advising council. There was also a weekly audience with the ulama. In the 1960s, Saud's health deteriorated; his eldest son, a known spender, tended to reach hasty economic decisions and tilted his support toward Gamal Abdul Nasser and Egypt. The leading group feared that he would bring instability to the regime, as regardless of the efforts made, the social integration of the tribes was only partly achieved.

The Hejaz acted as the hub of activity, supplying the largest portion of taxes and housing the king's foreign advisers, western businessmen looking for mineral resources, and rich local merchants planning the economic future of the kingdom. In contrast to this, the people of Najd were deprived of their former central role, and mostly served in the army, although they desired more lucrative jobs. The Asiris did not occupy any leading posts. Except for the rich merchants of al-Ahsa and al-Qasim, none of them achieved the high status enjoyed by the Hejazi traders.

IBN SHADDAD, ANTARAH (525–608). Antarah Ibn Shaddad, one of the seven great **pre-Islamic** Arab poets with a rare gift for **language**, was also considered a hero. He was born in Najd (northern Arabia). He was the son of a **Banu Abs** chieftain and an African slave named Zabiba. As a young man he was disregarded by the tribe, due to his dark complexion, so his father sent him to fight with the tribe warriors to prove himself and earn his freedom. His courage and fighting skills gained him the respect of his tribe, and his **poetry**, especially his romantic autobiographical life story, *Mu'allaqat*, distinguished him, which led to the famous love story Antar and Alba. Antarah is also known for being involved in the writing of the "Divan." His eloquence in the **Arabic language** led many Arabs to call him the "complete knight." His poems are included in the poetry collection known as the "Hanged Poems," which provided important historical cultural details of the time, especially those referring to the weaponry, **horses**, **desert**, and lifestyle. As a warrior he participated in several tribal wars at the time and was killed in battle during a war between the Banu Abs and the Tai.

IKHWAN. After 1912, but especially after 1916, tribal clans like the Utayba, Harb, Mutair, **Qahtan**, and other tribes, were expected to sell off their **camel** and sheep, give up their nomadic customs, settle in permanent sites, and join the Wahhabi religious revivalist movement, and spread it in order to attach other groups to the Saudi influence. **Ibn Saud** managed to persuade them to join his army, called the Ikhwan (brothers).

The Ikhwan were an important factor in the Saudi expansionary consolidation. They were among the corps that defeated the Rashidis, and in the forces that occupied Taif and Makkah in Hejaz. They were also involved in civilian projects as religious preachers and advocates of settling. Factions of the Ikhwan affiliated with the Mutair, Qahtan, Utayba, and Ujman tribes retained their tribal structure and **nomadic** lifestyle. They mixed *asabiyya* (tribal integrity) and religious fervor, including a change in appearance, which made them attractive and forceful.

The movement spread to the Rub el-Khali **desert**, the Gulf States, Transjordan, and **Iraq**, and caused difficulties for the local rulers. The activity of the Ikhwan created problems in the Saudi hierarchy, as they tried to force Ibn Saud to spread Wahhabi teachings in the **educational** institutions all over the kingdom. Their relations with the urban centers and clergy became tense. Ibn Saud was compelled to replace their teachers in the *hujar* and, in 1919, asked the senior Najdulama to pronounce a *fatwa* (legal opinion) that "Ikhwanist" **Islam** was not superior to ordinary Wahhabi practice. Their unrelenting religious zeal was a central factor in the internal struggle between the traditionalist and modernist elements within the Saudi upper class. *See also* IKHWAN REBELLION; SAUDI ARABIA.

IKHWAN REBELLION. After World War I the French and British wanted to limit Bedouin tribal power in the Middle East. The ruler of Najd, Abd al-Aziz ibn Abd al-Rahman Saud, and the Hashemite ruler of **Iraq** and Transjordan sought ways to settle the nomads and "release" vast stretches of land the Bedouins considered to be their territory. They forbade border crossing and fought smuggling. The Bedouins' traditional **migration** routes were blocked, and their assets of land and grazing areas were significantly reduced. **Ibn Saud** used the **Ikhwan** tribes from the *badiya* region of northern Arabia to attack territories outside his native Najd, and expand his territory.

The Ikhwan were an extreme Wahhabi group in the Najd who were encouraged to settle on the border with **Kuwait**. By adopting **agriculture** and joining religious revivalist movements, these tribes were expected to develop a new sense of cohesion and loyalty to Ibn Saud, who sought to benefit from their military skills by making them part of his army in the service of the state.

In October 1920, after certain provocations and accusations of blocking commerce, tampering with **trade**, and smuggling, the Ikhwan soldiers raided the camps of **nomad** tribes across the border and amassed troops to attack Kuwait City. However, the reinforcement forces of the Shamar tribe arrived in time and saved Kuwait from being pillaged and annexed to **Saudi Arabia**. Their revolt marked a new era in the Sunni/Shiite split. According to a neutral observer, "The fierce Sunni hatred of the Shia Iraqi tribes was evident; the puritanical Brotherhood had attacked a large encampment of **Bani Malik shepherds** here, killing 37 Iraqi men. The Ikhwan plundered many Iraqi families of all their possessions in a manner previously unparalleled in **desert** warfare."

IMRU-AL-QAIS. Qais was an Arabian poet in early 6th century AD. He was the youngest son of a local king, Hujr bin al-Harit, the last king of the Kindite line, who ruled the Nagd in central Arabia at the time. Some consider Qais the father of Arab **poetry**. His qaseeda (long poem) "Let Us Stop and Weep" is one of the seven Mu'allaqat poems prized as the best examples of **pre-Islamic** Arabian verse.

According to legend, his father disapproved of his writing and his lifestyle in general. Nevertheless, when his father was assassinated, he was the only son who attempted to avenge his death and fought the Asad tribe for the rest of his life. At that time there was no systematic recording of events in Arabia, and hence the exact details are not known. Therefore, historians have to compare oral stories and legends to ascertain the life story of this famous pre-Islamic poet.

INTIFADA, SHIITE. The term *intifada* means "people are resistance." The Shiite Intifada refers to the Shiite insurrection that broke out in 1991, in **Iraq**, on the grounds that the regime favored the Sunnis, the economically neglected southern area, and their opposition to the secularism of the Ba'ath party. **Saddam Hussein** criticized the Ba'ath apparatus for failing to control the masses of Shiites in southern Iraq and act against guerrilla activities and infiltration from Shiite **Iran**. He turned to the tribal **sheikhs** of some Kurdish tribes, who supported him against the Kurdish nationalists, and some Sunni tribes around Baghdad he could rely on.

However, in the south many Shiite tribes joined the intifada against the regime. The tribal chiefs of Bani Arid and the Khaza'il, Afak, and Sadah joined the leadership of the revolt and gave it a public standing. The sheikhs who led the revolt in Najaf wanted to march into Baghdad. However, a large part of the Khaffaja tribe near Nasiriyya supported Saddam Hussein, who had appointed one of their leaders as governor of **Kuwait**. In addition, the regime managed to ensure the support of the **Bani Hassan** tribe. By the end of March, the intifada lost its momentum. Many tribes, Sunni and Shiite alike, decided to back the regime. This enabled the Republican Guard to suppress the Intifada. In total, between 30,000 and 100,000 lives were lost in the Intifada.

IRAN. Nomadic tribes have entered Iran throughout history, or at least since 2,000 BC, when the Aryan tribes entered the Iranian mountains from the north; however, the tribes' composition and relation to the ruling regime changed due to **migrations**, invasions, and other social factors. The tribal society in contemporary Iran is composed of various ethnic groups and cultures. The main division is the differentiation between Iranians and non-Iranians.

The Iranian tribes are composed of six groups: the Lilar are composed of several groups that have merged with five big tribes—Lelek, Lalak, Zand, Bakhtiaria, Mamsinia (Mamsani); the Karous, Kahalar, and Mokaria; the Kurds of Khorasan, comprised of the following tribes—Zafranalu, Saadanalu, Koanalu, Daher Akuanalu, and Duanalu; the Galarion in Khorasan; the Karayoun; and the Jalayoun.

The **nomadic** tribes are also of diverse ethnic origin: Turks, Turkmen, Persians, Kurds, **Lurs**, Arabs, and **Baluchis**. The two provinces without nomadic tribes are Kurdistan and Yazd. The Kurdish nomads live in the **Bakhtiari** province. The non-Iranian tribes are divided according to the ethnic Arabs and Turks. The Arabs are comprised of six tribes: Kaab, Arab Hueida, Arab Fares, Arab Khorasan, Zankuein, and Amarein.

The Bedouin tribes in contemporary Iran are divided into three ethnic groups: Turks, Lilak (Lurs), and Arabs. The Turkish tribes are remnants of the Turkish conquest of the Turkistan region; the Lilak comes from hybrid Persian-Arabs, people who lived in the Persian Gulf; and the Arab tribes scattered in Iran are remnants of the Muslim Arab conquest of the 7th century and the tribes that followed in their wake.

Most of the Bedouins in Iran differ from Bedouins in the Arab countries, as the latter live or used to live as nomads, while the majority of the Bedouins of Iran live in the mountains and they are either sedentary or seminomadic, their **wandering** being very limited. Contemporary Iran has a population of three million Bedouins, and they used to have significant political power.

Toward the end of the 18th century, the Iranian central government began to intervene regularly in the internal political life of the tribes. Nasser el-Din Shah appointed Hussein Koli Khan Nazem from the Bakhtiari tribe as leader and commander of the tribes in the Zagros region in exchange for loyalty of the tribes to the throne. At the time, most of the regular Iranian army was comprised of Bedouins.

The leaders of the tribes who accumulated power were nicknamed "uncrowned kings." Leaders of the Bakhtiari tribe almost reached the Persian throne at the close of the 18th century and in the early 20th century. Once oil was found in Zagros, the Bakhtiari leaders held important political roles. However, in 1944, with the new constitution that forced them to settle and confiscated large portions of their land, they resisted, and several tribal leaders were arrested and some of them executed. Reza Shah adopted a policy designed to undermine the Bedouin economic base by confiscating lands and eliminating the Bedouin culture, forbidding them to wear their traditional clothing and grow beards.

This policy alienated the Bedouins. Moreover, the Shah kept changing his policy toward the Bedouins; for example, in 1953, he founded the "Supreme Council for Tribes" and compensated the Bakhtiari tribes for damages they sustained during the enforced nationalization; in 1954, he deported members of the Kashkai tribe; in 1956 he founded a military brigade designated to fight the tribes; and so on. When other components of the Iranian society rebelled against the Shah, some Bedouin tribes joined in. The White Revolution started in 1963 and continued until the dismissal of the Shah in 1979.

The Sunni tribes in Iran, except for the **Kurds**, who had their own agenda, did not play an important role in the revolution that led to the overthrow of the Shah in 1979, as despite the grudges they had against the regime, many of them served in the army. The revolution was carried out by the urban middle classes and students, and was hijacked by the religious Shiite ayatollahs. The non-Shiite Muslim Iranians (Baluch, Turkmen, Kurds, and some Arabs) resisted the Islamic Republic on religious grounds, and the **Qashqai** tribe joined them in response to discrimination and military aggression.

The Iran-**Iraq** War (1980–1988) heightened national Persian sentiment among the Shiite Persians, who classified Sunni Arabs as enemies. However, the only real resistance to the Khomeini regime was in Kurdistan and Baluchistan. The Soviet occupation of Afghanistan drove 1.8 million Afghans to flee across the border to Iran. The Afghan refugees renewed their longstanding alliances with the Baluchi tribes.

During the 1980s, 1990s, and early 21st century, the Iranian government showed an interest in the tribes in Iran and supported publication of research and literature dedicated to **tribalism** and nomads, while certain Iranian exiled factors, along with the U.S. State Department, tried to persuade the tribes to overthrow the regime and offered them assistance and military equipment. However, the factions failed to cooperate and could not be unified, as there were too many political and ethnic (including linguistic) differences between the diverse minority groups.

The 17 clauses of civil rights in the White Revolution manifesto did not refer to the Bedouin tribes; in fact, the new regime did its best to destroy tribal infrastructure and the Bedouin culture. For example, it issued an order forbidding growing animals near **water** sources, especially lakes; forests and grazing areas were nationalized; and uncultivated lands were confiscated by the state and closed to grazing animals. This policy caused migration of the poor Bedouins and the dispossessed *fellahin* to the cities, created shanty slams, and provided cheap workers to the industrial sector.

The Iranian nomadic tribes live mainly by raising grazing animals: sheep, goat, cattle, **camels**, **horses**, mules, and donkeys. However, many are semi-sedentary and grow wheat, barley, and vegetables in the rainy season. In the mountains they also plant orchards of gum and resin, almonds, and other nuts. They use acorn flour to produce a type of bread. Female members contribute to the home economy by weaving and sewing saddlebags. They also do embroidery and weave carpets, rugs, and canvas for family **tents**.

The tribes produce and sell animal products, such as, meat, wool, goat hair, and milk products. In the Statistics Center's census of 1974, the nomadic tribes were found to own only 10 percent of the livestock units in the country. The economic basis of these nomadic tribes is grazing animals such as sheep.

In Persian, the words *asira*, *qabila*, *il*, *tayefa*, *uymaq*, and *ulus* and their plurals are often used as synonyms for the word *tribe*, and sometimes they stand for *lineage*, **clan**, *family*, *community*, or even *body of troops*. *See also* PAHLAVI, MOHAMMAD REZA SHAH (1919–1980); PAHLAVI, REZA SHAH (1878–1944).

Historians believe that the first Arabian tribes arrived in Khuzestan from the Arabian Peninsula, when circumstances dictated the move. However, during the Sasanian period a number of large Arab tribes, including the Tanuk, Asad, Nezar, Bakr, Tamim, and Tagleb, moved into the Fertile Crescent and founded grazing territories on the edges of the Persian Empire. Another wave of mass immigration occurred in the 7th century. The migrating tribes scattered throughout the Middle East, and some of them penetrated Iran.

The Arabs did not plan to settle in the Persian dominion, but only pillage it. However, following the unrest in southern Iraq, the governor sent 50,000 Arab families to Khorasan in northeastern Persia. The Arabs who settled in this region intermarried with the local residents, shook off their cultural identity, and assimilated. During the 16th century the Ka'b tribe settled in Khuzestan, where they found few clans of the Asad tribe, who migrated there sometime during the 10th century AD. As this region was practically "Arabized" it was sometimes referred to as "Arabestan."

The largest and most important Arab tribe in Iran is the Bani-Kaab, whose clans populate the Minoo Island and Khorramshahr and Shadegan districts on both sides of the Karun River, and members of the Kassir family reside in the city of Ahwaz. The other main tribes are Bani-Lam, Bani-Saleh, Bani-Torof, Bani-Tamim, Bani-Marvan, Al-Khamiss, Bavi, and Kenane. The seminomadic **Arabic**-speaking tribes are called Araba and Koti. In 1976, the Arab tribal population in Iran was estimated to be around 300,000 people.

IRAQ. In ancient times, the society was divided into tribes and **clans**. Nomadic tribes have lived and gone through the area of modern Iraq since the dawn of civilization. People, nomads and sedentary alike, migrated to Iraq and from it, great armies crossed it, and the neighboring empires annexed parts of it and brought settlers to their new territories. Today, tribes of diverse ethnic origin live in all the provinces of Iraq.

Large portions of the Bedouin tribes who live in Iraq today are Arabs who came (or were pushed) from the adjacent Arabian Peninsula. Tribes of **Kurdish** and **Turkmen** origin also live in Iraq. Most of them found themselves in Iraq after the Ottoman Empire collapsed and the national borders were set. Others moved over for various reasons.

The big factor that led to the massive penetration of the Bedouin tribes from Arabia into Iraq was the Muslim conquest of the 7th century AD. Some Bedouin tribes settled, some had adopted a semisedentary lifestyle, while others remained nomads. Regardless of their lifestyle, the Bedouins in Iraq maintain their tribal values and tradition in marriage, festive ceremonies, robbery, and the tribal customary law system.

There are several major Arab tribes. The Tai tribes, of the Arab southern group (Al-Kahtaniun), live near Mosul, in the Al-Jazira plains, near the Syrian border, and beyond. Another group affiliated to the Tai, the Banu Lam and Al-Hazaal tribes, live near Baghdad. The Azena tribes of northern (Al Adanioun) Arabian descent are dispersed among several Arab States, including Iraq. They live in the Baghdad region near the Euphrates River. The Zubeid tribes, also called Abu Sultan, who are **Qahtan** (southern) Arabs, live in the Gulf States and in the Babylon district of Iraq. The Al-Jabour tribe lives in the districts of Bakouba, Baghdad, Al-Yosfia, Al-Hala, Mosul, Al-Zab, and El-Haboud.

During World War I, the Bedouin tribes joined the Arab national struggle against the Ottoman Empire. They also opposed the British presence in Iraq but later were used by the British to safeguard convoys that passed through their territories.

Kurdistan, the first independent Iraqi state, was not able to contain and subdue the tribes. Therefore, the British formed separate agreements with certain **sheikhs** to safeguard their interests. Sometimes the British officials were asked to mediate between the monarchy and the tribes.

In 1968, the Ba'ath Party gained control of Iraq. Its leadership perceived the tribes as a hindrance to political reform and economic progress; hence, it launched **agricultural** reforms, seized lands, and formed societies of peasants in order to undermine the sheikh's role and status. **Saddam Hussein** assumed patronage by means of bribes to gain their loyalty and support and harness them to the state's hegemony.

In the post-Saddam era, the tribes began to fill in the voids in the security tasks. Today in some urban centers, there is a social trend of people returning to their tribal identity; unfortunately, this trend increases the differences between the various components of Iraqi society.

The Americans, who were in control for a while, befriended the tribes and encouraged the tribe leaders' involvement in Iraqi politics. They also helped the revival of organizations such as Zahawat Al-Iraq and Abnaa el-Iraq and financed their activities, with the aim of suppressing the local branches of Al-Qaeda. The Kurdish tribes were actively involved in the Kurdish revolt, demanding Kurdish independence or at least autonomy, which they eventually achieved in the Iraqi part of Kurdistan. All things considered, the tribe in Iraq constitutes a factor of stability in times of crisis.

ISLAM. The appearance of the Islamic **religion** in the year AD 610 created a new reality. It weakened the tribal identity and created in its place an Islamic religious identity. It was the Prophet Muhammad who started the promulgation of the Islamic religion, something that aroused much opposition among the Arab tribes, as according to tribal culture, they saw him as someone who threatened their hegemony. The result was a resistance against him among Arab tribes, especially from members of the **Quraysh** tribe, as he was counted with this tribe.

By virtue of the leadership of the Prophet Muhammad and by virtue of the enthusiasm of his people for their new belief, Muhammad succeeded in defeating the corps of Quraysh soldiers and in the year 630 took control of the town of Makkah without a battle. After the conquest of the city, delegations of Arab tribes came to him, one after another, to express their loyalty to him and the new religion.

Muhammad received the delegations and demanded that the tribes accept the religion of Islam, and that now their loyalty be to the new religion and not to the tribe as it had been in the past. Thus, Muhammad became the leader of the Arab tribes, which the religion of Islam united.

When the whole of Arabia converted to Islam, it was impossible to implement any more *gazo* (robbery), as now everybody was part of one state and raids were executed outward, against Byzantium, the Sassanian kingdom, and the like. This was the fuel that the Islamic conquests needed at the start of their course.

The Muslim religion started to develop at the start of the 7th century (610), in the Arabian Peninsula, under the leadership of the Prophet Muhammad. The Holy Book of the Muslim religion is the Koran, considered by the Muslim believers as a wonderful divine book in which all the wisdom is included.

Islam is principally an orthopractic religion, that is, a religion of law that is based on practical commandments. Muslim law is called the *sharia* (the way of the honest). It directs the steps of the believer in every place and at every time; there is no separation between religion and life.

In the Islamic religion five basic commandments exist, called "the five pillars of Islam" (sort of pillars on which the religion is founded).

The first commandment is the testimony (from *to testify*). The Muslim testifies to his belief by saying the sentence—"There is no God without Allah and Muhammad is his envoy." This sentence is said during the prayer, in the ceremony of Islamization, and on every occasion.

The second commandment is the prayer. A Muslim needs to pray five times a day. The prayer is done with the face of the worshipper directed toward Mecca. It is possible to pray in any place and also in a mosque. On Friday, at noon, the Muslim tends to pray in a mosque.

The third commandment is charity (*el-zakaa*). Every Muslim is required to contribute from his money according to his economic situation. The alms are handed out to poor Muslims, to widows, and to orphans. Likewise the money is contributed to the needs of Islam, for example, toward building mosques.

The fourth commandment is fasting. A Muslim needs to fast during the month of Ramadan. There is fast from dawn until sunset. At the end of the month the Muslims celebrate the feast of breaking the fast—*Eid-ul-Fitr*.

The fifth commandment is pilgrimage. Every Muslim has to make a pilgrimage once in his life to the Kaaba in Mecca, in contemporary **Saudi Arabia**. The ceremony of the Haj is executed during the 12th Muslim month, and at its end the Muslims celebrate the Feast of the Sacrifice (*Eid-ul-Adha*).

The period before Islam was called *el-Jahaliya*—the period of ignorance, in which the people were polytheistic (they believed in a number of gods). The Islamic writings describe *el-Jahaliya* as a dark period, in which the people did not know how to worship the right God.

At the center of the religion in the Jahaliya period stood the worship of trees and springs, ghosts and spirits, holy stones and idols, belief in soothsayers and in fortune-tellers, and sacrifice of victims, such as animals, **food** products, and valuable objects. Each group of tribes had gods of their own, with no central god. The tribes had statues that represented their deities, which they carried in their **wandering**s or held in their houses.

The religion was syncretic, that is, it attached different ideas and views to one wholeness and recognized gods who were brought from outside.

The **nomads** believed in fate and did not think about the eternity of the soul or the next world. They believed in superstitions, and each tribe had a faith of its own—a creed of inanimate objects, to which mysterious forces would be ascribed. The nomad was indifferent to matters of religion and admired what he saw in the **desert**: stars, trees, mountains, valleys, and fire. "Allah," who in the Islamic period would be the name of the sole monotheistic god, was in this period one of the various deities. He was not the sole god, but he was considered as sovereign of el-Kaaba, the holy black stone in Mecca, in due course the holiest place for Islam.

Religious emotion filled a less important role than the tribal ideals in the pre-Islamic period. Worship of trees, springs, and holy stones was widespread. The most important of the stones was the black stone of Mecca on the eastern wall of the el-Kaaba building. Ceremonies of encirclement (*tawaf*) already existed then, and similarly there was pilgrimage once a year, and this was connected to the **Okaz Market**. There were four holy months: *Dhou el-Kaada*, *Dhou el-Hijja*, *Muharram*, and *Rajab*. In these months bloodshed was forbidden, and thus, it was possible to maintain commerce without disturbance. The Arabs before Islam believed in ghosts and spirits (*djinn*). They also recognized a supreme god called "Allah," the sovereign of the Kaaba, but ascribed three daughter deities to him, whose temples are found in various places in Hejaz. Their names were: *Allat* (the goddess of fertility), *Monat* (the goddess of fate), and *Al-Uzza* (the goddess of beauty).

The Kaaba already constituted a holy place for the Arabs before Islam. It is found in the city of Mecca, in contemporary Saudi Arabia. The annual ceremony of pilgrimage to Mecca and to the holy places close to it, like standing on Mt. Arafat (mercy), is considered a principal ceremony in the month of *Dhou el-Hijja*, one of the holy months. Tradition states that Hagar, the wife of Abraham, who was deported with her son Ishmael, set out to the desert, and when she saw her son dying from thirst, she abandoned him and went to look for **water**. She climbed on a hill, the name of which was *Tzafa*, and looked around, but did not see water; she descended and climbed another hill that stood in front by the name of *Marva*. Here also she did not see water. When the Archangel Gabriel saw her in her desperation he came down and cleaved a spring called the *Zamzam* spring, which exists even today. The pilgrims used to come to the spring before a religious ceremony. They would purify their flesh by washing. They took off their clothes and wrapped their bodies in white sheets without a stitch of needle or thread called *ahram*. They did *tawaf* (encirclement) seven times, kissed the black stone, and did all the actions that Hagar did. After the two hills they climbed Mt. Arafat near Mecca and sacrificed an animal. This occasion is called the "Mt. Arafat occasion"—the Prophet Muhammad sanctified this ceremony. It is still considered today a Muslim religious ceremony that precedes the Feast of the Sacrifice (*Eid ul-Adha*) by one day.

The most important of the stones was the black stone of Mecca on the eastern wall of the building. According to tradition, Abraham the Patriarch built the temple while Ishmael helped him. The black stone was given to them by Archangel Gabriel. They encircled the stone in a special ceremony called tawaf and afterward sacrificed animals. In order to enable the pilgrimage, which was always connected to commercial activity in **markets** close to Mecca, it was customary to stop the tribal wars for three months a year, and it turned out that during these four months (one for commercial activity) bloodshed was forbidden. The reason for the proclamation of these holy months was for the satisfaction of the needs of the nomad, who needed to barter for **camels**, sheep skins, fabrics, weapons, and the like. However, if the tribes were involved in wars in these months a lull was created in the economic goal, which was interwoven in religious and cultural goals.

Before the appearance of Islam there were tribes that believed in monotheistic religions—Judaism and **Christianity**. According to the testimony of the Muslim tradition, in the 6th and 7th centuries, a Jewish and Christian population was apparent in the Arabian Peninsula. One part of them converted to Islam when it appeared, another part left the region, and a third part, especially among the Christians who accepted the authority of Islam, stayed Christians, although they were compelled to pay a special tax, called "protection tax."

The Prophet Muhammad, in the name of Islam, succeeded at the start of the 7th century in turning the Arab society from a pagan society into a monotheistic society. Muhammad created the core of a new religious-political community—a Muslim nation—which united the divided tribal society in the Arabian Peninsula and placed the religious connection above the blood connection. In the process of Islamization the Arabic **language** was accepted, which was the language of the culture common to all the Muslims. In the huge territories of the Arab Empire an economic-cultural unit was created that linked the Mediterranean Sea and the Atlantic Ocean. Traffic for armies, traders, scholars, and pilgrims was created. The flourishing **trade** brought about the creation of big towns and an urban culture in Islam. The Muslim state was very dominant in the Middle Ages.

The last Muslim state was the Ottoman Empire, which collapsed during World War I. The Arab national states were founded in the Middle East and North Africa during the 20th century. Although the Islamic factor continues to constitute a challenge to nationalism and today it struggles with the national idea, it wants to return to the Muslim state and the Islamic caliphate in the Middle East.

Islam is divided into two principal factions: Sunna, regarded as orthodoxy of Islam, which includes 80 percent of the Muslims, and the Shia (faction), which split off from the Sunna following differences of opinion in the Islamic leadership after the death of Muhammad (in the year 632), which includes 15 percent of the Muslims. In addition to this, additional factions exist (roughly 5 percent of the Muslims) like the Huareg. In Sunni Islam itself there are various schools and branches such as the ***Wahabis***, which are a faction founded by Mohamed ibn Abed el-Wahab (1691–1787), ruling Saudi Arabia and interpreting Islam radically and the Muslim orthodoxy literally, and *Sufism*, which is a faction of Islam insisting more on the intention than on the deed. In the rest of the factions in Islam they think that Prophet Muhammad died and his heritage is engraved in the rock and it is impossible to change anything in it. The *Sufis* (*Sufism*) think that the Prophet continues to speak to his believers by means of the holy teachers of orthodoxy, connected in a mystic chain to Muhammad, and they are the ones who decide everything. According to the *Sufis*, these holy men can cause miracles during their lives and also after their death. It is customary to see in *Sufism* an esoteric Islam. Also other religions split off from Islam (especially from Shiite Islam), for example: the Druze, the Alawites (who are considered in their own eyes to be part of Shiite Islam), and the Bahais. It is possible to find remnants of Muslim customs in these religions, although they are considered separate religions, as they distance themselves to a significant extent from Islam, and they are seen in the eyes of the rest of the Muslims as "heresy."

ISRAEL. The Bedouin population in Israel constitutes a small but significant minority within the state. The Bedouins number 3.5 percent of the whole population of the state and number close to 210,000 people—80,000 of them living in the north and the rest in the **Negev Desert**, in the south of the state. This population is characterized by its social, cultural, and historical uniqueness, as a special group. Most of the Bedouins who are found today in the state of Israel entered this place at the end of the 16th century. They came from the Syrian Desert, from Transjordan, from the Arabian Peninsula, and from North Africa. The Bedouins in Israel started to establish permanent **settlements** by the end of the Ottoman period. They bought lands and erected their **tents** on their land. Their search for land suited for agricultural cultivation close to their tents necessarily brought about disruption in the tribal framework.

On account of the geographical location of the land of Israel, it was a meeting place between two cultures—the grazing and the **agriculture**. There were periods in which the grazing culture and the agricultural one lived in peace. This period was when there were strong governments that brought security to the country. When the regime was strong, it prevented the Bedouin penetration into the settled regions. It even created a settlement of **nomadic** populations. However, during periods of a weak government, it ended in Bedouin penetration into the settled region. During the past 1,400 years there were three upheavals among the Bedouin tribes in the Arab deserts and in the deserts delimiting the country, as a result of which the Bedouin tribes penetrated into **Palestine**.

1. The first incursion: This was in the 7th century, with the Muslim conquest of **Syria** and Palestine. After the appearance of **Islam** and the surrender of the inhabitants of the Arabian Peninsula, the Muslims moved into Syria and Palestine. The fighting armies of the new **religion** were composed mostly of Bedouin fighters, who advanced to Syria and Palestine with their families, their tents, and their herds; these Bedouins settled in **Sinai**, in the Negev, in the Mt. Grizim (Nablus) region, in the internal valleys of the country like the Beit- Shean Valley, in the Jezreel Valley, and on the Golan.
2. The second incursion was in the 9th century. The incursion came as a result of the incursion of the two big tribes Banu Hillal and Banu Salim, which moved suddenly northward from the Najd Plain and drove before them many tribes and remnants of tribes, part of whom also penetrated into the borders of the country. These tribes penetrated into Palestine through the Aravah and from there to **Egypt** and to North Africa. Among the tribes that the Banu Hillal and Banu Salim drove before them, there were also the forefathers of the Tiaha tribe, the big tribe of the Negev.
3. The third incursion was in the Ottoman period. It started at the end of the 16th century and reached its peak in the 17th century. This period was the start of the weakness in the Ottoman Empire. The disturbance started among the Bedouin tribes in the north of the Arabian Peninsula, when large parts of the tribes began to wander northward. Their previous masters had been conquered before them from the Syrian Desert. These **wanderings** had an influence on Palestine. They caused **migrations** of Bedouin tribes from the Syrian Desert to Palestine, chiefly due to the fear of the big tribes. Among these tribes it was worth noting the Ziadna tribe—a tribe that attained a high position in the 18th century and the **sheikh** of the tribe, **Daher el-Omar**, became the ruler of **Galilee**.

The penetration of Bedouins into Palestine continued throughout history until the start of the 20th century. They came from Syria, **Jordan**, Egypt, and North Africa.

The Bedouins originally lived in tents, and with the establishment of the state of Israel in the year 1948 they were forced to live in permanent residences and began to earn an income from hired work in nearby settlements. Under the Israeli government the **sedentarization** of the Bedouins was accelerated to a wide extent. Today there are 35 **Bedouin** settlements in Israel. Since the foundation of the state in 1948, the Bedouin population has undergone an immense change—from a society of nomads to an urbanized society. Permanent settlement brought great changes in the Bedouin society.

In recent years Bedouin society has undergone a process of social, economic, and internal political change. The Bedouins are not the only ones in the society, in Israel, who are undergoing processes of change. There are the others who are new immigrants, but the fact of their not being Jews is a burden on these processes, due to the special nature of relations that were formed between the Bedouins and the establishment and focus of the problem between them—illegal construction and a dispute over lands; the Bedouins claim ownership of lands in the northern and central Negev region of a total of 680,000 dunams (5.5 percent of the Negev), on the strength of the traditional law that existed under the auspices of the previous governments, and on the strength of the ancient possession, use, and settlement on that land. The state claims that most of the lands that the Bedouins demand belong to it as they are apparently *mawat* lands ("dead" according to Ottoman law), which are unsettled, uncultivated, and unregistered.

In fact, it is possible to define this as a conflict between the ethnic cultural identity of the Bedouins and their identity as citizens with equal rights in the state. This conflict is expressed in almost every field of development linked to the Bedouin sector. From the point of view of the nomadic Bedouin population, the relationship between them and the state became very complex. The complexity stands out especially in the light of the growth in the power of the states in the last century. Until the beginning of the 20th century, in the Middle East, the governments were only deployed for very limited control of the marginal regions. Therefore, marginal spatial positioning in remote desert regions gave an advantage to nomads as **shepherds**, and from their point of view created a very simple relationship with the state. Usually the Bedouins had it in their power to determine the conditions of their relationship with the villagers, who were the permanent settlers, and of course that with the state, and therefore, they constituted a threat to its political stability. This relationship was characterized many times by incursion into the agricultural lands of the villagers. Moreover, the tribal structure enabled nomadic societies to accumulate income as administrative agents of the state, in addition to their traditional income from grazing.

However, the development and spread of the modern means of transport and weapon technology gradually enabled the extension of the rule of the state to the desert margins. Consequently the status of the nomads changed from rulers to subjects. Therefore, the balance of power during the 20th century began to tilt in favor of the state, which gradually started to erode the power of the nomads. The nomads were now compressed into the socioeconomic margins, and due to this their spatial marginality turned from an advantage into a disadvantage.

This process not only forced the Bedouins to renounce their power, control, and their freedom of action in their traditional territories, but also even increased the complexity of their relations with the state. The governments imposed constraints of location, wandering, and use of resources on the nomads, with an attempt to rule and settle them. This was reflected in the growing and strengthening protests of the Bedouins against the government.

The state of Israel decided, in the year 1963, to concentrate the Bedouins in the north and south in permanent settlements, in modern villages; thus four settlements were established in the north: Bir el-Maksour, Ibtin, Wadi Hamam, and Bosmat Tivon. Simultaneously, the state founded the town of **Rahat** in the south, as well as the two settlements of **Kuseife** and Tel-Sheva. After a number of years the government decided to extend the recognition of the Bedouin settlements in Galilee and Negev. Today there are 35 Bedouin settlements in Israel, aside from the small settlements, which are part of regional councils or Bedouin neighborhoods in Arab villages and towns, and dozens of more settlements without municipal definition, called unrecognized villages.

The Israeli government took many decisions with regard to the development of the Bedouin settlements both in the south and the north of the country, to improve the social and economic situation of the population, with a view that this population was considered a beloved population of the state from a social and security point of view, and with an idea that investment in Bedouin settlements would reduce the feelings of oppression and inferiority among the Bedouins in Israel. In reality, the lifestyle of Bedouins and their conduct made it difficult for the state to develop their settlements suitably. Many Bedouins still live in illegal structures, and an additional part still lives in unrecognized settlements, which constitute more than 70 dispersed settlements in the north of the country.

In the state of Israel today, tens of thousands of citizens live in villages without municipal definition in the north and south of the country. They do not receive basic services from the state. The Israeli government has left these settlements outside the master plans. The authorities designated the lands on which these villages were founded for agricultural use, while refusing to change the designation of the land to "residential," despite the existence of these villages for generations. These villages were judged by the establishment as illegal. These communities have existed for years, and strive to survive and develop. In the light of the government policy to relocate the inhabitants, the inhabitants were forced to struggle in order to continue to live on their land. The insistence of the authorities to refrain from any solution, apart from expulsion of the residents from their villages, did not enable the state to issue building permits to the inhabitants. The attempts of the residents to ask for change of designation on the lands to residences and the presentation of plans that were prepared at their request by planners for this goal encountered refusal.

The residents of the unrecognized villages claim that as the land was classified by the state as having an agricultural designation, construction on it was forbidden, thus ignoring the dwelling of people on this land for decades. They note that this policy was biased, mainly when Jewish settlement was concerned. The residents of these villages note that at the end of the 1970s, many settlements were founded, and the authorities tried to evacuate the inhabitants from these villages, in order to found Jewish settlements in the same places or close to them. The governmental authorities claimed that the unrecognized settlements were too small and isolated to be supplied with services, and therefore, the residents would have to pass to recognized settlements, where they could enjoy the full services and also develop. As to the high cost of supply of services to settlements, the inhabitants of these villages claim that in most of the cases electricity, **water**, and telephone lines pass close to their villages. In a number of cases, the villagers note, the network, which was designed to serve a nearby Jewish settlement, literally passes in the territory and on the lands of the unrecognized village, which they refuse to connect to the network, and thereby deny its inhabitants the basic services.

Today, the Bedouins claim ownership of 1.5 million dunams of land in the Negev. Some 500,000 dunams of pastureland have not been recognized. In 2009, the Praver Committee recommended that the Bedouins receive 180,000–200,000 dunams of land, while they claimed possession of about 650,000 dunams. It also recommended the evacuation of 40,000 Bedouin squatters from dozens of unrecognized villages in the Negev.

From a traditional Bedouin society founded on **clannish** tribal frameworks with desert values, mentality, and customs, and on a traditional leadership, the Bedouin society becomes a society in transition, trying to cope with the extreme changes in lifestyles. The tribal clannish pride, which was the trademark and identity of every individual in this society, made way for the restricted family framework while stressing the concern for personal interest. Clannish tribal leadership in the figure of "the sheikh," who led the tribe and took care of representing it before the authorities, has already become obsolete, and apart from restricted social involvement, the tribe's sheikh has no special status today.

The long-standing neglect of the Bedouin population on the part of the establishment, with regards to the advancement of the treatment of the population, accompanied by the complex social processes derived from the extreme changes in lifestyles, invited the entry of nationalist and religious factions, which filled the vacuum.

Civilian society among the Bedouins in Israel got organized much later in comparison to Arab organizations in other regions in the country. However, one should note that some parts of these organizations are stronger and more active than their counterparts among the general Arab population.

The lack of help from the local government and representative institutions to supply services and protect the interests of the Bedouins pushed them into attempting to have local organizations. The first organization emerged in Bedouin society at the end of the 1970s and the beginning of the 1980s. The Civilian Bedouin Society strengthened in the light of the harsh reality prevailing in the unrecognized villages, the lack of local government in these villages, the weakness of the Bedouin local authorities, and the limited activity and movements of the Arab political parties, whose center was in the north (except for the Islamic movement). Today more than 150 Bedouin associations exist, almost all of which are associations for social change. It is possible to divide the organizations of the civilian society according to their fields of activity.

The issue of lands, the recognition of unrecognized villages, and the supply of services to villages are the central concerns in the activities of these organizations. The local council for unrecognized villages in the Negev and the umbrella organization of the local committees in the unrecognized villages are some of the leaders in the struggle for the lands. Many organizations focus on issues connected to **women**, their rights, and their empowerment, for example, the Al-Nuhud (revival) Association. Also **education** in the Bedouin society gains much attention. Among the organizations that act on this subject, the Bedouin Forum of Education under the auspices of STIHL-Support and Counseling Services for Advancement of Social Change can be named.

Tribalism is one of the prominent characteristics of Bedouin civil society. The managements of many organizations operate in the framework of the tribe and are influenced by it.

With regard to Bedouin political life, they have, down the years, protected internal tribal cohesiveness, on the one hand, and a very loose connection with the Israeli establishment and pan-national politics, on the other hand. The connection existed only through the "sheikh," the tribe's leader. The uniqueness of the Bedouins caused their disconnection from the rest of the Arab population and its problems.

There was intergenerational tension between a new stratum of educated youngsters, with a rising middle class and the traditional leadership of the sheikhs and heads of families in the tribes—a practical expression of the disruption of the tribes and a growth of civil society. The traditional leadership of the sheikhs made way for a new young leadership of heads of local authorities and heads of associations and organizations.

The Bedouins were introduced to national politics in the middle of the 1970s. The development of political awareness among the Bedouins was influenced by several factors:

1. Daily connections with the inhabitants of the occupied territories since 1967 exposed the Bedouins to the problems of the Palestinians and strengthened their Arab-Palestinian identity.
2. Exposure to political-national ideas—the Bedouin population in Israel was exposed to the political activity of the Arab citizens in Galilee and in the triangle area. Likewise Arab political parties and movements, for example, the Israeli Communist Party, held gatherings in the Bedouins' villages to note national events.
3. The process of **urbanization** weakened the traditional leadership. The status of the individual strengthened at the expense of the power of the tribal collective, and the process led to local elections and to intertribal competition. Likewise lists were founded that strengthened the connection with the national parties, especially with the government parties.
4. The growth of influence of the media, which expanded and reached all over the country. The Bedouins were exposed to their influence and capacity to help them in the advancement of their affairs.
5. The plight of the Bedouins and the lack of solutions to their problems by the various Israeli governments encouraged them to integrate into national politics. Bedouins from the young and intellectual generation looked for centers of influence for advancement of their personal status and for solving their plight. This process was also influenced by the crisis of leadership striking the Bedouin society. The young generation, which integrated and was educated at universities, demanded full equality with the Jewish society in Israel. By contrast to the generation of sheikhs, for whom Bedouin survival stood at the top of their priorities, the young and intellectual generation did not make do any more with basic conditions and expected more than this from the state.
6. The religious revival, which took place in the occupied territories and in Israel, did not pass over the Bedouin inhabitants of Israel. The religious discourse of the 1980s and 1990s found its way easily to the traditional Bedouin society.

Until 1977 the voting of the Bedouins to the Knesset was apolitical voting, and they gave their votes chiefly to Mapai (Israeli Labor Party) and to Mapam (United Workers' Party). These two parties had controlled the state until then. The process of partisan politicization of the Bedouins started when an independent Bedouin list to the Knesset was founded, under the leadership of Hammad Abu-Rabia, which for the first time succeeded in putting a Bedouin representative into the Legislative Assembly, in the year 1973. The murder of Knesset Member (MK) Abu-Rabia, in the year 1981, intensified the need for a Bedouin representation in the Knesset. This trend was expressed in the elections to the 12th Knesset, which took place in 1988, when a majority of the Bedouin voters gave their vote to the Arab Democratic Party—Mada. The insertion of the Bedouin Taleb el-Sana in the second place in the Mada list and his election in 1992 to the 13th Knesset marked a dramatic change in the political possibilities of the Bedouins. MK el-Sana, a Bedouin intellectual youngster, who was elected to the Knesset at age 32, serves as an MK and endeavors to represent the Bedouin population and express its needs and demands. The young MK presented a dialog that was mainly patriotic Arab nationalist and increased the cooperation of destiny between the Bedouins and the Arab population in Israel.

The entry of the Islamic movement into politics posed obstacles. The Islamic movement is very organized and active in all the Bedouin settlements, especially in the Bedouin townships in the Negev. In the past decade it managed to win in the elections for the leadership of the local authorities in all the Bedouin settlements in the south, except in Kuseife. As the Arab lists Mada and the Islamic Movement united, and as Taleb el-Sana was elected to the Knesset, Raam (United Arab List) has continued to pick up most of the Bedouin votes.

One of the characteristics of Bedouin politics is its reactiveness and lack of initiative. This derives from the depth of hardships that the Bedouins have to cope with, which creates an order of priorities. At the head of these is the concern for immediate and family needs, which leaves little space for initiated political action.

In opposition to the Arab National Identity, which was presented before, many Bedouins, before the establishment of the state, had already linked their fate to the Jewish population. Their dealings were characterized by good neighborly relations. At a time when these Bedouin tribes engaged in robbery and plunder, they did not touch the Jewish population. The Bedouins were considered good friends of the Jews and did not touch their property. The Bedouins were partners with the Jews in defense of the Jewish population before the foundation of the state. Many tribes linked their fate with the fate of the state, and therefore risked their lives on behalf of its security.

Individuals, families, and also whole tribes linked their fate with the fate of Jewish fighters and settlers, with whom they found a common language. These are the connections that often endangered their lives and property.

The first people who were recruited to help the Jews in the **War of Independence** of Israel as a consolidated group were the Bedouins from the Arab al-**Heib** tribe, a part of whom lived in the village of **Tuba** in upper Galilee. The Bedouin unit that fought next to the **Israel Defense Forces** (IDF) in the War of Independence was linked to the Palmach and was called ***Palhib***. From this cooperation the first alliance was born between Jews and the Bedouin population, an alliance that at a later stage produced the trackers' unit in the IDF, a unit in which officers and soldiers who were members of the Bedouin population became its main component over time.

Since the establishment of the IDF, the Bedouins have served in it, chiefly in tracking jobs. In the year 1970, the trackers' unit was founded in the south, and today it operates in additional zones. In the year 1986, the **desert rangers battalion— *Gadsar***—was founded, and today it plays a very important role in the fighting in the Gaza Strip zone. A memorial commemorating the unique contribution of the Bedouins to the state and to the IDF was placed in Galilee. However, despite their recruitment to military service, the integration of the Bedouins in Israeli society is very limited.

In spite of the positive connection and the identification with the state, the Bedouins feel an inequality and even discrimination and oppression. They emphasize the neglect by comparison to other settlements, and this increases the feeling of alienation among them toward the state. The matter is distinguished between the Bedouins in the south and Bedouins in the north, when the latter express identification, increasing the positive feeling toward the state of Israel. Feelings of oppression constitute an open door for penetration of undesirable parties, who can damage, in their case, the relations between the Bedouins and the state. This is significant in the conduct of the Bedouin inhabitants of the Negev versus the attitude of the state of Israel, and in the background of the controversies is the question of ownership of the land.

This forms the center of controversy and constitutes a central problem in the relation between the community and the state. This problem not only is connected to the conduct of the state versus the Bedouin sector, but also conceals within it the refusal of the Bedouins to accept the governmental plans to settle them and concentrate them in permanent settlements, to help them in everything connected with development and infrastructure. This still constitutes the bone of contention, as opposed to the fact that the decisive majority of the Bedouins in the north live in permanent settlements. *See also* ISRAEL, "ILLEGAL" SETTLEMENTS; ISRAEL DEFENSE FORCES (IDF); KHWALED; KUSEIFE; LAKIYA; PEACE LAW (1980); RAHAT; SALLAMA; SHIBLI-UMM AL-GHANAM; SUWAED; TEL AS SABI; TUBA-ZANGHARIYYA; ZARZIR or BEIT ZARZIR; ZBEIH.

ISRAEL, "ILLEGAL" SETTLEMENTS. This term refers to rural Arab Bedouin **settlements** in the **Negev** and **Galilee** districts that were built without permission (on state land or disputed land), and therefore, were not recognized by the **Israeli** government. As a result, they did not receive infrastructure like **water**, electricity, paved roads, and other regular municipal services. In recent years, some of these settlements have gone through a legitimization process, but some (especially in the Negev) are situated in areas that the government has allocated for other purposes.

As some of these "illegal" settlements are tiny settlements of one to a small number of improvised dwellings, and others are genuine communities of several families, it is impossible to determine the exact number, but official organizations, such as the Bedouins' Advocacy Organization and the Adva Center, state that there are around 40 to 45 such settlements, most of them in the Negev, and a single-digit number in Galilee. According to Maha Qupty, representing the Bedouin Advocacy Organization, in 2004, there were 45 unrecognized Bedouin villages in the Negev. According to the Human Rights Watch report, based upon the 2006 statistics offered by the Adva Center, approximately half of the Bedouin citizens of Israel (85,000 out of 210,000) live in 39 such villages, while according to another Bedouins' Advocacy Organization, the number of such settlements is much higher and is between 60 and 80.

Since 2003, a number of previously illegal Bedouin communities underwent procedures that led to state recognition and enabled them to receive state services. However, other such settlements are still in a legal limbo.

ISRAEL DEFENSE FORCES (IDF). Although the Bedouins are not committed to service in the IDF, from the 1950s on Bedouins were integrated as trackers in the Minorities Unit. Today, a minority of them choose to volunteer for the various units of the IDF.

Bedouins have two exclusive units: the **Desert Rangers Battalion** (Gadsar) or "the Desert Rangers," which include 20 percent of all the Bedouin soldiers and tracker units, and in which 40 percent of the Bedouin soldiers serve. In addition 7 percent are conscripted to the Border Guard.

Conscription among the community members is controversial. Following the outbreak of the Second **Intifada** (2000), and due to a feeling of discrimination among many in the sector and the strengthening of the Islamic movement among the inhabitants, a decline was recorded in the percentage of Bedouin conscripts. However since 2002, a rising trend was indicated in the proportion of conscripts, and it stabilized at three hundred to four hundred per year. Today, one thousand serve in the IDF, many of them in permanent service. *See also* PALHIB.

ISRAELI WAR OF INDEPENDENCE. Israel's War of Independence, in 1948, highlighted the complex relationship between the Bedouins and the Jewish population, as some Bedouin tribes that developed good relationships with the Jews fought with them against the **Palestinians** and invading Arab armies, while the others were part of the Palestinian struggle and fought on their side, and yet others were neutral and took no part in the war.

During and after the war, tribes from **Galilee** and the northern valleys who were affiliated with the militant gangs or collaborated with "the Saving Army," like the **Turkmen** tribes, Al-Dalaika, Al-Muwasi, Al-Zaker, and Al-KdAria, fled the country to **Lebanon**, **Syria**, and **Jordan**, while tribes like Arab el-**Gwarina** of the Hula Valley left their **settlements** before the war started, under the order of the emir of Arab Al-**Fadil** from the Golan Heights.

In the ballot of 1931, under the British mandate, the Bedouins' population count was 20,000 in northern Israel; in 1951, after the War of Independence, the population count of the Bedouins in Northern Israel was less than 6,500. These numbers reflect the extent of the escape and its impact on the distribution of Bedouin tribes in the north of the country, after establishment of the state.

The War of Independence influenced the economic situation of the Bedouins, as many of their sheep and goats were slaughtered to feed the troops of both sides, and much of their grazing lands were confiscated by the government of the victorious state of Israel. Thus, many Bedouins who remained in northern Israel had to change their lifestyle, to settle in the land they still owned, or near an existing Arab village, and look for employment to sustain their families.

The Bedouin tribes that remained in northern Israel are concentrated in five regions: Givat Alonim-Shfaram, Beit-Netufa (Al Butoof) Valley, the Zalmon block, Mt. Tabor region, and the Tuba region.

In central Israel and the coastal plains, despite the good relations that some Bedouin tribes had with the Jewish population, vast areas were empty of Bedouins, as they had either evacuated or were ordered to evacuate by the commanders of the Palestinian militant gangs, who refused to accept the existence of good relations with the Jews, whom they wanted dead or out of the country. Among the evacuees were the veteran Abu Kashk tribe, which lived near Petach Tikvah and maintained good relations with the Jewish colony. Those who were forced to leave hastily sold their possessions, especially livestock, to local Jewish farmers who were their friends. It turned out that the reason for this forced evacuation was the preparation for a large-scale attack about to be carried out by massed Arab forces on the entire region.

The war caused dramatic changes in the demographic composition of southern Israel. These changes affected the local Bedouins. The number of Bedouins in the **Negev** decreased from 90,000 on the eve of the War of

Independence to 12,500, while the Jewish factor in the Negev turned from a minority to a majority. The results of the war were traumatic for the Bedouins; tribal and family frameworks were destroyed, and the new borders reduced the spaces in which the Bedouins used to **wander**. A further impeding factor was the military control they opposed along with what they considered to be confiscation of land, and in some cases, forced transfer. The tribes that were forced to move away saw themselves as refugees in the state and developed feelings of bitterness and grudges against the government. Thus, many of the tribes that reached the Negev from **Sinai** and Egypt returned to their previous places.

The leaders of the tribes who stayed in the Negev initiated a meeting with representatives of the newly established Israeli government. In the meeting that took place on 2 November 1948, they expressed their willingness to live under Israeli authority and their desire to live quietly and till their land like before. As the war was still going on, the government representatives recommended that the Bedouins move as far away as possible from the army roads and disputed lands. In November 1948, at an official ceremony in Beer Sheva, 16 **sheikhs** swore loyalty to the state of Israel, and the government promised to protect and honor the rights of the Bedouins, promised to equip them with weapons for self-defense, and assured them their property and lands. In 1954, the Negev Bedouins received Israeli citizenship.

ISRAELITE TRIBES. The Israelite tribes, or the People of **Israel**, were a group of Semite-affiliated tribes who lived in the ancient past, in the western part of the Fertile Crescent (contemporary Israel, the **Palestinian Authority**, western **Jordan**, and southern **Syria**), which supposedly had converted into one nation, in which some of them had preserved their unique tribal heritage while others had not.

According to tradition, the 12+1 tribes originated from the 12 sons of Jacob, also called Israel, the third patriarch of the nation, grandson of the initial patriarch Abraham, son of Nahor, who migrated to the land of Cana'an in the early 19th century BC, with his entire tribe, perhaps as part of the large Habiru **migration**.

According to the ancient scriptures (the Old Testament), the 12 tribes turned to 13, as the twin sons of Josef, Ephraim and Menashe, received a tribe status, and their descendants were allocated by Joshua and the elders to their own district during the Israeli **settlement** in the land of Cana'an (believed to have occurred during the 13th century BC). Other scientific theories place the return of the Israelites back from **Egypt** a century earlier.

Historical archeological research has not yet provided absolute proof regarding the precise origin of the Israelite tribes. Some believe they penetrated the area either together (the Semite tribes that were forced to leave Egypt), or in small groups, over time, while another theory suggests that they were a separatist group that stemmed from the local population. Many scholars in the field suggest that the Israelites were a combination of the above, meaning certain Semite groups had entered the area during the 14th and 13th centuries BC and had merged with the local groups. Once they became the dominant culture, they merged with other local groups that shared the same **language** and perhaps other characteristics too.

Whatever the case, this group of tribes that came from the **Sinai Desert** was led by the two Levi Brothers, Moshe the great legislator and Aaron the first high priest, who may have designed and established the unique tribal organization and a different role for the Levi tribe in the nation. Under the leadership of Joshua, the tribes (except for Levi, whose people were to live among the other tribes and provide them services as priests, teachers, scribes, and law interpreters, to ensure cultural unity and a sense of kinship) received their allocated districts in order from north to south.

According to conventional counting, the number of the tribes corresponded with the number of months in the Semite annual calendar, which according to the ancient Assyrian tradition, was associated with a certain star or a specific star constellation. Each of the original Israelite tribes had a certain specific identification color and a special symbol that appeared on the flag of its color, which was supposed to correspond with the color of the tribal stone on the high priest's *Hoshen* (holy vest).

1. Dan was the most intriguing tribe, whose origin is debatable. The original district allocated to this tribe was the coastal plain and the low country in central contemporary Israel. However, they did not manage to conquer it, since another strong migrating group of sea people, the Philistines, had also settled in parts of that area. The Dans were able to secure and settle only in part of this district; therefore, a large portion of this tribe migrated northward and conquered the area in main Jordan's tributary sources including eastern **Galilee**, the northern Golan, Mount Hermon, the Iyun valley, and some part of contemporary southern **Lebanon**. This tribe was considered to provide the best warriors, as well as good sailors. They were also comprised of judiciary, masons, blacksmiths, craftsmen, and artists.
2. The Naftali received the central upper Galilee and the central and eastern lower Galilee. This tribe was the second richest and among the largest tribes in Israel; its people lived from **agriculture**, mostly orchards, and fishing (in the Sea of Galilee). They also operated a couple of natural spas.
3. Half of Menashe were a seminomadic tribe; they lived in the Golan and the Bashan areas (contemporary southern Syria) and combined agriculture and livestock. They were known to raise sheep, goats, cattle, and **camels**. Half of Menashe were allocated the north central mountain

range, including Mount Carmel, Menashe Heights, the Gilboa, Dotan valley, Iron valley, and north Samaria. They lived from combined agriculture, vines, olives (including vineries), and the olive oil industry, alongside fields of wheat, barley, and seasonal vegetables. According to the Old Testament, this tribe was responsible for the first attempt to unify the tribes and establish an Israeli kingdom.

4. The Asher were allocated the northern coastal area and western Galilee; they never subdued or replaced the Phoenicians who lived in the area, but intermixed with them. Some of them managed to maintain their separate identity for a couple of centuries, and some assimilated into the dominant groups.
5. The Zebulon were allocated the western lower Galilee and the corresponding coastal areas. Similar to their Phoenician neighbors, they were distinguished as merchants and **traders**. They were involved in the nautical industry and services and in fishery, and they may have discovered glass and glass manufacturing.
6. The Gad received the area of the Gilead Mountains (present-day northern Jordan). The Gad were a strong militant tribe and lived off field agriculture and livestock (both **herding** and transport of animals).
7. The Yissaschar were allocated the Jezre'el valley and its bordering heights. It was a docile agricultural tribe described as hardworking people who also invested in learning.
8. The Ephraim were allocated most of Samaria, its western lowland, and the corresponding coastal area. Ephraim was a powerful tribe. It was considered the largest or second largest (there are claims that Yehuda, its historical rival for leadership, was the largest) and was definitely the richest and most influential tribe, which later in history led the kingdom of Israel.
9. The Benjamin were the smallest tribe of Israel. The tribe was allocated the central mountain area, squeezed between Ephraim in the north, Yehuda in the south, and Dan in the west, and surrounded by Jerusalem. They were also a militant tribe who lived from combined agriculture. The first king of Israel, Soul son of Kish, was chosen by Prophet Samuel from this little tribe to circumvent the rivalry between Yehuda and Ephraim.
10. The Yehuda (Juda) was the largest or second largest tribe of the Israelites. Its district contained the southern part of the central mountain range (Judea) down eastward to the Dead Sea, parts of the northern **Negev**, and the corresponding coastal area, which was occupied by the Philistines, with whom they fought. Yehuda was a strong and dominant tribe that absorbed several small minorities that either lived in their district or invaded them. After a disastrous defeat and the death of king Soul, his son-in-law David, who was a Judean, became the new king of

Israel, and his dynasty ruled first the United Kingdom of Israel, and later the smaller kingdom of Judea, for nearly half a millennium. When Judea was conquered by the Babylon Empire, and its inhabitants were exiled eastward, others began to call all Israelites "Jews," after the name of this dominant tribe.

11. The Reuven were a **nomadic** or seminomadic tribe who settled in the area of contemporary southern Jordan and had intermixed with the local Hebrew-speaking small nations: the Moavites and the Edomites.
12. The Shimon were a nomadic tribe who lived in the Negev and intermixed partially with other local nomadic tribes and partially with its dominant neighbor, Yehuda. Eventually they lost their unique tribal identity; though certain Bedouin tribes in the Negev and Sinai claim to be their descendants.

According to the Old Testament, the second and highly successful attempt to unite the 12 Hebrew tribes into one nation occurred in the last quarter of the 11th century BC, and the various tribes had partially intermingled. The United Kingdom existed for about a century (under Soul, David, and Solomon). Toward the end of the 10th century BC it was split into two separate but interconnected sister kingdoms: the larger kingdom, Israel, comprised of the leading Ephraim tribe and all the tribes that lived in central and northern Israel, endured for almost two centuries. It was ruled by a number of individuals and dynasties and reached its peak under the rule of King Yerovam the second. The kingdom of Israel was destroyed in 722 BC by Sennacherib, king of Assyria, who exiled the leadership, the nobility, and the military (and their families) eastward. The Judean king, who was forced to become a vassal of the Egyptian pharaohs, invited the remnants of the Israeli kingdom to participate in religious duties and ceremonies conducted in Jerusalem, and in fact had accepted them as subordinates. The Davidian dynasty managed to lead a semi-independent state until the area was conquered by the Babylonian empire led by the emperor Nebuchadnezzar, who had most of its population exiled to various parts of his empire and replaced by people he previously conquered and exiled from their original homeland. Thus, in several cases, the new exiles joined and merged with the previously exiled Israelite communities, who managed to preserve their national identity and cultural heritage.

As there is no written evidence of this process, most of the Jewish people today are considered to be descendants of the exiled of Babylon, who included mostly three tribes—Yehuda, Levi, and Benjamin—and the descendants of the Israelites who were not exiled by the Assyrians.

This uncertainty regarding the fate of the Israelite tribes exiled by the Assyrians led to a constant quest for the alleged "ten lost tribes," since although some of the exiled Israelites settled in their new locations and even built towns and institutions, many others were either sent to distant locations, or drifted to the margins of the empire: east to Persia, Afghanistan, and India, north to Anatolia and the Caucasus, and south to the Arabian Peninsula, Abyssinia, and Egypt.

There are also legends that some Israelites found their way westward, like stories about the Gad exiles who settled in Majorca and the Bay of Cadis (in the Iberian Peninsula) and stories of Dan sailors who landed in England and Ireland. There is also evidence of an Israelite presence in North Africa, but due to the ruination of Carthage, there is no dependable written material.

The search for the alleged lost tribes still continues, and every distant Jewish community is checked and double-checked by enthusiastic scholars.

Toward the end of the 6th century BC, Cyrus, king of Persia, allowed the Israelites who desired it to return to their homeland and rebuild Jerusalem. As the Jewish/Israelite communities in his empire were already mixed tribe-wise, except for the Levi tribe, and certain individuals who were proud of their personal heritage, very few of the returning masses were absolutely sure of their personal tribal origin. Since then, there is no tribal distinction among the people of Israel, except for descendants of the Levi tribe, who preserve their tribal identity for cultural and religious reasons.

J

JANJAWEED. *Janjaweed* or *Janjawid* is the name of the Sudanese **Baggara** (cattle herder)-based militia that operate in the **Darfur** region in **Sudan** and eastern Chad. The name is a combination of three **Arabic** words, meaning "man," "gun," and "**horse**," although the core of these units is based on the *Abbala* (**camel** herder) groups of these people. These nomad tribes were in conflicts with the sedentary population for the use of land. Years of continuing drought in the area had worsened the **struggle** over the land and dwindling resources. The civil war between the government-supported Arabs and the indigenous non-Arab people caused this self-appointed militia to attack, raid and loot, and expel the non-Arab sedentary population.

JAZZAR, AHMED (1720–1804). Ahmed Jazzar was the Ottoman-appointed governor of northern **Palestine** from 1775 to 1804 who fortified Acre and entered history as the successful defender of the city that stopped the Napoleonic invasion in 1799.

Northern Palestine was supposed to be governed from Damascus, but when the central administration was weak, such regional governance often disintegrated into local autonomous provinces, which, when proved to be efficient, gained Ottoman recognition. El-Jazzar, who considered himself the son of the Inawiya tribe, was one of these local rulers. One of his main concerns was the penetration of the Bedouin tribes from the Syrian **Desert** and the plains of Transjordan.

He fortified strategic positions in **Galilee**, especially near and around Lake Kinneret, and posted cavalry units in these posts. He sent the army to suppress nonorderly tribes, enforce tax payments on "free" tribes, and limit the roaming territory of the Bedouin tribes of Hula and Golan. On the other hand, he formed friendships and alliances with some local tribes and brought over from **Egypt** additional **clans** from his own tribe to help him fight the **Zidanes**. The warriors from these clans also fought with his army against Napoleon's invasion.

JORDAN. The tribes in Jordan played a significant part in molding the modern Hashemite state. The Jordanian tribes demonstrated their loyalty to the state and its government throughout the years of its existence. The majority of the Bedouin tribes in Jordan migrated there from the Arabian Peninsula between the 14th and 18th centuries. After World War I and the decline of the Ottoman Empire, the British, who received mandates of the area between **Egypt** and **Syria**, decided to separate the area into **Palestine**, west of the Jordan, for the Jews, and Transjordan, east of the river, for the Arabs. This decision created the Hashemite kingdom of Transjordan, which later became Jordan.

Emir Abdullah, the first king of Jordan, recruited the tribal confederations of the **Bani Sakhr** and the Huwaytat to prevent the threat of the encroaching tribes from **Saudi Arabia**. Emir Abdullah also mediated and sponsored an agreement between the veteran rivals, the Bani Sakhr and Adwan tribes, and two years later between the Bani Sakhr and Huwaytat.

Since the foundation of the Jordanian kingdom, the Bedouins accepted the central government and became its main loyalists. Abdullah the First, the son of Sheriff Hussein, who reached Jordan from the Arabian Peninsula in order to establish the kingdom of Jordan, relied on the loyalty of the various Jordanian tribes. He integrated the tribesmen in the army and in the various government ministries. Over the years the influence of the tribe grew in the Jordanian kingdom, especially in the army circles. The Bedouin youths tended to join the Jordanian army and proved themselves as outstanding fighters. They were very disciplined, well-organized, loyal to the regime, and were prepared to defend it. Service in the army was for a salary, and therefore, it also served them as a source of income. A special situation was created in Jordan in which the Bedouins were loyalists of the king, and the group of officers grew out of them. They had senior positions in Jordanian politics.

In 1923, the **Balqa** tribe, which was discontented with the rights the other tribes received, rebelled against Amir Abdullah. After this rebellion, the British instituted reforms that transferred the power from the hands of emir Abdullah and the tribes to the central government. The authorities implemented their rule in the populated region between the Hejaz railway and the Jordan River, enforced their authority on the **nomads** entering the region during the summer, levied taxes on the animals and land of the **sheikhs**, and enforced **law** and judicial decisions, even on powerful sheikhs, who were traditionally exempted.

During the years 1929 to 1936, there was a period of drought and a worldwide economic slump. The Jordanian Bedouins lost men and property, mostly stock animals, due to the Saudi raids and droughts. The nomadic tribes and their livestock suffered poverty and hunger. The central government helped them to obtain **food**, clothing, and employment, to survive the harsh times.

Later the state provided economic, political, and administrative infrastructure to the tribes. Thus, to overcome dissatisfaction of the tribal sheikhs, due to the erosion of their power, the tribal hierarchy was reinforced by drafting young men into the king's patrol and by appointing the sheikhs as judges and magistrates in newly founded tribal courts.

In the sedentary regions, the state delegated authority to the sheikhs and entrusted law and order, levying of taxes, and settling of disputes to them, by making them official employees of the state.

When domination over the **desert** had been achieved, Glubb led the Arab Legion in several operations against the Bani Sakhr and Huwaytat and transferred the Juhur **clan** of the Bani Sakhr, by force, to another territory and punished the sheikh of the Zaban tribe from the same confederation by banishing him.

Tribal chiefs made contact with foreign powers, sometimes hostile to Transjordan, such as Saudi Arabia, the Zionist entity, and Palestinian nationalists. The nomads also took advantage of the enmity between the Hashemites and Saudis. The main reason for the loyalty problems was derived from the border demarcations that ignored the traditional routes of tribal **migration** and sometimes even split certain clans from the main body of the tribe.

In 1936, the **Arab Revolt** against British rule started in Palestine and spread to Jordan, where telephone lines were knocked down, oil pipelines were damaged, rebels received money, arms were smuggled, and anti-British demonstrations were frequent. The Palestinian rebels gained the support of the tribes along the Jordan River, and when the rebels disintegrated, their fighters found refuge in the region of al-Salt and Ajloun. Members of the northern Bani Sakhr tribe and Mithqal al-Fayiz supported the Palestinian cause and cooperated with the Grand Mufti and Haj Amin al-Husseini.

When World War II broke out, the participation of the Arab Legion in fights against the bordering states caused further discord, especially during the time of the 1941 Arab Revolt. When the legion conquered the Syrian Desert, in July 1941, the Bani Sakhr showed signs of dissent and attacked the Amman-Madaba telephone line, which crossed their domain.

Finally, in the 1940s the tribes were integrated into the fabric of the state, thousands of the tribesmen joined the legion, others came in to own their land and tilled it, with government help. They were given health, veterinary, and **education** services. The chiefs became judges, ministers, and parliament members. The tribes served as a pipeline for supply of resources from the central government to the periphery, and the tribal confederations stayed as the most important social and political entities.

Today, 33–40 percent of the Jordanian population is composed of Bedouins. The Bedouins of the east breed **camel**s and are herders, while the Bedouins of the west graze sheep and goats. They live mostly in the arid region stretching east from the Desert Highway. Some of them are seminomadic; they **wander** during some of the year and practice **agriculture** on their lands and near their homes.

The biggest nomadic tribes in Jordan are the Banu (Bani) Laith, who live in and around Petra, the Bani Sakhr, and the Banu al-Huwaytat. There are many smaller groups, like the al-Sirhan, who live near the **Iraqi** frontier, Banu Hasan, Banu Khalid, Hawazim, 'Atiyyah, and Sharafat. These have a tradition of paying protection money to the bigger groups. The Ruwalah (Rwala) tribe is not indigenous to the country, but it crosses Jordan annually on its way from **Syria** to Saudi Arabia.

The relations between the Bedouins of Jordan and the Bedouins in **Israel** varied. Part of the Bedouins who live today in Israel, especially in the **Negev**, had come to these regions from eastern Transjordan (the present-day kingdom of Jordan) in the Ottoman period. The Bedouins used to graze their flocks on both sides of the Arava River without disturbance, but when the state of Israel was founded in the year 1948, a separation was created between the two sides. In 1948, part of the tribes and families who escaped to Jordan joined the Bedouins who lived in eastern Transjordan. Following the peace agreement between Jordan and Israel in the year 1994, the connections between the Bedouins in Israel and the Bedouins in Jordan tightened.

In 1948, the indigenous nomadic tribes in Jordan were joined by refugees from Israel, who voluntarily joined their brothers on the East Bank, and those suffering from extreme hardship in the **Sinai** infiltrated to Jordan via the Negev. In the East Bank, these nomads had no land of their own, and therefore had difficulty in forming large concentrations or raising livestock. In the 1950s, **tents** and animals were donated in a project called "**Azazme** Mobile Villages," designed to lodge 1,025 families at Karak, near the Dead Sea shore. Some Bedouin refugees received grants of livestock in order to rehabilitate them in the framework of the United Nations Relief and Works Agency (UNRWA) Bedouin Livestock Project.

By contrast to the traditional position of the Bedouins throughout history, and also in the neighboring Arab states, which is opposed at its base to any central government, the Bedouins in Jordan became great supporters of the Jordanian government and of the Jordanian royal family, and eventually even its main support versus the unrest of various factions within Jordan, and had at their head the Palestinian faction (the Palestinians constitute today 60–65 percent of the whole population of Jordan, which numbers eight million). This role was very noticeable mainly in the period of King Hussein (1952–1999), and especially after the Palestinian faction established a state within a state in Jordan, which threatened the security of the Jordanian state. This resulted in a conflict in September 1970, in which the Jordanian army won, that is, the Bedouins. However, King Hussein, throughout the entire period of his government, declared equality between the whole Jordanian population, without any distinction as to origin.

He always spoke about cohesion of ranks, for he always feared the Palestinian factor within the kingdom, especially after the decision of the Arab summit in 1974, in Rabat, **Morocco**, which decided that the Palestinian Liberation Organization (PLO) was the sole unique representative of the Palestinian people. This did not help the king to keep unity of ranks, especially when the PLO declared that it was also the representative of the Palestinians in Jordan and that the PLO could hold negotiations as to their future and fate. This forced the Jordanian royal family to rely more and more on the Bedouins for protection of the state and its stability.

King Abdullah, who was assassinated as he was leaving the El-Aksa Mosque, and King Hussein, who succeeded him, encouraged this practice of settling the Bedouins, who were Palestinian refugees, in refugee camps in Jordan, and in 1970 after the Six-Day War between Israel and Jordan, Egypt, and Syria, there was an increase in terrorist activity by Palestinian paramilitary elements (*fedayeen*) within Jordan, and in June 1970 fighting erupted between the Jordanian government and the Palestinians. As a consequence of this, Palestinian fighters were expelled from Jordan in a battle known as Black September.

King Abdullah the Second ascended the throne in the year 1999. He enacted social, economic, and political amendments. He adopted a policy of equality between the citizens without any connection to their origin—including the Palestinians. The Bedouin faction did not like this policy and saw in it a damage to their status, which caused them to criticize the royal family. The Bedouins claimed that this policy would lead to turning Jordan into a homeland for Palestinians. In April 2014, the Bedouin factions appealed to King Abdullah to reduce the political influence and role of his wife, Queen Rania, who was of Palestinian origin, with a claim that she had established bases of power that she would perhaps use in the future against the interests of the kingdom. They accused her of using public money for these goals, without taking into consideration the economic difficulties facing the state. The declaration was signed by 36 tribal leaders mainly from Beni Sakhr and Abbadi. The content of the declaration reflected the deep split between the Jordanians on the one hand and the population of Palestinian origin on the other, more than it reflected a challenge to the government of King Abdullah.

In 2011, the Arab Spring discord spread to Jordan, and the Bedouins participated in some unrest. However, the Hashemite kingdom is still not expecting a full revolution as in other Arab countries, due to a clever and calculated response of the state leadership.

JUBUR. Jubur was previously a nomadic confederation of people, and was one of the Zubaydi Yemeni Arab tribal groups of **Iraq** that lived throughout central and northern Iraq. Part of the tribe settled in Kirkuk near the **Kurdish** zone. The Jubur has several subtribes, which are the Al-Jiburi, 'Azza, Dulaym, Janabi, and 'Ubadi. Until the 19th century, most of the Jubur were Sunni Muslims, but since then, some have converted to Shi'ism, especially in southern Iraq.

K

KHALDUN, ABDURRAHIM BIN MUHAMMAD IBN (1332–1406). Ibn Khaldun was a notable scholar, philosopher, poet, historian, and Islamic lecturer. Born in Tunis, he studied in Fez and Andalusia, and taught in the al-Azhar University in Cairo and other academic institutions of the time. He published *Muqqddimmah*, the first **Arabic** version of universal history. His other important work is a philosophic analysis of the *asabiyyah* or "social cohesion," which refers to group solidarity or **tribalism** and explains that this phenomenon evolves when small groups unite in a kinship society, which can be reinforced by a religious creed. It is the first analysis of the tribal heritage of culture and society. Ibn Khaldun was known to the great rulers of his time and was welcomed to express his opinions and discuss important matters. He passed away in Cairo, at age 74, and was buried in the Sufi Cemetery outside Bab an-Nasr, Cairo. *See also* TUNISIA; URBANIZATION.

KHAZRAJ. The Khazraj tribe lived in the town of Yathrib (al-Madinah), in the north of the Arabian Peninsula. It penetrated into this region from the **Yemen** region in the south of the Arabian Peninsula. This tribe is known in Muslim history, together with the **Aws**, as supporting the Prophet Muhammad and the new **religion**—**Islam**—and helping him while he emigrated to the town of Yathrib in the year 622, following resistance of the **Quraysh** tribe to him and to his new religion. They gave him a significant supplement of power, and they joined him in his wars against his opponents, thereby helping him to spread the new religion.

KHLOUT. Khlout is an Arabic tribe of Jacham of Bani Hilal, originating from present-day **Bahrain**. It settled in **Egypt** and then in **Tunisia**, under the restriction of the Targhlib tribes. In the 12th century, the Almohad caliph Yakoub Al Mansour made them come to **Morocco** and settled them in Tamesna (Shawiya). The Khlout lived in the region of Tadla (which was a part of Tamesna) at the start of the Saadian dynasty. Toward 1540, they entered the service of Muammed Esh-Sheikh and then they rebelled against him to join the Turkish army of Wattasid Abou Hassoun.

After becoming the ruler of Morocco, Muammed Esh-Sheikh removed the military control of the Khlout, submitted them to payment of taxes, and deported their **sheikh** to Marrakesh. On the advent of Ahmed El Mansour, in 1578, and due to their heroic conduct in the battle of Wadi El Makhazen, he reintegrated the tribe under army control. The others received an order to settle in Azghar.

KHWALED. Khwaled is a small Bedouin village found in northern **Israel**. Members of the Hawaled tribe live in the village, which is named after the Muslim military leader Khalid ibn Al-Walid (592–642). The tribe's members received municipal recognition in their place of **settlement** in the year 1993. The village counts seven hundred people today. *See also* GALILEE.

KINDAH. Kindah is an ancient Arab tribe that lived in Najd, Northen Arabia, at least since the 2nd century BC, where they established a kingdom whose capital was the city Qaryat Dhāt Kāhil, today called Qaryat Al-Fāw.

Until the 6th century AD they were polytheistic pagans. There is historical evidence of rituals that were dedicated to gods named Athtar and Kāhil. It is not clear whether they converted to **Judaism**; however, archeological evidence shows that they were among the tribes who fought with the Jewish king's attempt to suppress **Christianity** in **Yemen**. In the mid-7th century they converted to **Islam** and played a crucial role during the Arab conquest of Arabia. *See also* SAUDI ARABIA.

KURDS. The Kurds are non-Semitic people who have lived in the same place since the **pre-Islamic era** and have all the characteristic of a nation; however, they do not have a country of their own, as unlike other nations, their country, Kurdistan, was split up by demarcation lines drawn by foreign rulers, between Russia, **Turkey**, **Iraq**, **Iran**, and **Syria**. The Kurds are a relatively large nation of about 20 to 25 million. They have been fighting for independence or at least autonomy since the late 19th century.

In 1946, Qazi Mohammad, a Kurdish leader, established the People's Republic of Kurdistan in its Iranian part, with Mahabad as the capital. When the Red Army withdrew from Iran, the Iranian army crushed the new state.

The Kurds are Sunni Muslims. Most Kurds in Iran are of the Shafe'I sect, including the sedentary and urban, who are subdivided into tribes and **clans**, such as the Mokri in northern Kurdistan, the Bani-Ardalan in the south (with Sanandaj at the center), and the Jaaf at the extreme south, with their overall number in Iran estimated to be about 1.5 million. They live in northeastern

Kurdistan in the provinces of Baktaran, Kurdistan, West Azerbaijan, Ilam, and northern Khorasan. In Turkey, the Kurds have long struggled for independence or at least autonomy, and their organization, the Kurdistan Workers' Party (PKK), has been caught in many skirmishes with the Turkish army and air force in the eastern mountains. In Iraq, however, they recently managed to establish a semiautonomous region, while in Syria they are facing encroachments from the Islamic State.

KUSEIFE. Kuseife is a **Bedouin** town founded in 1982 as part of a government project to settle Bedouins in the **Israeli Negev**. The town was acknowledged as a local municipality in 1996, and was home to members of several Bedouin family **clans** including Abu-Rabi'a, Abu Ajaj, Elamor, Al-Zabarka, Al-Nasasra, Azbarga, El-Dada, Abu Juda, and Abu Anam. Two other clans, the Al-Nasasra and Elamor, reside outside Kuseife, close to the Nevatim air base.

According to the Israel Central Bureau of Statistics, in January 2011, the population of Kuseife was 17,400. *See also* RAHAT.

KUTHAYYIR AZZAH. Kuthayyir ibn 'Abd al-Raḥman (660–723), known as Kuthayyir Azzah, was an Arab poet of the **Azd** tribe in the Umayyad period. He was born in the city of Medina and lived in Hijaz and **Egypt**. The major subjects of his **poetry** were love and panegyrics, and much of it was dedicated to his unfulfilled love to a married woman named Azza.

KUWAIT. In ancient times the **nomads** and seamen settled in the harbor of Kut (Kuwait), which was a natural harbor. They thrived on fishing, **pearl** diving, and shipbuilding soon after. Merchandise from local ships was offloaded, and it was a good place for merchants to **trade**. There was some trade in **camels** and sheep, and trading relations with Bedouins living inland.

The Bedouins went north in the summer, toward **Iran**, **Iraq**, and **Syria,** including **Jordan**; and then they went south in the winter. Each nomadic tribe was connected to an area called the *dira*, which was a sort of homeland: the Adwani and the Otaibi tribes were based in Taif and **Saudi Arabia**; the Ajmi were from Al-Wadi, Saudi Arabia; the Mutairi were from an area near Kuwait.

The people who had settled inside the Kut city walls received the name *Hadhar*, an **Arabic** word meaning urban or civilized, whereas, the Bedouins, who were called *Bedu* because of their nomadic life and their insistence on it, lived outside the Kut city walls. Thus Kuwaiti society was founded on social division between the Bedu, who lived off livestock and lived outside the city, and the Hadhar, who were refugees and settled in Kuwait. Some of the merchant families had links with Saudi Arabia, Iran, and Iraq.

Nomadic tribes settled in Kuwait between the end of the 17th century and the middle of the 18th century. In 1762, the merchant families of Kuwait selected **Sheikh** Sabah bin Jaber bin Adhbi as their leader, and so the al-Sabah family became the ruling family of Kuwait, which is one of the three principal families of the Utub. The Al-Sabah family, which had come to Kuwait via **Bahrain** and Basra, had an agreement with the merchants, who would knock on the door of the family's house above the **market**. Kuwait was on the trade crossroads between India and Iraq and India and Iran; thus the merchants had a lot of influence.

After the death of the Bani Khalid emir Suleiman Al Hamid, in 1752, the Utub built a mud wall around the town to protect it against Bedouin attacks. Due to the lack of centralized power in Persia and the waning of the Ottoman Empire, Kuwait enjoyed limited political autonomy in the 18th century. Al-Sabah used the Bedouins to protect them as a defensive force, and the merchant tribes who had good relations with the ruling families gained special economic commissions or arrangements.

The Persian occupation of Basra in 1775–1779 and the weakening of the Ottoman Empire brought good relations with the British. The latter saw Kuwait as influenced by **Turkey** but had strategic interests in the area, as it was on the way to India. Mubarak Al-Sabah came to the throne in 1896. He reigned until 1915. He played Turkey, Great Britain, and Russia against each other, and by killing two of his pro-Ottoman brothers took over power. He made secret agreements with the British. In 1913, Kuwait signed the Oil Exploration Agreement with Britain, while Germany was negotiating to make Kuwait the outlet for the Berlin–Baghdad railway, which the Germans were building. Mubarak died in 1915, while Britain still suspected him of supporting Turkey.

The *bidoon* are descendants of nomadic families who lived near Kuwait. They settled down and abandoned nomadism but are now unable to obtain legal papers or citizenship documents from the authorities. They serve in the oil industry, the bureaucracy, and the army. Some claim that the armed forces in Kuwait are principally mixed between local Awazim and Reshayda tribes, and other roaming tribes—both northern and southern—like the Anazah (which extends to Syria, Iraq, and Jordan), or the **Shammar**, which is a northern tribe. Many bidoon were Bedu from the Shammar and Anayzah tribes, which were two deeply rooted and extensive tribes, whom the emir encouraged to settle outside the city walls.

The oil industry, which sprouted at the time of the formation of the state, had a big influence on institutions, and on the organization and construction of the modern city of Kuwait. It was also the foundation of the welfare state, which encouraged obedience to the government and helped pay off debts by companies and citizens. The territories of **settlements** in Kuwait multiplied after the inception of the oil industry and it also mobilized thousands of the nomads into the ranks of its workers.

Some nomads went back to sheep grazing while their wives and children kept animals, and some nomads joined the army. These Bedouins were classed as seasonal workers. The enclosure of the oil refiners and oil wells reduced the land available to the tribes for grazing. The Bedouins would become Hadhars—that is, as one writer commented, it was impossible to describe those "who work for wages, live in a house, eat regularly and well, find amusement in the cinema" as a *badawin* (Bedouins).

Bedu families who still keep sheep do this mostly as a hobby. Some of them travel abroad to Syria or Saudi Arabia, for example, to buy aesthetically pleasing sheep, and enter them into competitions, like the annual one in Saudi Arabia. They treat camels in the same manner.

Kuwait itself is a society with multiple components and its leaders (the Al-Sabah family) have managed to satisfy the diverse elements composing its society, to achieve stability.

It is composed of six main subgroups, the Muslim Sunni Arab tribes, including some nomadic tribes, Muslim Sunni nontribal Arabs, Muslim Shiite Arab tribes, Muslim Shiite nontribal Arabs, and non-Arab Muslim Shiites.

The discovery of oil and the huge revenues this yielded deeply affected Kuwaiti society; as the sudden abundance of money had a complex impact on the traditional values and criteria, since wealth provided other options to the individual and weakened his dependency and reliance on the collective tribe.

Before the oil industry transformed the economy, Kuwaiti society was based on the pastoral, marine (fishermen and pearl divers), and farming components, with few urban centers that facilitated commerce, trade, and other services. The discovery of oil changed the way of life; it brought foreign experts and foreign workers, and changes in the relationship between the government and various components of society, and it affected the lifestyle of social groups like the Bedouins and the *fellahin*, who moved to city neighborhoods founded by the state, and in due course adjusted to the circumstances and filled all the state employment sectors. They enjoyed **education**, social services, and modern technology, but they also did their best to keep their tribal affiliation.

Political life in Kuwait recognizes the diverse interests of three major groups, and each of them chooses its own representatives: *Qebla* (Sunni) representatives, *Sharq* (Shiite) representatives, and tribal representatives. A recent amendment has increased the number of constituencies from 10 to 25, so that it can guarantee a Sunni majority in certain areas and a Shiite majority in others. It also ensures the representation of specific tribes, to make them loyal and grateful to the government. In recent times, Kuwaiti **women** were given the right to participate in elections.

The **Iranian** revolution caused tension between the Kuwaiti Sunnis and Shiites, which worsened during the Iran–Iraq War (1980–1988), and instigated terrorist attacks, including a car bomb, in an attempt to assassinate the then emir of Kuwait. The downfall of **Saddam Hussein**, in 2003, increased sectarianism in Kuwait.

The situation worsened significantly when Saddam Hussein attacked Kuwait in April 1990 and annexed it as the 19th province of Iraq. He was subsequently driven out by a U.S.-led coalition under the auspices of the United Nations, after the Gulf War of January–February 1991. But the downfall of Hussein in 2003 led eventually to an eruption of protests in the Arab Spring of 2011–2012. The parliament was dissolved in December 2011, and the prime minister resigned.

L

LAHEIWAT. Laheiwat is an Egyptian tribe that is relatively small, subdivided into three **clans** living in three separate territories in the **Sinai** in **Egypt**: one is posted in southeast Sinai near the coast of the Red Sea, another near the coast of the Mediterranean, and the third dwells on the northern shore of the Suez Canal.

LAKIYA. Lakiya is an **Israeli** Bedouin semi-urban municipal authority founded in 1982, providing services to a number of nearby Bedouin **settlements**, and has development plans that aim to make it a city. Unlike other towns built in the Israeli **Negev**, to settle the nomadic and **wandering** population, Lakiya is less successful economically, and the Interior Ministry, along with the local community leaders, looks for possible ways to bring in **trade** and industry, in order to boost the average income of the residents. *See also* RAHAT.

LANGUAGE. In the Middle East there are five main groups of people: The Indo-European group is found in the east, with whom the **Iranians**-Persians, the **Kurds**, and the Armenians are numbered. The Altaic group is found in the north, which includes the Turks and additional peoples who were not included in the Middle East, among them the Uzbeks and the Kirghizians. The Afro-Asiatic group is found in the center and the west of the Middle East, which includes the Arab and Jewish Semitic peoples. The Nubians in southern **Egypt** and **Sudan** are counted with the fourth group. Finally, there are members of the Caucasian peoples who are dispersed all over the region and to which the Circassians belong, who constitute the fifth group.

Each one of these groups has its own language. Below are the four central languages that are spoken in the Middle East as mother tongue and official languages in the various states:

1. Arabic: the language of the Arab peoples. Arabic is a language that developed on the Arabian Peninsula. It is the main spoken language in the Middle East. This is a Semitic language and it is the language of the

Koran, and therefore it is considered in the eyes of the Muslims to be a holy language. Over the years different dialects developed in various places. For example, Lebanese Arabic is different from Egyptian Arabic.

2. Turkish: the language of the Turkish peoples. From the Turkish Islamization in the Middle Ages until 1928 Turkish was written by means of a version of the Arabic alphabet and was called "Ottoman Turkish," but since then until the present Turkish has been written in a Turkish alphabet based on the Latin alphabet.
3. Persian: This language is spoken in Iran, and in the regions close to Iran such as Afghanistan. The language is written by means of a version of the Arabic alphabet adapted to Persian writing. Persian is the official language of the Islamic Republic of Iran.
4. Hebrew: Hebrew is a Semitic language, from the family of Afro-Asiatic Semitic languages, known as the language of the Jews and of the Samaritans. Hebrew constitutes the dialect in which the inhabitants of Palestine spoke starting from the 2nd millennium BC in the heart of a region called in the Bible the Land of Canaan, or the Levant including today the territories of **Lebanon**, Syria, **Palestine**, and **Jordan**. According to Jewish tradition, the 10 divine sayings with which the world was created were in Hebrew, and the angels used this language. Therefore the language is called the Holy Language. Hebrew serves as the official and main language of the state of **Israel**.

LAW, BEDOUIN. Traditional Bedouin law is part of the **desert** culture, derived from the severe conditions prevailing in it. With the absence of a central government and law-imposing mechanisms, Bedouin society created its own law system—*El-Kanoun el-Orfi.* This law system is not written anywhere. It is an oral tradition all tribal societies respect. It is based on the principle of right and wrong: if someone wrongs you, you have the right to respond and punish him or his family, **clan**, tribe, or the like. It depends on the severity of the offense and the accepted punitive measures. In most cases it is better to resolve a conflict rather than let it fester, where each side responds to the last punitive act of the other. Therefore, the law provides for a compensation that will end the conflict.

The trial takes place before a judge, who is a man both sides accept as the judicial authority. He must be a person known for his knowledge of tradition and Bedouin customs and has investigation powers and decision-making ability, and is also able to listen to both sides objectively.

Legal actions have rules and specific procedures; the injured party is the plaintiff. He must present evidence or witnesses against the wrongdoer. When there is no substantial evidence and the accused denies the accusation, the judge can use other methods to get to the truth, like demanding an oath—

Halphan el-Yamin. The oath has a unique place in Bedouin law, due to its magical and deterrent power. The Bedouins believe that a person who swears to a lie will be severely punished by God. Sometimes, a Bedouin may deny connection to a given act, until the moment he is required to swear, after which he takes no chances with God and confesses.

The second option is the test by fire, *Lahas el-Nar* or *Al-Bisha'a* (licking the fire). This is an extreme measure that was used only when all other means did not work. Today, it has almost vanished as Bedouins often choose to stand trial by the legal system of the state they live in rather than be judged by the tribal method.

In the past, the compensation set for the injured party would be animals, since animals constituted the main property of the Bedouin. However, in modern times, money has become the most frequent means of payment, as most Bedouin income and property is no longer animal-based. *See also* VENDETTA.

LEBANON. In the **Arabic language** the Lebanese differentiate between the *Bedu* (Bedouins), whose name is derived from the word *Badia*, the semi-arid steppe land in northern Arabia, and the sedentary population (*badar*). In Lebanon, the Bedouins are called Arabs, as the term Bedu is considered insulting.

The Bekaa Valley is located between Mount Lebanon (on the west) and the Anti-Lebanon Mountain Ranges (to the east) separating Lebanon from **Syria**. Many Bedouin tribes come into and go out of the Bekaa during their seasonal **migration.** Reports of Bedouins in the Bekaa have been recorded from the 13th century onward.

In Lebanon, most Bedouins are not considered citizens. They are "stateless" people, have no identity documents, and do not receive anything, nor are they entitled to any government services. Most of them can no longer conduct their previous lifestyle, but they have retained their sense of tribal loyalty.

Among the Bedouins found in Lebanon today, most of them are counted with the Muslim camp (Sunna and Shia), and several tens of thousands are counted with the **Christian** camp. The Bedouins in Lebanon originated from the Arab tribes, who came chiefly from the south of the Arabian Peninsula, from **Yemen**, in various historical periods. They migrated due to natural causes and struggles between tribes. They migrated first from Yemen to the region called **Saudi Arabia** today, and afterward to **Iraq** and Syria, and then reached Lebanon. They live today mostly on the Lebanon-Syria border, in the Baalbek/Al-Harmal region. Some of the tribes who lived in this region are: the Muslim tribes Zaitar, Nasser el-Din, Alawa, Dandash, Jaffer, Alam, Hamadeh, and Makdad; and the Christian tribes Kiruz, Rahma, Fahri, Suker, Tok, and Jaja. The Christian and Muslim tribes are similar from the point of tribal **fanaticism**. The Bedouins in Lebanon today do not match the pastoral image of Bedouins: riding on **camels** and **wandering** to search for pasture for herds. This picture matched the reality of the Lebanese tribes at the start of the 20th century. Today the population already lives in permanent settlements.

The Bedouins in Lebanon include the following tribes: the Anazah Hasana (bu 'Eed, 'Eedeen), Fadl (Huruuk, Haramisha, **Faour**), Mawali, Bani Khalid, and Naim. When the Ottoman Empire weakened, and Arab nationalism rose, many Bedouin tribes joined the **Arab Revolt** and supported the foundation of an Arab independent state under Amir Faisal in Greater Syria. Therefore, they opposed the creation of Lebanon for the **Christian** population and **Israel/Palestine** for the Jewish population.

On the social and cultural plane the Bedouins in Lebanon underwent changes and transformations as a result of the processes of modernization that the Lebanese state was undergoing. They underwent a process of **settlement**, integrated in the labor market, and likewise they integrated with the surrounding society in marital connections; several of them assimilated into Lebanese families. However, tribal fanaticism did not disappear, and this was because all the forms of tribe, family, and fanaticism continue to exist in Lebanon. In Lebanon, ethnicity was perpetuated, and this was based on the national covenant—an unwritten agreement that the leaders of the sects in Lebanon accepted after negotiations, in the year 1943.

The agreement laid the foundations for a nonsectarian Lebanon. The principles of the agreement included that the president of the republic would always be a Maronite Christian; the prime minister would be a Sunni Muslim; the speaker of the parliament would be a Shiite Muslim; the deputy parliament speaker would be a Greek-Orthodox; the defense minister would be a Druze; the army commander would be a Maronite Christian; and the parliament seats would be divided in an equal ratio (6:6) between the Christians and the Muslims (the Druze were included in the Muslim group). The division of political posts at the lowest levels was executed in a 5:6 ratio. The division of the central jobs in the state, including membership of parliament, is according to an ethnic key. Thus it turns out that the conditions for maintenance of **tribalism** still exist in present-day Lebanese society, and this sectarian affiliation is very strong. Likewise, part of the tribe still has authority in the regions in which they live, from a geographical point of view. The tribe's leader is the person who represents the tribesmen in all events and with foreign bodies, and the tribe still exists as one social unit.

The French mandatory regime in Syria-Lebanon (1920–1945) provided some services to the Bedouin population: it dug wells in the **desert**, opened schools, and operated mobile health clinics, but the Bedouins in the *Bekaa* and their needs were practically ignored. The French allocated large areas of pastoral land in the Bekaa Valley for **agricultural** purposes, a policy that had a significant impact on the Bedouin residents of the Bekaa, such that the foundation of Lebanon cut off the tribes from their brethren in Syria and dramatically reduced their seasonal migration range.

Thus, many Bedouins in Lebanon evaded the national census of 1932, and others were not included, since seasonal migration caused them to be elsewhere. As a result, the Bekaa Bedouins, who were not registered, had no nationality, so they could not buy land or be recognized as lawful owners. They had no rights for state services, and the state tried hard to force them to settle and abandon their traditional lifestyle.

Modern Lebanon has no place for **nomads**. The government uses means such as privatization of land and harassment of Bedouins by police, government officials, and sedentary locals in order to force the Bedouins to settle, but on the other hand, they do not supply these new Bedouin settlements with state services, like **education**, health care, piped **water**, roads, and electricity. Their villages are considered unrecognized settlements, and they do not exist on government maps.

Although the last official census in Lebanon was conducted in 1932, the number of Bedouins today is estimated to be anywhere between 100,000 to 150,000 adults. In 1994, those counted in a study project, about 10,000 (all registered as single bachelors or spinsters regardless of their real marital status), were granted nationality, as according to Lebanese law, unmarried **women** cannot pass on nationality to their children. Today, their children are *Maqtumeen al Qayd*, or stateless.

Thus, Lebanese Bedouins are generally poor, stateless people, who live in dilapidated houses, without sanitation facilities. They have the right to be employed as teachers or in the army, but they are not allowed to practice law or similar professions. In recent times, they have started to benefit from services like public education and some are given limited rights to receive health services, but only those who are recognized as Lebanese nationals.

The Bedouins in Lebanon played a significant role in Lebanese history; they participated in the struggle for Lebanese independence. The tribes participated in a few battles against the Turkish army and the French mandate. They were integrated into the political life in Lebanon, and since the state received its independence in the year 1943, many of the tribesmen joined religious, secular, and nationalist political parties. The tribes have a significant role in the political life of the state. Sabri Hamadeh (1902–1976), a member of the Hamadeh tribe from the Al-Harmal region, held the post of speaker of the Lebanese Parliament for many years (1943–1950, 1959–1970).

The Bedouins, in the period of the events that struck Lebanon—the Lebanese War of the year 1958 and the Civil War that broke out in the year 1976—joined the broader coalitions; the Muslim Bedouins joined the Muslim camp while the Christian Bedouins joined the Christian camp. These are their positions today also.

The Civil War was between the Muslims, Druze, and Christians in Lebanon, which ended with the dispatch of the Syrian Arab Deterrent Force by the Arab League. The Palestinian refugees, among whom there were many ex-Bedouins from Palestine, lived in camps and had joined the Palestinian Liberation Organization (PLO), under the leadership of Yasser Arafat. In 1982, after an attempted assassination of the Israeli ambassador to London and much PLO shelling of northern **Galilee** with Katyusha rockets, the Israeli army invaded Lebanon, and after the assassination of the Lebanese president, Bashir Jemayel, the Christians massacred Palestinian refugees in the Sabra and Shatila refugee camps. Israel became embroiled in a messy situation, and withdrew in 1983, after Arafat and his fighters had left for **Tunis** in August 1982.

In 1932 the French conducted a population census, but many of the Bedouin inhabitants did not register. In 1958, such Bedouins were given "understudy" status under the provisions of a Lebanese law, and in 1994 the government endowed these people with Lebanese nationality; they represented approximately 10,000 out of the 100,000 to 150,000 Lebanese Bedouin inhabitants. But many of these registered in 1994 as being single, and their children are now Maqtumeem al Qayd.

Bedouins in Lebanon were among the first to take advantage of modern technology in order to excel as farmers, and if they are citizens they are entitled to public health services and public education, but are not entitled to study law. But the dispossession of Bedouins from their land, which was given to landowning families, and the restrictions on granting nationality to some wives of Lebanese Bedouin men cause difficulty and complaints about lack of provision of adequate public services.

LIBYA. President Muammar Gadhafi of Libya had a strict rule for the Bedouin tribes under his regime. He kept contacts with smaller tribes linked to the officers who formed his Revolutionary Command Council, who had instigated the coup in 1969. But the main element in this strategy was the connection between his own **clan**, the **Gaddadfa**, and the other two biggest tribes in the country.

There are an estimated 140 tribes in Libya, of which 30 are influential. They are scattered among three main areas: Tripolitania, which is the location of the Libyan capital of Tripoli by the Mediterranean Sea in the northwest; Cyrenaica, stretching from the Mediterranean into the Sahara and containing the 2011 revolution in Benghazi, and Fezzan, which is completely in the **desert**.

In 4200 BC, in the third Egyptian dynasty, the Temcu tribe was reported to have invaded Libya. In the 18th dynasty (1703–1462 BC), the mother of Amenhotep, who was probably a Libyan called "Taia," was painted with blue eyes. An important **migration** of the Libyan tribes took place in 1300 BC, where an inscription of Meneptah II on the wall of the temple of Ammon at Api states that King Mar-ajui of Libit led a big army east into Egypt, starting at the town of Prosopis. He and many thousands of his soldiers were killed. Herodotus counted the tribes of Cyrenaica: from east to west, the Adyrmachae, the Giligammae, the Asbystae, and the Auschisae, and in the south the Garamantes. These were seminomadic tribes, grazing sheep and **camels** in the summer, but living in **settlements** in the winter, and most of the tribesmen were sedentary, living in nuclear **agricultural** villages.

The Libyans are from a mixed Arab-**Berber** origin, although some Bedouins take pride in their pure Arab descent. The Banu Hilal settled in Tripolitania in the 11th century, and simultaneously the Banu Salim settled in Cyrenaica as landowners and they were powerful. The Murabitin used the land without owning it. During the Turkish rule, the tribal people in Libya were led by the the Qaramanli dynasty (1711–1835). The Ottomans divided Libya into two provinces—Tripolitania and Cyrenaica.

At present, the largest tribe in the country is the **Warfallah**, with over a million members, which is based around Tripoli, whereas Cyrenaica contains the Kargala, Tawajeer, and Ramla tribes. In Cyrenaica the tribes were divided into two major types: the Saadi, who were landowners and powerful, and the Murabitin, who used the land without owning it.

The **Magariha** tribe is greatly indebted to the Gadhafi regime for the legal support it promised to Abdel Baset al-Megrahi, who was convicted in Great Britain for the Lockerby airplane bombing. His promise to return him was kept. This tribe's members have key roles in the state and security apparatus. The former region has often looked toward western **Islam** and the Maghreb, whereas the latter has ties with **Egypt** and eastern Islam. It was the home region of King Idris I, who was toppled by Gadhafi in 1969. Idris was a member of the leading family of the **Sanusiyah order**, which had been established by his grandfather, Muhammad ibn Al-Sanussi, in 1842, in Al Bayda, which constituted a religious Sufi brotherhood of conservative Islam.

The most active followers of the Sanusiyah were of a mixed Arab-Berber breed, based on the Arabic tribes Banu Hilal and Banu Sulaym, who migrated from Najd to North Africa in the 11th century and intermarried with the native Berber population. This movement played a great part in freeing Libya from the colonial domination of the Ottoman Empire (1551–1911) and the Italian rule, which existed from 1912 to 1943. The tribes clashed with colonial powers in two periods: the first occurred in 1911, and again during the period of 1923–1932, when tribal resistance against the Italians was led by the Sanusiyah order. After nine years of fighting, the Italians defeated the tribes, and then they crushed and destroyed the order, to prevent another war.

The United Nations proclaimed Libyan independence on Christmas Eve, 1951, and Muhammad Idris, head of the Sanusi order, became King Idris I, the constitutional ruler of the United Kingdom of Libya. This was the first time that Cyrenaica, Fezzan, and Tripolitania were ruled as a part of the united state under the Sanusiyah. Until World War II, no Bedouin leader was able to undermine the European rule and power in Libya. It also played a big part in the Libyan *jihad* led by the Libyan Islamic Fighting Group, which likewise overthrew Gadhafi in the 2011 Arab Spring revolution.

In the early 20th century, the Libyan Bedouin population was estimated as numbering anywhere between 800,000 and two million people, and was composed of **nomads** (*badawi*) and seminomads (*uruba*). **Tribalism** played a big part in the economic advances of the Gadhafi regime after the coup d'etat of 1969, as although the ruler tried to limit tribal authority, he intensified the tribal roots in the country and also involved them in employment and career-seeking. He based much of his authoritarian regime on tribal groups but reduced their power by granting them economic benefits and sometimes imposing punishments. He also balanced the power between the tribes within his own regime's institutions.

He notably, like another Arab despot, **Saddam Hussein**, used a policy of "divide and rule," and gathered members of his own tribe—the Gaddadfa tribe—around him, but this discriminatory attitude alienated many tribes, particularly among the Magariha, which were liable to revolt against him.

He rewarded cooperative tribes and reprimanded unruly ones. There was a culture of patronage, in which loyal generals were materially rewarded and gained significant social status among their elders, when Gadhafi showered the tribal **sheikhs** with prestige, wealth, and jobs, and practiced a kinship strategy. In March 1997, the parliament legislated the "code of honor," which enabled it to punish a tribe collectively usually by restricting public services if it acted against the regime.

When the oil industry developed, Libyan society was transformed, as most of the tribes became sedentary and sought modernization. Nevertheless, tribalism remained a major factor and the regime allowed tribal loyalties to persist. The revolutionary leadership craved modernization and regarded Bedouin traditions as anachronistic. Thus, the state divided tribal areas into common zones in order to weaken their power. The economic change affected hierarchy formation, as tribal leadership changed from lineage and wealth to capability and **education**.

Gadhafi managed to marginalize many tribal sheikhs, but when he felt threatened by opposing powers, he renewed tribal sentiments and reinforced the loyalty of his own clan and clans he had an alliance with. As the urban population maintained its tribal loyalties, Gadhafi and his regime could draw support from the Tripoli suburbs, inhabited by people from the Warfallah and Gaddadfa clans, which were loyal to him, but in cities with a long urban history, like **Misrata** and Benghazi, tribal features were a lesser factor. Therefore, these cities led the February 2011 revolution that ousted Gadhafi's regime.

Unfortunately, no one ever attempted to unite all the tribes and other social components of Libya into one nation. Thus tribal disputes, ethnic conflict, and disagreement regarding control of the oil industry and revenue prevent instilling order and stability in Libya today.

LURS. Lurs (or Lors) are a group of Iranian tribes living in the southwest mountainous areas of the Lorestan, Khurasan, and Kerman provinces. They may be ethnically related to the **Kurds**. The Lori **language** is linked to the ancient Iranian and also to the Kurdish, indicating that they are ancient people who lived in the area since **pre-Islamic** times. The main Lur groups are the Bala Geriva, the Delfan, the Selseleh, and the Tarhan.

The Bakhtiari or Great Lur tribes are some of **Iran**'s most important seasonal **migrant** groups located in the central Zagros Mountains. The Bakhtiari are subdivided into two major groups: the Haft Lang and the Cahar Lang. The Haft Lang tribes **wander** annually between the southeastern districts of Khuzestan.

The smaller Lur tribes live in the ostans (the 31 provinces of Iran) of Lorestan and Ilam near the **Iraqi** border. Over the years the implementation of settling projects fragmented these tribes. The Bala Geriva tribe roams in the Malavi district, in the vicinity of Korramabad. The main remnant of the Dirakvand tribe settled in this area. Tarhan district lies between the Seymara and Kasgan Rivers in the west of the Lorestan as far as the suburbs of Korramabad. The Lor tribes of Tarhan are the Suri and Emra'i.

M

MADFUNA. Madfuna is a traditional main course. Its name meant "buried." A whole chicken is filled with rice and snobar or a dish of rice and is squeezed into a pot and buried in the earth under hot coals for three to four hours. In the modern version the cook wraps the chicken with aluminum foil. There are those who fill the chicken with vegetables and serve it on a layer of steaming rice. *See also* FOOD.

MADI, HOUSE OF. The House of Madi denotes members of a Bedouin family from the Wahidat tribe of south **Palestine**. At the beginning of the 18th century, this family lived in **Galilee**, in the north, and controlled Nazareth, Jesreel Valley, Zebulun Valley, Mt. Carmel, and the western part of the central mountain ridge (Samaria). In 1735, they fought the Bedouin force of **Daher el-Omar**. They were defeated and did not regain power until the early 19th century, when they managed to take over the coastal plain, south of Haifa. In time they also regained some control over western Samaria.

The House of Madi opposed the Egyptian conquest of 1831, and their **sheikh** led a revolt against the Egyptians, which was suppressed. The House of Madi paid dearly for this attempt, but when the Ottomans returned, the Madi were reinstated and their new sheikh was appointed by the Ottomans as governor of Gaza; one of his brothers was appointed governor of Safed, and a third brother was appointed governor of Haifa. In the second half of the 19th century the family lost its prominent position and influence in the country.

MAGARIHA. This Libyan tribe is the second biggest tribe in the country, inhabiting not only the region of Fezzan, but also the main cities of Tripoli on the coast, like almost all other Arab-**Berber** tribes in **Libya**. It produced Abdessalam Jalloud, who was once number two in the regime after Muammar Gadhafi and prime minister for five years in the 1970s, but he got into a quarrel with Gadhafi in the 1990s when the tribe joined the 1993 coup attempt. He was one of the 12 members of the Revolutionary Command Council in 2011. Negotiations following that coup brought the tribe back in proximity with Gadhafi.

The most powerful man of the Magariha tribe was Colonel Abdullah al-Sanussi, head of the Jamahiriya Security Organization (JSO), which consisted of both the Internal Security Organization and the External Security Organization, which backed Abdel Basset Ali al-Megrahi, whose surname indicated that he too was from this tribe. Abdel Basset Ali al-Megrahi was arrested for the Lockerby bombing. Al-Sanussi married Gadhafi's sister-in-law, sister of his second wife, Safia Farkash, and he was the guiding hand behind the Abu Salim prison massacre in 1996, in which more than 100 Islamist prisoners were executed. He remained loyal to Gadhafi and directed the rebellion's suppression in 2011 in **Misrata**.

In Zawiya, in February 2011, opponents told reporters that an aide of Gadhafi named Abdullah Megrahi (obviously of this tribe) had warned them, saying: Stop the resistance or there will be a massacre. On the following day Libyan soldiers used anti-aircraft missiles and automatic machine guns to attack a mosque in Zawiya, which sheltered the opponents.

MAJNUN LAYLA. Majnun Layla was the Kais Ibn al-Mulaweh (645–688), a poet from the Middle Ages who lived in the Arabian Peninsula in the Najd region—the region of contemporary **Saudi Arabia**. His poems were love poems. He fell in love with his cousin Layla, who also returned his love. Layla's parents refused to let her marry her beloved Kais and wanted her to marry another person. However, their love was very strong. Due to the refusal Kais lost his sanity, and he wandered in the Arabian **deserts**; he went from place to place and wrote poems in which he described his strong love for Layla, which gained him the name *Majnun Layla* or Layla's madman. The suffering killed him. One day the members of his tribe found him dead in the desert by a heap of stones. *See also* POETRY.

MANASIR. Manasir was a collective name for a group of Sunni, **Arabic**-speaking tribes of northern **Sudan** whose homeland was located near the Fourth Cataract of the Nile River. The Manasir were of indigenous Nile culture and adapted **Islam** along with the Arabic **language**. Although several groups of the Manasir lived near the Nile, a considerable part of their population were nomadic Bedouins, **herding** goats, sheep, and **camels**, who lived in the adjacent Bayudah **Desert**, due to the annual flooding of the Nile.

MANSAF. Mansaf is a splendid **food** that is offered to important guests and served on holidays and feasts. The method of preparation: 5 kilograms of rice are placed in a big pot; a cup of oil is added to the rice and stirred well; later, **water** is added in a quantity that will cover the rice. It is then cooked on a big flame for 20 minutes, and for seven more minutes on a small flame. Every so often the dish is stirred. During the cooking, pepper and salt are added.

Toward the end of the cooking a big tray is covered with thin pita. Slices of mutton are added, as well as yoghurt or water. The tray is decorated with slices of meat and with fried pine nuts from all sides. This food is usually eaten with their hands. The *mansaf* is one of the most prestigious and important foods of the Bedouins. It has a social importance and is of very significant value in Bedouin culture.

MAQUIL. Maquil is one of the former Arabian nomadic tribes that migrated through the entire Middle East in the 11th century and settled in north Africa, bringing with them **Islam** and other aspects of cultural influence. Although they claimed to be decedents of the prestigious Hashemite dynasty, the fact that they were **nomads** contradicted such a claim. Therefore, and due to other characteristics, most scholars believed that their origin was in **Yemen**. The tribe settled in and around the Sahara **desert**, but some subtribes related to them continued westward and settled in **Mauritania**. The Maquil were originally a relatively small tribe, but during their **migration** they were joined by many other Arabian tribes, such as the Fezara of Asheja, the Chetha of Kurfa, the Mehaya of Iyad (or Ayad), the Shuara of Hassin, the Sabah of al-Akhdar, and some of the Banu Sulaym.

The subtribes of the Maquil include the Bani Ubayd Allah, which is the largest subgroup of the Maquil, and they are also subdivided into two groups: the Haraj and the Kharaj. These two groups had been involved in wars with the **Berber** tribes, with which they sometimes fought and sometimes allied. Bani Mansour, the second largest subgroup of the Maquil tribe, used to roam and live in the territories between the Taourirt and the Draa Valley in Mauritania. **Bani Hassan** was a subtribe related to the former two but also included groups descending from other branches of the main dynasty.

They came to their present territory by invitation of the local governor of the time, who needed their military help in fighting rebels in his realm. The Thaaliba subgroup gave up their nomadic ways and settled in the mountainous area near **Algeria**, where they lived for about four centuries, until they were conquered and oppressed by the Berbers, and eventually succumbed and became extinct.

To date, the people who live in western Algeria, Mauritania, southern **Morocco**, and western Sahara speak a unique version of **Arabic** called Hassaniya, named after the Bani Hassan subgroup of the Maquils.

MARINID DYNASTY. Mariniyun was an offshoot of the nomadic Zenta **Berber** tribe, which was the ruling dynasty of Berber descent that ruled **Morocco** for almost two hundred years (13th to 15th century). They ruled Morocco from 1244, and in the 14th century led the entire Maghreb for a while, supported the kingdom of Granada in Andalusia, and tried to take over control of the **trade** routes, including the commercial traffic of the Strait of Gibraltar. The Marinids rulers were overthrown in the 1465 revolt and were later replaced by a related dynasty of the Wassin, which had risen to power in 1472.

The Marinids arrived in Morocco during the 11th century and initially submitted to the Almohads, the rulers of the time, and settled in the north-eastern parts, near the Rif mountain range, where they began to tax farming, until they were recognized as a leading power. When they came to power they founded Fes Jdid and made it their administrative and military center.

The Marinids played an important role in shaping and influencing the Moroccan history. As rulers, they brought progress by building several *madrassas* (schools), enlarging the army, fortifying ports, and building road posts and castles at strategic locations. In the 14th century they were defeated by the Castilian armies and lost their glory. The revolt that ensued broke Morocco into fragments, which brought anarchy, loss of territory, and financial crisis.

In 1459, the heir to the Marinid dynasty and his troops managed to massacre the ruling Wattasid family; however, he himself was murdered in 1465, and with that came the end of the Marinid regime.

MARKET, BEDOUIN. In the year 1905, a livestock market was opened in Beer Sheva (**Israel**) in the **Negev Desert**, which was designed to be a place of commerce for nomadic Bedouins. Market day also proved to be a golden opportunity for social meetings of Bedouins from various tribes, during which deals were made using the barter system. Over the years the market received a more urban character, and Jewish **traders** and vendors joined the staff.

Beyond the authentic merchandise, it was possible to find in the colorful market a variety of goods like household utensils, clothes, various cloths, and so on, side by side with objects characteristic of the Bedouin culture, like Bedouin carpets, woven cloths, *nargilas*, copper utensils, jewels, and so on. The area of the market was sizable and it was possible, after or before buying vegetables and fruit in the nearby town market, to go for cheap and experiential shopping; if not to buy, then at least to feast one's eyes on the splendid colors. The market was held every week on Thursdays, and therefore, there were those who called it *Souk al-Khamis* (the Thursday market).

MAURITANIA. According to historical records, the first settlers in the area were the **Berber** tribes, who landed on the coasts of north Africa around 2000 BC and expanded inland and westward. The ancient Egyptians built the Audogost Kingdom on the Arguin Island, and then they expanded inland and enslaved the Berbers. Several centuries later, the Arabic forces conquered the region and Islamized its population. The population of Mauritania was a new hybrid nation of an Arabic-Berber mix, which called itself "Beidanes" in order to be distinguished from the black people who lived in the southern regions.

Most of the state's society is made of Bedouin tribes who **wander** in order to look for **water** and income. The tribal cultures that vanished or became subdued in several Arab countries still exist in Mauritania. Until 2010, there was no revolution and no significant civil unrest in the state, until the regional civil unrest that began in 2010 called the Arab Spring, which spread from north Africa to several other countries in the Middle East.

In the 15th century the Portuguese conquered coastal north Africa and established trading posts in Mauritania, in the small islands around it, and in **Egypt**. A few years later, the **nomadic** tribes penetrated Mauritania, ousted the Portuguese, and conquered the entire country, including its inland territories. They ruled the country until the French invaded the area and occupied Mauritania as well. In 1960 the French withdrew, and since then Mauritania has been an independent state.

Mauritania comprises four proto-state emirates: Trarza, Brakna, Adrar, and Tagant, which were indirectly connected by these small regional **market** towns, as **urbanization** started only with the French colonial rule, in the early 20th century.

The population in Mauritania is composed of three main population groups: Black Africans (Negroes), Berbers, and Arabs. The Arabs brought with them their **language**, their specific **Arabic** dialect, and **Islam**.

The first Arab tribes arrived in the region with the Muslim conquest. However, their number was small, and therefore, they did not influence the composition of the local population. The **migration** of Arabic **Maquil** tribes from **Morocco**, in the 13th century, had a significant impact on the composition of the population, as they intermarried with the Berbers and, by doing so, created a new people. The nomadic Arab tribes Banu Hilal, Banu Sulaym, and Banu Maquil arrived in north Africa in the 11th century. They intermixed with the local population and caused an "Arabization" of many local people. The common dialect is called Hassaniyya Arabic after Banu Hassan, a subtribe of the Banu Ma'qil. In the past, there were many tribal conflicts and alliances, the end result of which was eradication of the Zenaga language and the Berber identity.

Throughout history, the tribes in Mauritania conducted bloody wars among themselves. They attacked one another, robbed one another, and also fought for influence and hegemony. The situation led the principal **sheikhs** to issue religious legal *fatwas* in favor of a foreign conquest of the state in order to stabilize security. Such an event was conditioned on the rule that the foreign conqueror would not intervene in the religious matters of the inhabitants. However, the French, who eventually occupied Mauritania, failed to subdue the tribes and stabilize the state. The tribesmen refused to convert their loyalty to the tribe to loyalty to the state.

To date, the tribes, especially the leadership of the large ones, carry a significant influence on the decision makers of the state, to obtain their needs and achieve status and legal rights. The rulers of the state always ensured representation of the tribes in their governments, in order to gain their support. **Tribalism** fulfills a central role in the inner politics of the state; the parties also are founded on a tribal basis.

Thus, despite the efforts of the liberal intellectuals in their struggle with tribalism, their influence is small, and the dominance of tribalism is still firm and valid. The so-called Arab Spring reminded everyone of this traditional cultural characteristic and there is evidence of returning to tribalism in some Arabic states that managed to subdue it, with the birth of national Arab states.

Nouakchott, the capital of Mauritania, was founded in 1957, three years before Mauritania received independence. Today it has 750,000 inhabitants, indicating the modernization of the country, which in the beginning of the 20th century had 95 percent of its population as nomads. Today, almost 80 percent of its population is sedentary, and only a small number of its original tribes are still nomads and preserve their traditional culture and Arabic language. In Mauritania, most of the farming population is black, whereas the nomadic herdsmen are white, of Berber descent, from the Zenete (**Tuareg**) and the Zenaga (**Sanhaja**) tribes of western Sahara. Each group speaks its own dialect.

MEDICINE. In ancient times, Bedouin healers used medicinal plants according to their similarity to the human organs. They believed that the Lord shaped a given plant in a given shape, as a hint for the healer, to know what to use; therefore, they used a plant resembling the organ to cure that particular organ. Over time medicine developed, defining which plant was good to cure a particular ailment. The healers also found out the correct method to use a given medicine: eating parts of it, drinking an extract of some sort, applying it as a balm, or inhaling its fumes.

Years of experience, acute observation, and knowledge were passed on and taught to popular healers. They learned about poisonous plants and possible remedies to cure certain types of poison. As Bedouins tend to believe that diseases are caused by spirits and devils, popular acts of healing are often accompanied by various rituals of sorcery. The Bedouin used to believe that most of the diseases are divine punishment for one's sins, including neglecting the rules of hygiene, **religion**, and moral behavior.

Traditional medicine has two segments: preventive medicine and correlative medicine. Preventive medicine includes the aforementioned rules and specific steps like hanging amulets on the body, writing verses from the Koran, commitment by a vow, visits to holy men, or misleading the evil eye by tricks, lighting incense, and so on. Correlative medicine uses the knowledge of the healers and individual knowledge of cures. It also includes the use of **music** that affects the soul and the inner feeling of the person, as in order to heal, a person must be tuned completely, body and soul, for the cure to succeed. Various medicinal plants are used.

The onion is a disinfecting and curing material. It is used as medicine for colds, mostly as a preventive medicine. It is also used to treat wounds, after being boiled in olive oil. It is both a spice and a medicine, used for treating throat infections, colds, gas, and liver ailments. Sesame products are used for stomachache, sugar balance, as a pregnancy aid, and for milk production of nursing **women**. Sage (*marmiya*) (in a hot drink) is used as a medicine for stomachache, diarrhea, gastroenteritis, and gas. Mint is used in the same manner and for the same purpose, and additionally for treating nausea and vomiting. It is also supposed to help regulate menstruation in women who do not have regular menstruation.

Potherb (*blan*) roots, boiled for a long time on a small flame, are used to treat diabetes. Skinned thyme (Persian hyssop) leaves added to boiling **water** is a popular medicine for cold, sore throat, and coughing. Garlic (*thum*) is used as a spice, and is also perceived as an effective medicine against intestinal worms or cold, and as a pain killer for scorpion stings and snakebites.

The Bedouins consider caramel trees to be holy; damaging caramel trees is forbidden, and these trees are visited by the faithful, who read verses from the Koran, especially *Surat el-Fatiha*, and even make vows on its behalf, and slaughter goats or sheep. They hang white pieces of cloth on the tree to mark their visit and notify God so he might reward them and grant their requests. The fruits of the caramel tree serve as a medicine for diarrhea. The female Bedouins believe that such visits to the caramel tree can bestow blessing on barren women and help them get pregnant. Juice produced from crushed eucalyptus (*kina*) leaves is used as cough medicine. Leaves and branches of the buckthorn are used to prepare medicine for jaundice. The extract of laurel (*rand*) fruits is used to treat muscular dystrophy and rheumatic fever.

There are also medicines of animal origin: **camel** milk is considered nutritious and is healthy for the body; it is used to cure children suffering from liver problems, and for people who are stung by a scorpion or bitten by a snake. It is also reputed to increase sexual potency, especially in the elderly. Camel urine is used to disinfect wounds, serves as medicine against dandruff, and strengthens the hair roots. Donkey milk is supposed to help stuttering children, and cooked donkey meat is a medicine for hysterical (or crazed) women. Lemur droppings (*tzon*) and old donkey droppings are used to prepare a disincentive solution; a small quantity of porcupine blood is used for heart pains; an extract of boiled yellow scorpions can immunize a newborn baby against future scorpion stings; the slough of a snake is used to cure allergies; and goat's milk is given to somebody who is stung by a scorpion or bitten by a snake.

MESSIRIA. Messiria or Misseriya Arabs are a branch of the **Baggara** tribes. The Baggaras, who speak Chadic **Arabic**, are the second largest population group in western **Sudan**, extending into eastern Chad. Most of them are nomadic cattle **herders**, and their journeys are season-dependent. In the past the Baggara were known as **slave** raiders, but today they prefer to be called Messiria.

MHALLAMI. Mhallamia is the name for one of the old Arab tribes that lived in the Taurus Mountains, close to the region of Mardin in **Turkey**. They are named after the father of the tribe, Mhallam ben Dahal (Tahal) ben Shiban el-Bakri ben Vail. The Mhallami Un is a big tribe who number today 1.5 million inhabitants. Many of the members of this tribe still live in their customary region of **wandering** in the Mardin region in southeast Turkey, and groups of the tribe live in part of the Arab states. The tribe members have retained their Arabness, especially those who live in Turkey.

The Western Orientalists and travelers who visited the land of Mardin mentioned the Mhallami and its identity, and they always noted the Arabness of this tribe. Thus, Mark Sykes (1878–1919), the British diplomat who made long visits to Turkey, wrote travel books about this. When dealing with the Mhallami he noted that they were Arabs, their **dress** was similar to that of the **Kurds**, they lived by the side of the **Christians** in the Taurus Mountains, they say that they are sons of Ishmael, and they speak **Arabic**.

MIGRATION. Throughout history the states of the Middle East and north Africa were exposed to incursions on the part of the Bedouin inhabitants of the **desert** who strove to raid the sown lands. Borders that were breached or blocked before the Bedouins were conditional on two basic causes. The first, they depended on the existence of strong or weak central government: when the central government was strong, then the border was blocked, but in periods when the central government was weak, then any incursion of Bedouins ended in conquest. The second basic factor is connected to the conditions that prevailed inside the desert: the pressure of the Bedouins on the borders of the countries close to the desert like **Iraq**, **Jordan**, **Syria**, and **Palestine** grew during upheavals and sudden shifts of large blocks of tribes out of the great reserve of **nomads** of the Arabian Peninsula. It is difficult to reconstruct exactly the factors that brought every so often **wanderings** of groups of big tribes from the heart of the Arabian Peninsula northward.

In the 1930s, the theory was common among researchers that these incursions of nomads derived from constant climatic changes, striking the Arabian deserts with a periodic frequency of six hundred years. According to this theory certain areas of the Arabian Desert following certain climatic changes become especially arid, and consequently their dwellers are forced to move and wander northward. This theory, with all its logic, was proven to be incorrect. It was proven that in the historic periods concerned, no cyclical climatic change of the type described took place, and the Arabian Peninsula did not become more arid than it was four or five thousand years ago. Even if we cannot grasp exactly the system causing upheavals among the Bedouin tribes, then the very existence of this phenomenon of wandering is what needs to occupy us.

Every incursion of Bedouins into the Arabian Peninsula causes a chain reaction, as tribes moving with much power northward drive other tribes before them. This is similar to a landslide from a mountaintop, when the stone collapsing at the top pushes and rolls stones and blocks of earth down the slope, and those on the side collect with them everything that is found on their way.

The research literature notes that a number of big migrations took place before **Islam** that went out from the Arabian Peninsula in the direction of Syria and Iraq. One migration was in the 4th millennium BC; among the migrants were the Canaanites, who settled in the region of Greater Syria (*Balad el-Sham*). A second migration was the migration of the Akkadians, who migrated to Iraq. A third migration was in the 3rd millennium BC; this was the migration of the Amorites, who migrated to Iraq and Syria. A fourth migration took place in the 1st millennium BC, and this was the migration of the Arameans, who settled in the Syrian region (*see* PRE-ISLAMIC PERIOD).

Migration of tribes from the Arabian Peninsula took place all the time; the peninsula was regarded as a tireless treasury of Bedouin tribes that always moved northward. The migration of the Arab tribes into the Syrian region was a phenomenon that took place all the time: it started mainly about the year 200 BC, when they came to what is now Jordan and was then Greater Syria, which was being taken over by the Roman Empire from the vestiges of the Greek Empire colonies ruled by the Seleucid branch.

The tribes that moved northward from the desert founded buffer states between the **agricultural** region and the desert; out of these states it is possible to indicate the **Ghassanian Kingdom**, which ruled the Syrian

Desert, a kingdom that enjoyed the support of the Byzantines for a long time, who supported it as it filled for them a role of buffer state between the fertile sown areas of Syria and Palestine and the desert.

During the past 1,400 years we knew of three upheavals among the Bedouin tribes in the Arabian Peninsula that caused a Bedouin penetration into the Syrian and north Africa region.

The first incursion came with the rise of Islam in the 7th century. The warring armies of the new **religion** were composed mostly of fighters who were Bedouin tribesmen, and these went north to Syria and Palestine and continued from there to **Egypt** and the rest of the states of north Africa. They did this together with their families, their tents, and their herds.

The second incursion was in the 9th century. This was an incursion of the two big tribes Banu Hilal and Banu Salim, which moved northward from the region of Najd, the north of the Arabian Peninsula (the region of contemporary **Saudi Arabia**), and drove before them many tribes and fragments of tribes, part of which penetrated into Palestine. Their wandering was so influential that legends about their heroes became an inseparable part of the stories of Arab storytellers (*see* FOLK STORY). These Bedouins penetrated through southern Palestine to the heart of the **Sinai Desert** and moved quickly until they reached upper Egypt in the 10th century. From Egypt they continued on their way west and reached north Africa in the 11th century. This wandering, which brought destruction in its wake, left its imprints on the land of Egypt and north Africa for many generations, until it influenced the historical viewpoint of one of the great Muslim historians, **Ibn Khaldun** (he died in the year 1406), who described the course of human history as an interaction between the life of the settled country and the wandering tribes, when natives of the settled country build a civilization and sons of the desert strive to destroy it. With the tribes that Banu Hilal and Banu Salim drove before them were numbered the forefathers of the Tiaha tribe, the big tribe of the Negev and central Sinai.

The third incursion started at the end of the 16th century and reached its peak in the 17th century. The upheaval started among the **Shammar** tribe, which wandered in northern Najd, northern Arabian Peninsula, in a region called "Jabal Shammar" (the mountain of Shammar). When big parts of the Shammar started to wander north, its previous masters, the Mawali tribes, who wandered in Horan, were driven before them from the Syrian Desert. The Shammar took the place of the Mawali for a short time, but the movement that they caused within the Arabian Peninsula did not cease. Twenty years after the wandering of the Shammar came the wandering northward of the **Anazah** tribe, who drove the Shammar again from the Syrian desert toward the region of Aljazeera between Iraq and Syria. The Anneza, which was a large block of tribes, conquered the Syrian desert.

It is worth noting that apart from migrations of tribes out of the Arabian Peninsula northward, there were also migrations from north Africa to the Syrian region like, for example, the migration of Egyptian tribes into Palestine and Syria as part of the Egyptian conquest of Syria in the 1830s. There were also internal migrations; this means within the regions themselves as, for example, the migration of tribes within greater Syria, or within the Arabian Peninsula, or in the north African region as well. With the foundation of national states, there were migrations within the states and this concerns especially the oil states, when Bedouin tribes migrated to the new towns that were established due to the oil. An example of this is the kingdom of **Bahrain**, which **nomads** reached by the beginning of the 20th century and settled there in order to earn an income from the oil industry and **pearl diving**.

Also, Palestinian Arabs who are citizens and natives of Israel often recount that they are of Bedouin origin, and are descendants, even though they live in the north of **Israel**, of Bedouin tribes in the **Negev** that migrated to Ottoman Palestine from places like Iraq and the Arabian Peninsula in the 17th and 18th centuries. *See also* SETTLEMENT.

M'INAEANS. The M'inaeans were one of the main tribes that lived in the area of contemporary **Yemen**. In the Middle Ages, they were independent and ruled their own kingdom/principality, which had a monopoly on major **trade** routes that ran through the Arabian Peninsula. Their capital city was Qarnaw (now Ma'īn). Their second most important city, Yathill (contemporary Baraqish), still exists. The third important city in their kingdom was the trading post Dedan. Most of the rock inscriptions mentioning Ma'īn are found in these three cities and their immediate vicinity, hinting at its possible territory. It also appears that, at that time, these cities served as "caravan cities." M'inaean inscriptions are found in **Egypt** and in the island of Delos, indicating the scope of the kingdom's trading connections, Some such inscriptions refer to the interruption of trade during the war between Egypt and the Syrian Seleucids.

There are references to M'inaean caravans in a number of medieval texts, of Middle East context. However, scholars know nothing at all about the early history of this Yemenite tribe. Ma'īn was mentioned for the first time in history during the reign of the Sabaean *mukarrib* Karib'il Watar I. The M'inaean **language** dating from this period is inscribed in texts from the city state of Haram. The kingdom of Ma'īn was first mentioned in the 6th century BC, but as a vassal state of Saba. About AD 400, the M'inaeans were no longer vassals; they moved their capital to Yathill, conquered Najrān, Asir, and Hejaz, which gave them control of the "Perfume Road," and forged an alliance with Ḥaḍrama. Their caravans carried exotic commodities. They reached the Dead Sea and traded their merchandise in north Africa and the Aegean Sea.

All we know is that the structure of the M'inaean society was different from the rest of the tribal societies in the Peninsula. The king was the sole legislator, together with a council of elders composed of priests and the upper-class families. The kingdom was subdivided into large units ruled by an official who was appointed every two years, and who supervised one or maybe all of the transit stations.

MISRATA. The Misrata are supposedly the biggest tribe in eastern **Libya**, in Cyrenaica, although numbers do not exist to prove this. They are based in the eastern town of Misrata, and not in the western town of that name, which is situated opposite it, across the Gulf of Sidra, which was bombarded. This is where the tribe used to live before they migrated after the World War II to the east. They also live in Benghazi and Darnah.

MOROCCO. Morocco is a kingdom located at the northwest tip of the African continent, bordered by the Atlantic Ocean on the west and the Mediterranean Sea on the north, and has a mountainous interior. It is a relatively large country and homeland to 33 million people mostly of **Berber** and Arab origin. Its name derives from either the **Arabic** term for the western kingdom, Al-Maghrib, or from the Spanish name for the people who lived there in the Middle Ages, the "Marruecos."

Tribalism played a central role in the history of Morocco. The initial native inhabitants of Morocco were the Berbers, who had a lighter skin than the Arabs. They had a complex society that was subdivided into tribes, some of which were sedentary while others had a nomadic or seminomadic lifestyle. The Arabs who conquered the area in the 7th century AD were also composed of sedentary and nomadic elements.

The first Arab tribes arrived in North Africa with or soon after the Muslim conquest. However, their impact on the population was rather minor until the 11th century, when masses of Arab Bedouin tribes invaded the country and brought with them their culture, **language**, and **religion**, and competed with the Berber pastoral herders for the plains that accommodated grazing herds. Massive Arab immigration continued throughout the 12th and 13th centuries.

Some of the Berbers fled into the **desert**, where they enslaved black Africans. The mountain tribes held their own and kept their unique language and culture for a much longer period, but the rest were Arabized in language, culture, and religion. The third stage of Arabization occurred when refugees from Muslim Andalusia fled to Morocco and integrated with the local population.

The Moroccan Bedouins depend economically on the livestock they raise, including goats, **camels**, sheep, and cattle. Many of them maintain their traditional lifestyle. They settle around secure **water** sources (**oases**), and in the rainy season they penetrate deep into the desert (*see* OULED BOU SBAA; OULED EL HAJ).

Morocco in the 11th–13th centuries was ruled by the Almohad and Almoravid dynasties, and it dominated the Maghreb and parts of Spain and Portugal. The Reconquista in the 15th century resulted in the mass expulsion of hundreds of thousands of Arabs from Spain to Morocco in 1492. In 1666 Morocco fell under the rule of the Alawite dynasty, and in 1904 Spain and France divided zones of influence among themselves. In 1912 the Treaty of Fez made Morocco a French protectorate, and tens of thousands of French colonists (*pieds-noirs*) entered its territory and settled there.

Morocco is a constitutional monarchy. The king has wide legislative and executive powers, including the power to dissolve the parliament. France granted Morocco independence in 1956, and it has been ruled since then by kings of the Alawite dynasty (the dynasty that has governed Morocco since 1666), namely Mohammed V (1956–1961), Hassan II (1961–1999), and Mohammed VI (1999–). The rulers have skillfully kept control of the country's establishment, but they let winds of change blow in the country and let its people move with the times, so that the people did not rise up against them during the events of the Arab Spring. The estimated Bedouin population (the Yahyia tribe) in Morocco today is 105,000 people, and they have been encouraged by the authorities to found camps for tourism in the Sahara Desert with tents and camels where children can ride and play. *See also* ALGERIA; MAURITANIA.

MUNTHERIDS. Muntherids are Arab tribes whose origin is from the south of the Arabian Peninsula. They founded the kingdom of Al-Hira in the 3rd century AD, in the southwest of contemporary **Iraq** (268–633). This kingdom received its governmental authority from the Persians, who ruled and dominated Persia and Iraq. The Manadra helped the Persians. Their state constituted a buffer state, which blocked the penetration of Bedouin tribes that threatened the Persian state from the north of the Arabian Peninsula.

The Manadra participated in the Sassanian Persian wars against the Byzantines, and the ruler of the kingdom from the Banu Lakhm Dynasty usually gained significant influence at the court of the Persian state.

The Manadra believed in various **religions** and chiefly the religion that prevailed in the circles of the Persian government: Nestorians-**Christians**, pagans of various sorts, and Zoroastrians.

The Manadra left behind remnants that were used in the period of the Abbasi government, chiefly palaces like the Al-Abeid (white) Palace, the Ben Balila Palace, the El-Zoraa Palace, and the El-Hurnak Palace. In the kingdom there were also **Christian** monasteries like the Al-Harik Monastery, Deir Hana Monastery, Hand Al-Koba (the great) Monastery, and Hand Al-Zogara (the small) Monastery.

The government of this Arab dynasty came to an end in the year 602. When the Persians murdered the king of the Manadra, Nuaman III, after they accused him of treason, the kingdom was annexed to the Persian state, and a route was opened before the Bedouin tribes from the **desert** to carry out attacks and raids against the Persians. The situation on the southwest border of Iraq stayed fragile until the Muslim conquest at the start of the 7th century. The Manadra served as spies for the Muslims, and they contributed to the downfall of the Persian state.

MURRAH. The Murrah was a relatively small tribe of about 15,000 members. It is one of the subtribes descended from the famous tribe of **Banu Yam**. Traditionally, they were **camel -herding nomads**; however, in recent years some of them have settled down in and around a traditional **oasis**. This tribe is found all over Arabia but mostly in the southeast parts of the peninsula.

Historically, the Al Murrah tribe made up a large proportion of Qatar, but today they constitute about 2.5 to 5 percent of the Qatari population. The reasons for this are the historical events that occurred in the very last years of the 20th century.

A majority of tribe members supported **Sheikh** Khalifa Al Thani, the former emir of Qatar, who was deposed by his son in 1995. The Al Murrah tried to depose the new emir and retrieve who they thought was the right ruler, but failed. Some of them were captured, and the others had to flee to neighboring countries.

In 2004, the emir published a decree that stripped all the Al Murrah clan of their Qatari nationality and expelled them from Qatar. Most of them left for **Saudi Arabia**.

MUSIC AND DANCE. Traditional Bedouin music is a music of the heart. It emerged from the **desert** in the Arabian Peninsula. This music expressed human life, the seasons of the year, the connection to the person, to **water**, to the tribe's heroism, to Bedouin nobility.

One of the characteristics of the music is the rhyming technique, according to the rule: poem-story. A poet declaims and is accompanied by playing on the **rababa**. Bedouin music includes, in fact, singing and playing together. Music with the Bedouins is mainly collective music—music of all, of the family, society, the tribe. The music is created within the tribe and on behalf of the tribe, whereby the life situations and conditions of existence influence the writing and the performance. Therefore it is possible to find in music song and dance sections of different repertoires: home and family songs, work songs, grazing songs, desert and camel songs, hero and tribal war songs, songs of sheikhs and legendary figures, historical and traditional events. The Bedouins use the rababa for performance of the music, which is more than a musical instrument; it is a loyal escort and an inseparable part of the life of the poet-composer-singer-player.

Bedouin music is functional music. Similar to the status of music with the peoples of nature in general, it is designed to serve goals and events deriving from the essence of the tribe's life. The music has no goals of entertainment. It does not exist for its own sake. It is not examined by the yardstick of artistic music. The quality of performance does not stand under judgment here. Its quality and use are determined according to its functions and connections. Below are a number of examples for illustration of the functions of the music in the lifestyles of the Bedouins.

(1) Hojeini: The name Hojeini comes from the Bedouin riding on the camel (*hojein*—a riding camel) who sings in a guttural voice about the desert, the landscape, the continuing road. The name of this type of music comes from here. Not only does the Bedouin riding on the camel sing this music, but also people sing it during journeys; **women** sing it when they collect twigs for a fire, or draw water from the well or from springs; shepherds sing it while grazing. The Hojeini music is a sort of psychological relief for a Bedouin required by him in order to overcome the loneliness surrounding him and in order to conquer his fear.

Below is a *hojeini* song of a woman who directs her words to a man who seeks her hand but whom she does not want:

Itzha tajini waana ma ahbak Beware of coming to me. I do not love you.

La shuftani wala taartzini You did not see me and will not stand in my way.

Tavalt rav al-mala yaatik I prayed to the almighty to give you your desired,

Waana asa Allah yeutzini and God will reward me with plenty.

(2) The songs of the well and the flock: the shepherd draws water from the well and calls the flock to come and drink when he praises the well's water. The following is an excerpt from the song: "*Ya bir kither hirk, badur girk*" [Oh well, thank you for your bounty; tomorrow I will ask your fellow].

(3) Beat music: this type of music is performed at parties, and it is performed with a mortar and handle (pestle). The music has a social-traditional function. This is, in fact, beating with a pestle on the walls of the mortar while grinding coffee beans in its preparation for guests. It is accepted that every tribe or every family will have somebody knowledgeable in the grind-

ing craft. The desert's tradition states that grinding the **coffee** is executed aloud in order for it to be heard at a distance and will constitute an invitation to guests to come.

(4) *Dahaya* dance: This is a dance performed at a barbecue and accompanied by a song performed with common singing tactics. The song is of a call-response nature, and a group with a soloist performs it. This is an example of collective/tribal song. The dahaya was danced before setting out for journeys of robbery or war with the goal of exciting the tribesmen, likewise after the end of battles, in which they describe what took place in battle and to demonstrate the heroism of the tribesmen. Today the dahaya is danced in festive events: weddings, holidays. The dahaya is a group dance in which the men are arranged in a row or in two parallel rows. The poet located in the middle sings his poetry, and both rows answer him when they repeat one expression, which was agreed on before. The dahaya includes songs of praise.

Below is an excerpt of a dahaya song:

Lula mazvana ma jina wala katana arachina Without our host we did not come and we did not cross our land.

Ya ahal el-bait el-jadidi lita mavrouk wasaidi Oh, the new home's family let them be lucky and happy.

Hatha bitek ya abu ali ba el-kaharev matchoya This is your house Abu Ali in which the lights are lit up.

Hala halal bak ya hala la ya halifi yua walad Welcome, welcome—no, not my ally child.

The processes of change and the transition from **nomadic** life to life in permanent settlements have generated changes and transformations in traditional Bedouin music and dance. Music and dance from the surrounding Arab urban society are now penetrating into Bedouin society. On the background of the process of globalization, Western (English and French) music is also penetrating into Bedouin society. It is possible to find this type of Western music and dance among the Bedouin youths, while the adults are still loyal to traditional music. *See also* DABKA; DAHIYA.

MUSZEINA. Muszeina is an **Egyptian** tribe that is the largest tribe in the **Sinai**. They dwell in the southernmost part of the peninsula, in and around Sharm el-Sheik. They live near all habitual areas (near **water** sources) in the southern part of Sinai and near various development centers (hotels, mines, oil fields, army compounds, etc.).

MUZZEZIENA. This Egyptian tribe is a Bedouin tribe from **Saudi Arabia**; some of its **clans** moved westward to **Jordan**, the West Bank, **Israel**, and the **Sinai Desert** (**Egypt**), mostly in and around the town of Dahab, situated where there had been a small **oasis**, before **water** was brought in by a pipe system. In recent years their way of life has been challenged, and it is gradually changing, causing them to lose their cultural heritage.

N

NABATEANS. The Nabateans (Al-Anbat) were tribes whose origin was thought to be near the Gulf Coast of the Arabian Peninsula. They were **trading** people who led **camel** caravans from the coast of the Indian Ocean to the Red Sea and eastern coasts of the Mediterranean. In the 3rd century BC, they migrated to the Edom mountain range, on the routes of the major **trade** roads, pushed the native Edomites out of their capital, Sela Edom (in contemporary **Jordan**), made it their capital, and called it Petra.

They handled much of the trade from India and Africa to the Persian Empire, the Middle East, and **Egypt**. During the autonomous regime in Judea and when it was still a functioning Roman province, they brought their merchandise to Jericho and Ein Gedi, where it was processed, rebaggaged, and sent over to ports on the Mediterranean. They had a unique knowledge of the **desert** and how to reach and use hidden **water**. They dug water cisterns and built transit stations along the major trade roads. They also developed a unique **agriculture** system based on their knowledge of water and dew. When the Judean revolt was subdued by the Roman Empire and several towns and villages were ruined and abandoned (2nd century AD), they moved westward and built new cities in the **Negev**, on the two main routes from Petra to the port towns of Gaza and El-Arish. They managed to remain independent by reaching agreements and paying taxes to kingdoms and countries they crossed on their way.

The Nabateans' control of trade diminished when ships became a major factor in commerce. As their main profit was made by trade of incense and perfumes, specifically frankincense and myrrh, used in large quantities in pagan temples, the spread of **Christianity** inevitably reduced their main source of income, and they had to rely more on their indigenous desert agriculture. Toward the end of the Roman Empire, most Nabateans were sedentary. Under Byzantine rule they accepted Christianity, lost their unique identity, and blended with the rest of the local population. *See also* ISRAEL.

NEGEV BEDOUINS. Negev Bedouins are **clans** and tribes that used to be **nomadic shepherds** and seminomadic tribes who cultivated some of the land in the winter and **wandered** around during the dry season. This population was affected by the 1948 war between **Israel** and the Arabs, and many of them were forced to relocate and move to other parts of the Negev. Like all nomadic societies in the world, the Negev Bedouins were forced to change their way of life. Some were willing to adapt to the change, but others clung to their cultural tradition and refused to settle in large town-like **settlements**.

Exposure to modern life affected the Negev Bedouins in other respects too. Their birthrate has been the highest in the world. According to statistics, this population doubles its size every 15 years.

The Negev Bedouin tribes were divided into three classes, according to their origin: descendants of ancient Arabian nomads, who came from the **Arabian** Peninsula; descendants of the **Sinai** Bedouins; and descendants of impoverished Palestinian peasants (fellahin), who leased land from the Bedouins and cultivated it for settling rights. The large Negev Bedouin tribes are the **Tarabin**, the Al-Tayaha, and the Al-Azazme.

Today, many Bedouins call themselves "Negev Arabs" rather than "Bedouins," as for them, the word *Bedouins* means "nomads." *See also* NEGEV BEDOUINS AND PARTITION.

NEGEV BEDOUINS AND PARTITION. The United Nations' decision of 29 November 1947, on the partition of **Palestine**, did not come as a surprise to the Bedouins of Negev, as a preliminary report of the Recommending Committee included Negev in the future **Israel**. The **Negev Bedouins** opposed the fact that no one thought to ask them about their views, they protested in public, and they later joined the campaign against the Jewish population in Negev for two reasons: The main reason was the pressure of the Supreme Arab Committee and the Palestinian National Movement to choose sides and join the armed struggle. The second was that although many of them had good relations with the Jews, they had long-standing connections with the Arabs of the Mt. Hebron region, which led to their participation in past events (the **Arab Revolt** of 1936–1939), and many of them were reluctant to be included within the realm of the future Jewish state.

In 1932, in a meeting between the Palestinian leader, the Mufti Haj Amin El Husseini, and prominent Negev Bedouin leaders, an agreement was signed and endorsed that stated: "Not to sell Arab land to Jews, and declared that he who sells land to Jews, or even mediates such a transaction, will be regarded as a traitor and ostracized, and if he would be murdered for this his blood would not be avenged."

Consequently, Bedouin attacks and harassment of the Jewish population became common. The novelty of this period was the fact that for the first time Negev Bedouins participated in actions against the British; they sabotaged the railway and attacked small isolated police posts, after which they simply packed and fled to **Egypt** or **Jordan**.

Following the declaration of the partition plan in the UN, in November 1947, the Negev Bedouins increased their violent attacks and harassment of Jews, mainly under the leadership of the Bedouin-Arab society. They set ambushes on roads, harassed farmers and small working groups on the fields, raided small **settlements**, attacked the long transport lines, and sabotaged the **water** pipelines, which, having brought water from the north, stretched for several kilometers.

NOMADS. Nomadic people and tribes were groups of people whose lifestyle consisted in **wandering** from place to place. They did not live in a permanent manner in a certain place. The nomads wandered according to the availability of **water**, **food**, pasture, security, and the like. Mostly the wandering was done in a defined area, or in a cyclic track. The lifestyle of the nomads was very prevalent in the past, mainly with people who lived in the **desert**, but today this phenomenon is diminishing. *See also* MIGRATION; NOMADS, SETTLEMENT.

NOMADS, SETTLEMENT. The phenomenon of the **settlement** of **nomads** is an old one that exists in several variations and as a result of various factors, in various places in the Middle Eastern and North African space. There are examples from history where settlement of nomads was carried out in the region as a result of political, strategic, and economic factors that operated on the whole region, as during the Muslim conquest at the start of the 7th century. There were cases of settlements that were forced on the nomads, as in the **Egypt** of Muhammad Ali, in the first half of the 19th century. In other places, what happened in the **desert** itself had a great influence on their settlement, whether by God's hands or human hands, for example, drought, famine, tribes that lost in wars, and so on.

In the modern era, settlement has taken place as a result of losses of nomads in the historical struggle that was carried out between the nomad and the farmer, and as a result of the intensification of Western culture, the culture of the residents of towns and villages. Today the governments treat the subject of settlement of Bedouins in a central form, as they understand that one should solve the problem in an orderly fashion. *See also* WANDERING.

NUAIM. Nuaim is a large Arab Bedouin tribe that can be found in several countries in the Middle East. They used to live mostly in the Arab states located on the western side of the Persian Gulf, where they were subdivided into branches called Al Muhanna, Al Sayad, Al Mansoor, Al Jaffali, Al Rahma, Al Jaber, Al Ali, Al-**Shamsi**, Al Majed, Al Alaaq, and Al Bukhraiban. However, their **clans** and subtribes can be found in **Syria**, **Jordan**, and **Iraq**.

Al Nuaim was one of the Bedouin tribes that moved to **Bahrain** in 1783. After Al Khalifa conquered the island, some clans returned to the Gulf States when circumstances changed, while others chose to stay and their descendants still live in Bahrain.

O

OASIS. This is an area in the heart of the **desert** that contains a source of **water**. The view of the oasis stands out very much in its arid environment; it served as a home of growth for animals and a focus of attraction for man including for the Bedouin tribes. The water sources of the oasis are connected to the groundwater level. In most of the oases the water rises to the surface by its own strength, in the form of springs. Most of the oases were already settled in a very ancient period. Oases were always settled by man, as they were blessed with water in the heart of an arid region. Tens of thousands of oases are scattered in the deserts in the Middle East and below are four examples:

1. Al-Ahsa. It is a historical oasis region in eastern **Saudi Arabia**. Al-Ahsa is a segment of the area known traditionally as Eastern Arabia, which includes the eastern coast of the Arabian Peninsula descending to the borders of **Oman**, and also contains the island of Awal (present-day Bahrain). Al-Ahsa has been settled since prehistoric times, due to its proliferation of water in an otherwise barren region. Natural freshwater springs have surfaced at oases in the region for millennia, encouraging human residence and agricultural efforts (date palm cultivation especially) since prehistoric times.
2. Qatif. It is a governorate and urban region located in Eastern Province, Saudi Arabia. It stretches from Ras Tanura and Jubail in the north to Dammam in the south, and from the Persian Gulf in the east to King Fahd International Airport in the west. This region has its own municipality and includes the Qatif downtown and many other smaller towns and townships. It is one of the oldest **settlements** in Eastern Arabia; its history started around 3500 BC. Before the discovery of oil, Qatifi people used to work as **tradesmen**, farmers, and fishermen. However, in recent years, after the discovery of oil and the foundation of Jubail Industrial City, most of Qatifi's people work in the oil industry, public services, education, and health-care systems.

3. Ein Gedi. This is an oasis in **Israel**, located west of the Dead Sea, near Masada.
4. Tafilalt. This is a region and the most important oasis of the **Moroccan** Sahara; it is also considered to be one of the largest oases in the world. Entirely located along the Ziz River, the oasis is 10 days' journey south of Fez, across the Atlas Mountains. It is celebrated for its large and juicy dates. Al Hassan Addakhil, the forefather of the incumbent Alaouite Dynasty of **Morocco**, cultivated these with much success around 1250 so that he could fund the dynasty's rise to power.

OKAZ, MARKET. The Okaz market was a large and important market in the Makkah region. The Arabs would come to it once a year in the **pre-Islamic period** (Al-Jahaliya). The market would be open for a month. Aside from being a fair of merchandise, where they **traded** dates, honey, wine, clothes, and beasts, it was also a tribal meeting place. Arab tribes gathered for a month in the market region and exchanged their experiences. Likewise the fair was cultural. There were **poetry** competitions. Poets composed poems (some of which were composed by the greatest poets of Arabia) and came and presented their poetry before a committee of tribes, who chose the winning poems. *See also* SAUDI ARABIA.

OMAN. Archeological findings reveal that Oman was inhabited in prehistoric times. Sumerian tablets mention a country called Magan in reference to copper mining. However, there is no evidence regarding the lifestyle of the inhabitants in these ancient times. From about 600 BC until the 3rd century AD the entire area was under the rule of various manifestations of the Persian Empire, but since then Oman, or at least the coastal area of modern Oman, was semi-independent and was ruled by local dynasties. The sultanate of Oman converted to **Islam** in AD 630 and practiced its own version of Islam called Ibadhism. At present the country has a mixed population of sedentary people and Bedouins of **nomadic** origin.

The pastoral nomadic tribes that live in Oman today raise grazing animals, mostly sheep and **camels**, and follow an annual **migration** according to the seasons. The Bedouin tribes in Oman are divided into two major groups that arrived and settled in the area separately using two different routes: the **Qahtani** tribes Mahra, Jebena, Beit Kathir, and Harasis, who came from **Yemen** and moved gradually northward via Hadramaut to Oman, and the Adnani or Nizar tribes including the Duru and the Wahiba, who came originally from Arabia and entered Oman through the Buraimi Pass in the north, during the 2nd and 3rd centuries AD.

In the 16th century, the region was conquered and ruled by the Portuguese, who were later ousted by the rebelling tribes, who reestablished their semi-independent status. In the 18th century, the area was again conquered by the Yemenite militant tribes, who made it a sultanate. Some people of these tribes remained in the area and imprinted their genes on the complex texture of Oman's population.

The Bedouin tribes in Oman possess vast lands, and some of it can be cultivated. The presence of mineral **water** in their land and the development of modern roads and large modern trading centers contributed to their nomadic existence. Some tribes like the Duru expanded their grazing areas and their new territories touched the cities and enabled them to visit urban centers and purchase various commodities.

The modern state of Oman adopted a humanitarian action toward the Bedouins through its relevant ministries and built a veterinary hospital, a boarding school, and petrol stations in the Bedouin areas. The Ministry of Water and Electricity has supplied water to the Harasis since the 1980s. The government has paved the **desert** roads to enable the nomadic tribes to bring water to their livestock by trucks. Thus, the Bedouins of Oman can keep their traditional lifestyle and raise sheep and camels, and they also benefit from the modern services and facilities provided by the state. *See also* HERDING; SAUDI ARABIA.

OMAR, DAHER EL- (1689–1775). The **sheikh** of the **Zidanes** who ruled northern **Palestine** in the 18th century, Daher el-Omar was born apparently in the year 1689. At an early age he strove to be the family head and started to distance his elder brothers from a position of influence in the family. He also began to weave friendly relations with the members of the nearby villages, help them in their struggle with their Bedouin neighbors, and protect the environment from the Ottoman clerks. The goal he had in mind was to lease the levy of taxes from the governor of Sidon for himself.

Daher succeeded in keeping his government running for 50 years continuously, and furthermore was considered to be generous and courageous, a seasoned politician, and a charismatic leader. At his peak, in the middle of the 18th century, he ruled extensive areas, from the north of the country to its south and from the sea in the west to Transjordan in the east. One of the most important characteristics of his period was the security and order that he provided. He succeeded in subjugating the local rulers and heads of the Bedouin tribes to his authority and required them to keep road security.

Out of his familiarity with the country's natives, he knew how to bring members of other people, like Jews and **Christians**, closer. He believed that with their knowledge they could add to his subjects' prosperity. Therefore, he allowed the Jewish population to renew in Tiberias and in Kfar Yasif. He permitted Christians to renovate the ruined churches. The stoppage of robbery on the roads, the orderly levy of taxes, and help to tradesmen in collecting debts brought a transfer of the center of gravity of **trade** from Europe to Acre, instead of Sidon. Acre became the center of trade of the Eastern basin of the Mediterranean Sea. All these fixed his place and status as one of the greatest rulers in the Ottoman period in Palestine. It is possible to see his mark in Palestine even today, in the network of castles and fortresses that he built, and chiefly in the towns of Tiberias, Nazareth, Acre, Haifa, and Jaffa. *See also* GALILEE.

OTAIBAH. Sometimes spelled Otaiba, Utaybah, or Uteibah. This is one of the largest Arab tribes of the Arabian Peninsula. Similar to other large tribal confederations in the region, the name Otaibah appeared in the region only in the last centuries. The original territory of the tribe was around Taif, but in time had extended as far as central Nejd.

The tribe has no chief and it is led by a council of leaders. In the 18th century, a large section of Otaibah moved eastward to Nejd, and this move led to a bitter war with the **Qahtan**, who were the dominant tribal federation before the Otaibah moved over. The Otaibah won control of the vast grazing lands of the Qahtan and pushed them southeastward. The majority of the tribe was nomad Bedouin, until they reached Nejd. Today, some sections of the tribe live in the vicinity where many of them settled.

At present, the Otaibah live in all of central **Saudi Arabia**, from Riyadh in the east to Qassim. The Otaibah are all Sunni Muslims. They cooperate with the rulers of Saudi Arabia, and many of them serve in its armed forces and in the National Guard. Their exact count is unknown, since no reliable statistics exist.

OUDAYA. Oudaya is a **Moroccan** tribe, and was formerly a very powerful Arab tribe that formed a large confederation, founded by the Meknassa tribe, which settled in the region of Taza. As there was only one *reha* (contingent of soldiers) left in the region, in the 20th century, the rest of the tribe left the region of Taza at the time of the Idrissid to settle around Meknes, and another fraction settled in Larach. The Oudayas are divided into three groups: the first around Fez and Meknes, another in the neighborhood of Rabat, and the third in the region of Marrakesh.

They served under the Alawites, from Moulay Sliman until Moulay Abderrahman, the *makhzen* (the royal guard) of the sultan. Very troublesome, they played an active role in the change of reigns and imposed their will on the sultans. Moulay Abderrahman dispersed them into fractions and divided them into three tribes that carried their name, in the regions of Fez and Meknes, Rabat, and Marrakesh.

OULAD DELIM. This tribe is a Moorish tribe that **wanders** along the Atlantic coast of Cape Timiris and of Arguin Bay and at the estuary of Seguia-Al-Hamra River and Dra River. In the east and northeast, the Oulad Delim border with the Reguiebat and the Aroussiin, in the north with the Reguiebat-Sahel and **Tekna**-Sahel, and in the south with the Oulad-bou-Sba. This is a **Sahrawi** tribe, with origins from pure fighting Arab invaders, forming part of the Hassane's ruling, fighting, and social stratum, and fluent in Hassaniya **Arabic**.

The ancestors of the tribe are thought to be: Oudei, the son of Hassan (maybe the Prophet Muhammad's grandson), who had a son by his little servant girl Delima, who grew up and put to flight his enemies. However, there is another legend that Delim was the son of Hassan himself. This is a legend taken from the Arabic novel *Antar*. They were involved in the Arab invasions of **Mauritania** in the 14th, 16th, and 17th centuries. In 1913, according to a book by P. Marty (1913), the Oulad Delim were divided into two groups: the Remeithia, descendants of Remaith, and the Oulad-Chouikh, descendants of Chouikh. Both groups numbered approximately six hundred **tents** each at that time.

In 1860, Captain Vincent, officer of General Louis Faidherbe, met them while going up the Adrar River. The tribe attacked the French explorers, who noted that the Moors were mounted on **camels**, they had excellent **horses**, and they would be informed of any caravan passing within their reach. Tribesmen as young as 12 were known to the French to carry guns. Two main cities in the region were St. Louis and Port-Etienne. From 1909, there is a record of a certificate of submission (deed of surrender) that the Oulad Delim signed with the French army. There is also a record of battles with the Reguiebat in which 350 fighters were slain.

The Oulad Delim are mainly concentrated in the southern regions of the western Sahara, in the city of Dakhla. They have many tribal contacts with the northern Mauritanian population and are Muslims, belonging to the Maliki Islamic school. They are **nomadic**, rear camels, and resisted European colonization in the 19th century. But after Spain gained control over Spanish Sahara, they resided in the Rio-de-Oro region and joined the Tropas Nomadas or Spanish auxiliary forces.

The Oulad-Delim had no **agriculture** and no industry, except for the manufacture of artifacts of wood, iron, and leather. They had a small fishing industry and imported tobacco, sugar, and tea from Guinea. *See also* MOROCCO.

OULED BOU SBAA. The Ouled Bou Sbaa is a **Moroccan** tribe. The tribe mixed with the **Sanhaja** tribes and the **Berber** tribes of Haouz of Marrakesh. They formed part of the Hamdana **Himyari** tribe of **Yemen**. They based themselves in Fez, in the reign of the Lemtouna (Almoravids). On their arrival they first mixed with the Sanhaja. Youssef Ben Tashfin confided the command of the Sanhaja to one Ouled Bou Sbaa member. The latter died, leaving children. The sultan then decided that the name Ouled Bou Sbaa would be given to a group of Sanhaja, of Berbers and converted Jews commanded by the deceased, and his progeny disappeared in the mass.

In 1782, under the reign of Sidi Muammed Ben Abdullah, an important colony of the tribe lived in Marrakesh. The perpetual brawls that they raised in the town tired the sultan, who expelled them in little groups to the Moroccan south. They descended gradually to the south and at the end of the 18th century reached Adrar. They were **traders** and got by with raising beasts.

OULED EL HAJ. Ouled El Haj is a **Moroccan** tribe. This is a semisedentary, seminomadic tribe of Arab origin. It recognized the authority of Sultan Moulay Hassan I. They had a *caid* elected from among them who was recognized by the sultan. He was denounced by one of his cousins, Moulay Hassan, and was put in prison. The denunciator took the title of caid. He was killed in 1882, and since then the tribe has been leaderless; each faction rules itself as it pleases. Only three factions, those of Bani Riis, Ahl Rashid, and Ouled Admer, submit to the caid of Taza.

P

PAHLAVI, MOHAMMAD REZA SHAH (1919–1980). Mohammad Reza Shah Pahlavi wanted to consolidate **Iran** under his rule. As the first step, he got rid of Prime Minister Mohammed Mossadeq, who had led the attempt to nationalize the oil industry. This move was aided by the Central Intelligence Agency (CIA), which protected the American interests. His second political move was aimed to reduce the tribal strength in Iran. The shah was fairly successful in his policies due to military and economic support of his new protector, the United States. He published decrees of land reforms and nationalization of grazing land in an attempt to force the **nomad** tribes to settle. He also tried to integrate them by assimilation and the erasing of their culture; schools were permitted to teach only in Persian, and the same rule was applied to publishing houses and broadcasting.

These efforts to undermine tribal integrity led to resentment and rejection of the regime, especially among the **Kurds**, Baluch, **Turkmen**, and **Qashqai** tribes, who sought help from beyond the borders. The dissident Baluch received support from **Iraq** in retaliation of the shah's support of their rebellious Kurds. The tribes had many objections; they lost property and were marginalized. However, as it happens in other countries, regardless of the enforced use of Persian **language** on the young generation, increasing literacy caused an increase of ethnic awareness and the educated well-traveled circles developed "high" political consciousness. *See also* PAHLAVI, REZA SHAH (1878–1944); QAJAR DYNASTY.

PAHLAVI, REZA SHAH (1878–1944). Reza Shah Pahlavi tried to forge a modern nation-state by reducing competition among powers and political loyalties; therefore, he paid special attention to the tribes. His efforts were supported by the urban intellectuals, who perceived **tribalism** as an anachronism. Reza Shah Pahlavi took advantage of enmities among tribes by using tribal elements in his army to suppress local tribes in other parts of the country and sent the **Qashqai** forces against the Lur. Later, he founded a modern army, with no tribal elements, and used it to crush them all. It adopted strict measures against tribal leaders, like execution, imprisonment, or exile, installed military governors, disarmed some groups, settled **nomads** by force, issued rules against traditional **dress**, outlawed the official usage of non-Persian **languages**, and imposed other discriminating rules.

These policies politicized tribal ethnic identity among the non-Persins tribes, and in fact, they reduced the minorities' loyalty to the state. After his abdication (1941), foreign powers renewed their interests in **Iran** and interfered in its internal politics. The tribes were given room to recover from the repressive policies of the previous regime. They were recognized, and their leaders were allowed to participate in state administration and represent their tribes on the political scene. Families of previously condemned people were partially compensated, and people in exile were allowed to return. The **Qajar** regime even encouraged tribes to collaborate with agents of foreign powers. *See also* PAHLAVI, MOHAMMAD REZA SHAH (1919–1980).

PALESTINE. When the Ottomans conquered the area they recognized its importance as a bridge between continents, and its special status as a holy land for three **religions**: Judaism, **Christianity**, and **Islam**. At the beginning of their rule, they invested in development of the country and the well-being of its residents. They restrained the Bedouins and stopped their penetrations. However, when the empire's interest was shifted elsewhere, due to external threats, the Ottomans withdrew their troops from the area, and thus security dwindled and the Bedouins gained power and practically "ruled the land." The increase of their power was a result of a weakening of the central control and the flow of weapons they received both from Ottoman officials and from European **traders**. They also stole weaponry from the army storage. By trading, toward the end of the 19th century, other elements got involved, and the Bedouins lost their dominance over the land.

Muhammad Ali, the ruler of **Egypt**, was involved in the power struggle with the Ottomans and conquered **Syria** and Palestine and ruled these provinces for 10 years from 1831 to 1840. He left the region only after intervention of the superpowers, notably Great Britain and Austria-Hungary, who supported the Ottoman Empire. The Bedouin tribes opposed every government, and similarly they opposed the Egyptian rule. They raided places, attacked commerce and travelers, and caused instability in security. One of the main triggers to their revolt was taxation (until then, Muslim residents were exempt) and rules against protection fees, which for many Bedouins were the main source of income.

The governor Ibrahim Pasha (son of Muhammad Ali) used the army to impose law and order. His conduct led to several local clashes and an open revolt in north Palestine, in 1934, when the governor stopped payments to the Huara tribe for their contribution to the security of the roads and the passage of the *hajj* convoys.

The inhabitants of the coastal plain between Carmel and Atlit, led by the **Madi** house, which was the principal dynasty in the area, joined the revolt, and when it was suppressed, they lost their leader and their status. As a result of these events, the Egyptians used a firm hand against all the Bedouin tribes that participated in the revolt. Many of them were conscripted into the army or sent to be employed in the dockyards in hard labor.

Ibrahim Pasha forced the sedentary population to help the Egyptians against the Bedouins. He managed to convince the **sheikhs** of the central mountain ridge to disarm the people and leave the security to the army. They succeeded in disarming the villagers but failed to disarm the Bedouins. Thus, Ibrahim Pasha changed his policy and made efforts to settle the Bedouins in order to control them. The project began in the Horan region, and was also implemented in the Jordan Valley and in the Gaza region, but it was not very successful, as his rule was short lived. Later Ibrahim Pasha renewed previous arrangements and paid the Bedouins a protection tax to ensure a convoy's safe passage.

The British conquered Palestine in 1918, and this brought a marked change to government–Bedouin relations under the British mandate of the League of Nations. For the first time, a government initiated action designed to help and improve the Bedouins' life. It provided help in years of drought, established schools, initiated the foundation of tribal courts, recognized the legality of tribal law, and founded schools for Bedouin children. It expanded the **educational** system in the Beer Sheva district and, for the first time, built high schools for the Bedouin population.

It also protected their rights to their land, or at least partially so in some disputed areas. It even gave some Bedouin tribes a *kushan* (bill of purchase) on their land.

The actions of the British in the land disputes brought forth an improvement of the relations between Bedouins and Jews, who accepted the rights of tenant farmers and looked for adequate satisfactory solutions in undetermined situations. Therefore, Jewish–Bedouin relations did not create friction between the Jews and British.

The mandate authorities abandoned the sympathetic policy when the Bedouins participated in the Palestinian revolt of 1936–1939, which was carried out against the Jewish population and against the mandate authorities. The British used harsh measures against the militant gangs and against the villages that provided assistance to them. As tribal villages gave refuge to rebels, the British fined their sheikhs. Before the riots broke out, the sheikhs whose tribes lived near the Iraq Petroleum Company (IPC) oil pipeline were paid to safeguard it from attacks. However, when the terror activity was renewed on a large scale, the preventive measures failed. As a result, the

British built roads to enable military vehicles to penetrate the mountainous interior in pursuit of terrorist gangs. The British also increased punitive measures against villages suspected of facilitating sabotage actions.

As the terror continued, the British activated both army and police. They undertook searches, confiscated arms, made arrests, and so on. Eventually they established military courts that were permitted to pass a death sentence for actions of sabotage and murder. The first execution took place on November 1937, and the first gang militant who was executed was the Bedouin sheikh Farhan al-Saadi.

Prior to the Israeli War of Independence in 1948, the British were sympathetic to the **Negev Bedouins** in "return" for their help. They tried to persuade the sheikhs to remain where they were and equipped them with arms to fight off the Jews to prevent them from taking over the Negev and making it part of the new Jewish state since they wanted to create a large neutral zone as a strategic backing for their interest in the Suez Canal.

The relations between the Jews (and later Israelis) and Bedouins in Palestine changed during different periods, according to circumstances, other environmental factors, prejudices, and the precise groups they belonged to. The Jews who emigrated from Europe looked down on the Bedouins, but on the other hand, they were willing to help improve their situation, while other Jews who spoke the **language** either formed good relations with them or were afraid of them, depending on their previous history.

The Bedouin attitude toward the Jews was not uniform, as some treated them as they treated other farming people: they raided their **settlements**, ruined fields, or asked for protection fees, while others appreciated services or identified mutual interests and chose to cooperate with them. Fights ensued mostly over grazing rights, as the settlers acted according to the principle of a landowner, whereas the Bedouins wondered how their animals could be prevented from grazing on grass given by God, which they considered ownerless, as oftentimes the previous owner did not reside in the country and the land was neglected for generations. Other disputes arose with seminomadic people who were either squatters or land tenants, who after land transactions were often evacuated from their homes without warning.

Nevertheless, other types of relations also developed between these two populations, as when a group of Bedouin leaders from the Negev, who sought development that would improve their economic situation, sent a delegation to the Jewish leadership and offered to allocate land to Jews for settlement in the region. Soon enough, the settlers and their Bedouin neighbors cooperated and shared objectives and ownership of livestock. Jewish colonies employed Bedouins as guards and escorts, and used their **camels** as means of transportation for their produce.

The mutual dependency that developed strengthened relations between the Jews and the Bedouins and led to some outlandish ideas to form an alliance to throw off the Ottoman regime. Also, the Jewish Israeli-born youth romanticized the brave Bedouin on his noble **horse** and imitated his appearance to a degree.

The evolution of national sentiment among Palestinian Arabs and rise of the Arab National movement affected the bilateral Jewish–Bedouin relations, as some Bedouin tribes that had good relations with the Jews fought on their side, while other tribes that had long-standing connections with the Palestinian elements fought on the Palestinian side. The attitudes of the Jews also were modified due to increased settlement and Zionism. *See also* AL-HASI, AQIL AGA (?–1870); DABKA; FOOD; ISRAEL; JAZZAR, AHMED (1720–1804); MUSIC AND DANCE; OMAR, DAHER EL- (1689–1775); PALESTINIAN AUTHORITY; PALHIB; URBANIZATION.

PALESTINIAN AUTHORITY. The Bedouins in the Palestinian Authority live in the two main regions of the Gaza Strip and on the West Bank. As for the Gaza Strip, most of the Bedouins who live today in the region originate from the **Negev**. They had passed into the region after the 1948 war. They lived in the refugee camps in the Gaza Strip; likewise parts of them live in the eastern region of the Gaza Strip, mainly in the region between the Gaza River and the city of Rafiah. The Bedouins in the strip founded a number of Bedouin villages such as Hajr el-Dik, Matzadra, Netzer, Karara, Wadi el-Dik, Tzarara, and so on.

On the West Bank they live in the Jerusalem/Bethlehem region. The tribes in the bank region had already penetrated into the region during the period of the Ottoman rule. They underwent a process of permanent **settlement** and they founded a number of villages such as **Sawahra** east of Jerusalem, Arab Abid east of Sawahra, Arab **Taamra** east of the town of Bethlehem, Arab Kaabna east of Hebron, and Arab Jahalin in the Hebron region. Likewise there are Bedouins in the villages of Yata, Samua, and Bani Naim, and in the refugee camps in Hebron and Bethlehem.

The history of the Bedouins in **Palestine** goes back a long way. It started with the Arab invasion of Palestine in the 7th century, following which the Bedouins settled in some of the coastal villages and coastal plain areas. This continued into the Mameluke period from the 13th to 16th centuries, in those same lowland areas. Scholars say that environmental factors determined the decline of the existing populations in settlements in these regions. In the Baysan valley south of Lake Kinneret, the Bedouin tribe Arab al-Sakhr originated from Hejaz or Najd in the Arabian Peninsula and the Ghazawiyya traced its ancestry to the Misl al-Jizel tribes in Houran.

There is a striking historical-geographical study of Palestine toward the end of the 16th century, a short time after the Ottoman occupation, with a map of the Bedouin tribes at that time. In this study, Wolf-Dieter Hutteroth and Kamal Abdulfattah examined the Ottoman tax lists of 1596, and found details of 43 **nomadic** tribes, some coming from **Turkey** and Kurdistan. These tribes determined the stability of the rural settlement, and they used the loss of centralized governmental authority to reinforce their settlement. These tribes no longer existed in the region in the 19th century.

A geographical survey by the British Palestine Exploration Fund (PEF) from 1880, which was the most detailed map of that country of the time, showed about 67 Bedouin tribes within the borders of what became Mandatory Palestine, after the defeat of the Ottomans in 1917, by General Edmund Allenby's army. The regions dominated by the Bedouins had enlarged, so the rural landscape was less settled and cultivated than four hundred years previously. On the other hand, one of the members of the PEF, Claude R. Conder, noted that the settlers were gaining ground and eroding the Bedouin presence.

The Ottomans made great efforts to settle the Bedouins on land in the Negev **Desert** and in the Jordan Valley, in the Wadi Besor, in Asluj, which is the site of a *makam* (holy place) and a well (*Bir Asluj*), where the Ottomans constructed a railway bridge. There was also the presence of Bedouin tribes in the Sharon Valley, like the Ghawarina, who had been imported as **slaves** from **Egypt** and lived in malaria-ridden reed swamps (like the Kabara swamp in this region) and raised buffaloes. In another well-known part, Antuan Bishara al-Tayan, a Lebanese Maronite, purchased 30,826 dunams of land in Wadi Hawarith for the Hawarith tribe.

Also in the Hula marshland, three thousand Ghawarina tribesmen, who had come in 1830, during the Egyptian occupation under Mohamed Ali, experienced a "high degree of **sedentarization**." The Ottoman government gave 1,500 of them 15,000 dunams out of the 52,000 dunams swamp, on which they could live. This centered around the village of Zawiya by the Zawiya stream. The Zionists and the British government later drained the reed-covered marshes. Later in the Ottoman period, the arrival of new technology weakened the Bedouin dominance in this region.

In the 1922 census, the mandate authorities registered 120 members of a tribe they erroneously called "Nabi Rubin" and four hundred of a tribe called "Sutariyeh," who had settled around the Rubin River near the great shrine of Nabi Rubin, in Palestine. In contrast to this, in the Baysan subdistrict, 40 percent of the population was Bedouin; most of the lowland had been owned by the sultan, and the high commissioner Sir Herbert Samuel took notice of this. The government signed the Ghor-Mudawarra Land Agreement (GMLA), and 179,545 dunams of land were transferred to the Bedouins to settle, in three tribal areas. Later, much of this was sold to the Jewish National Fund and other Arab effendis or Jewish groups. However, the Bedouins had built several small villages here.

The Bedouins also settled in three settlements by the springs in the Jericho district, in the Nablus subdistrict, and in the Haifa district in the Jezreel Valley. Thus, until the last few years of the 19th century, the Bedouins controlled and had authority in large areas of Palestine, but the introduction of modern technology and the destruction of the forests curtailed this. Land deals paved the way for the creation of new Bedouin villages, which contained 27,844 inhabitants according to the census of 1945. The Bedouin raids (*ghazzu*) occurred for the last time in 1920 and then stopped.

In present-day Palestine, 15 percent of the population derives from a tribal origin, and in Gaza the proportion is 25 percent. There are three **clan**-like structures in the Palestinian society. The first is the tribes themselves, which have undergone a process of detribalization due to the end of the mobility of the Bedouin community in Palestine. In Gaza, the tribes are grouped into six tribal confederations (*saffs*), each of which contains a dozen or more individual tribes (*asha'ira*). The main confederations in Gaza are the Hayawat, **Tarabin**, Tiyaha, Ijbara, Azazme, and Jahalin. The tribes in the West Bank are concentrated in the hills east of Hebron, with a small part in the east of Jerusalem and in the western part of the Jordan Valley.

The second is the clan-like structure, and the clans have increased in importance since the collapse of the structure of the Palestinian Authority, after the second intifada that started in 2000. The clan or *hamula* contains several interconnected extended families (*a'ila*), with common forefathers, in the father's male lineage. The *a'ila* includes males first, and then second cousins and female children who marry outside the *hamula* will join the other *hamula*. Clans are historically organized in order to cultivate shared lands (*musha'a*). This changed with the Ottoman Land Law of 1858, which recognized private property.

The third clan-like element is the urban elite family, which exists throughout the former Ottoman Empire countries. Many prominent Palestinian families come from this notable, or *a'yan*, class, like the Husseini, Nashashibi, Dajani, Khouri, Khatib, Masri, Barghouti, and others. They previously dominated the Palestinian political life until the 1980s. The Ottomans used these families to mediate between them and the local population, and the notables included military officers, religious *'ulama*, and merchants. They also, since the Ottoman Land Law of 1858, became major landowners. **Israel** undermined their authority, as it confiscated land in order to establish Israeli settlements on the West Bank. Also the emergence of an educated middle class, which supported the Palestine Liberation Organization (PLO), eroded their influence. As opposed to the clans, when the state was weak the notables were weak, and only a strong state would enable the notables to use political stability to exert their power.

After the Oslo accords of 1994, Yasser Arafat endorsed a "policy of antithesis" so as to consolidate the power of the PLO elite, which returned from **Tunis**. He implemented the "tribalization" of PLO politics by encouraging patronage and a personality cult. When parliamentary elections to the Palestinian Assembly were held in January 1996, clans became kingmakers in their own districts, and **sheikhs** and local patriarchs were favored by the home district, first-past-the-post electoral system. Also the Palestinian Authority (PA) established the Department of Tribal Affairs, which legitimized and empowered clans, and enforced the Bedouin "informal" method of justice, the ***sulha***.

However, during this period, after the start of the second intifada in 2000, Israel destroyed many Palestinian police stations and security force buildings, and infighting started between the Palestinian tribal factions. When income became scarce, the clans often provided jobs for their own unemployed, but there was prevalent malnutrition and deprivation. Smuggling of fuel, consumer goods, and cigarettes via tunnels from Egypt and kidnapping became common sources of revenue for some clans in the Gaza Strip.

After Arafat's death, the last source of control of the PA over the clans lapsed, and the new PA chairman, Mahmoud Abbas, is known to have fewer links with these clans. By 1995, most of the Bedouin population in the West Bank lived in area C, which was determined as comprising 60 percent of the West Bank territory under the Oslo Agreement. On account of the barriers imposed by military checkpoints and the Wall of Separation, the Bedouins have difficulty in gaining access to sources of **water** and pastures for grazing. Also recently, in 2007, 2008, and 2009, drought caused a severe problem for farming livestock in Palestine, and water prices have increased from 5 NIS (New Israeli Shekels) per cubic meter to 20 NIS for transportation to their camps, and the price of fodder has grown by 300 percent.

After the Hamas victory in the January 2006 parliamentary elections, lawlessness decreased for a time in Gaza, as before then the murder rate had risen by 50 percent from 2005 to 2006; the use by the clans of roadblocks and accompanying extortion was banned, the use of gunfire at weddings was also banned, and people were not permitted to wear masks in public. Hamas freed the BBC journalist Alan Johnston from a kidnapping in 2007. Hamas also learned how to play off the clans, one against the other, by the "divide-and-conquer" method, and supported smaller clans against larger ones. It is necessary to wait and see what effect the current (July 2014) conflict with Israel in the Protective Edge Operation will have on the Gaza clan structure and on Palestine in general. *See also* JORDAN; URBANIZATION; WANDERING.

PALHIB. Palhib was a Bedouin unit of the Arab el-**Heib** in the **Israeli** Upper **Galilee** that joined the **Israel Defense Forces** (IDF) in 1948, during the War of Independence. They were part of the Palmah, the fighting unit of the *Hagana* (defense) organization, long before the war started. They mediated between the Jews and Druze, performed reconnaissance actions, and helped to protect the Jewish population in the Galilee from attacks.

The **tribe** tied its fate to the fate of the Jewish population, as both parties helped each other in times of need. The Palhib unit began as a company, grew to a platoon, and later became a battalion, which served directly under Igal Alon, the Israeli Galilee commander, who spoke their **language** and gained their trust. Their first commanding officers were Jewish, but in time, many Bedouins became officers. The Bedouins' military cooperation with the IDF led to the formation of tracker units, which eventually developed into reconnaissance units and special commandos.

The Palhib was the first minority unit that openly joined the IDF, to be followed later by other Bedouin tribes and other minorities like the Druze and the Circassians. Today most Bedouin youth serve in the Israeli Army and in other law enforcement organizations, like the police, the border police private agencies, and the Municipal Security System.

PEACE LAW (1980). This law, which was legislated by the state of **Israel**, was designed to confiscate the territory in the Arad Valley (Tel-Malhata) and to enable the transfer of a military airport from **Sinai** to **Negev**, as provided for by the peace agreement with Egypt. The law was passed in light of the unwillingness of the Bedouins to be evacuated from a territory that Israel claimed was state land but that the Bedouins claimed they were the owners of, although they had no legal documents testifying to this, or their claim that they had lived in this territory since the period of the Ottoman Empire.

The state legislated the law after it saw that the Bedouins were not prepared to evacuate willingly and in light of the fact that the evacuation of the land was urgent for the establishment of the airport. In the framework of the law, the Bedouins were offered a real financial return for land, which was significantly large. The possessors of the land received free plots from the state in the Bedouin townships of **Kuseife** and Ararah in the Negev.

The Peace Law determined for the first time that the state recognized the right of the Bedouins to the land, to which they did not have a *tabu* (ownership). Despite the innovations in the Peace Law, the state implemented it defectively—the registration of the land was done negligently, many Bedouins did not obtain registration of their lands in the tabu, and the planning of the **settlements** was done poorly.

On the one hand, the Peace Law constituted an important precedent in the attitude of the state of Israel toward its Bedouin citizens, but at the end of the day, it did not constitute a true model of achieving compromises of land and helping to end the land conflict between the Bedouins and the state.

PEARL DIVING. Before the discovery of oil in the 20th century, the local population in **Bahrain** dealt, as a principal occupation, with extraction of pearls from the sea, and it constituted an important factor in the foreign **trade** of Bahrain. Pearl diving in the region was an ancient occupation. There exists evidence of pearl diving from the Persian Gulf sea floor since the Neolithic period, both for local needs and also for goals of trade, apparently with Mesopotamia. After a lull during the Bronze Age, an extensive and well-organized pearl industry emerged whose center was in Bahrain, although this concept at that time dealt with a much more extensive area than that of the modern state of Bahrain. This industry gave an answer to the great demand for pearls in the Roman Empire. In the Middle Ages the trade in pearls grew. The pearls were taken out from Bahrain and designated for the elite layers of society, during the days under the rule of the Umayyad caliphate and the start of the rule of the **Abbasid** caliphate. Starting at the end of the 15th century until the start of the 17th century a decline took place in the scope of the industry, apparently due to the discovery of alternative sources of pearls in America. However, this competition was short-lived, and after the Safavid Empire (Iran) conquered Bahrain in the year 1602, approximately, the pearls served for financing the spread of the Shia all over the empire.

During the 17th century the religious and commercial elite in Bahrain took over the industry and started to manage pearl diving. In addition, the rise in demand for pearls in India brought migrants to Bahrain. In the 18th century the industry became the main factor that underlined the power struggles in the region, during which it caused great harm, and the municipal centers in it declined. Alongside this, competitive industrial centers developed in Qatar and **Kuwait**. However, in 1820, the British Empire gave the control of the state to the Al-Khalifa family, which rules it even today, and this move stabilized the security situation in the state and also brought development of trade in additional fields.

In this period the town of Muharraq started to stand out as the center of the pearl industry, and it became the biggest city in the Persian Gulf, with six thousand inhabitants in it. The pearl industry in Bahrain reached its peak in the last quarter of the 19th century and at the start of the 20th century, until the state supplied 80 percent of the world's consumption and the industry employed 30,000 people. In the 1930s, the pearl industry of Bahrain collapsed totally, within a short time, when Japan started commercial growth of freshwater oysters for the extraction of pearls. The end of the industry and the discovery of **oil** in the central island of Bahrain brought mass emigration from Muharraq, and the city lost its centrality.

It is worth noting that the Al-Khalifa tribe, which rules Bahrain today, and which succeeded in becoming rich from pearl diving while they still lived in Qatar, succeeded—thanks to their wealth—in conquering Bahrain from the Persians at the end of the 18th century. Furthermore, with their domination of the region, they also controlled the pearl market and with the discovery of oil during the 20th century, they took control of the oil industry, and today they control the economy and politics in the kingdom of Bahrain, together with their allies—the members of the Sunni tribes.

PERISHED. This term refers to Arab tribes that no longer exist, but some of them are mentioned in the Koran, and some early historians mentioned others. A list of the perished tribes include **Aad**, **Thamud**, Tasm, Jadis, Imlaq, and others. Two of these tribes, Taam and Jadis, perished by genocide, while the others were defeated, driven away, or scattered. Recent archaeological excavations in the ruins of ancient Iram, a major city of the perished Aad and Imlaq, disclosed inscriptions suggesting that this name is the singular form of Amaleeq, which may have been the biblical Amalek. *See also* PRE-ISLAMIC PERIOD.

POETRY. Bedouin poetry has many functions. By means of poetry the Bedouin expresses his problems and his joys, transmits essential information to those found at a distance, sends messages to his allies, and sends warnings to his rivals. Bedouin poetry is the fruit of a **desert** tradition, four thousand years old.

Bedouin poetry truly transfers the tradition like the legend, the **fable**, the saying, and the judgment tradition. Bedouin poetry is a poetry of rhymes. It is personal and intimate poetry, which is mainly directed at a small public audience—for example, a small group around a bonfire.

The Bedouins see this poetry, which is called *qasida*, as serious poetry. It is written on an emotional background, whether it is joy or sadness. The motives for the composition of poetry may be anger, fear, astonishment, joy, or pride. Bedouin poetry is folk poetry, and the folk poet builds his poem from stereotypical expressions and familiar patterns of **language** and figures that suit the subject of discussion. It is possible that these expressions have existed already from the **pre-Islamic period**.

The world of Bedouin poetry is wide and rich in variations. Its essence depends on its transfer by word of mouth, from **tent** to tent, and from generation to generation. A good poem would be passed around in tents and become common. An unsuccessful poem was forgotten as soon as it was born. *See also* FOLK STORY; MUSIC AND DANCE.

POLYGAMY. Polygamy is a marital connection with several **women**, usually two but sometimes three. Polygamy was practiced in the past in various cultures, and today it is widespread chiefly in Africa, Asia, and the Middle East especially among Muslims. Among the Bedouin population, polygamy is still a central social institution, which, to a great extent, is connected to the patriarchal social structure, and to the importance of the group and the tribe. Polygamy is a pattern of life in which a man manages a household with a number of wives. This lifestyle is widespread among the Bedouin society. This custom exists also among other populations.

The Koran permits the Muslim man to marry up to four wives. The man is permitted to choose a new wife if he believes that his former wife is infertile, cannot give birth to sons, is physically or mentally sick, or cannot satisfy him sexually. If one of these reasons does not exist he can declare his desire to increase the number of children. The prohibition fixed in criminal law against polygamous marriage does not deter the Bedouins in **Israel** from maintaining such a lifestyle.

The status of a woman living in the framework of a polygamous family is inferior to that of women living in a system in which there are two spouses alone. This relationship leads to competition and unjust division of the resources found in the hands of the family, leading to jealousy and hostility between the wives and the children of every wife. Beyond this, in most of the cases, it is possible to find a difference in the difficulty that the first or senior wife encounters, as to who the husband preferred over them, in relation to the second and newer wives. Although in certain societies the status of the first wife is higher than that of the second wife, in Bedouin society in Israel the situation is just the opposite.

Many times the connection of the husband with a new wife leads to neglect and ignoring of the first wife and her children. In this situation, the wife feels a need to struggle for her existence and status in the extended family framework. Thus, a polygamous marriage many times leads to a decrease in social and economic status of both the first wife and her children.

The children constitute a primary factor in fixing the status of a woman in Bedouin society. The power and status of a Bedouin woman are measured according to the number of children she brings to the world, and chiefly the number of boys.

A large number of boys is essential to society in order to strengthen the physical and economic power of the family, and chiefly in order to increase the extended Bedouin family, as the size of the family influences the location of the family in the social hierarchy. Therefore, the more sons the woman gives birth to, the higher her value in the eyes of her husband, her family members, and the extended family. The other skills of the woman, like handiwork, cooking, and cleaning, are less important than her capacity to give birth to as many children as possible. This is the situation in a Bedouin society in general, and among others in a polygamous family. *See also* EDUCATION; FOOD; HOSPITALITY; LAW, BEDOUIN.

PRE-ISLAMIC PERIOD. In the pre-Islamic period (*Al-Jahiliyya*) the Arabian Peninsula was inhabited by a tribal society of common ethnic origin and a common **language**. In ancient times some groups of tribes got organized under a strong leadership and built a kingdom that lasted either until environmental circumstances changed or they were invaded by armies of foreign countries. However, around the 1st century AD, the stronger kingdom in the peninsula disintegrated (the central dam had collapsed) and only small kingdoms remained at the fringes: in **Yemen** and Hadrmout. The vast expanse of the center was inhabited by nomadic tribes and a number of sedentary tribes, which cultivated the areas near and around the **water** sources. The tribe became the largest reference group, but within the tribes there were smaller units, parts of clans, to which the individual felt a link and identification and in whose framework he gained protection.

The scarcity of water and grazing land and control of strategic locations caused disputes and wars among the tribes, and family members protected each other. The lack of a central legal system and courts led the tribes to develop alternative laws and characteristic manners and behavior patterns. In the pre-Islamic period the tribes in the Arabian Peninsula followed various religious convictions: some were pagans worshipping man-made idols, some accepted Judaism, and others adopted a modified version of **Christianity**. Non-monotheist tribes worshiped trees, springs, and spirits. Those who worshipped Allah believed that he is superior to all other Gods. From the start of civilization, the holiest site in the peninsula was believed to be and still is the *Kaabah*, in the town of Makkah (today know as Mecca).

The nomadic tribes in the Arabian Peninsula followed their herds in an endless search for water and grazing areas. They used **camels** for transport, but they also used their milk, fed on their flesh, and used their droppings to light a fire. The sedentary population lived in stone houses in towns like Yatrib (the former name of Medina) and Makkah, and in mud houses in small villages, built near constant water sources. The nomads traded wool, mutton, and milk for grain, dates, vegetables, and other commodities made in the city or brought over from other places.

Other tribes, which lived in the coastal area of the Gulf, developed some maritime skills such as fishing and **pearl diving**. As Makkah attracted pilgrims and commerce, its residents made a pact with the tribe to secure and defend the caravans and **trade** routes.

As all tribes worshipped the *Kaabah*, the months of pilgrimage and worship were sanctioned, and tribe members were forbidden to fight among themselves. As Makkah became the central focus for all, the rulers of the city who were members of the **Quraysh** tribe, who were protectors of the *Kaabah* and organizers of the ceremonies, gained immense power and respect. See also ISLAM; SAUDI ARABIA.

Q

QAHTANITES. Qahtanis or Qahtanites are a group of Arab people who descended from tribes originating in the southern (Yemenite) part of the Arabian Peninsula. It is claimed that according to Arab tradition a mythical figure called Qahtan (and his 24 sons) was the forefather of these inhabitants of southern Arabia, and he is identified with Yoktan son of Eber of the Hebrew Bible. Azaal and Hadramaut were two of the principal sons of Qahtan, and another was Yarub, who was the father of Yashjub and the grandfather of Abd Shams, or Saba. All the Yemenite tribes trace their origins back to Saba, through Himyar or Kahlan, his two sons.

The Qahtan tribe is divided into two subtribes: the Himyar and the Kahlan, who make up the settled Arab population of southern Arabia and some nomadic brethren. The Kahlan in itself is divided into four subgroups: the Tayy; the **Azd**, which conquered **Oman**; the Amila-Judham of Palestine; and the Hamdan-Madhhij, which stayed chiefly in **Yemen**.

Between the 7th and 14th centuries, there was Arab expansionism and colonization of territories stretching between Spain and China, and the Qahtan formed part of this process. They intermingled with the local populations but preserved their knowledge of their ancestry. Arabs of a Qahtanite origin can be found in **Morocco** or **Iran**, and many of them are familiar with their genealogy, which has been thoroughly researched. A distinguished scion of the Qahtan tribe was the scholar **Ibn Khaldun**, who was born in **Tunisia** from parents who had left Andalusian Islamic Spain. *See also* PRE-ISLAMIC PERIOD; SAUDI ARABIA.

QAJAR DYNASTY. The Qajar dynasty ruled in **Iran** from 1796 to 1925 and sought to administer tribes while relying on their support. A third to one-half of Iran's population was then tribal, and the rulers tried to send the tribes to frontier regions, which was an ineffective and overly expensive policy. It adopted a principle of indirect rule through appointed tribal leaders, who were responsible for raising taxes, collecting military levies, and managing security in their own territories. The rule of the Qajars did not reach much beyond Tehran; they lacked physical means of enforcement and a standing army; and princes, tribal leaders, and clerics had considerable authority in the provinces. As in the case of **Iraq** under **Saddam Hussein**, the rulers sowed dissent between their subordinate tribes in order to apply the principle of divide-and-rule, so the quarreling tribes would not trust each other and would turn to the government for support. Tribal leaders competed against one another, and their relocation changed the tribal formations, so that the local leaders became powerful and formed some of the country's elite. Qajars also used a tactic of holding tribal leaders or their relatives hostage at court or in provincial capitals and making alliances of **marriage** with tribal and elite families. This family made links with representatives of and identified with the **Qashqai** people, whose policy was thus established.

In the second half of the 19th century, European powers vied for strategic, commercial, and political ties to Iran. After 1860, European superpowers including Great Britain and Russia applied the same tactics as the shahs had used in relation to the tribal leaders, by appointing and replacing them, by promising them rewards and punishing them for failure to implement their requests. In this period, the provincial tribes were still in total stronger than the Qajar central government: the foreign bodies undermined Qajar legitimacy, but in the long term delayed the overthrow of the Qajar regime and challenges to it, and sustained it. The Qajar rulers continued to conscript tribal forces to their military, but the foreign powers gradually brought a lesser dependence of the Iranian army on the tribes and strengthened it without them.

In the constitutional revolution of 1906–1911, tribes, particularly the **Bakhtiari**, had great influence in the struggle against Qajar rule, and formed intertribal alliances and alliances with foreign powers. The British, Russians, and Germans took advantage of the tribes for their own interests in the period of World War I, and at the beginning of the 20th century these had more influence than the central Iranian government on the tribes themselves. *See also* PAHLAVI, MOHAMMAD REZA SHAH (1919–1980); PAHLAVI, REZA SHAH (1878–1944).

QASHQAI TRIBE. This Turkish-speaking tribe has a high reputation in the south of **Iran** and stretches from Abadeh and Shahreza in the province of Isfahan to the Persian Gulf. Its main **clans** are Kashkooli, Sheesh Blocki, Khalaj, Farsi Madan, Safi Khani, Bayat, and Darreh Shuyee.

Scholars claim that their ancestors were the Turkish Khalaj clan, who lived between India and the Sistan area of Iran, and then migrated to central and southern Iran. Each clan has a chief, and there was a general leader appointed in historical times. Although they did not play a decisive role in politics, they caused trouble for many regimes.

In the 19th century, the names of 22 Qashqai *tiras* (lineages) were given by the historian Fasa'i, some of which had Lor or Lak origin, as can be seen from their names. The number of *taifas* (clans) in the Qashqai confederacy in 1941 was said to be 27, but this fell to nine in 1962–1963. The number of tiras rose, and a certain *khan* was appointed to manage the affairs of each group of tiras or each taifa. The number of tiras in 1932 was reported to be 90, but in 1961 it had grown to between 180 and 200. In the Qashqai confederacy, each tira was divided into smaller units called *bonki*, and *abonku* is a group of families who migrate seasonally together and share a common pasture.

QURAYSH TRIBE. The Quraysh tribe existed on the Arabian Peninsula, in the city of Makkah, from the 6th until the 8th centuries. Its people were **shepherds** and traders. In the **pre-Islamic period**, the tribe was considered to be one of the strongest tribes in Hijaz, the northwestern part of the Arabian Peninsula.

In the second half of the 4th century, members of the tribe conquered the city of Makkah. According to tradition, Qusai ibn Kilab (400–480), the tribe's leader, rehabilitated the Kaabah and took into his hands the religious posts and the leadership of the city.

His grandson, Hashim ibn 'Abd Manaf (464–497), who was the great-grandfather of the Prophet Muhammad, changed the economic status of Makkah, and according to tradition was responsible for its becoming a center of **trade** and passage. Hashim received a security writ from the Byzantine emperor, called "the Ilaf agreement," which enabled Makkah tradesmen to come with their wares, leather skins, and clothes, up to the Byzantine territory.

According to tradition, the eminent families of the Quraysh tribe in Makkah competed among themselves for the provision of various services to the pilgrims to Makkah, like hosting and the supply of **water**. They levied taxes from the pilgrims and traders, who took advantage of the armistice of El-Haj, the period of pilgrimage, for the purpose of making deals in fairs.

The people of the Quraysh tribe held great prestige in the Arabian Peninsula, and they mediated between the tribes. The members of the tribe did not hold raids for the sake of plunder and robbery, did not have sexual intercourse with **women** prisoners, and did not bury girl babies alive, as was customary among other tribes in periods of hunger.

The most famous member of the Quraysh tribe, by virtue of whom this tribe is remembered in the pages of history, was the Prophet Muhammad. The tribe has an important role in the rise of **Islam**, but in the period of the first wave, apart from some lone persons, all the members of the tribe opposed Muhammad's new **religion**.

At the start of his prophecies, Muhammad set out against the pagan belief of his tribe and the other inhabitants of Makkah. He saw them as heretics, and they saw him as somebody harming their gods, insulting their religion, and scorning their lifestyle. Nonetheless, due to his family pedigree, and due to the defense of his uncle, Abu Talib ibn Abdul Muttalib (c. 549–619), they did not harm him.

After *el-Hijra* and Muhammad's **migration** to the city of al-Madinah in the year AD 622, he returned to Makkah to fight in it. Muhammad, who defeated the townsmen and among them members of his tribe, gained recognition from them as somebody who stood at the head of an independent political, super-tribal factor, which was united around religion and not tied to tribal origin. Muhammad, who did not want a **vendetta**, recruited several members of the Quraysh tribe to his ranks and made them senior officers in his army.

After Muhammad's death in the year 632, the difficult question was who would succeed him in the position of leader of the young Islamic nation. Affiliation to the descendants of the Quraysh tribe became almost a necessary criterion to serve as *khalifa*. All the first four caliphs, after the death of the Prophet Muhammad, were members of the Quraysh tribe: Abu Bakr, Umar ibn Al-Khattāb, Uthman ibn Affan, and Alī ibn Abī Ṭālib.

In the Sunni tradition, affiliation to the Quraysh tribe was a condition for caliphate. In the Shiite tradition, the imams had to be not only members of the Quraysh tribe but also descendants of Ali ibn Abi Talib, Muhammad's cousin, who according to the Shiite tradition, was the heir of Muhammad according to divine order.

R

RABABA. A one-stringed string instrument producing a monotonous magical sound; it is possible to play it for a long time. The sound is a sound of the **desert** atmosphere. It is original and special. The *rababa* is made of leather, and the string is made usually of horsehair. It is customary to play it from twilight until the evening hours. *See also* MUSIC AND DANCE.

RABI'AH. This is the name of the patriarch of one of the two main branches of the so-called "North Arabian" (**Adnanite**) tribes, who according to legend came originally from the Tihamah region of western Arabia. Classical Arab genealogists list the following as descendants of Abd al-Qays of **Bahrain**, in eastern Arabia: the Bakr whose Bedouin sections migrated eastward, but its sedentary section lives in and around Riyadh; the Bani Hanifa in **Saudi Arabia**; the Taghlib who moved to the Al-Jazirah region (northern **Iraq** and northeastern Syria); the Anz who lived in southern Arabia and are said to have perished in the 13th century by the plague, although a tribe named "Rabi'ah" in present-day Asir might be its descendant; and the Anizzah, which was subdivided into a sedentary section called Yamama and a Bedouin section in northern Arabia.

During the **Abbasid** era, many members of Bani Hanifa and related tribesmen from Bakr ibn Wa'il migrated to southern **Egypt**, where they dominated the gold mines of Wadi Allaqi near Aswan. In Egypt all these people were called "Rabi'ah." However, over the years they intermarried with the local tribes, and some of their descendants are called Banu Kanz or Kunooz, after Kanz al-Dawlah, one of the historical leaders of the Bani Hanifa.

RAHAT. This is a large town in southern **Israel**, built specifically for Bedouins and other Arab groups that had no permanent domicile (former **slaves**, work immigrants etc.). According to the Israeli Central Bureau of Statistics, by January 2012, the population count in Rahat was 54,882. It is the largest Bedouin **settlement** in the world, and the only one in Israel to have the status of a city. It is built in a region formerly owned by the Al-Hezeel **clan** of the Al-Tayaha tribe. *See also* NEGEV BEDOUINS; URBANIZATION.

RASHAIDA. This tribe, which is also called Bani Rashid, dwells in Eritrea and northeast **Sudan**, where the tribe migrated in 1846 from Hejaz in contemporary **Saudi Arabia** following tribal fighting there. In their present country they live close to the Beja population, but many are still found on the Arabian Peninsula.

They practice the traditional customs and folklore of Sunni **Islam**. The tribe, which is related to the **Banu Abs** tribe, are proud Arabs, who still keep their traditional **dress**, culture, customs, **camel** breeds, and **religion** (Sunni Islam), and speak "*Hejazi*" **Arabic**. They sell racing camels throughout Sudan and Saudi Arabia for very high prices.

REGUIBAT. This is a **Sahrawi** tribe of the **Berber Sanhaja** confederation that absorbed a number of tribes of Arab origin, which influenced its culture and **language**. The Reguibat speak the Hassaniya Arabic dialect and belong to the Maliki school of Sunni **Islam**. This tribe is historically seminomadic and is famous for its **camel** rearing and its relatively good military success, which has turned it into the most dominant and powerful warrior tribe in the area. This status led to its expansion, and today it is the largest Sahrawi tribe.

The grazing lands of the Reguibat fractions extended from the plains of Western Sahara to northern **Mauritania**, southern **Morocco**, northern Mali, and largely, western **Algeria**.

Reguibat Sahrawi played an important role in the local resistance to European colonialism, and since the 1970s, many of them are active in the Polisario Front resisting Moroccan rule over the sovereignty of Western Sahara.

RELIGION. The main religion in the Middle East is **Islam**. More than 90 percent of the inhabitants of the Middle East are Muslims. Some 80 percent of the Muslims in the area belong to the main faction in Islam—the Sunna. Twenty percent of the Muslims belong to the Shiite faction, and they are concentrated mainly in **Iran**, **Iraq**, and **Lebanon**. Four percent of the inhabitants of the region are **Christians** who are split into various sects: Copts in **Egypt** (who constitute half of the Christians in the Middle East), Maronites in Lebanon (who constitute a third of the population of the Lebanese state), and Catholics and Orthodox in **Israel**, **Jordan**, **Syria**, and Lebanon. Jews make up 2 percent of the inhabitants of the Middle East, and they are concentrated in Israel. The rest are various minorities.

RHAMNA. This is an Arab tribe whose origins date back to the **Yemenite** tribe Bani Maqil, who settled in North Sahara from the 13th to the 15th centuries. In 1525, the Rhamna were conscripted, like other tribes, by the Saadians of Muhammad **Sheikh**, to fight the Portuguese in Agadir, Essaouira, Safi, and El Jadida. In the second half of the 16th century, and after the end of their conscription, the Rhamna occupied a huge area north of Marrakesh, inhabited in the past by the **Berber** Haskoura. They are the brothers of the Yagout living today in Northern Sahara.

In 1912, the Rhamna were on the scene of the battle between Sid Bou Othman, who opposed the French troops under the command of Colonel Charles Mangin, and the troops of Ahmed Al Hiba, son of the chief Ma Al Anain; the defeat of the latter was sealed by the occupation of Marrakesh on the following day. *See also* MOROCCO.

RIZEIGAT. Or Rizigat, or Rezeigat. This is a nomadic tribe of Arab ancestry, one of the **Baggara** (standard Arabic: Baqqara) people in **Sudan**, who live in the region of **Darfur**. The Baggara are the second largest population group in Western Sudan, numbering more than one million members. The Rizeigat are primarily nomadic cattle herders whose movements depend on season and rainfall. The ecological differences between north and south Sudan led to the evolution of two different types of nomadic lifestyle: **camel** herders in the north and cattle herders in the south. Thus, the Rizeigat are subdivided into two major groups: the Abbala (camel **herders**) and the Baggara (cattle -herders), who are subdivided into several large **clans**. The Rizeigat are Muslim Arabs, called **Janjaweed**, a synonym for nomads.

During the conflict with the Sudan People's Liberation Army, the Rizeigat backed the Sudanese government and participated in raids directed at non-Arab people, looting their property and enslaving **women** and children. Thousands of Dinka women and children and an unknown number of children from the Nuba were abducted and subsequently enslaved by members of the **Messiria** and Rizeigat tribes. However, in the recent Darfur conflict the Baggara Rizeigat refused to join the government troops in the persecution of the non-Arab population.

The Abbala Rizeigat people live in northern Sudan, close to the Libyan border. *See also* SLAVERY.

RUWALLAH. Ruwallah is a large Arab tribe residing in northern Arabia and the bordering parts of **Syria** and **Jordan**. The Ruwallah used to be a warrior tribe whose territories stretched from al-Jauf and Wadi al-Sirhan in northern **Saudi Arabia**, southward to al-Qasim, and northwestward to the outskirts of Damascus. The demarcation lines that drew borders in the Middle East in the early 20th century cut off several groups and **clans** from this previously strong tribe, and weakened it considerably. Historically this tribe was a branch of the Dhana Maslam branch of the large Anizzah confederation.

Today, most of the tribe have changed their lifestyle and settled in their countries of residence, Saudi Arabia, Jordan, and Syria. Some of the tribe's members left the Middle East and migrated to faraway countries such as the United States, Australia, Canada, and New Zealand.

S

SABA. Saba was an ancient kingdom (1200 BC–AD 275) whose territory encompassed most of contemporary **Yemen** and parts of the adjacent provinces of contemporary **Saudi Arabia**. The kingdom went through ups and downs, and it is considered to be one of the long-lived kingdoms in history. Its economy was based on **trade** and **agriculture**, as a dam and **water** constructions regulated irrigation-based agriculture, and this kingdom was situated on the fringe of the vast Arabian **Desert**, providing logistic support to caravans. Wealth was accumulated, and the kingdom thrived. The capital of Saba was Ma'rib, whose impressive ruins can be seen in the site, and its secondary city was called Ṣirwāḥ.

The kingdom is mentioned in several ancient scripts, including the Hebrew Bible (the Old Testament) in the story referring to the visit of the queen of Saba to the court of King Solomon. It is also mentioned by Greek, Roman, and Persian historians, who were impressed by its wealth and described its leading role in the spice trade and commerce in general, due to its geographic location, which gave it control over land caravans and sea traffic in the Red Sea. It established colonies in Abyssinia, and during the Roman era had some control over Hadarmout and the rest of Yemen.

When the great dam of Ma'rib collapsed, what ensued was a colossal disaster: towns and villages and cultivated land were flooded, and many people left, never to return. In the 4th century AD, the kingdom of Aksum in East Africa competed with Saba and gained control over the Red Sea traffic and conquered some of its land in Yemen. By the 6th century the declining kingdom of Saba was overcome by Persian and Muslim powers.

SAHRAWI. The Sahrawi are a people of mixed origin, composed of Berber, Bedouin, and Black tribes, who live in the western part of the Sahara, some parts of **Morocco**, including the territories claimed by the Polisario, at the edge of southwestern **Algeria**, and **Mauritania**. Their culture has mixed elements of Bedouin and Tuareg tradition; thus, although most Sahrawi speak Hassaniya **Arabic**, there are groups who speak in the Berber dialect. In addition, certain subgroups of Sahrawi preserve the African cultural characteristics.

SALLAMA. Sallama is a Bedouin village in **Israel**, found in western **Galilee** in the territories of the Misgav Regional Council. The village was recognized by the state of Israel in 1976. The two tribes of **Suwaed** and Marisat live in the village. It counts 3,500 people today.

SANHAJA. The Sanhaja (Ṣanhājah) was in the past one of the largest **Berber nomad** tribes. Today, several tribes and regions in the Berber territory in the Maghreb are still called Sanhaja . Ever since the 9th century *the Sanhaja* has been an inclusive term to several tribes, including the **Tuareg** and the Kutama in Niger and Mali, which established itself in the central area of the Atlas mountain range, in the Rif mountains and at the Atlantic coast of **Morocco**, while another group of the tribe wandered inland and settled in the Kabylie mountains in western **Algeria** and northern Niger. The tribe played an important role in the Almoravids' alliance that dominated Morocco and conquered western Algeria and the region of Andalusia in Spain.

In addition, some small groups of the Zenaga tribe, believed to be descendants of the southernmost Sanhaja subgroups, live today in **Mauritania** and in parts of northern Senegal.

SANUSI, MUHAMMAD AL- (1787–1859). Muhammad al-Sanusi was the founder and first leader of the brotherhood named after him. Born in **Algeria**, he went to Makkah to study and later was teaching Islamic studies with the great Ibn Idris. When the latter died, he was appointed caliph. In the late 1840s he left Makkah and moved with his students to Cyrenaica, where he founded his Sanusiyah Order, to bring an Islamic touch to the backward area, which at the time was detached from Islamic religious influences.

In the early stages of their settling in Cyrenaica, Sanusi had no military aspirations. His wish was to bring peace and harmony to the native Saharan tribes as a mediator between the tribes and the Ottoman rulers. He established good relations with the Ottoman governor and was granted a semi-autonomous status.

When French and Italian forces threatened Ottoman rule in **Libya**, he turned the order's teaching centers into military facilities and prepared his followers for *jihad.* In 1895, his son and successor, Muhammad al-Mahdi, moved his headquarters first from Jaghbub to Kufra, far from the Turkish sphere of influence, and later to other locations, to avoid conflict with the Ottomans. The members of his family led the order he founded until 1933. *See also* SANUSIYAH ORDER, LIBYA.

SANUSIYAH ORDER, LIBYA. Sanusiyah is a Sufi religious brotherhood based in the northern Sahara. The order is named after its founder and first leader, **Muhammad al-Sanusi**. The brotherhood used tribal power to fight colonialism in **Libya**, a goal it finally achieved in the early 20th century.

When Sanusi and his followers came to Cyrenaica they built lodges (*zawiyah*). At the first stage the lodges became Islamic Centers where they taught Sufi **Islam**, a combination of simple puritanical Islam mixed with mysticism. In the early days of their settling, Sanusi's goal was to spread his version of Islam and bring peace and harmony to the native Saharan tribes. Each lodge was run by a **sheikh** and many **Ikhwan** (brothers) who taught children and organized Friday prayers. The sheikh could mediate among the tribes and between the tribes and the Ottoman authorities.

These *zawiyahs* (groups) not only instilled peace and stability in the area but also stimulated **trade** between Cyrenaica and the southern Sahara **desert**. The brothers collected payments that were used to finance the maintenance of lodges and their families, as also the upkeep of the Koranic university at Jaghbub. When the movement turned against the colonial powers, these centers became military recruiting and training compounds.

The Grand Sanusi passed away in 1859, but his son, Sayyid Muhammad al-Mahdi, took over the order, which prospered under his leadership. Together with his nephew, Ahmad al-Sharif, he founded many additional lodges. The brotherhood took part in the power struggle in Libya and its immediate neighboring countries. They collaborated with the Turks against European colonialist forces.

In 1912, the Ottomans granted autonomy to the local Arabs, and the Sanusi family started to speak about a local government—*Hakuma al-Sanusiyah*. However, the Turks withdrew from Libya at the end of 1912 and left the locals to fend for themselves. Ahmad al-Sharif declared a jihad against the Italians; he published a Sanusiyah manifesto (*Manshur*) and summoned all the Bedouin tribes and inhabitants of the region to resist the foreign invaders. In 1918, when the Ottoman Empire was defeated, Muhammad Idris signed a treaty with the British and Italians, and the leader, al-Sharif, went into exile in Istanbul.

The second war between the Sanusis and the Italians occurred in the period between 1923 and 1932. The order led the tribes in their war against the Italian colonial forces, and after nine years of struggle, the Italians prevailed and crushed the order to prevent another wave of tribal resistance.

In 1947 the Italians left North Africa with the rest of the defeated Axis powers, and in 1951, Libya was declared an independent state, and Muhammad Idris, head of the Sanusi order, became King Idris I. But he was overthrown by a coup in 1969 by Colonel Muammar Gadhafi. This movement is an excellent example of a tribal group that fought colonial invasion under a religious jihad formation, initiated Libyan nationalism, and had a crucial role in tribal integration.

SAUDI ARABIA. Saudi Arabia is the largest state on the **Arabian Peninsula**, the original homeland of all Arab Bedouin tribes. Before the 20th century, territories were organized along tribal lines. The majority of the population was **nomadic**, ruled by tribal **sheikhs**. The principal sheikhs established a balance of power and a cooperative coalition among the autonomous factions, rural tribes, urban dwellers, and the city-based ruler. The tribes were important guards of the **trade** caravans, provided warriors to fend off enemies, and encroached on foreign territories. A power base was dominated by the *umara*, the lay rulers, and the *ulama*, clergy, who had dominated the leadership and the spiritual and political factors.

The nomadic tribes roamed according to seasons and circumstances, and more often than not, followed their herd way beyond their official territory. The concept of borders changed dramatically in the vast expanses of the peninsula, as the British introduced their own concept of borders in contrast to the former nondemarcated limits set for grazing areas. The first modern ruler, Ibn Saud, signed the treaty that divided the vast area into today's states in the autumn of 1925. The Saudis expanded the initial territory allotted to them, and included Makkah, and the final demarcation was sealed in 1930. Thus, Saudi Arabia became the center of pilgrimage and trade, under the control of the Hejazi, the urban upper class.

Ibn Saud took certain steps to subdue the tribes, such as preventing them from trading and grazing animals through neighboring states, and by increasing taxation. He also managed to exclude the chiefs of the Najdi tribe from high administrative positions. He did not appoint leaders of important tribes such as Faisal al-Dawish of the Mutair tribe and Sultan Ibn Humayd of the Utayba tribe as governors of the Hejaz. The new policies threatened tribal autonomy. The tribesmen thought that transportation and communication installations would hamper their control of their domains and of the caravan routes. They claimed that this leader, who once adhered to tribal tradition and Wahhabi austerity, had become a follower of foreign ways.

Between 1927 and 1929 the **Ikhwan** (brothers) openly challenged Ibn Saud's principles of government and chose to support the Najdi clans; but during 1929–1930, in a series of encounters, Ibn Saud prevailed. In the 1930s, there were revolts of a smaller order, the Billi tribe in northern Hejaz rebelled in 1932, and the Asiri tribes rebelled in 1933. The trigger for these occurrences, which the government managed to suppress, was heavy taxation and arbitrary provincial governors. Development and modernization along with state-initiated population transfers and the rapid growth of urban centers and **education** opportunities affected the life of the nomadic tribes, and many of them turned sedentary. The share of nomads dropped from more than 50 percent in 1900 to less than 25 percent today.

Modern Saudi Arabia developed a new class order: the royal family, the higher *ulama*, and wealthy merchants are on the top; professionals and technocrats are the new middle class; and unskilled city workers, nomads, and the rural population, including most of the two million immigrant workers, comprise the lower class. The traditional egalitarian values of society fell apart. Also the influx of two million foreign workers to man the huge construction projects formed a completely new component in society.

Today tribal chiefs have become vast landowners and joined the upper echelon; many Bedouins are working for the state, serving in the National Guard and other law enforcement agencies; others adapted to modern life by switching their **camels** for cars and trucks, either for private use or as employees of the state and private companies. Thus, modernization improved the Bedouins' life in many ways.

Nevertheless, some Bedouins who were deprived of their traditional lifestyle were forced to move into shantytowns near the big cities and became alienated from the state. However, members of the royal family patronized the tribes and their leaders, and endowed them with subsidies and privileges to make them feel part of the state and ensure their loyalty.

SAWAHRA. Sawahra is a Bedouin tribe that lives in the Jerusalem region. The Sawahra constitute a coalition of Bedouin families, part of whom came from Transjordan, and another part came from the south of **Palestine**—from the Beer Sheva region. They entered the region in the 19th century, and they received their name due to their **wanderings** in the region via the village of Beit Sahur. The tribesmen today number more than 30,000 people and they live in several villages in the Jerusalem district, including Jabal Mukhbar and Kafr el-Sawahra El-Sharqiya. *See also* ISRAEL.

SAWARKA. The members of the Sawarka tribe are located in the north of the **Sinai** Peninsula, in the region bordering between the Gaza Strip and el-Arish, a strategic region where, among other things, the gas pipeline to **Israel** and **Jordan** passes. The tribe counts 10,000 people today. The tribe imposes terror on the rest of the tribes and on all the businessmen in the region. There is a concern that the tribe, in its distant past, had some members of Jewish origin, and until this day they follow part of the customs of Judaism, including circumcision, lighting Sabbath candles, and so on. Part of the tribe's members live in the Bedouin diaspora in Israel and in the territories of Judea and Samaria, and they have family connections with the members of the tribe dwelling in Sinai.

The breached border, which not long ago existed between Israel and Egypt, enabled the tribe members to become smuggler kings, undisturbed. The paradise of smuggling, which they built by means of very sophisticated networks, raised several hundreds of millions of dollars for the tribe's treasury, which made them the richest tribe in the Sinai.

SAYYID. *Sayyid* (master) was the name that was given in the **pre-Islamic period** (*Al-Jahiliyya*) to somebody who stood at the head of the tribe, a concept that over time developed to the concept of a **sheikh**. The sayyid is a dominant figure who grows out of the tribe, with a sort of general acceptance of the members of the tribe, and he manages the tribe within the general agreement of the rest of the tribe's members. A tribe member who refuses decisions is liable to expulsion from the tribe. The sayyid was characterized by strong roles and positive traits: a leader, a fighter, a host, polite, and manager of the public relations of the tribe.

SEDENTARIZATION. The process of sedentarization of nomadic societies in the Middle East and north Africa, to a wide extent, has taken place since the end of the 19th century and has strengthened during the 20th century. The process of transition from **nomadism** to permanent **settlement** is the most prominent out of the processes of change taking place in Bedouin/nomadic society. Bedouin settlement has two different forms of development. The first is spontaneous settlement: settlement with the initiative of the nomads when the models of the settlements are fixed according to their social conceptions and needs; the second is planned settlement, which comes at the initiative of the governments, and therefore there are those who call it initiated settlement.

The reasons for sedentarization are a strong central government, technological development, and development of means of transport, which caused changes in the traditional branches of the nomads' economy. In parallel, the importance of the livestock farm and the beasts of burden and riding of the Bedouins declined. The Bedouins lost their relative advantage, following damage to their freedom of **wandering**. Consequently, but also from self-initiative, the Bedouins integrated in external and modern branches of employment, which reduced their dependence on the traditional farm but increased their economic dependence on the general labor **market**.

The settlement of nomads is an ancient phenomenon in the region. It takes place in several variations, and as a result of different factors, in the Middle Eastern space. There are examples from history in which the settlement of nomads is carried out as a result of political, strategic, and economic factors, which operated on the whole region, as during the Muslim Arab conquest in the 7th century AD. There were cases of settlement that was imposed on the nomads as in **Egypt** and **Syria** of Mohamed Ali in the first half of the 19th century. In other cases what happened in the desert itself, whether due to divine or human hands, had much influence—droughts, tribes that lost in war, and so on—and of course in the modern era, as a result of losses of the nomads in the historical struggle that was engaged between the nomad and the farmer, and as a result of the strengthening of western culture—the culture of townsmen and villagers—and due to the control of western technology. *See also* MIGRATION; NOMADS; NOMADS, SETTLEMENT.

SETTLEMENT. The process of settlement of **nomadic** societies has been taking place on a wide scope from the start of the 20th century, in countries of the Middle East. The reasons for this are a strong central government, technological development, and development of transport means, which caused changes in the traditional branches of the economy of nomads. In parallel, the importance of the **market** for livestock, beasts of burden, and riding beasts of the Bedouins decreased, and therefore they lost their relative advantage, which curtailed their freedom to wander. Consequently, but also from independent initiatives, the Bedouins integrated into the external and modern branches of employment, which reduced their dependence on the traditional economy but increased their economic dependence on the general labor market.

The settlement of Bedouins took place in two forms: spontaneous settlement, executed with the initiative of the society of nomads; and settlement with initiative of governments.

By trying to settle the nomads forever, the authorities aroused conflicts between the two sides. The conflict was derived from the conceptual gap in relation to the uses of land. The nomads made use of the land for needs of grazing, while the state saw the problems of nomads as secondary to the needs of the overall society.

It is possible to close the gap of conceptions and needs between these two sides by three factors:

1. Dispersal of the nomads over an extensive area, which causes taking extensive areas and preventing their designation for the general needs of all the citizens of the state, and refusal of the nomadic population to give up their lands or to compromise over them. In the past the Bedouins could realize their territorial rights, as the state was weak against their power. Today, in contrast to this, the power of the nomads is null versus the power of the state. They have become dependent on the will of the state, where every state solves its problem in its own unique way. The coping also used coercive means, by the use of force or by way of a policy of giving benefits and encouragement.

2. Government's encouragement of permanent settlement, derived from considerations of security and demographic balance, as it was expressed in the Gulf states, where the regimes encouraged **migration** of the nomadic population to the towns where government institutions were concentrated, with the goal of balancing the growing number of foreigners and reducing their political and religious weight.
3. The coping entailed settlement of the Bedouins. It used both coercive means by the use of force, for example, the case of **Iran**, which settled nomads by force along the border with the former USSR and Afghanistan. **Reza Shah Pahlavi** as part of his policy to supervise the nomads forced them to build permanent houses. In contrast to this a policy could be adopted of giving benefits and encouragement, as in **Jordan**, where King Hussein tried to settle the Bedouins by creating preferential conditions for them, like building a school, hospital, and so on.

There are different processes to bring the Bedouins to a transition to permanent settlement. Four models can be mentioned:

1. Drought and decline: Drought causes destruction of the Bedouin economic life. Loss of pasture means loss of the economic existential basis, which cancels the need for continuation of **wandering** and transfers them to permanent settlements.
2. Defeat and degradation: Disputes between tribes, whereby strong tribes defeat tribes weaker than them and deport them from their area of residence. Consequently the latter are pushed into agricultural life and for a lack of an alternative they go to a permanent settlement, whereas the strong tribes that constitute a threat to the central government are fixated by force.
3. Failing and falling away: Loners, or small groups, are discharged from nomadic society due to various reasons, such as murder, crime, and failure in attempts to build economic units of property from which it is possible to subsist, and these are absorbed in a society of permanent settlement.
4. Adaptation and response: A voluntary transition to **agriculture** and to permanent settlement. This usually occurs when the external economic and political conditions are suitable. This model is less reversible than the three previous ones.

The Bedouins in the Middle Eastern region started to pass to a permanent settlement at the end of the Ottoman period. The Bedouin tribes began to cultivate the lands at their disposal. The search for land fit for agricultural cultivation close to the **tent** brought out the necessity of dismantling the tribal frameworks.

In the second half of the 19th century the Ottoman authorities adopted several reforms, which were designed to curb the power of the Bedouins in the Middle Eastern region. Among the reforms that were introduced for this sake were:

(1) The Law of Lands: During the years of anarchy all the land arrangements in the Middle East region were undermined. Many areas good for cultivation were abandoned by their owners due to wars and due to raids, expulsion of the population, and natural disasters and diseases. The Ottoman government, most of whose income was from the taxes that were imposed on the land and on its crops, was interested in terminating the anarchy in this field, and therefore, in 1858, it published the "Land Law" and in the year 1861 the "Taboo Law." The goals of these laws were to define the types of lands and the rights of ownership to them. By issuing land laws, the Ottoman government intended to register the lands in the name of those holding it, and to define their rights next to its rights. This was done to arrange the levying of taxes. Among other things it was laid down in law that if any land fit for cultivation stayed fallow for three years running, its owners would lose their right to it and it would pass to the state.

The Ottoman government acted with the full severity of the law against the Bedouins, mainly toward tribes destined for raids, which caused unrest and public insecurity. If these abandoned areas were not cultivated, the government would confiscate them from the Bedouins. The government also confiscated lands on which the Bedouins dwelled. This was a punishment imposed on Bedouins who did not register their lands in the taboo offices. For example, the state confiscated lands from the **Bani Sakhr** tribe in the Jezreel Valley in **Palestine**, as no legal ownership documents were at their disposal for corroboration of their demands.

(2) Transport: As long as the **camel** was the sole means of transport for heavy goods, the Bedouins filled an important role in the economic life, as they were the growers of camels and the main suppliers of **trade** caravans. At the end of the 19th century the Ottoman government paved routes and roads; for example, in Palestine, the Haifa-Nazareth-Tiberias road was laid, as also the Jaffa-Nablus, Jerusalem-Jericho, Jerusalem-Bethlehem roads. Likewise they built railways like the Hejaz railway, which linked **Syria** to Hejaz (present-day northwest **Saudi Arabia**) as well as the Jaffa-Jerusalem railway in Palestine.

The transport systems caused a decrease in the value of the Bedouin economy and of the services that they supplied, so the price of beasts was reduced for convoys and for transport in the villages, and the demand for guarding the caravans decreased. The modern transport system compelled the Bedouins to find an alternative source of income.

(3) Settlement of the population of migrants in regions under Bedouin control: One of the methods that the authorities adopted for weakening the power of the Bedouins was the settlement of refugees within the Bedouin regions. In 1878, Sultan Abed el-Hamid the Second (1876–1908) took Circassian refugees who had escaped from the Russian government in the Caucasus under his auspices. Many of them were settled in the region of contemporary Jordan, especially in the Amman region. In Syria and Palestine, Sultan Abed el-Hamid encouraged the Circassians to settle in the empire, and they were settled on the border of the Syrian **Desert** or in barren regions, as a shield from invasion of the Bedouins.

(4) Attempts to settle the Bedouin tribes by coercion: In the year 1869 there was an attempt to settle the Bedouins in all the Ottoman districts in Syria. The first step was in Gaza, but the Bedouins resisted this intervention by force, and all 15 soldiers who reached the Bedouins were killed. A further attempt to settle the Bedouins was made in 1896. The Ottomans set out just as in the previous instance, with a plan to settle the Bedouins in the Ottoman districts in Syria. In other places also, such as Palestine, they founded army delegations within the districts to supervise the execution of the plan. However, this plan failed, as the Ottoman government did not succeed in defending the Bedouins, who belonged to the strong and big tribes.

(5) The founding of cities in the border regions: The Ottoman authorities strove to impose a government with validity on the border territories, which were found on the margins of the empire. In this period towns were established in Kurdistan, Iraq, Syria, contemporary Jordan, and Palestine. In this period, too, the town of Jerash was rebuilt and Amman in eastern Transjordan developed. Likewise the city of Beer Sheva was built in the year 1900, in the **Negev** district, most of which was controlled by Bedouin tribes. Similarly, military forts were founded along the Syrian Hajj road (from Syria to contemporary Saudi Arabia) at a distance of one day's walking from one to the other. The goal of building the cities and of these forts after they were constructed was to supervise the Bedouins.

A new reality was created for the Bedouins after World War I. The regime of mandates that were introduced in the countries of the Middle East, and partition of the countries between a British mandate and a French mandate, influenced the Bedouins greatly. The demarcation of borders between the countries of the Middle East influenced the Bedouins, as there were no more open spaces, and this affected the wandering of Bedouin tribes. Following this the wandering became limited. The security situation improved in the period between the two world wars when the British and French authorities operated a policy of restraint toward the Bedouins. For example, in the year 1942 the British imposed on the Bedouins in Palestine the "supervision regulations on the Bedouins," whose goal was to control the Bedouins and to cause them to pass to a permanent settlement. These regulations stated that a

Regional Committee would formulate regulations to which the Bedouin tribes in the region would be subject. The wandering of the Bedouins would be under supervision of the authorities. Similarly, it would be possible to investigate the tribesmen, to make arrests, to confiscate the property of a Bedouin, and to return thefts. According to the regulations a possibility also existed of imposing collective punishment on the Bedouin tribe.

The effective government of the British mandate and the French mandate forced the Bedouins to look for alternatives to their traditional sources of income. They started to work in laying roads, erecting buildings, and so on. Another part of them started to cultivate the lands, and next to them they continued grazing. Most of the Bedouins curtailed their wanderings and started living in a permanent settlement. The mandate authorities used to note the ownership on the lands in a new way, something that they treated with scorn in the Ottoman period. For example, the British in Palestine issued certificates of ownership of lands to individuals, in contrast to the registration in the past, which was in the name of the tribe or sheikh, if a record like this existed at all.

The tribal territories were demarcated for the first time on maps, and this reduced the wandering of the tribes and caused a breach in the tribal framework.

The improvement in the security situation, which took place in the mandate period, and following the improvement in the economic situation, enabled the Bedouins to gradually build structures, testifying to permanence.

With the foundation of the national states all over the Middle East from the end of World War II onward, every state of the region coped in its own way with the fixation and settlement of the Bedouin tribes.

The intervention of various governments in the Middle Eastern states caused the settlement of the nomadic population all over the Middle East. Part of the nomads "settled" on the edges of towns and cities in an attempt to find income within the urban areas; for example, in Jordan around Amman, in Syria around Halb and Homs, in **Egypt** around El-Arish, and in the Persian Gulf states they settled around such towns as Doha, Manama, **Kuwait**, and Dubai. The various states made efforts to settle the nomads in permanent settlements according to their own actions, similar to what was done in Jordan, **Iraq**, Syria, and also in **Israel**, where they founded Bedouin towns and villages like the city of **Rahat**, villages like Tel-Sheva, Segev Shalom, Bir el-Maksour, Salama, **Zarzir**, and so on.

In the Middle East and in contemporary north Africa, the phenomenon of wandering is disappearing, and its characteristics such as the tent, camel, **horse**, and goats and sheep grazing in the *wadis* of the desert are becoming a very rare phenomenon. The Bedouin society today is a society in crisis, as it lives between a vanishing magnificent and ancient tradition and modernization, with its advantages and disadvantages, but which obliterates the tradition. *See also* URBANIZATION.

SHAMMAR. Shammar is one of the largest Arab tribes. They are known to be descendants of the Tayy tribe of **Yemen**. They moved northward in **pre-Islamic** times and lived in the area called Nejd, where most of them remain **nomadic** and live as **shepherds**, **camel** herders, and **horse** breeders (in northern Nejd), while the others have settled down in the city of Hail in **Saudi Arabia**. Toward the end of the 19th century, this tribe ruled a significant part of Arabia from Riyadh to today's Syrian border and the vast area known as Al Jazira in northern **Iraq**. Today, there are about 1.5 million members of the tribe living in Saudi Arabia. Its main body is estimated to be more than three million, who live in Iraq, and relatively large groups live in **Kuwait**, **Syria**, and **Jordan**.

Ancient non-Arab sources refer to Arabs (Hebrew for people from the wastelands) as Taits. The name Shammar is attributed to their point of origin in Yemen, the area near their main city, Hail, which is today called Jabal Shammar.

Hatim Al-Ta, a famous leader of the pre-Islamic Tayy Shammar, who was a **Christian**, is referred to by historians, storytellers, and poets. His son Adiyy ibn Hatim, known in his time as the King of Tayy, accepted Muhammad the Prophet and converted to **Islam**.

The Shammar participated in the early Muslim conquest and settled all over the Muslim empire, from the Arabian Peninsula to the Mediterranean and throughout north Africa. As many abandoned their nomadic lifestyle, most of them assimilated in the local population, while some groups joined other tribes.

The Shammars who remain in Saudi Arabia are all Sunni Muslims, while in Iraq, they are split between the two sects: the northern branch, Shammar al-Jarba, is mainly Sunni, while the southern branch, Shammar Toga, is Shiite.

Although in Saudi Arabia and **Kuwait** the Shammar are mostly urbanized, and have adapted to modern life, the vast majority of the Shammar retain a strong tribal identity and tribal loyalty. They are proud of their Bedouin heritage and preserve their cultural characteristics. In Iraq, the Shammar are one of the most powerful tribes, they have won a considerable part of the land, and their support is sought by the rulers. Their close relations with Saudi Arabia put them at odds with the regime of **Saddam Hussein**; thus, after his overthrow the unanimously chosen interim president was Ghazi al-Yawar, from the Al Jarbah clan of the Shammar.

SHAMSI. Shamsi is a large Arabian tribe (with many subtribes) that lives today mostly in the northeastern part of Arabia. They live in northern **Oman**, the **United Arab Emirates**, **Kuwait**, **Qatar**, eastern **Saudi Arabia**, and **Bahrain**. This expansive tribe has many subtribes and secondary branches that trace themselves to the Al-Shamsi.

It is believed that the Al-Shamsi lived originally in Ma'rib, from which they migrated after the destruction of the dam. Until the second part of the 20th century, the Al-Shamsi family ruled Al-Hamriyah. Today, many of them fill important positions there and in other countries in northern Arabia.

SHARARAT. The Shararat trace their genealogy back to the ancient Arab *Kalb* ("dog") tribe, which ruled north Arabia in the 7th century; thus they are considered of noble origin. At the close of the 19th century, they were praised for breeding the best **camels** in Arabia. The Shararat were a **nomadic** tribe whose seasonal **migration** crossed the borders between **Saudi Arabia** and the kingdom of Transjordan. They became part of Saudi Arabia in 1921 but abandoned the nomadic lifestyle only in 1956.

The tribe controlled a huge territory stretching from Kaf to Dumat al-Jandal; its members were known to be hospitable and chivalrous. In the past, they used to collect protection fees from the tribes of south **Jordan**.

Arid conditions and pressure of other tribes forced the Shararat, who were a relatively small tribe, to migrate somewhere else. Today, their number is estimated at 35,000 people, living in many towns and **settlements** in Wadi Sirhan. Their principal town, Tabarjal, has a population of about 23,000. Most tribe members live from **agriculture**, especially livestock breeding, related professions, and services.

The tribe is subdivided into four leading clans: the Azam, Dhubayyin, Hlessa, and Fulaihan. The first two descended from the Kalb tribe, and the other two joined later. Each of these clans has a **sheikh**, who represents it with government ministries and municipal offices. The first school for tribe children was opened in 1956. Recent data show that now there are 20 schools for boys and 15 for girls in their district, with a total of 8,500 pupils. The region received social and medical services from the state that also helped to finance the move from nomadic to sedentary life by allotting lots for home building.

SHEIKH. A sheikh is the head of the tribe, the tribe's leader. He is the last judge on any matter in the tribe. But his role varies. In wartime he and his sons must stand at the head of the campaign with heroism and courage, and in peacetime he is a supreme judge and leads his tribe's members to grazing places.

From a theoretical point of view, the sheikh's authority was founded on the counsel of a tribe's elders; from an operative point of view, he was the absolute governor, all of them submitted to his words, and in his hands there was a decisive right of veto.

Bedouin tradition places conditions for a position of *mashaikh* (leadership), like the sheikh. He should be healthy, strong, and an exemplary hero. Therefore, he is a sort of military leader for the tribe. Only if he does not have the suitable talent is another person chosen to fill the job of leadership of the forces of the tribe during wartime. He also needs to be a well-known judge, but in cases when the sheikh cannot judge and there is a person more experienced than he, the job of judgment is entrusted to that person. The person who meets the conditions will be the tribe's head, but from a practical point of view usually the *mashaikh* passes in inheritance and only in rare cases does a strong man from the tribe's members take control. The sheikh is regarded as the outward representative of the tribe, both toward other tribes and also toward the government. Inward, he judges his tribe's members according to Bedouin tradition.

SHEPHERD. Grazing is one of the most ancient professions. The first man was regarded as the first shepherd and also his son Abel. The prophet Moses is mentioned as a shepherd; he was a shepherd of the flock of his father-in-law, Jethro. Also it is mentioned that Prophet Muhammad dealt with grazing. As the **nomadic** Bedouins grew beasts, they employed shepherds. The shepherd is a person who supervises the flock every day of the year, usually by using a shepherd dog, in the pasture areas, the **desert**, or the mountains. The job of the shepherd is to find **food**, **water**, and shelter for the flock, to protect it from predators, natural disasters, and robbers, and also to maintain its unity and wholeness.

The status of the shepherd was usually inferior: the shepherds had to stay most days of the year with the flock; hence, they were isolated and disconnected from society. Due to this special form of life, the shepherds were considered exceptional. The girls preferred not to marry shepherds, except if they lost their chance to find another groom.

The shepherds devoted themselves with all their might to their vocation, and the flock was entrusted to them. They stayed in the company of the beasts every day of the year, and their work continued from sunrise to sunset. The dependence of the flock on the shepherd was great, and his connection to the animal was very close. The shepherd knew each one of the animals of the flock by its name and knew how to tell its history. Every morning he would choose the pasture lot and lead the flock to the sources of water. In the evening hours he would return the flock to the encampment or lodge it in the field or in caves. The hut in the field was surrounded by a fence of stones and held up by thorny plum branches.

The shepherd learned his profession over many years. Children started to help the scattered shepherds from the age of three, but only after age 10 were they allowed to manage a flock independently. **Women** and girls only drifted close to the tribe's encampment.

The shepherds did their work under very severe conditions. Usually they were orphans or from among the poor or penniless strangers, and their wages were low, but in addition to payment, they received clothes and assorted food commodities, like salt, flour, sugar, and lentils.

The salary of the shepherd was annual, and the shepherd received his wages in the form of beasts: For the treatment of 100 sheep, the shepherds received 8–10 head. Thus, the shepherd was permitted to cover his needs. *See also* CAMEL; HORSE; WANDERING.

SHIBLI-UMM AL-GHANAM. This is a local council in the northern district in **Israel**. It was declared a local council in the year 1984. The two **settlements** that the council was composed of are very close to one another and are found in the eastern (Shibli) and southeastern (Umm al-Ghanam) slopes of Mt. Tabor. The Shibli are descendants of nomads who came from **Syria** and southern **Turkey**, and a small part are the descendants of Sudanese who reached the region in the 1830s.

Seven thousand inhabitants live in Shibli-Umm al-Ghanam today.

SHRARDA. Shrarda is a **Moroccan** tribe. This is a tribe, situated around Mechnes, of Arab origin, composed of various Arab Saharan tribes, of Tafilalet and of Dra. They were brought to the region by the Alawite dynasty, to serve as Guich (Moroccan tribes). These are soldier tribes, who are found around the big towns of the kingdom (Marrakesh, Rabat, Fez). This is one of the reasons that part of the Shrarda is based in the southwest of Fez. As compensation for their services, the Guich benefit from usufruct of "Guich" lands whose property (*Raqaba*) only the sovereign retains.

SINAI BEDOUINS. About 300,000 Bedouins live in the Sinai today, and most of them still follow a nomadic lifestyle; some segments that live near the shores of the Red Sea or the Mediterranean adapted to fishing and smuggling. In recent years **Egypt** has found it difficult to maintain full control of the peninsula. The Bedouin enmity for the authorities has deepened, and with the encouragement of external parties the Bedouins attack central government facilities, like police stations, and create roadblocks and kidnap foreign tourists.

Although the Sinai Peninsula has constituted an integral part of Egypt since the dawn of history, the Bedouin tribes living in it have enjoyed semi-autonomous status, and the central government has intervened little in their affairs. They have their own legal system based on ancient customs. Only in the second half of the 19th century did the government begin to pay attention to the distant Sinai, whose unruly presence caused security problems: damage to the **trade** routes or a threat to pilgrims. During the period of the **Israeli** presence in the Sinai (1967–1982), the Israeli government held an ongoing dialog with the Bedouins, took care of their needs, and left positive memories behind. Tourists discovered the Sinai, the foundation for tourist infrastructure was laid, and the local population thrived. The Egyptians developed it further and made the Sinai one of the main income sources of foreign currency for Egypt.

After the Sinai was returned to Egypt, the Egyptian government accelerated economic development, and the Bedouins found themselves outside the development cycle. They were not involved in the labor force, which was brought from Cairo, and in El-Arish; tourism villages were founded on the shores for the Egyptian wealthy. The Bedouins continued to graze their flocks and to get by with inferior work. Moreover, they had difficulties obtaining electricity and **water**.

Extremists and terrorist groups always find a discontented population and exploit the situation. The terrorist attacks in Taba and in Sharm el-Sheikh in recent years reflect the conflict between the Bedouins and the authorities, as the vast Sinai mountainous **desert** expanse provides refuge and shelter for those receiving the support of discontented residents.

In the past couple of years, the Sinai Bedouins began to organize demonstrations and demanded the release of their detainees. In addition, they demanded that the government allocate resources to construct housing complexes, give study scholarships to their youngsters, and register ownership on their lands.

SLAVERY. Slavery and slaves existed among the Bedouins throughout history. This phenomenon vanished during the 20th century, and this was due to the influence of democratic values and the development of an awareness of human and civil rights. *Slavery* is a term that denotes a work regime, characterized by ownership, and great control of one person over another person, who is considered his property. In slavery, the enslaved person is not let loose or free to determine his conduct or his daily routine, and his master is the one who fixes all or most of his lifestyle and his way of conduct for him. The slave receives his **food** and other needs from his master, and he must execute all the work that will be required of him.

The slaves in history were usually of a different racial, ethnic, or religious origin from that of their enslavers. The period of their slavery started by way of a kidnapping or by being taken as a captive in a war. The reasons for the slavery of people to people of their own race were usually conviction of a crime or incapacity to pay a debt. Often an abandoned baby was collected for the home of a family, who raised him as a slave. The children of slaves mostly became slaves themselves.

Slavery in the Middle East in general, and in the Arabian Peninsula in particular, was a common phenomenon in the **pre-Islamic period**. It was widespread and very common, similar to most of the areas of the world during the ancient periods and at the start of the Middle Ages. Most of the slaves in the Arabian Peninsula were of an African origin, mainly from central and eastern Africa. A minority among the slaves were white, of a foreign race, who were apparently bought by Arab **nomads**. There were also Arab slaves.

The slaves in the countries of the Middle East were employed in housework. Female serfs were given preference, as they could also serve as mistresses. The slaves were brought to the Islamic countries from Africa by Arab **traders**. For example, some of the slaves were brought from **Sudan** to **Palestine** and integrated over generations among the Arabs of Palestine—they started to speak **Arabic**, to give their children Arab names, and also accepted the Muslim **religion**. In the Muslim writings there is condemnation of the enslavement of Muslims by Muslims, but conversion of religion did not ensure the slave his freedom.

An important institution of slaves in Islam was the Mamelukes. These were slaves who served as soldiers in the Ottoman Empire. They were brought as children from the Euro-Asiatic plain, were converted to Islam, and worked in the service of the caliph. Later on they dominated **Egypt** and turned from slaves to rulers (1250–1517).

Slavery among the Bedouin tribes existed throughout history. The heads of the tribes and rich people within the tribe had in their ownership a number of slaves and female mistresses—their numbers usually ranged from five to seven slaves. They carried out difficult work, grazed flock, carried **water** from the spring, drew water from the well, built and dismantled **tents**, collected branches for a fire, and prepared **coffee**; the female slaves prepared the food, they escorted the traders, and they also executed guarding tasks in the Bedouin encampments. The slaves could become free in several cases: a token of esteem for the generous service of the slave to his master after a number of years of devoted work; in cases where the slave had displayed heroism, for example, during a robbery or plunder, the slave displayed heroism and protected the tribe; and in case of the death of the master of the slave. Slaves did get married. The slave's master took care of marrying him off, usually after he was freed. Generally they married the members of their own class or their own color. The slave class was the most inferior in the social hierarchy of the Bedouins. Many of the slaves who were released and became free were still called slaves.

SUDAN. The Sudanese population today is more than 34 million, of which 70 percent are Arabs or Muslim "Arabized" tribes. The rest include Nubians, Zaghawa, and Copts. There are 597 tribal groups in Sudan, speaking more than four hundred **language**s and dialects. The Sudanese Arabs are clearly the biggest ethnic group in the country: They are almost all Muslims; most of them speak Sudanese **Arabic** while others like the Awadia and Fadnia tribes speak other Arabic dialects: the Bani Arak tribes speak Najdi Arabic; the Rufa'a, **Bani Hassan**, Al-Ashraf, Kinanah, and **Rashaida** tribes speak Hejazi Arabic. In northern Sudan, a few Bedouin Arabs of the **Rizeigat** speak Sudanese Arabic and share the culture of the majority.

Most of the Arabized and indigenous tribes like the Fur, Zaghawa, Masalit, and some **Baggara** tribes speak Chadian Arabic, and they are less culturally integrated with other Arabized tribes. The Sudanese Arabs have descended mainly from tribes that migrated from the Arabian Peninsula and some of the primeval native Sudanese population, in particular the Nubians, who have a joint history with Egypt. Some **pre-Islamic** Arab tribes moved to Sudan in an earlier period from Western Arabia, while the majority of the Arab ancestors of modern Sudan arrived there during and after the 12th century. The latter practiced mixed marriages with the indigenous Nubian and other African people and spread the **Islamic religion**.

Since the 12th century, there was process of Arabization in Sudan, enforced by further immigration of Arabs from the other shore of the Red Sea and the spreading of mixed marriages.

Tribal culture had a great influence on Sudanese society, affecting almost all social, political, and behavioral conventions. Most Sudanese tribes are proud that they belong to the Arab-Muslim culture, although this view is not shared by the black African groups, which broke away to form South Sudan in 2011. *See also* EGYPT.

SULHA. *Sulha* (reconciliation) is a traditional custom for imposing peace between aggressive sides—be these people, families, or tribes. The sulha is held according to clear and predetermined rules. The sulha constitutes an unwritten social law, the roots of which are in the **desert** life of the Arab tribes, and it is still valid in our days, not instead of the official law of the state, but alongside it.

From a historical point of view, disputes were always a natural factor in human society, and therefore the need was born to develop methods of reconciliation side by side, to stop the destructive effects of the quarrels and return to a proper course of life.

The sulha is built on principles that are effective in shortening the negotiation process in disputes. The rules are predetermined and detailed, up to the dictation of the versions of sentences that should be stated at various stages. Therefore, for example, when one family member hurts another family member, the sulha tradition determines that in a case like this, the attacking family must turn immediately to the delegation that would be composed of neutral notables, known to all for their honesty and reliability, and ask that somebody arbitrate in the quarrel—this in order to prevent possible revenge. The term in **Arabic** for a delegation is *jaha*. The authority of the jaha derives from the fact that its members have social influence and are familiar and acceptable to everybody.

The essence of the sulha is forgiveness. Forgiveness of the injured party is essential for the success of the sulha, and in the imposition of peace, the goal of the jaha is to obtain this forgiveness from the family that was injured. This is often not achieved in the first meeting, and two, three, or more visits like these may be necessary.

When all the parties reach an agreement, they decide on the peacemaking day. One should invite many notables from all over the **settlement**. The peace has to be made openly: all of them need to see it, to know its conditions, and to be witnesses. A fixed protocol exists for holding the ceremony. It includes a meeting of both families involved under the auspices of the delegation and under a white flag.

On the morning of the ceremony the mediators accompany the injuring party to the home of the injured party. The mediator ties a white handkerchief on a wooden rod. The mediator, the injuring party, and the injured party each tie one knot in the handkerchief, symbolizing the healing of the rift.

Following this the mediator reads the terms of the sulha, and the injuring side pays him the compensation sum. The injured party agrees to decrease the sum as long as it does not fall below the true minimum to which he aspires. Next, the mediator transfers the compensation to the injured party and reads again the terms of the sulha. Following this all the guests go and eat the sulha meal.

Sulha Sabaean mukarrib Karib'il Watar I—"peace"—is a popular ceremony in the Middle Eastern society, in which both parties involved in the dispute forge an alliance of peace and the injured party forgives the injuring party. The injured party needs to agree to hold the sulha and he also is the one who determines the sum that will be paid to him as compensation. In the case of murder, the compensation is *daya*—a ransom.

SUWAED. The Suwaed is a Bedouin tribe that was considered one of the biggest tribes in the north of **Israel**. They live in several places in the **Galilee**: in Kfar Salame, Ras el-Ayin, Kamana, Husseiniya, Hamiram, and so on. The tribesmen note that the father of the tribe was the Muslim military leader Sa'd ibn Abi Waqqas (595–674). The tribe was also named after him. The tribesmen reached **Palestine** from **Syria** apparently during the 17th century.

At the start they **wandered** in the Hula region, and during the 19th century they reached central Galilee, where their villages are found today. At present the tribesmen number seven thousand.

SYRIA, EARLY. The state of Syria is situated in the middle of the Fertile Crescent, where ancient civilizations bloomed, declined, or were destroyed for thousands of years. As the entire area borders the **desert** or semiarid plains, the competition between nomadic herders and farmers was present throughout the history of human civilization. Its geographical location, between the two major civilization centers of the ancient word—those that developed on the shores and the delta of the Nile and those that rose and developed on the shores and between the two great rivers, the Euphrates and the Tigris—made Syria and its southern neighbors, **Israel/Palestine**, the main highway for all conquering armies that passed the region in the past five thousand years. These two major factors affected the culture and ethnic composition of the population of Syria in the past and in the present.

The first Arab tribes arrived in Aljazeera, from where they moved to other parts of Syria and the area of modern **Jordan** in about 200 BC, when the emerging Roman Empire was replacing the declining Greek Empire and its Seleucid branch ruled Greater Syria.

Under Byzantine rule, some of the Bedouin tribes in south Syria accepted **Christianity**, but when their brother Bedouins fought the Byzantines for control of the region, the Bedouins chose to assist the Arabs, and eventually all of them converted to **Islam**. Some of them joined the Muslim forces, some settled and changed their lifestyle, and others kept their cultural tradition and remained nomadic herders.

Under Muslim rule, the Bedouin tribes provided warriors to the rulers, and they were also trusted with security for trading caravans. A number of Bedouins reached high positions within the administration. During the Ottoman rule the Bedouin way of life was respected, and in some districts they became semiautonomous: they collected taxes, secured the highways, and controlled a large segment of the **trade**. The central administration did not intervene in their lives and seldom interfered in tribal conflicts.

Syria is situated northwest of the Arabian Peninsula; thus, throughout history, many tribes that migrated from the Arabian Peninsula went to or through Syria. Since much of Syria was already inhabited by Arabic tribes, it was the first target chosen by the Prophet to spread Islam. He sent over envoys to convince them to convert, and he also sent military delegations or *gazawat* to force the people to join Islam as preliminary actions for its conquest at a later stage. Therefore, the military delegation sent by the Prophet did not conduct too many battles but busied itself in intelligence gathering to "pave the way" for the conquest.

The interest of the Prophet Muhammad in the Syrian region pressured the Syrian tribes, especially when some of them began to accept the new **religion**, while others that were under the influence of the Byzantines accepted Christianity. Thus, the tribes had a loyalty crisis, especially for those who were declared allies of the Byzantines and were paid to defend the borders of the empire from the threat of the Bedouins, who moved to Syria from the Arabian Desert.

Bedouin tribes from Greater Syria (Bilad Al-Sham), like the Jodam tribe, which roamed through various territories in the area, in contemporary Syria, **Jordan**, Israel, and the **Palestinian authority**, sent delegations to the Prophet Muhammad in Heja offering support and willingness to join Islam. Their delegation reached the city of Medina in the seventh year, by the Muslim count (AD 629). The Byzantines responded by stopping the salary given to the Jodam to defend the borders of the empire from the Bedouin encroachment.

The second group of tribes to convert to Islam was the Lahm tribes, which had previously accepted a "light" version of Christianity, like several tribes under Byzantine rule. They were followed by the group of the Tayy tribes who lived in the Gaza region, Hebron hills, and on the coastal plain of the south of Haifa.

At the time these tribes converted to Islam, the Ghassan, Taglab, and Kaleb tribes kept their Christian religion and were loyal to the Byzantine Empire. These tribes accepted Islam much later, after the Muslims under the leadership of the caliphs Abu Bakr and Omar ben Al-Khatab defeated Byzantium and became the rulers of the entire region.

In the 18th and 19th centuries a wave of Bedouin **migration** from the Arabian Peninsula, mostly from the Anazah and **Shammar** tribes, moved into the Badia area in Syria. Today, these two are the largest Bedouin tribes in Syria, with more than half a million members each. In the 19th century a special boarding school was built in Constantinople for the sons of tribal leaders throughout the Ottoman Empire. In time, many graduates of this school became **sheikhs**. Every tribe appointed a sheikh to mediate between it and the Ottoman government, although **camel-herding** tribes like the Fid'an and the Sba'a did not recognize its authority over them. They paid no taxes and were considered "free." However they were permitted to control their district and levy taxes on passing travelers. *See also* SYRIA, MODERN.

SYRIA, MODERN. Toward the end of the Ottoman Empire (1880–1915) Arab nationalism was endorsed by some of the Bedouin elite, who supported the foundation of an independent Arab state under Amir Faisal. The leaders of the three tribes that were closest to Damascus—the Ruwala, the Fadl, and the Hasana—supported the Hashemite Kingdom in Syria (1919–1920) and opposed the French mandate on the land.

The French (1920–1947) adopted their traditional policy of "divide and rule." They supported religious minorities and also divided the country into semiautonomous districts. Their attitude toward the Bedouins was also marked with "divide-and-rule" management: they provided the tribes certain social services and enforced arms control. However, they also encouraged the traditional Bedouins to manage their own affairs, which meant fighting only between themselves and not in populated areas. They encouraged the Bedouins to set up a mini-state in the *Badia*, which would ensure a continuous and safe passage through **Lebanon**, security in the area, controlling **trade** and travel routes to Baghdad, and protecting the flow of oil from Mosul and the southern pipeline to Haifa. They also annexed parts of the territory of greater Syria to Mt. Lebanon, creating a separate Christian country of Lebanon.

In 1947, the French mandate expired, and Syria became an independent state. The new government decided to settle the nomads. The constitution of 1950 devoted a special section to the Bedouin issue, declaring that the government would allocate funds to settle the nomads and safeguard their culture. The government also published a new law of tribes that permitted the Badia tribes, Anazah and Shammar, and a few other tribes, including the Hadidi yin and Mawali, and a number of seminomadic tribes to carry arms. On the other hand, the number of deputies representing the Bedouins in parliament (Tribal Bloc) was reduced from nine to six, four of whom were reserved for the large tribes of major districts: the Mawali, the Hadidi yin, the Shammar, and the Hasana.

Under the United Arab Republic (UAR) the government ruled that the Bedouins have no separate identity, and they should obey the laws of the land. Some of the tribes, like parts of the Anazah and sections of the Fid'an and the Sba'a, left Syria for **Saudi Arabia**.

When the UAR dissolved, the Ba'ath Party came to power in 1963. The Ba'ath government wanted to form one united, homogeneous, egalitarian society. They tried to suppress the wealthy landowners, by changing the land laws, and confiscated 1.5 million hectares of land, mostly from tribal leaders.

The Bedouin tribes in modern Syria are found in every corner of the state, in the rural region and in the towns. In some big towns in Syria, it is possible to find whole neighborhoods or suburbs, like the "Hai Al-Baqara" in Aleppo, inhabited by el-Atasi tribes, and All-el-Haraki, in the town of Homs, members of el-Youssefi, maarat el-Nuaman, Aal-el-Jundi in Damascus, and so on.

As the government plans to force the Bedouins to cultivate the land failed and demands to return to raising grazing animals were heard, the government came up with a new idea: to create livestock cooperative farms supervised by government employees. Thus, most of the Bedouin tribes felt discontent throughout the **Bashar al-Assad** regime, and when the Arab Spring reached Syria, many of them joined the ranks of the rebels.

The organizations on a tribal basis proved to be an essential component of the Syrian social fabric. As the Bedouin tribes in Syria constituted 45 percent of the Syrian people since the outbreak of the riots in Syria, the tribes became a significant factor. The Syrian government succeeded in preventing the tribes in the north and east of Syria from joining the rebels but failed to prevent the tribes in the south from joining the opposition forces. *See also* SYRIA, EARLY.

T

TAAMRA. The Taamra tribesmen live today in a region between Jerusalem and Bethlehem. The Taamra originate from the north of the Arabian Peninsula, from Hejaz. They penetrated into the region at the end of the 16th century and lived initially in Hirbat Beit Taamir. Over time they took control of the village of Beit Taamir and merged with its local inhabitants. In that period all the settlers of the place received their common name—the name of Khirbat Beit Taamir. In the years between the 16th century and the 19th century, the Taamra turned from a bunch of families into a real Bedouin tribe that ruled the whole space stretching from southwest of Bethlehem up to the Dead Sea.

The tribesmen today number in the tens of thousands of inhabitants. They live in several places, some in the city of Bethlehem, some in the villages of Bethlehem region like Dar Salah, Shawaura, Ras el-Wad, Zaatra, Beit Taamar, Britzaa, Asachra, Tanua, and Handaza, and there are also thousands of tribesmen who live today in **Jordan**. *See also* SAUDI ARABIA.

TA'ISHA. Ta'isha is one of the **Baggara** tribes, which are all part of the Guhayna Bedouin groups who came from Arabia across the **Sinai** Peninsula to eastern north Africa. The Ta'isha moved into the Nile region of upper **Egypt** at the beginning of the 16th century, and from there moved to **Sudan** and settled in the southern part of **Darfur**. They participated in the Mahadia revolt against the Ottoman/Egyptian occupation of Sudan and Egyptian occupation of Sudan during the 19th century. After the death of the Al-Mahdi, Khalifa Abdulla Al Ta'ishi was the ruler of Sudan until it was recaptured by Anglo-Egyptian forces. He was the leader of the Ta'isha tribe.

Today, the Ta'isha are concentrated in and around the city of Reheid Al Berdi, a beautiful city that inspired several artists. Like most Arab tribes in the area, the Ta'isha people are Sunni Muslim. Some segments of the Ta'isha became sedentary and even established important cities in Sudan, while others kept their traditional **nomadic** lifestyle and cross political borders during their seasonal **migration**.

TAJAKANT. The Tajakant is an Arab-**Berber** tribe with Moorish origins, speaking Hassaniya **Arabic** and chiefly dwelling in the Western Sahara, **Mauritania**, and **Algeria**. According to some, they are descendants of the Almoravids, who ruled **Morocco** in the 11th century. They are Sunni Muslims and belong to the Maliki school of **Islam**. They were warriors and traders in the 19th century, and established in 1852 near an **oasis**, and then in Algeria, near the commercial city and trading crossroads of Tindouf. However, in 1895, the **Reguibat**, who had been in conflict with the Tajakant since 1820, attacked and destroyed this town, and so they abandoned Tindouf and retreated, mostly to the Mauritanian territory, and gained fame due to religious erudition.

Today they are sedentarized and devote their time to petty **trade** and **agriculture** in Mali, Morocco, Mauritania, and Tindouf. However, one source on the Internet claims that there are 1,480,000 Tajakant in Algeria today, almost 99 percent of their population.

TARABIA. The tribe members of Tarabia originated from the north of the Arabian Peninsula, from the region of the town of Makkah. The exact date when they penetrated into **Palestine** is unknown. They chiefly dominated the region between the Carmel Mountains, the Yizrael Valley, and Nablus. The tribe members were part of the Mameluke administration, and some of them were commanders in the Mameluke army, for example, Abdullah Tarabia, Tarabia el-Dahari, and El-Ashkar el-Ibrahimi, in the 17th century, in the period of the Ottoman government. The Tarabia members received the income from taxes of various districts north and west of Nablus on lease from the Ottomans.

In the second half of the 16th century the tribe's leader, **Sheikh** Asaf, became prominent, as he was appointed keeper of security in the north of Palestine on behalf of the Ottoman government. He accepted to guard the **trade** caravans passing in his domain, and also to supervise the Syrian Hajj route and to protect the safety of the Muslim pilgrims to Hejaz (contemporary northwest **Saudi Arabia**).

In the first half of the 17th century Emir Ahmed ben Tarabia was prominent. His government took over in the period of renewed ascent and the expansion of the government of the Druze House of Ma'an in **Lebanon**, under the leadership of their leader, Fakhr el-Din the Ma'anid II. The Ma'anids tried to penetrate from Lebanon to Palestine, and therefore threatened the House of Tarabia. Open wars broke out between the sides; the House of Tarabia and their allies defeated Fakhr el-Din and repulsed him back to Lebanon. Following this Ahmed conquered large parts of Samaria, the lower **Galilee**, around Haifa up to Jaffa, and levied a special tax (*hawa*) on anyone passing in his territory.

In the second half of the 17th century Emir Muhammad became famous. This emir lived permanently in an encampment on Mt. Carmel, and his income came from the villages of the region and from the franchises in use at the port of Acre. The Ottoman sultan did not demand percentages of his income but expected in return that the emir would secure freedom of movement on the roads and would take care of the caravans of traders, which the Bedouins used to plunder.

Toward the end of the 17th century the star of the House of Tarabia waned. It was weakened and lost most of its assets. The descendants of the House of Tarabia are today found in several states: in **Israel**, in the **Palestinian Authority**, in **Syria**, and in Lebanon.

TARABIN. During the 19th century and early 20th century, the Tarabin were the most important Bedouin tribe in the **Sinai** Peninsula and the second largest in the British mandatory **Palestine**. Today, the majority of the tribe lives in **Egypt**, mostly in the Sinai, but also on the other side of the Suez, near Cairo, and sections of this tribe live in areas bordering the Sinai in **Israel**, **Jordan**, the Gaza Strip, and **Saudi Arabia**. A township named Tirabin al-Sana was built in Israel in 2004 for members of this tribe as part of the Israeli government's project to settle the Bedouin **nomads**.

TEKNA. Tekna is a name referring to two **Berber** nomadic tribes whose origin is probably southern **Morocco**, consisting of the Lamta Sahara tribal federation. Today these tribes count to approximately 670,000, and their roaming territories have expanded over most of the northwestern Sahara. All Tekna are Sunni Muslim, but some subgroups cling to the Berber **language** and preserve certain cultural traditions, while other subgroups speak Hassaniya, a unique version of **Arabic** brought to the area by the **Bani Hassan** tribe.

The Tekna **settlements** control important routes of the Saharan caravan **trade**, while other subgroups are still nomadic or seminomadic, and their economy is based on **camels** and goat **herding**.

These tribes had been involved in many local and regional wars. They managed to preserve their independence for centuries. However, when the colonial powers left north Africa, they recognized the sovereignty of Morocco over their territory and accepted its rulers as their leaders. *See also* MAURITANIA.

TEL AS SABI. The Bedouin semi-urban center in the **Negev** district that was established on the outskirts of Beer Sheva, the major city in southern **Israel**. Tel As Sabi was the first Bedouin township built in Israel as part of a government project of building permanent **settlements**. It received the status of municipal authority in 1984. At first the project had been in an experimental state, and from mistakes and successes in Tel As Sabi, both the government and communities learned how to do things better.

According to the Israeli Central Bureau of Statistics, the population of Tel As Sabi in January 2011 was 15,700.

TENT. The tent is the traditional home of **wandering** Bedouins. The residential home has an important and central place in the culture of every society, including the Bedouin society, in its various representations: the **nomadic**, the seminomadic, and the permanent dweller. The dwelling place is made of building materials that can be obtained from their surrounding environment. It is clear that a nomadic person will erect a mobile home, and in contrast a permanent settler will not live in a temporary or mobile home, but only live in a fixed home. The rich person or one of a high class will build a spacious and splendid house for himself, whereas the poor man will make do with a simple and modest house, which will reflect his lifestyle and his means. Thus, there is a parallel between a person's lodging and his social and economic status.

The nomadic Bedouin, due to his nomadic lifestyle, needs a residence that will answer his demands, namely a home that will be convenient to dismantle and erect; a home that is possible to be built from the materials found in the environment where the nomadic Bedouin chooses to camp; a home that can be built and repaired by his own strength and with minimal expenses; a residence that fulfill the needs of the Bedouin family: it must suit the weather conditions, it must be a convenient residence suitable for a family to host its guests, and as much as possible it must be a pleasant and comfortable residence under the weather conditions. A solution was found to these demands in the image of the tent, known to the Bedouins as *Beit Al-Shaar*, which means the house made of hair. It is called so because its canvases are woven from the hair of black goats. This tent is also called the winter tent or *Beit Al-Mashta* as the nomad lives in it in the winter season.

The tent is divided into two parts: the men's section (*Makad Al-Rajah*) and the **women**'s section (*Mahram*).

The men's section: This section is designed to serve the men and the family and their guests. The men's section is called by the Bedouins **sheikh**. It is a known fact that the men's section is found in the northern part of the tent, that is, the right side when one comes in from the direction of the entrance to the tent. It is covered frequently by a front canvas called *satar* closing its opening. These characteristics were designed in order not to let guests make a mistake and know where the men's section is found.

As the men's section is designed to serve as a place of **hospitality**, it is obvious that the suitable facilities necessary for this will be found in it: mattresses, woven carpets and pillows, the fireplace, and the system of **coffee** vessels.

The women's section: This section is located always at the southern edge of the tent, that is, on the left side of the tent when one is standing in front of its opening. The *mahram* is the section that houses most of the actions connected to the economic life of the family. The mahram is also the place of raising and care of the children; it also serves as a sleeping place of the family members, a storeroom for the family equipment, a place in which the family keeps its **food**, a kitchen, and a place in which the family holds all the bedclothes and hospitality instruments.

When the nomadic Bedouin looked for materials for building his home's walls, he turned to goat's hair, and from this hair he prepared the canvases of his tent. He prepared the other parts of the tent from plants and trees common in the **desert**.

With the transition of the Bedouin from nomadic life to permanent **settlement** there also came a transition from the tent life to living in a house made of stone. The stone house, with its various types and forms, was the last word in the field of a dwelling place for the Bedouin society, whoever and whatever it may be. However, it is worth noting that there are more traditional Bedouin societies, where despite the transition to a permanent settlement, it is still possible to see a tent built beside a stone house, as they still see in it a symbol and part of their heritage and culture, and therefore, do not give it away.

THAMUD. The Thamud were a cluster of tribes who came from the Arabian Peninsula a long time ago and formed a big kingdom, which prospered from about 3000 BC to 200 BC. In **Yemen** and all over central Arabia many Thamudic rock writings and paintings have been discovered.

The Thamud settled on the slopes of Mt. Athlab, and here also rock inscriptions have been encountered. The Koran cites the Thamud as an example of the transitory nature of worldly power. The Prophet Ṣāliḥ warned the Thamud to worship Allah; when they refused, an earthquake or a thunderbolt eliminated them. In fact, a volcanic outbreak whose origin was in one of the many Arabian lava fields might have caused their disappearance.

The Koran, old Arabian **poetry**, and Assyrian annals (Tamudi) mention this tribe, along with a Greek temple inscription from northwestern Hejaz, from AD 169, a Byzantine source from the 5th century AD, and old north Arabian wall writings around Tayma.

The annals of the Neo-Assyrian king Sargon II (8th century BC) mention them as he overcame this people in battle in a campaign in northern Arabia. They are also mentioned by the Greeks, who called them "Tamudaei" and "Thamud" in the works of Aristotle, Ptolemy, and Pliny. The Thamud disappeared prior to the onset of **Islam**, between AD 400 and 600.

TOUBOU. The Toubou live in small clusters in severe **desert** conditions, in southeastern **Libya**, close to the Tibesti Mountains by the Chad frontier and near to the Al Kufrah **Oasis**. They resemble the sub-Saharan black Africans more than Libyan Arabs in their skin color, and were thought at first to be those black troops whom Muammar Gadhafi used to suppress the unrest. In 2008, a group called the Toubou Front for the Salvation of Libya threatened to attack the Sarir oilfield, almost 400 kilometers away from Al Kufrah. At first the Toubou backed Gadhafi on the strength of financial support but later sided with the rebels.

TRADE. The Bedouin **wandering** all over the desert needs a fixed **market** to sell the surpluses of his produce and to be equipped with all that he requires. Therefore every Bedouin tribe already from the historical periods was connected with a nearby town, to which he sold his produce surpluses and from which he bought his necessary supplies. A good example is the Bedouins in the **Negev** region in the south of Israel today. In the past Bedouins of the Negev turned to the markets of Gaza and Hebron. With the foundation of the city of Beer Sheva in the year 1900, the Bedouin market was founded in the town called *Sukh al-Hamis* (Thursday market). In the market, the Bedouin sold his surpluses of sheep, the sheep's wool, goats' hair, and wheat and barley. The market thronged with life in the autumn season, when the Bedouin made his purchases for the winter: wooden plows, metal blades, ropes, and canvases prepared for the winter **tent**. The Bedouins buy in the market to this day: cloths, sugar, tea, rice, cooking and baking utensils, work tools, and so on.

Trade has been known as the hallmark of Bedouin society in the past. From the 2nd century BC to the 4th century AD, the **Himyar** kingdom, located on the Arabian Peninsula in the site of contemporary **Yemen**, was on the thoroughfare and trade route of spices and sapphires from India to the West, and from Africa of ivory and furs. Also the Nabateans in a similar period in the area of modern **Jordan** dealt with most of the commerce from India and Africa to the Middle East, Persian Empire, and **Egypt**. During this period they brought their goods to Ein Gedi and Jericho, where they were reloaded and sent to ports on the Mediterranean Sea.

The **Okaz Market** was an important market in historical times, to which Arabs would flock in the **pre-Islamic period**. It was a meeting place that was open for one month a year, and there dates, honey, clothes, beasts, and wine could be traded.

In the areas of a market in a certain region, the Bedouin **women** trade in new and old jewels. The jewels are the sole property of the woman. If the woman has money, she will buy a gold coin and will combine it among her ornaments. If she needs money, she will sell the coin in the market.

The animal market was, and still is, the heart of the market. In the past the market thronged with **camels**, donkeys, sheep, and goats. But recently, with the transition of the Bedouins to permanent **settlements**, a reduction has taken place in the extent of the growth of livestock, and therefore many buy a sheep or lamb in this market for slaughter in festive events.

TRAVELERS LITERATURE, WESTERN. The Holy Land is part of the Fertile Crescents, situated between the **desert** and the sea, and like its neighboring countries, always attracted nomadic tribes following grazing flocks or looking for easy loot. Arab Bedouins appeared in the area during the Roman era, but as long as the country was densely settled and cultivated, they stayed on its fringes, mostly on the eastern side of **Jordan**. When the urban and farming population left, for whatever reasons, the vacancy invited the nomads. Most Bedouin groups came from **Syria**, but during the last centuries, some Bedouins came to **Israel/Palestine** via **Sinai**.

From the end of the 16th century onward when the population was scarce, the Bedouins moved in decisively and found grazing land for their flocks in the most fertile districts of the country, and practically controlled the roads and **trading** routes that crossed from the desert to the sea.

During the 18th and mostly the 19th century, the holy sites, especially those holy to **Christianity**, attracted European travelers, who met the Bedouins and told about their novel experience when they got home. They recounted tales of robbery and plunder, about their **hospitality**, and about their **tents** and lifestyle. They wrote stories about their bravery and courage, about acting as guides and traveling escorts, about exotic meals and riding **camels**. They wrote or told an audience about the contacts they formed with them, how they functioned as service providers to trading caravans, transporters of goods, and other commodities. Their written reports along with pictures of the land and its inhabitants provide a unique source of information, as some of them also describe the mundane traits and characteristics of the Bedouins, their **food**, their **dress**, their residence, and their occupations, as seen by an eye witness.

Until the 18th century, the literature describing Arabs in general and Bedouins in particular as concerns their life, customs, and behavior had many faults. The change occurred with the publication of the French count Volney titled *A Voyage in* ***Egypt*** *and in Syria* (1787). His book was the first publication with a humanist and scientific view of the subject matter. Soon his book became the most qualified reference book on Greater Syria, *Bilad el-Sham*. Other travelers began to show interest in the archaeological sites of the country, in its residents, in its fauna and flora, and so on. Thus, many travelers were no longer just pilgrims; some of them had a scientific background that caused them to visit holy sites and look for evidence of classic geographic and historical scripts of the theological texts.

The trend brought to the area important Oriental scholars of the time, and the publication of their books influenced many travelers of the later years, in the 19th century. From that time onward the travelers' literature got richer and far more scientific with regard to the Orient and biblical studies, topographic research of the land, and historical insights and analysis. One book of special interest regarding the Bedouins of the Holy Land was *Domestic Life in Palestine* by Mary Eliza Rogers, who was the first Westerner who managed to penetrate, study, and provide information about the world of the Bedouin **women**.

According to reports of travelers in the late 19th century, the Bedouins were feared by the sedentary population. This state of affairs occurred whenever the local administration of the Ottoman Empire was weak; the Bedouins had the run of the land, and security was practically nonexistent. The Bedouins had full control of the roads: they plundered the trade convoys and the Haj convoys; they robbed travelers and imposed a "protection tax" on them, but they also served as guides and escorts themselves, and their camels were used to transport goods and commodities.

The Bedouin tribes stamped their imprint on the **settlements** of all the districts of the country. They collected protection fees, they moved with their herds on cultivated areas, and they raided villages and robbed the *fellahin* (peasants), causing the abandonment of several villages. However, in some cases they settled and intermingled with the locals.

At the close of the 19th century, as the security situation got better, due to reforms introduced by the Ottoman government, the Bedouins' power declined, and the travelers' literature reflects the change. The government backed strong, wealthy landowners, and they started to charge Bedouins for the use of their land. The influx of Jewish immigrants who bought land from these *effendis* (wealthy owners) and settled down there pushed the Bedouins further from the fertile valleys to uncultivated areas.

TRIBALISM. Tribe (*kabila*) is an alliance between **clans** from one origin who have a common interest. This alliance gives the clan members in it more power to protect the areas of land and the sources of **water** at their disposal.

At the head of the tribe stands one person called the ***Sheikh**-ul-Mashaikh* (the leader of leaders), representing the important needs of the clan members in the tribe.

Many tribal societies have more than one legal system, as various subgroups have their own unique set of rules. In many Arab states, the regimes learned to respect these legal subsystems, like the Tribal Customary **Law** or specific laws of a given religious group. In the tribal law system, the value of a person is determined by his patriarchal lineage; thus, as the kinship creates no hierarchy among brothers, rights to property can cause competition within families.

There are 14 strata within the tribes—from the smallest unit of the family, to the extended family, the clan, the tribe, the group of tribes, and so forth. A sheikh is a respected member of a lineage group who has the power to exert authority over the members of that group. The larger the group, the higher the authority of the given sheikh. In many modern states, tribal sheikhs function as representatives of their people, as mediators between the government and the tribe, and often also as the local judicial authority.

One of the measures rulers used to control Bedouins and to block their encroachment on fertile lands was to recruit them into the army or to organize them into tribal fighting units assigned for specific missions rewarded by the state.

The tribe (*ashira*) is a union of families grazing their flock jointly, tilling the lands together, and even fighting together in order to protect their land and their sources of water. Their common origin is one ancestor. His memory unites the tribesmen, who tend to make a pilgrimage to his grave in order to keep contacts between the families. The most important person in the tribe is the head of the tribe, the sheikh.

In most of the cases the tribesmen live in a certain region regarded as their homeland; they speak a uniform dialect, which distinguishes them from the rest of the tribes; and they have a homogeneous culture and common solidarity—mainly **fanaticism** against external parties.

Tribalism is found in all continents of the world; part of it disappeared as happened to the European tribes—the Alemannic tribes and the Franks—and similar to tribes that are disappearing like the Indian tribes in North and South America, and some are absorbed in settled societies, as in the states of southwest Asia.

The existence of a tribe has to have two components: one is the emotional component and the second the geographic space. Even if the tribe wanders and the territory changes, it still has its own tribal territory. The tribesmen are protective of one another due to the proximity that exists between the tribe's members and because they live in one region.

The tribesmen are connected socially among themselves and especially by blood, which is the strongest connection between the tribesmen. The ties are strengthened also as a result of marital ties. The tribesmen usually marry within the tribe, with exceptions only in special cases, for example, marriage between children of sheikhs, where the goal of marriage is designed to reinforce ties and alliances between tribes.

A large portion of the Middle Eastern cultures are tribal and organized as tribes. It is possible to say that tribalism is one of the characteristics making the Middle East unique from other areas in the world.

The tribes and tribalism filled a central role in the history of the Middle East and north Africa. The fact is that most of the Arab population in the Arabian Peninsula in the **pre-Islamic period** (the *el-Jahaliya* period) was tribal. Most of the warriors of the Muslim armies that conquered the Middle East and north Africa came from tribes of Bedouins, who had left the imprint of their culture and concepts on the societies that were founded later, which we know as Arab societies.

Even today there are phenomena in Middle Eastern societies that can be explained by tribal heritage (tribalism). There are states that were founded on a tribal basis or whose heritage is tribal, such as **Saudi Arabia**, **Jordan**, the Gulf principalities, **Libya**, and **Iraq**.

Tribal culture has a strong influence on the shaping of society and the politics of Middle Eastern and north African countries. The Bedouin tribes, throughout the history of the region, filled a central role in the life of the society and state in that region. They constituted a factor threatening the central government and they played an important role in the formation and collapse of dynasties.

The tribes constitute a very serious challenge to the political elites of the independent Arab states. He who thinks that the Bedouins are tribesmen, **nomads**, and riders on camels, and live in the **desert**, are sadly mistaken, as this picture does not match the reality of the Middle East. Indeed there is a distinction between settlers and nomads, but despite the **settlement** of the nomadic population, amazingly, tribal identity in the region still lives on the political and social consciousness of millions of Arabs inhabiting modern cities and towns. This unique phenomenon is one of the good examples that reflect the phenomenon of tribalism in the Arab world, which is not their way of life. Instead of this, it is an identity, grounded in cultural psychology and politics. Thus, tribalism in the Middle East is firmly established from a political and social point of view.

The relations between the political government and the tribes, no matter if this be a local or foreign government, were subject to reactions of the changes in security. When the central government was weakened, the tribes were strengthened; the power of the tribe was connected closely to the amount of power of the central government of the state.

As for the part and the role of the tribe in building the national state, certain states oppressed the tribes, forcing them to settle permanently. However, in certain states the tribes stayed as a central political protagonist, for example, Saudi Arabia, the Gulf principalities, Jordan, Iraq, **Yemen**, and Libya. In these states the tribal identity continues to play an important role in shaping the process of decision making of the state, and also in the construction of a national identity. The tribal identity in these states is so strong that it competes with two other identities in the state—the religious/Islamic identity and the national identity.

The impressive political influence of tribes in the region illustrates how such "modern" systems can remain very vulnerable to the reality of tribal culture, and how tribalism constitutes a central part of the political behavior in various states.

States like Libya and Yemen could not exist as independent political units; they could not manage without the support of the tribes. Decades after independence, loyalty to the tribe and to the sheikh in these states has stayed much stronger than loyalty to the state.

The stubborn persistence of the tribal identity in the Arab Middle East is a result of the failure of the national project and of political modernization as well as the addiction of Arab autocrats to the politics of survival. Following the outbreak of the Arab Spring revolutions in December 2010, it can be seen that the phenomenon of tribalism returned to its dominance in the Arab states. Loyalty to the tribe is still an important motif in the Bedouin life—this proves that blood ties are stronger than political ties. During a clash between the political interests and tribal interests, the Bedouins choose tribal interests. They see in the tribe stability, the same support that gives them the power, while they perceive political interest to be a passing phenomenon.

TUAREG. Nomadic Tuareg wander in a number of states in the Sahara region and also in the Sahel region. Being a **Berber** people, they have a different culture, **language**, **dress**, facial appearance, and history from the Arabic people on **Libya**'s coast, and also from the "pure" Arab Bedouins of the Libyan **Desert**. They live in little clusters, chiefly in the southwest of the country, centered mainly around the Ghadamis and Ghat oases. Tuaregs live close to the Waha natural gas fields on the Algerian border, in addition to being close to the big Elephant oilfield under the partial ownership of the Italian nationalized oil company, ENI, and Libya's state-owned company, the National Oil Corporation.

The Tuaregs attacked the Saharan governments and oil installations in order to achieve independence but did not confront the Libyan government, which some claim proves that Muammar Gadhafi armed them. Non-Libyan Tuaregs sought and obtained asylum in Libya, and they were partly loyal to Gadhafi in the 2011 conflict, and it was claimed that he was hiding among them trying to cross the southern border of the state. However, later they joined with the **Warfallah** and other tribes to demand Gadhafi's resignation and clashed with the police in the towns of Ghat and Ubary. *See also* ALGERIA; MAURITANIA; MOROCCO.

TUBA-ZANGHARIYYA. Tuba-Zanghariyya is a Bedouin town in lower **Galilee** in northern **Israel**, consisting of about 8,000 residents, all members of the ***Al Heib*** tribe. The town was formed by a merger of two neighboring villages, Tuba and Zanghariyya

The Bedouin tribes 'Arab al-Zanghariyya and 'Arab al-Heib used to encamp near the spring Ein Tuba, and were semi-settled by 1903. Initially they used to live in **tents** but later settled formally and built villages.

As Tuba was an Al Heib village, it suffered no harm in the 1948 war, since this tribe had long-standing ties with the Jews in **Palestine**/Israel and was allied with the Jewish Haganah organization. The tribe members helped defend Jewish villages in Galilee during the 1936–1939 Arab Revolt and fought alongside the Jews in the 1948 war. However, unlike their neighbors, members of Arab Al Zanghariyya took part in the Arab Revolt and fought with the Arab and Syrian forces during the 1948 war.

Therefore, in May 1948, when it had become obvious that the Jews were going to win the war in the Galilee, most of its population fled to **Syria**, while others fled into nearby Tuba. After the war, the government added the site of Zanghariyya to Tuba, and the two previously large camps became flourishing villages until they merged into one municipal township.

TUNIS. From 1930 to 1956 there was a considerable influx of **wandering** Bedouins from the **Tunisian** countryside to the capital, Tunis, which grew from a population of 220,000 in 1936 to 410,000 in 1956. Tens of thousands of people migrated from their **nomadic sheikhdoms** to the shantytowns in the suburbs of Tunis. This led to a considerable number of social problems, and the migrants, judged as undesirables, were imprisoned or sent back to their place of origin. The seasonal **migration** took place normally toward the end of the month of May, when peasants quit their miserable habitation and looked for harvest work in the governorates of Mateur, Beja, Souk El Erbaa, and Souk El Khemis. During this journey, they went through the town of Tunis in search of work or income.

Also, in years of drought and bad harvest of cereals, as in 1930, 1945, and 1948, the conditions caused an exodus of tribesmen with their flocks of sheep and their beasts of burden from the south and center of the country to its north. They adopted certain professions like porter, harvester, shoe shiner, secondhand goods dealers, itinerant salesman, and thief. They sold off their **camels** and ate their donkeys in order to survive.

This situation often caused problems of hygiene as well as serious security issues, as they took part in armed robberies, attempted murders, and the like. They lived in slums or *mamra* made of wood, mud, and straw shacks. In 1956, there were 105,000 migrants like this living in the capital, Tunis. Some who were fit for work were recruited and others who were unfit were given assistance.

There was a problem of return of the vagrants to their homes. The government made the following cases an exception, for those who did not have to return to their sheikhdoms: war veterans; all families whose head was employed; all families living in a stone hut, which was not frail; old people, pregnant **women** in the last months of pregnancy, and parents of patients at Sadiki; tenants of a rural plot possessing livestock, especially dairy cows; and people originating from Tunis.

Those who were sent back were transported by train, except when the distance was short, when they went by foot. The sick went by train. Most of the vagrants spent time in the civil prison of Tunis, which in 1940 housed 1,400 people. An accommodation camp of vagrants was founded in 1941, in the camel **market** and the **horses**' square, by the municipal bureau of hygiene. However, the efforts of repatriation were often in vain, as in 1937, it was noted in a statistical document that 20 percent of those repatriated had returned to Tunis. *See also* KHALDUN, ABDURRAHIM BIN MUHAMMAD IBN (1332–1406); PALESTINIAN AUTHORITY; SETTLEMENT; TUNISIA; URBANIZATION.

TUNISIA. The first people in recorded history who settled in **Tunis** were the **Berber**s. In the 9th century BC Phoenician settlers founded the city of Carthage, which became the dominant power in the western Mediterranean. The city and its surrounding area were conquered and destroyed by the Romans after the third Punic War. Later the city was reestablished and conquered by the Vandals, who controlled the area for a little more than a century. Arab Muslims conquered the country in the 7th century AD. They founded the city of Kairouan.

The country was ruled by the Aghlabid dynasty from 800 to 909. They had been replaced by the Fatimids, who were ousted by the Zirid. The Fatimids retaliated by sending the Banu Hilal, a warlike Arab **tribe**, to the Maghreb, and these people ravaged the countryside, laying it to waste: the lands became a **desert**. After the demise of the Zirid dynasty the country disintegrated into a number of micro-sheikhdoms.

One of the major rulers made a treaty with the Arab tribes, who were paid to keep the peace. Since then, tax payment was always associated with Arab cavalry. Thus, for centuries to come the **nomadic** tribes controlled the space between the cities; the nomads robbed or made themselves indispensable to power. They carried out raids and exerted pressure on the oases. Sometimes, they settled near them, becoming the armed wing of a sedentary group wanting to base its power in a town.

The Ottoman Empire conquered the country in 1534 and ruled it until the establishment of a French protectorate in 1881. Historical accounts tell of the intensity of the raids and rivalries between the tribal groups in rural Tunisia.

Between 1930 and 1956 the city of Tunis grew from a population of 220,000 in 1936 to 410,000 in 1956. **Urbanization** changed the character of the state. Modern life attracted several groups, including nomadic Bedouins, who migrated to the big cities to improve their living conditions.

Between 1945 and 1948, Tunisia endured a harsh drought that damaged the harvest and provoked an exodus of nomads with their livestock to the urban centers. This influx led to sanitary problems as well as to acts of aggression and begging. They joined gangs of thieves and lived in mud and wooden shacks of suburban shantytowns. When the authorities attempted to send the migrant population back, land ownership disputes caused further trouble in the rural provinces.

In 1956, Tunisia achieved independence from France under Habib Bourguiba and elected its own government, which had ups and downs. In December 2010, civil unrest started there that spread over much of the Arabic world and became known as the Arab Spring. In January 2011 President Zine El Abidine Ben Ali was forced to flee the country and seek asylum in **Saudi Arabia** with his wife and three children. He was sentenced to life imprisonment in absentia by a Tunisian court for inciting violence and murder. Democracy is now starting to develop in Tunisia, with the end of the corrupt previous regime. Therefore, the status of today's Bedouins in Tunisia is yet to unfold. *See also* SETTLEMENT.

TURKEY. Turkey is named after the **Turkmen** tribes, which migrated to Anatolia from central Asia during the 10th century AD. A century later, they were followed by the Saljuk, who penetrated Asia Minor and fought the Byzantines until they established a presence in Anatolia, where they founded a High Sultanate whose capital was the town of Konya. In the middle of the 13th century, right after the Mongol invasion, the Sultanate fragmented into principalities (*beyliks*) ruled by a prince (*bey*). One of those principalities, Osmanoglu (the sons of Osman), was named after the Bey Otman I, who was a charismatic leader and skilled soldier and who declared independence of his principality and established his capital in Bursa.

After his passing, the Ottomans took over the entire Asia Minor. They conquered the Balkans and kept expanding until the Ottoman Empire ruled most of the Middle East, most of Muslim north Africa, parts of Europe, and a number of islands in the Mediterranean. The ruler of the empire was called the sultan. In the mid-15th century, after several years of war, Sultan Mehmet the First defeated Byzantine and conquered Constantinople, which became his new capital, Istanbul.

In the era of the Ottoman Empire, the Bedouin **tribes wandered** from region to region according to circumstances. There were no political borders, and even the size of the provinces was flexible. Bedouin tribes were present in Asia Minor (contemporary Turkey) since **pre-Islamic** times. They came from **Iraq** and **Syria**, or followed in the wake of conquering armies.

Today, Arabs constitute approximately 5 percent of Turkey's population, estimated at 70 million people. They live near the Syrian and the Iraqi borders. The redemarcation of 1939 that attached the Syrian district of Iskenderun to Iraq had split the Bedouin tribes, who lived in the area between Syria, Turkey, and Iraq. Turkish Arabs were exposed to a "Turkization" policy, but the tribes still speak **Arabic**, although with a certain Turkish influence.

The Arabs have a long history in Asia Minor. They even founded the cities of Urfa and Mardin, whose residents still speak a special Arab dialect affected by Syrian and Saudi dialects, since most of the tribes in Turkey came from the northern Arab Peninsula. Many, especially those who live in the Mardin region, are descendants of the Bakr and Taglab tribes.

A coalition of Bedouin tribes lives in the districts of Haran, Bir Ajeik, and Sawirak. The largest, or most known, are the Jamila, Banu Ajal or Al-Ajlin, Abade, Jarmadli, Banu Yousef, and Banu Zaid. Other Arab tribes in Turkey include the Jabour, Adwan, Bakara, and Sharabin. *See also* ISRAEL; KURDS; PALESTINE.

TURKMEN, IRAN. The Turkmen in Iran include seven tribes: Afshar (Shamlu, Karhalu, Saruanalu); Biat and Dunbali; Kajar; Rajar (Gajar); Shakakain; Karakuzlu; and Sha Sivan (Shah Soun).

TURKMEN, ISRAELI. Arab Turkmen lived in the period of the British mandate in the Yizrael Valley region (Marj Even Aamar) in the north of **Palestine**. Their name testifies to their non-Arab origin. They belong to the Turkish peoples. The Turkmen were already found in the territories of **Syria** and Palestine in the 12th century. The penetration into the region continued in the period of the Mamelukes and also in the period of the Ottoman government. One should note that the Turkmen **tribes** lived on the Golan Heights until the **Israeli** conquest in 1967.

Turkmen are a minority of Turkish origin, speaking Turkish with the eastern Oghoz dialect spoken in the Republic of Turkmenistan. They are all Sunni Muslims; most of them are of the Hanafi sect, but some follow the Sufi version. They live mainly in the *sahrestans* of Gorgan and Gonbad-e Qabus in Mazandaran and Bojnurd in the Khorasan province, and in the Turkoman

Sahra and Gorgan Plain, a fertile region along the Iranian-Turkmenistan border, between the Atrak River in the north and the Caspian Sea in the west, and the Quchan Mountains in the east and the Gorgan River in the south.

Turkmen are Turks who came to **Iran** during the Turkish invasion of the 6th century AD, settled there, and kept their ethnic identity during the Mongol invasion. Turkmen tribes can also be found in Russia, Syria, and Afghanistan. The most important Turkmen tribe in Iran is the Guklan tribe, who live in central and eastern Turkoman Sahra, and the Yamotes, who live in the west of the same region. Their overall number in Iran is estimated to be about one million. Their main towns are: Gonbad Qabs, Bandar Turkoman, Aq-Qala, and Gomisan.

They have a history of resistance to central governments, and one of their revolts was crushed by **Reza Shah Pahlavi** in 1925. *See also* IRAN; TURKEY; TURKMEN, IRAN; TURKMEN, ISRAELI.

U

UMAYYAD DYNASTY (661–750). The Umayyad Dynasty was the first Muslim dynasty. It used the method of "divide and rule" and exploited tribal disputes to gain power, as the Arab **tribes** were crucial to any leader who wished to conquer new territories. The first three Umayyad caliphs were Mu'awiyah (661–680), Yazid (680–683), and Mu'awiyah II (683–684). They supported the southern tribes, who were more sedentary compared to the **nomadic** northern tribes. For example: Mu'awiyah ordered the settling of 50,000 **Azd** families in Khurasan. The northern tribes opposed the project but did not rebel. Yazid was threatened by a *fitna* (rebellion) by Abd Allah ibn Al Zubayr. Some northern tribes in the Hejaz supported him since Yazid was pro-**Qahtan**. Marwan (684–685) succeeded Mu'awiyah ibn Yazid, who started the Marwanid Umayyad dynasty, which was the second and last Umayyad royal house.

According to the historian Al-Baladhuri Ibn Ziyad, the governor of Khurasan province was not honored or accepted by the tribes; thus, many southern Arabs who came to settle in Khurasan found that the best plots in the province were already taken by the northern tribes. In those times there were many intertribal disputes.

Both northern and southern tribes were avid participants in **Islamic** expansion. But the expansion was executed mainly by the northern tribes, including the conquering of **Syria** and **Palestine** by the forces of the caliph 'Umar, as they were the first to arrive in the new territories. The same applied to the fall of Jazirah (**Iraq**) after the Battle of Qadisiyyah (637). The Mudar or Qays gained a large part of the booty and the best lands, as the Qahtan (southern tribes) were not privileged and received a far smaller share of the plunder.

Therefore, when the southern tribes realized that their northern enemies were blocking them in the east, they moved to North Africa and Al-Andalus (Spain), where the tribe members excelled and held major positions in the army and the governance. Al-Hajjaj ibn Yusuf (661–714), the minister of defense of the Ummayad kingdom, maintained a power balance between the two tribal confederations by calculated political appointments.

As by tradition, all imams had originated from the **Quraysh**, the tribe of the Prophet Muhammad, which belonged to a northern group, the northern group gained more prominence. In contrast to this, the southern tribes boasted of their past greatness, and claimed that Qahtan was a son of Prophet Hud and a direct descendant of Ismail, the "father of all Arabs."

The local administration of northern Arabia was controlled by the northern tribes, which had good connections with the Umayyad ruling class in Damascus, and they were granted privileges and positions by all Muslim rulers who succeeded them (including the Ottomans and **Saddam Hussein**).

Marwan tried to introduce a centralized system of government. He also founded local armies to enable local governors to contribute to the defense of the empire. For the first time in history there was an Arab army loyal to the caliph. He initiated the postal system (*barid*) and the writing and sealing of documents, and his descendants introduced a special Muslim coinage.

Abd Al-Malik ibn Marwan (685–705) married a Qaysi woman and relied on the Qays tribal confederation and appointed members of this tribe to high administrative positions. He sent Syrian forces to suppress the **Berber** revolt in North Africa and Andalusia, and also put down a revolt of discriminated non-Arab Muslim tribes in Iraq,

Two of the last four caliphs, Hisham (724–743) and Marwan II (744–750), relied on the northern Mudar tribes and triggered the anger of the **Yemenites**, who regarded this as harming their own interests. *See also* EGYPT; SAUDI ARABIA.

UNITED ARAB EMIRATES (UAE). Historical evidence indicates that society and contacts with other human groups go back to around 3000 BC, where evidence indicates the presence of **trade** centers and mining. Foreign trade developed when **camels** became a means of transportation. By AD 100 there was trade over land on the route between **Syria** and **Iraq**, and combined sea and land trade routes with India and China. The area converted to **Islam** in the mid-7th century AD. In the 16th century AD, the Portuguese conquered several major ports in the Gulf, but they had been ousted by the rebelling local **tribes**, some of which were **nomadic herding** tribes and others were sedentary, engaged in various maritime occupations. During the 18th and the 19th centuries, the Emirates were part of the first and second Saudi states that fought with the Ottoman Empire for their independent status. In 1892, British interventions led to a treaty with the allied **sheikhdoms**. Cooperation between the two parties created the framework that enabled the protection of the area from piracy and other threats. In 1971, the Emirates received their independence, and the country was formed as a Federation of Seven Emirates. In 1962, **Abu Dhabi** was the first emirate to export oil, and today the country is regarded as possessing the seventh largest oil reserves in the world.

The Bedouins constitute the main segment of the inhabitants of the state. Oil had a great influence on the lifestyles of the Bedouins in the state, especially from the 1970s onward, with the growth of oil income. They settled permanently. They do not wander in the **desert** anymore or look for pasture and **water** for their livestock. Today they are permanent settlers; they live in palaces and drive in magnificent cars.

A central milestone and essential change in Bedouin life took place in the year 1966, with the rise to power of Sheikh Zayed bin Sultan Aal Nahyan (1918–2004). Since then they have undergone accelerated processes of change, the results of which we see today. Sheikh Zayed took care of their welfare and opened schools and clinics for them. Today they live a life of plenty. The life of poverty in the past had an influence on the security. As a result of the shortage, the tribes would perpetrate robbery and plunder, as this was a legitimate source of income in those days. They would plunder for camels and sheep. Today as a result of the prosperity, there is security and there is no more robbery due to the income.

The materialistic oil revolution delivered the inhabitants of the Gulf, including the United Arab Emirates, at great speed from the **tent**-hair home life to life in the villas and Mercedes cars. However, despite the transition to a life of **urbanization**, the Bedouins still maintain the higher Bedouin values, like morality, generosity, and nobility; they act to conserve these positive social values.

Before the discovery of oil, at the start of the 20th century, the inhabitants of the region tried to acclimatize to the environment in which they lived. Despite the harsh conditions of the region, a desert climate, the inhabitants adopted professions for themselves in order to earn an income—for example, if the region was found on the coast, they would fish and pull out **pearl**s from the sea. The pearls were an important source of income. The income from the trade in pearls was a central support of the economy of the Arab Emirates in the Gulf before the discovery of oil.

The inhabitants who lived in the coastal region lived a life of almost permanent **settlement**, while those who lived far from the sea and within the desert led a nomadic life.

After the discovery of oil and the natural resources and the arrival of foreign companies, which came to look for oil in the region, together with the slow transition to occupation with **agriculture**, a process began of permanent settlement among the nomads, and they started to live in villages and towns, and also to obtain employment in varied professions. Similarly, the state began to take an interest in what was going on among the Bedouins. It took care of their welfare, and opened clinics and schools for them.

The oil wealth contributed its part to change of Bedouin culture; the Bedouin tribes abandoned nomadic life and passed on to a permanent settlement.

URBANIZATION. Traditionally, the Bedouins wandered in **desert** areas but moved closer to towns in the summer months when there was less or no **water** available. The process of settling of Bedouins is called **sedentarization**, where Bedouins abandon their **nomadic** ways of life and tend to build homes for themselves, which are not mobile like the **tent** but are fixed on the ground, like mud huts and the like, so that they do not need to travel away from them. Thus, the nomadic habits of grazing and **migration** with flocks of sheep, goats, **camel**s, and **horse**s have become less prominent. However, there is another process influencing the Bedouin way of life and in which the Bedouins participate these days: it is the process of urbanization, that is, the process of building towns where the Bedouins will settle and the process of Bedouins settling in a new or already-built town.

The Middle East is mostly a desert region, and therefore, for hundreds of years inhabitants wandered from place to place in order to find water and fertile land. Part of the inhabitants turned this into a permanent custom, where the most prominent population group in this field was the Bedouin group. The Bedouins lived in the region and earned an income from escorting caravans and levying road tolls on the desert roads. Today, now that states with clear borders have been founded, the Bedouins find it difficult to deal with these occupations, and they are forced to gain an income from **agriculture**, building, and service in the army in the same state in which they live. This state caused part of the Bedouins to stop **wandering** and to settle permanently in or around existing towns like Amman (the capital of **Jordan**) or if the state in which they live founded new towns for them like **Rahat** and Tel Sheva in **Israel**.

In **Kuwait**, the process of settling in towns and migration to the city from the countryside is called *hadar*. Urbanization has been taking place in Kuwait for more than a hundred years. Bedouins were attracted to Kuwait City and the water there for reasons of **trade** (by water), and they were joined in their new city by Persians, Indians, and Arab-African slaves. The latter searched for trading routes in the Arabian Gulf and the Indian Ocean. A number of traders from Bastak, **Iran**, settled in Dubai, in the Bastakiya quarters.

The settlers brought tradition, **language**, and architecture of their own to the cities. Their ancestry defines them in the eyes of the locals, and in Qatar there are three categories: (1) *arab*, from Bedouin or tribal ancestry; (2) *ajam*, descended from Persian forefathers; and (3) *abd*, descended from slaves.

In the United Arab Emirates (UAE), Emiratis are encouraged to go to any of the seven emirates that constitute the UAE, or **Ajman**, and Dubai. The settlers choose the emirate according to the tribe from which they originate, and their **settlement** and the choice of location are linked significantly with the **clan** to which the settlers belong.

In Kuwait, the merchants (*hadar*) settled in the center of Kuwait City, while the *bedu* (recent Bedouin citizens) settled on its outskirts. There were winding pedestrian streets that provided shade from the sun in open areas. Every community had a mosque of its own and maybe a *madrassa* or school attached to it. There were also *suqs*, or **markets**, which contained **coffee** houses for conversations between residents, where there was trade in copper pots and kettles, textiles, spices, **food**, animals, and clothes. Lastly, there were castles or forts, which gave the inhabitants protection in wartime.

In modern urban living, all the troubles that frequent Western countries are present, such as inflation, unemployment, poor or expensive housing or lack of it, traffic problems, and costs of **education**. National housing projects have been designated for young couples and other youngsters, and they can live in integrated or mixed-ethnic apartment buildings, or choose to live within the family territory. Some national families have bought farms outside the cities, but expatriates cannot buy property, as the law forbids them to do this.

The daily life is concentrated on the waterfront, where restaurants and high-rise buildings have replaced trade areas, and there are corniches and promenades. New downtowns have replaced traditional commercial centers, with foci of international business, and small shops for specific goods have sprouted. Nearly every neighborhood has a mall of its own, carrying fashions of every international brand. **Women** reveal their faces in the mall, except when they meet local men, when they cover their face with a *shayla*. The Mall of the Emirates (in the UAE) contains an indoor ski slope, and the Bellagio Mall, Qatar, contains a Venetian canal and gondola system.

There are many roundabouts in the Gulf States, and traffic spreads over three- or four-lane highways. There are watchtowers that guide traffic at intersections, and landscape architects have turned barren areas into green areas, full of grass, plants, and palm trees.

The building materials for the Bedouin houses were palm trees, *sarooj* (mud blended with hay and manure), *juss* (limestone mortar blend), and coral or gypsum molded into building bricks. Cement for single-story and multi-story houses started to be used in the 1950s. The houses had ventilation systems for the summer, *majlises*, and courtyards. Date palms were used in the early years for construction, particularly near the oases, and these houses were called *barasti* in English and *khayamah or 'arishah* in **Arabic**. Palm trunks were used as supports for walls and beams in the house, and their branches, stripped of leaves, were made into mats, which became walls.

In summer, the buildings relied on non-mechanized ventilation systems, which circulated and cooled air. Date palm and coral are porous and prevent a buildup of hot air. There were two ventilation systems: (1) the *barjeel* or wind tower, which rose above the house and trapped cool air into it, and (2) a *badqeer* or wall wind-puller system, which was composed of two walls five inches apart, which pushed cool air into the rooms through windows and let warm air escape.

In addition, the production of oil in **Saudi Arabia** and other Gulf countries by British, American, and other companies influenced the Bedouin a lot, as the wealth that flowed into these once-poor countries hurled these states into the modern world, and generated pressures and tensions between the old and new. This had an extreme implication on the traditional Bedouin culture and endangered the survival of Bedouins as a separate community in the Middle East.

Two-thirds of the 170,000 Bedouins living in Israel live in the **Negev**, of which approximately 54,000 live in the town of Rahat, which is the largest **Bedouin settlement** in the world. It is one of the seven developed Bedouin townships in the Negev, which include **Hura**, Kseife, and Tel Sheva (Tel as-Sabi). The city's population rose from 30,000 in 2000 to 40,000 in 2006. It has an industrial park, health and educational facilities, transport lines, and a railway station. The average salaries paid to workers are half the average income of the other inhabitants of Israel (3,900 as opposed to 7,000 Israeli New Shekels). There is a school and leadership program for local school students designed to promote participation, and Harvard University is planning to establish a campus in the industrial area, which will be managed by the Ben-Gurion University of Negev.

In this city of Rahat, there are problems caused by the urbanization and sedentarization of Bedouin Arabs, like high crime rates, unemployment, and the fact that only 46 percent of the school students in 12th-grade classes are eligible for graduation. **Polygamy** is practiced by Bedouin men, despite its illegality in Israel; thus, the men receive generous child allowances from the state. The Bedouins engage in theft of agricultural equipment, car thefts, and drug smuggling. The expansion of cities limits the freedom of movement of the nomads. Also, the illiteracy rate has dropped from 95 percent to 25 percent. Bedouins can own their own land, and they have access to excellent health services.

Until the middle of the 1920s, most of the population in the countries of the Middle East lived in villages; the urban population ranged between 2 percent and 30 percent. The accelerated urbanization took place in the second half of the 20th century. The urbanization process received a push from the big migration movement from the village to the town. Villagers left for towns in order to improve their standard of living. By comparison to the village, the town offers better health services, better education, more varied possibilities of employment, and easier access to the various achievements of modern technology. The result is a growth in the urban population at the expense of the village one. Thus, for example, the percentage of urban population in **Oman** grew from 2 percent in the year 1950 to 15 percent in the year 1998,

Yemen from 6 percent to 36 percent, Saudi Arabia from 16 percent to 81 percent, the UAE from 25 percent to 85 percent, **Iran** from 27 percent to 60 percent, **Syria** from 31 percent to 53 percent, and **Egypt** from 32 percent to 45 percent, and the percentages today are much greater.

The most interesting change regarding urbanization took place in the oil-producing states and especially in the Gulf States, as desert countries are largely without an agricultural hinterland and sources of existence aside from the oil, and the population was crowded before the oil era into a small number of oases. As a result of the oil, cities like Doha, Manama, Kuwait, Dubai, and so on underwent an accelerated process of building, and within a short time they grew from tiny oases to large and densely populated cities. For example, in the year 1965 **Abu Dhabi** was an encampment alone. In the year 1972 it was already a town with 30,000 people; in the year 1976 it had 200,000 inhabitants and in the year 1990 some 300,000 inhabitants. In the 1950s Manama in **Bahrain** numbered a few hundred inhabitants. At the start of the 1980s it already counted 121,000 inhabitants and today 3.7 million people. The same process took place all over the Gulf States.

V

VENDETTA. Bloody disputes are a widespread and very significant phenomenon in traditional Middle Eastern society. Quarrels like these clash with the conceptions, norms, and laws of the modern state and raise for discussion questions concerning the borders of the autonomy of private individuals versus the sovereignty of the state.

The custom of vendetta, *Al-Tar*, is regarded as one of the prominent customs of the Bedouins. With part of the tribes it is also grounded in tribal **law**. The Bedouins see it as a duty on them to avenge the blood of their relatives. Any act of enmity against one of the tribe's members is regarded as desecration of the purity of the tribe.

Blood vengeance is the strongest with regard to revenges and is imposed on all the tribe's members if this is between tribes and on every family member if it is between families. They do not give up blood vengeance until the last day of their human life.

In order for a Bedouin to sweeten the feeling of vengeance, he will leave his house and lie in wait for his rival for a great period of time and with patience. The waiting period can even continue for 40 years.

The act of blood vengeance is not hidden as it is a matter of honor. Although murder in the Bedouin tribes is something despised by everyone, killing the murderer (revenge) is something praiseworthy, and the murderer will rise to the rank of hero and will be respected by all as such.

The custom of blood libel is different among the Bedouins from any other custom, as it is also a belief and not only a custom. The Bedouins believe that the soul of the victim will not stay in its place until his relatives avenge his blood. This soul demands revenge.

The revenge derives from the fact that in the past Bedouin society was basically a military society: if a man is killed, the group numbered one less soldier. The vengeance comes for settling scores and for creation of balance. Moreover, the Bedouin balance states, "Grave versus grave."

The custom of blood vengeance still exists today in Middle Eastern Bedouin society. Blood vengeance is considered an ancient custom—the roots of which come from the **pre-Islamic period**.

Blood vengeance with the Bedouins is absolute, and they have to avenge in order to get back their honor and the trust of their tribe's members; otherwise they will be considered cowards and weak.

The revenge of the victim's family becomes a festive ceremony—the avengers dip their keffiyeh in the victim's blood, wrap the cloth on a spear, and return to the tribe. The **women** welcome them with songs of praise, "*Ahdu Althar wamahu aar*"—avenge and wipe out the shame from us. The tribe members bless one another, slaughter sheep and rejoice, and heap praises for having avenged and returned their honor.

The phenomenon of blood vengeance places before the modern state entangled questions: How do the authorities need to cope with the phenomenon, which on the one hand expresses a cultural phenomenon of an ethnic group and on the other denies human rights? What should be the limit of cultural patience and pluralism that the state needs to apply versus the phenomenon of murder for blood vengeance? *See also* SULHA.

W

WAHHABISM. About the year 1744, Prince Muammed Ibn Saud, the ruler of Al-Deriah, answered the appeal of Muslim preacher Imam Ibn Abdul-Wahhab and started to spread the faith among the Arabian population. Abdul-Wahhab was born in 1702 in Uyna some 50 kilometers north of Al-Deriah. He had learned the Koran by heart as a child. He traveled to many states in order to study Islamic law, the *sharia.* He was removed in 1744 from his hometown, as his preaching and *fatwa* were too radical. Prince ibn Saud accepted him due to his wife's persuasion; he also ruled southern **Iraq** and parts of the Syrian **Desert**, which he had attached to the first Saudi state with tribal help. The Wahhabies believed only in the teachings of the Koran, in one God and in the words of the *hadith*, Muhammad's doctrine. They denied the later developments in Islamic theology and mysticism. They refused to honor saints and tombs, as there was no intercession between man and God, and banned philosophy and cogitation "because they lead to heresy and infidelity." Ornamentation of mosques and graves was banned too, as well as luxuries and lavishness. All those who denied Wahhabism were considered "heretics" and had to be reconverted to **Islam**.

Prince Muammed Ibn Saud promulgated Wahhabism through his invasions and expansion in Arabia. In 1803, his son took Karbala, the holiest town in **Iraq,** and destroyed the grave of Hussein, in which the Shiites believed. After he attacked Makkah and Medina, the Ottoman Sultan ordered his ruler in Egypt, Muammed Ali Pasha, to retake these towns from him. The campaign spread to the western regions of Arabia, and in 1818, Al-Deriah, the Saudis' capital, was seized, and the Saudi prince Abdullah was sent to prison in Istanbul and later executed there. The first Saudi state terminated together with the Wahhabi revivalist movement.

A second Saudi state was initiated in 1824 but fell when the Rashidis from the **Shammar** confederacy ruled central Arabia. The Saudi princes were exiled to **Bahrain**, and then **Kuwait**, after Riyadh was conquered in 1891. However, in 1902, after King **Abdulaziz Ibn Saud** reconquered Riyadh from the Rashidis, Wahhabism became its dominant ideology. In 1912, Ibn Saud applied this ideology in order to settle the Bedouins.

Ibn Saud tried to persuade the Bedouin tribes to give up raiding and **nomadism**, which he said were contrary to the Wahhabi pure faith of Islam. Some of the verses of the Koran accuse the nomads of being ignorant and conceited. He persuaded each tribe to settle on the agricultural land of a *dira.* He claimed he was going to use "loyal tribes" who would return to "the true Islam" to unify Arabia, as Wahhabism demanded. Three powerful tribes answered his call and promised to spread Wahhabism through a jihad, which was an alternative option to raiding and sheep grazing. *See also* SAUDI ARABIA.

WANDERING. The main economic activity of the **nomads** was growth of beasts like **camel**s, goats, **horse**s, and cattle. The growth of beasts had a close connection with the pasture areas, and they were replaced according to the seasons of the year. The distances between the grazing plots demanded wandering for days and weeks and required a very flexible form of life. The most important factor of nomadism was the need to search for sources of **water** for man and beast and for new grazing fields. This forced the Bedouins to wander large distances over extensive areas and even to invade regions not their own while carrying out armed struggles.

Among the factors of wandering were also the search for cool places in the summer and relatively hot and protected places in the winter. There was wandering of tribes into the **desert** during the rainy years and into fertile regions in the years of drought.

The wandering was in the past the estate of all the Bedouin tribes, and only changes in their economic conditions brought them to change their lifestyle (the wandering) and in part they became seminomads and settlers. Each tribe had its own wandering territory called *dire*. Many wars broke out between tribes and **clans**, and all this was due to penetrations and incursions of one tribe into the territory of another tribe. Quarrels and wars like these were very common among the tribes in the various periods and in the various regions.

The wandering season is not the same for all the tribes. For example the wandering of the tribes in the **Sinai** Peninsula and in Transjordan in the past took place in the spring and summer periods in the northern direction, whereas, in the winter, the tribes were found in more southerly territories. In the Syrian Desert and in **Iraq** in the past the tribes wandered in the winter and also in the summer. In the winter they wandered southward due to the cold, and in the summer northward, from the hot regions to the colder ones.

On the day the wandering is executed, in the morning they start to unload the **tents**. The unloading is done after the dew has dried on the canvases of the tent. The Bedouins prefer to set out for wandering on Mondays or Thursdays, for these days are considered holders of good luck.

During the wandering the tribesmen help one another. The owner of camels lends some of his camels to poor families in order to load their tents and belongings on them. The mutual help between the nomads during the wandering is commendable. The camp is one overall unit.

On account of the rivalry between the tribes, a tribe during the wandering is always ready for any trouble that can arise. The fights between the tribes are always based on disputes over grazing areas and water wells. Each tribe protects its water at a great risk, because it knows that that water is the basis of their life.

The tribe's **sheikh** is the one who chooses the encampment place called "manual." The king's servants erect his tent. The rest of the tribesmen encamp in the neighborhood of the sheikh's tent.

The wandering of seminomads is slower due to their herds and flocks of sheep and goats. The nomads have to water them once a day and also permit them eating hours during the wandering. Since the seminomads move in order to reach their summer or winter place of residence, the wandering is often also done during the night hours.

WARFALLAH. Warfallah is a Libyan tribe. This is the largest tribe in Tripolitania, with an estimated one million members or one-sixth of **Libya**'s whole population. It resides chiefly in Tripoli and Benghazi, but its main base is in Wadi Warfallah and Bani Walid extending to Sirte, with its origins in **Misrata**. This tribe was allied to the **Gaddadfa** tribe for most of Muammar Gadhafi's 41 years of rule, but in 1993, when 55 army officers from the tribe failed in a coup attempt, he ordered the arrest of many of its members. There was a violent reaction from the tribe, centered mostly in the Bani Walid, but following it in March 1997, the parliament legislated a "Code of Honor," which stipulated a collective punishment of cancellation of government services as the penalty for rebellious behavior and as a deterrent to future unrest.

In February 2011, shortly after violence erupted in eastern Libya, the Warfallah tribe elders issued a statement condemning Muammar Gadhafi, his sons, and all members of his tribe. This group spoke in the name of the Warfallah confederation, made up of six subtribes: Matarfa, Zakarwa, Lotyyin, Fogyyin, Faladna, and Mrabtin.

WATER. Water is the origin of all forms of life. Humans, animals, and plants need water for the sake of their existence. Water served the Bedouins in a variety of ways, for domestic consumption: drinking, hygiene, and cooking and agricultural use, as well as for irrigation and drinking water for the animals that they take care of. On the strength of the many uses of water, a close mutual influence exists between water and the fields of demography and economics. The existence of potable water for drinking and for irrigation influences the human tendency of **settlement**. Mostly humans prefer to settle close to the source of potable water, although various technological developments, for example, agricultural improvements, development of transport technologies, desalination of salt water, and the like, have changed these tendencies.

Even in ancient times man knew that water was necessary for life, and without it there was no life. The lack of water dictated the lifestyle of the Bedouins. At the start they maintained the sources of water at their disposal. Second, they were constantly in perpetual **wandering** to look for sources of water for them and their flocks. Moreover, the Bedouin tribes set out on voyages of conquest in order to take over sources of water. For example, the Bedouin tribes from both sides of **Jordan**, in the historical periods, competed among themselves for control of the sources of water in Jordan. They also drew profits from this: at the start, anybody who wanted to pass in this territory was supposed to pay a passage tax to them. Similarly, the strong tribes received payments from the authorities for not injuring passers in their territory, as the **trade** and Haj caravans passed close to the sources of water.

Water constituted a common property in the eastern culture, including Bedouin culture, and therefore there was no ownership of water; anybody who was thirsty could come and drink undisturbed.

The water spring constituted a source of courting between men and **women**. As Bedouin society is very strict regarding meetings between men and women, this was done when the woman went to the spring to bring water and there she met with the men, and the conversation was conducted by hints, and from this the man could gather if the woman wanted him or not.

Water is considered holy among the Bedouins, and therefore, during robbery and plunder, if they reach a source of water on a chase they stop and do not continue.

WOMEN. Bedouin society in the Middle East and North Africa is undergoing economic, social, and political changes affecting the status of Bedouin women—their roles, living conditions, and expectations. In the past, the role and place of Bedouin women was clear: the women were responsible for the land, grazing, bringing **water**, making clothes, washing, raising children, and cooking. Transition to a permanent residence improved their living standards. However, so far a significant improvement of living conditions (running water, electricity, modern equipment, access to medical services, **education**, etc.) has not brought a significant improvement in the social status of the Bedouin woman. In many countries, the law provides women with basic rights and privileges. They are entitled to vote, to receive education, to be employed, to drive cars, and so on. It is also supposed to protect them from exploitation and abuse. However, this aspect is often neglected or cannot be enforced by the state.

In contrast to the rapid change in family functioning, the change in the social status of the Bedouin woman is very slow. Social behavior is still dictated by ancient traditions. She is still obliged to fulfill the role and conduct herself as expected by her family and her tribe. Obedience and subjugation to male authority are absolute. However, there are distinctive differences between the lifestyle and options according to the country they live in and the tribe they belong to. Moreover, in recent years, young females have relatively more freedom—they go to school and enjoy social contacts, but a young spinster's life is very restricted. She is expected to fulfill several house-maintenance chores and she is not allowed to step out without a male family escort. In some countries, a married woman is not supposed to go out without her husband.

The education of girls in Bedouin society depends on the decision of their father or the local sheikh, but today several countries have compulsory education laws, so male authority can no longer keep them ignorant and submissive within the home's walls as most of them would prefer, but they can prevent them from obtaining continuing education and choice of profession. They also dictate whom they marry. An important factor regarding a woman's ability to learn or acquire skills is the education level of the head of the family, as the patriarchal structure dictates male superiority and reinforces the inferiority of the woman in all aspects of life. Another important factor is the status and economic situation of the immediate family of the given woman.

Bedouin society makes a clear distinction between boys and girls from the time of their birth. The Bedouin welcomes the birth of a son, holds a party to celebrate the arrival of the infant, but when the newborn is a girl, he does not even announce it.

Ancient tradition forbids an unmarried woman to live in the company of men, who might push her to immoral behavior, as her honor and dignity must be preserved, to prevent shame on her, and more importantly, on her family

Compulsory education that includes education of girls causes a change in the balance of power between men and women. Thus, in many countries today, Bedouin women have gone ahead a good part of the way. For example, in **Israel**, the Bedouin woman, unlike her counterparts in other Bedouin societies, is far more involved and connected with the other components of the state's society: She has acquired education, works outside, and sometimes drives her own car to work. She acquires skills and goes to various outside places. Similar trends exist although somewhat slower among Bedouin women in other countries like **Jordan**, **Syria**, and a number of North

African states. To date, many Bedouin women have not yet realized their potential, but rapid social change and modern progress may enable more of them to do so in the coming generation. *See also* DRESS.

Y

YARKONI, AMOS (1920–1991). Amos Yarkoni was an Israeli military person, son of a Bedouin family, and one of the **Israel Defense Forces** (IDF) fighters. His original name, before he changed it, was Abd el-Majid Hidr. Yarkoni was born in the village of Na'ura, a son of the Bedouin tribe el-Mazarib, in the north of **Israel**. In the year 1936, he joined the Palestinian militant gangs, which fought with the Jewish **settlements**. On account of an internal dispute within the gang, he escaped and joined the Zionist camp, and since then tied his fate with them.

After the **Israeli War of Independence** in 1948, he was conscripted to the IDF and changed his name to Amos Yarkoni. In the IDF he served in the minorities corps and was known as an excellent tracker and ranger. He was wounded twice during his service in encounters, lost his left hand, and was injured in his leg. In the year 1953, he passed an officers' course. As time passed, he integrated into the command of the Minorities Unit and later into the Sayeret Shaked, which operated as a very small independent unit of the Southern command for locating, thwarting, and catching squads of infiltrators, spies, and intelligence operatives, from the borders of **Egypt** and **Jordan**. During his military service the medal of distinguished service was given to him as well as three other medals.

At the end of his job as commander of Sayeret Shaked, he was appointed governor of Central **Sinai**. Yarkoni was discharged from the army in 1969, at the level of lieutenant colonel. He died in 1991 and was buried in the military cemetery Kiryat Shaul.

YEMEN. Yemen has a very long history, including periods of prosperity and periods of subjugation and decline, long before the Islamic era. It is considered the original land of the **Qahtan**, one of the two main branches of the Arab Bedouin tribes, who are considered the ancient ancestors of several historical and modern Bedouin tribes.

Ancient Yemen had a unique conversion history: it was a prosperous pagan kingdom that converted to Judaism in the 4th century AD, and then was conquered by Ethiopia and was forced to convert to **Christianity** in the 5th century; In the 7th century it was conquered again by Islamic forces and coerced to convert to **Islam**.

These events are the cause for the presence of Jewish Bedouin tribes in Arabia and Africa, which later vanished due to religious intolerance (unlike the historical presence of Christian Bedouin tribes in the Jesirah region, attributed to the influence of the Byzantine Empire, who eventually converted to Islam).

Modern Yemen society includes an urban population, *fellahin* (farmers) along with nomadic and settled people with tribal affiliation, people who live in the mountainous western part, where there is rich **agriculture**, based on the terraced land, and where **tribalism** is weaker, in contrast to the flat lands. Most of the southern part is nontribal, and agriculture is still prosperous there. The villages in the north are grouped into tribes whose territories are clearly demarcated—not as village groups, but as families or individuals. They mainly grow sorghum and barley. Clans that have been less successful have left the tribe and moved to other areas, where they have settled or kept on the move. Those who are wealthy also settle down. Thus, most of those above and below the average income level do not stay in the north with the exception of the rich **sheikhs**, who own good land in other parts of the country.

In the past, the two largest blocs of tribes in Yemen were the Hashid and Baqil, who descended from two brothers: the first has seven main tribes, and the other 14, each with separate territories. There is another bloc of tribes called the Hamdan. The imams of Yemen, who had to be from the ***sayyid*** dynasty and a descendant of the Prophet, came traditionally from the Zaydi tribe. Naturally the imams depended on the backing of their tribe since AD 1150 onward in the form of the **Hijra**, which was a tribally protected area where scholars and sayyids dwelled.

They also ran small study centers from which they spread the literature and recorded historical events. The famous scholar Al-Hamdani (AD 893–945) wrote in the Iklil, which is a part of his work (AD 930–940), dedicated to the northern tribes of Hashid and Baqil tribes. He also defined the concepts of chivalry and honor, recorded genealogy lists, and wrote the biography of the first imam (al-Hadila I-Haqq, d. 941). His work was the beginning of a historiographical tradition that still goes on.

The dominance of the country in and around **Saba** (the capital of Yemen) and in the rich fertile areas and the port of Aden switched from one dynasty to another and changed hands several times, after accepting Islam.

In the 16th century the Ottoman Empire overwhelmed north Yemen and taxed it heavily. In the 17th century the Zaydis led by the Qasimi imams (descendants of al-Qasim bin Muhammad, d. 1620) assembled armies from the northern tribes, repulsed the invader, and occupied lower Yemen and Hadramawt. The Qasimis founded an Ottoman-style state: they kept **slave** soldiers and an ornate court, and also managed by means of slaves and used tribesmen to man their armies.

The Qasimi, *dawla*, fell apart in the 19th century, when the Red Sea ports were occupied by the **Wahhabis**. A period of chaos set in called *ayyam al-jasad* or a time of corruption. Drought, famine, and locusts drove tribes into nontribal territory. This period ended with a second Turkish occupation in 1872, when the imams were repulsed to the north. A new dynasty of imams, the Hamid al-Din dynasty, led the tribe against the colonial power, and laid siege to Sanaa, with huge forces. A ceasefire was reached in 1911 that legitimized Imam Yahya's rule of the districts north of Sanaa. The Turks were forced to abandon Yemen in 1918, and the imam led armies to the west and south, and reconquered the evacuated territory. The last imams of the Hamid al-Din (1918–1962) ran very simple courts, managed the country by personal decision and by imprisoning vast numbers of hostages, thereby installing order. However, modernization and the example of other Arab countries led to a revolution and overthrowing of the anachronistic regime and the establishment of a republic.

The foundation of the Republic of Yemen was followed by civil war between the royalists (supported by **Saudi Arabia** mainly) and the republicans (supported by Nasserite **Egypt**) between 1962 and 1970. Both sides used the sheikhs in their military forces, and they received important government posts, backed by tribal power and governmental authority. The tribes could switch sides during the struggle, and as both Egypt and Saudi Arabia paid them in money and arms, they accrued large quantities of both and thereby became an autonomous social power that could influence Yemenite politics.

In the first years after the war, the sheikhs were prominent in the government. Tribes were represented and employed in all governmental branches of the army, administrative echelons, legislative and executive institutions, and politics in general. Thus they managed to prevent the government from penetrating the society and disbanding the tribes. President Ibrahim al-Hamdi (1974–1977), who tried to limit tribal power, was assassinated, and the president who followed him, Ahmad al-Ghashmi (1977–1978), was also assassinated, perhaps for different reasons.

North Yemen became a puppet regime of Saudi Arabia; its strategic location and the size of its population, which was the largest on the Arabian Peninsula, made it a key player in Saudi and the Gulf, and a buffer state between these monarchies and the Marxist South Yemen. The Saudis ensured the support and financial dependency of northern Yemen by paying the government, the army, and the tribes, which became more autonomous. During the period 1972–1982, tribalism practically boomed. The tribes benefited from the income paid by emigrant workers and from oil that was discovered in eastern Yemen.

In 1990, external circumstances led the leaders of the two parts of Yemen to agree on the unification of the two countries. Rivalry between the two major parties of unified Yemen led to another civil war that ended a few months later; however, unification was maintained.

There are a few leaders of modern Yemen who are of tribal origin, like the speaker in the Yemenite Parliament, Sheikh Abdullah Al Ahmar, and President Ali Abdullah Saleh, both from the Hashid tribe, and the leader of the Ba'ath Party, Sheikh Abu Lahum of the Baqil tribe. However, a small influential class of people promoting their own interests rather than their original family and communal origin has emerged.

In 2011, a Yemenite revolution echoed the Arab Spring, and there were mass protests against unemployment and corruption. The inner pressure forced President Saleh to concede all his power to Vice President Abdrabuh Mansoor Hadi. The unrest continued, and the tribes were very much involved. In the north there was a confrontation between the Zaydi rebellious Houthi group that led to a violent conflict between the Houthis and a Salafist group. In addition, the Al-Qaeda organization gained control of cities in the districts of Abyan and a foothold in the district of Shabwah.

In March 2011, the governor of Marib was compelled to leave the city after his guards killed a demonstrator from the Abeedah tribe. Hundreds of armed tribesmen from Jahm, the governor's tribe, hurried to his office, and gunmen from the Ashraf and Abeedah tribes surrounded the governor's building.

In January 2012, hundreds of Ansar al-Sharia activists, linked to al-Qaeda, conquered an old castle and the mosque of al-Ameriya in Radaa and liberated hundreds of prisoners from the local prison. The tribes of the Radaa area adopted a strategy to avoid the occupation of the city by the activists, and big tribes, like the Qaifah, al-Hattaimah, and Aal Sarhan, placed armed guards to protect government institutions and security installations from the militants. A Tribal Mediation Committee persuaded the militants to withdraw. The tribe Ansar al-Sharia withdrew its favor and protection from the leader of the militants and declared that he shamed the tribe. Later, this leader was killed by one of his brothers. After the country's general elections, the Yemenite army recaptured the Shabwah governor's building.

Despite changes in the state, Yemenites have used native tribal traditions to solve disputes and impose justice for centuries, if not thousands of years. Tribal law deals with disputes among tribes, between tribes and oil and mining companies, and between tribes and the government. It deals with ordinary disputes and even handles murder cases.

The tribal mediators conduct political discourse and form agreements and political entities. When the regime is too weak to handle security issues, the tribes provide protection in their domains and along the main roads. Tribal methods of conflict resolution are integrated within the state system and coordinated with its officials. In recent times, due to the Arab Spring events, violence escalated in Yemen, and the public demand to deal with the situation was brought before the sheikhs.

For a long time, tribes in Yemen have declared their independence and refused to allow state agents in their domains. As the state actors in Yemen are generally weak and corrupt, the tribes have amassed strength and political power, and tribal justice often acts as an alternative to the nonfunctioning state legal system. The carrier of tribal justice is a sheikh, who is authorized to pass judgment when his capacity to solve conflicts and protect tribal interests is proven. Tribal justice leaves room for arbitration and appeal.

Customary law is a social contract between the tribe and its leadership, and between the different tribes. It regulates politics, defends joint interests, and gives protection and economic backing to the tribe's members. It emphasizes the aspects of collective responsibility, solidarity, accountability, safeguarding of public interests, and helping the weak elements in society.

When the Arab Spring led to the retreat of national military forces from the main roads in tribal areas and security deteriorated, the tribes took over the checkpoints and placed their own armed men to ensure security. In some areas, they created local militia to protect government installations. Tribal law and political powers are recognized by the central government of Yemen, and when real trouble occurs, the president approaches the most important sheikhs in the area and asks them to appoint a mediation committee. Nevertheless, some tribal chiefs hold the position that it is time to put an end to the unrest and return to the proper functioning of state legal institutions in their regions.

However, while the tribes in Yemen constitute 20 percent of the state's population and play an important role in Yemen politics, they differ from each other, and their concerns and priorities change according to their location, size, access to resources, and other factors. For example, the tribes in the north want to preserve their military prowess, whereas those in the south and east, toward Hadramaut, concentrate more on social development. Thus, some tribes choose to support a certain political party, while others may support another.

Tribes also differ in their relations with the regime. For example, the Sanhan tribe occupies high positions in the security and military systems, but most of the rural tribes, which hardly get basic services and are last in the resource allocation, do not trust the government and keep their agents at bay. Nevertheless modern technology has spread from the large urban centers to the countryside and has begun to affect the life of all Yemenite people. It seems that as has happened in other countries, technological developments may change traditional social structures and weaken tribalism. *See also* BAHRAIN; KUWAIT.

Z

ZAHRAN. Zahran is a tribe of farmers, and therefore, cannot be counted as a Bedouin tribe. However, it is an Arab tribe from the **Arabian Peninsula**, but clans and families of this tribe can be found all over the Middle East and beyond. They are found in **Egypt**, **Lebanon**, **Israel**, **Syria**, **Jordan**, **Palestinian** territories, and among Arab communities all around the globe. The Zahran and Ghamid are pre-Islamic tribes, which are offshoots of the large Al **Azd** tribe. They come from the Kingdom of Saba (or Sheba) in the Yatriv district of modern **Yemen**. The shortage of **water** in their land pushed them to Arabia, where they settled in Al Baha, a region called by travelers and historians "The Garden of Hijaz," and eventually converted to **Islam**. Arab scholars claim that the dialect used by the Hejaz tribes, the Zahran and the Ghamid, is the closest to classical **Arabic**.

Modern times have affected the Zahran cultural tradition. Some members have adopted the modern attire, and there are concessions regarding festivities, wedding traditions, and dowry requirements.

ZARZIR or BEIT ZARZIR. This is a Bedouin local council in the northern district in **Israel**. Zarzir was declared a local council in the year 1996. The **settlement** population is composed of the members of five Bedouin tribes: Gawamis, Mazarib, Grifat, Iyadat, and El-**Heib**. The inhabitants who live in the settlement today number 8,000.

ZBEIH. Zbeih is a Bedouin tribe that was considered one of the strongest and biggest tribes in the north of **Palestine**. The tribe was dominant in the region of eastern lower **Galilee** in the period of the Ottoman Empire and in the period of the British mandate. The origin of the tribe was from the north of the Arabian Peninsula—the Hejaz region. The tribe entered Palestine through the Yarmoukh Valley at the end of the 17th century. The tribesmen levied protection money from anybody who passed into the tribe's territory in the Ottoman period. In the period of the British mandate, many of the tribesmen joined the Palestinian national struggle against the Jewish population. During the **Israeli War of Independence** in 1948, many of the tribesmen escaped to **Jordan**, and they live there even today; the section of the tribesmen that stayed in **Israel** live mainly in Kfar Shibli today.

ZENTAN. Zentan is a **Libyan** tribe. The Zentan dwell around the towns of Nalut and Zentan, 100 kilometers southwest of Tripoli, in the Nafusa Mountain range, close to the Tunisian border. They are well mixed into the Libyan army but also tend to side with the demonstrators. In their areas of residence there were scuffles between demonstrators and police in February 2011, when people burned photos of Muammar al-Gadhafi and burned a military armored personnel carrier.

ZIDANES. The Zidanes originated from the Arabian Peninsula. They are ascribed as the descendants of Ali bin Abi Talib, the son-in-law of the Prophet Muhammad. The Zidanes were forced to leave Hejaz at the end of the 17th century for unknown reasons. They wandered to **Palestine** and settled in **Galilee**. The tribe's head in those years was Omar a-Zidanei, who helped Bashir a-Shahabi, the governor of **Lebanon**, to suppress the revolt of the Metwalis, who settled in the Safed region and in northern Galilee. After suppression of the revolt, Bashir received the job of governor of Safed and the land of Galilee, and as a token of thanks appointed Omar a-Zidanei as the levier of taxes in Tiberias and around it.

A legend spread in the Arab villages in Galilee that tells of a Druze **sheikh** whose place of residence was in the village of Salama and who coveted one of the daughters of Arabe. The inhabitants of Arabe explained to him that their **religion** prevented a marriage of this sort, but the sheikh did not give up. The inhabitants turned to the Zidane members with a request for help. The Zidane members acceded, and the struggle ended with the ruin of Salama until its foundation.

The help that the Zidanes gave to the Arab villages paid off for them. As a result they enhanced their status and became the dominant power in the region. The important sheikh of this tribe was **Daher el-Omar**, who ruled northern Palestine from the 1730s until the middle of the 1770s. Several times, the authorities sent forces to fight Daher, but did not succeed in overcoming him. Not only did he defeat the Ottoman corps, but he also managed to expand his government over the whole of Galilee, South Lebanon, Jaffa, Ramle, and Gaza.

In August 1775, Daher el-Omar was killed in his capital, Acre, by the authorities and an end was put to his government and his family. Until this day there are remnants of the government of Zidanes in various **settlements** in Galilee, mainly mosques and castles.

Bibliography

CONTENTS

INTRODUCTION

Bedouin society has long interested researchers and writers. Those who came to know Bedouin society, particularly the peoples of Europe, were charmed by it. Thus, it is not surprising if researchers and writers today see Bedouin society as a human laboratory fit for description and research. Life in the desert and the Bedouins' perpetual struggle for survival, in the midst of which they have developed a rich spiritual culture and a closely connected material culture and grazing economy, constitute a focus of interest even today.

Ancient norms and values continue to exist in Bedouin society. However, the Bedouins underwent far-reaching processes of change in all fields as modernization—with its principal elements of technology and urbanization—began to influence their contemporary lifestyle. Despite the significant influence and power of these factors, Bedouin identity is not blurred; it continues to exist alongside modernization in contemporary Middle East and North Africa as they integrate their heritage in the life systems of society. These phenomena have attracted the attention of historians, geographers, anthropologists, and culture researchers, and thus a wide and varied literature exists on Bedouin society. Part of this literature discusses the Bedouins in a general sense, while another part discusses the Bedouins in certain regions or in certain states and certain periods.

The literature about the Bedouins in the Middle East and North Africa is large and varied. Furthermore, it is found in a number of languages, particularly in English, French, Arabic, and Hebrew.

As the list of bibliography is large, below are a number of recommended sources for each one of the following subjects:

General

Chatty, Dawn, ed. *Nomadic Societies in the Middle East and North Africa: Entering the 21st Century*. Leiden, Netherlands; and Boston: Brill, 2006. A book that is built from a number of articles that discuss Bedouin society in the Arab states in the Middle East and in North Africa in the 20th century and at the start of the 21st century. The articles discuss the social, cultural, and economic changes nomadic society underwent in the various states.

Khoury, Philip, and Joseph Kostiner. *Tribes and State Formation in the Middle East*. Berkeley: University of California Press, 1990. A book built from a number of articles discussing relations between tribe and state in the Middle East and in North Africa from various aspects: history, sociology, anthropology, and political sciences.

Ancient Period (Pre-Islamic Era)

Eph'al, Israel. *The Ancient Arabs: Nomads on the Borders of the Fertile Crescent 9th to 5th Centuries B.C.* Jerusalem: Magnes Press; Leiden, Netherlands: Brill, 1982. The book discusses history of the nomadic population in the Middle East in the ancient era and the part of the Bedouins in the history of the region, including their relationship with the outside world.

Hoyland, Robert G. *Arabia and the Arabs: From the Bronze Age to the Coming of Islam*. London: Routledge, 2001. The book discusses the social and cultural history of the region of the Arabian Peninsula in the pre-Islamic period.

Medieval and Early Modern Period

Gil, Moshe. *A History of Palestine, 634–1099*. Cambridge: Cambridge University Press, 1997. The book discusses the social and political history of Palestine from the Muslim conquest in 634 until the Crusaders in 1099. It discusses the history of the country and the background of the political and military events of the period.

Hasan, Naji. *The Role of the Arab Tribes in the East during the Period of the Umayyads*. Baghdad: Al-Jamea's Press, 1978. The book discusses the place and part of the Arab tribes in the period of the government of the Umayyad House (660–749) in the Muslim state.

Oppenheim, Max von F. *Die Beduinen.* 4 vols. Leipzig: Otto Harrassowitz, 1939. The fruit of research of 40 years, this is a selection of information that the author collected in his various visits to the Middle East. It is rich in information on the Bedouins in the Middle East and contains historical, social, and cultural information on Arab tribes including the wandering places of the various tribes (the book is in the German language).

Suwaed, Muhammad. *Al-Budo Fi Falastin Al-Hakba Al-Otmaniya: 1516–1914*. Amman, Jordan: Dar Zahran, 2008. The book discusses the social, cultural, and political history of the Bedouin population from the beginning of the 7th century until the end of World War I, while focusing on Palestine in the Ottoman era. It discusses Bedouin migrations from countries of the Middle East to and from Palestine; the government of the Bedouin sheikhs in Palestine; relations of settled Bedouins; tribe-state relations; and relations of the Bedouins with the Western travelers and pilgrims who visited Palestine in the Ottoman era. (The book is in Arabic.)

Algeria

Algeron, Charles-Robert. *Modern Algeria: A History from 1830 to the Present.* Translated from the French and edited by M. Brett. London: C. Hurst, 1991. The book is a comprehensive history of Algeria, dealing with the period of French occupation until independence and the armed Muslim struggle. The book was translated from French to English.

Despois, Jean. *L'Afrique du Nord.* Paris: Presses Universitaires de France, 1949. The book is a description of geographic and historical processes that occurred in the French territories in North Africa during French rule. (It is written in French.)

Bahrain

Khuri, Fuad I. *Tribe and State in Bahrain: The Transformation of Social and Political Authority in an Arab State*. Chicago: University of Chicago Press. 1980. The book discusses social, economic, and political changes of tribal society in Bahrain in the last century.

Egypt

Hobbs, Joseph. *Bedouin Life in the Egyptian Wilderness.* Austin: Texas University Press, 1992. The book discusses tribal tradition and culture of the Bedouins in Egypt.

Marx, Emanuel. *Bedouin of Mount Sinai: An Anthropological Study of Their Political Economy.* Oxford: Berghahn Books, 2013. The book discusses Bedouin life in the Sinai Desert. It contains considerable information about the history, society, and culture of the Bedouin tribes in the Sinai Peninsula.

Iran

Salzman, Philip Carl. *Black Tents of Baluchistan.* Washington, DC: Smithsonian Institution Press, 2000. The book discusses the daily life, family, and tribal organization of the nomads in the mountainous region of southeast Iran.

Tapper, Richard. *Tribe and State in Iran and Afghanistan.* London: Routledge, 2011. The book discusses tribal history in Iran from the start of the 18th century until the end of the 20th century, including the quality of relations between the tribes and the Iranian authorities.

Tapper, Richard, and Jon Thompson, eds. *The Nomadic Peoples of Iran.* London: Azimuth Press, 2002. The book discusses nomadic life in Iran.

Iraq

Baram, Amatzia. "Neo-Tribalism in Iraq: Saddam Hussein's Tribal Policies 1991–96." *International Journal of Middle East Studies* 29, no. 1 (1997): 1–31. The article deals with the quality of relations between the Bedouins and the regime of Saddam Hussein in the1990s.

Haj, Samira. "The Problems of Tribalism: The Case of Nineteenth-Century Iraqi History." *Social History* 16, no. 1 (1991): 45–58. The article discusses the tribal problem in Iraq in the 19th century, during the Ottoman period.

Israel

Abu-Rabia, Aref. *A Bedouin Century: Education and Development Among the Negev Tribes in the 20th Century.* Oxford: Berghahn Books, 2001. The book speaks about the social and educational changes that Bedouin society in the Negev underwent during the 20th century.

Marx, Emanuel. *Bedouin of the Negev*. Manchester: Manchester University Press, 1967. The book discusses the social demographic and cultural characteristics of the Bedouin population in the Negev in Israel.

Suwaed, Muhammad. *Relations between the Bedouins and the Jewish Settlement in Palestine during the British Mandate: 1918–1948*. New York: Edwin Mellen Press, 2014. A book discussing Bedouin history from the beginning of the British government in Palestine in the year 1918, until the year 1948, with the establishment of the state of Israel. It deals with the quality of relations between the Bedouins and the Jewish and Arab population and the relations with the Israeli authorities from the beginning of the state.

Jordan

Alon, Yoav. *The Making of Jordan: Tribes, Colonialism and the Modern State*. London: Tauris, 2007. The book discusses tribal history in Jordan during a discussion of the place of the Bedouins in the establishment of the Jordanian kingdom.

Layne, Linda. *Home and Home Land: The Dialogics of Tribal and National Identities in Jordan*. Princeton, NJ: Princeton University Press, 2001. The book discusses the issue of identity in Jordan with regard to tribal identity and national identity.

Kuwait

Al-Kandari, Yagoub Yousif, and Ibrahim Naji Al-Hadben. "Tribalism, Sectarianism and Democracy in Kuwaiti Culture." *Digest of Middle Eastern Studies* 19, no. 2 (2010): 268–85. The article deals with the place of tribalism in the political culture of Kuwait.

Lebanon

Chatty, Dawn, Nisrine Mansour, and Nasser Yassin. "Bedouin in Lebanon: Social Discrimination, Political Exclusion, and Compromised Health Care." *Social Science & Medicine* 82 (April 2013): 43–50. The article discusses migration, settlement, and health of the Bedouins in Lebanon.

Libya

Hweio, Haalo. "Tribes in Libya: From Social Organization to Political Power." *African Conflict & Peacebuilding Review* 2, no. 1 (Spring 2012): 111–21.

Toktamış, Kumru. "Tribes and Democratization/De-democratization in Libya." *Challenges to Democratic Governance in Developing Countries* 11 (2014): 121–36. The two articles discuss the social and political power of tribalism in Libya.

Mauritania

Bousquet, Georges-Henri. *Les Berbères*. Paris: Presses Universitaires de France, 1957. The book discusses political, sociological, historical, and linguistic factors that cover the term *Berber*, which is not a race or a nation. It deals with the ancient Berber language, which is still spoken in the nation. (The book is written in French.)

Marty, Paul. *Les Tribus de la Haute Mauritanie*. Paris: Comité de l'Afrique Française, 1945. The book contains a description of the various Mauritanian tribes while the North Saharan region was under French control. It claims to provide lessons for the rulers in the future. (The book is written in French.)

Morocco

Gellner, Ernest. *The Saints of the Atlas*. Chicago: University of Chicago Press, 1969. The book studies how a few holy men kept order among a hundred thousand shepherds who transferred their sheep in the springtime from the anti-Atlas plains to the high steppe and back in autumn. There was plenty of opportunity for theft, and the holy men were there to keep the peace.

Norris, Harry T. *The Arab Conquest of the Western Sahara*. Harlow, Essex, England: Longman; and Beirut, Lebanon: Librairie du Liban, 1986. The book contains a description of the historical events, religious beliefs, and social customs that made one of the remotest areas of the Sahara part of the Arab world.

Oman

Chatty, Dawn. "The Bedouin of Central Oman." *Journal of Oman Studies* 6, no. 1 (1984): 149–63.

Janzen, Jorg. *Nomads in the Sultanate of Oman*. Boulder, CO: Westview Press, 1986. The two works discuss the life of nomads in Oman while referring to tradition as opposed to social and cultural changes.

Saudi Arabia

Alabbadi, Ahmad. *Nomadic Settlement in Saudi Arabia: A Semi-Historical and Analytical Case Study*. Lansing: Michigan State University, 1981. The book discusses tribes in the settlement processes of the Bedouin nomads in Saudi Arabia.

Kostiner, Joseph. *The Making of Saudi Arabia, 1916–1936*. New York: Oxford University Press, 1993. A book discussing the modern history of Saudi Arabia while referring to changes that nomadic Bedouin society in the kingdom underwent.

Sudan

Cunnison, Ian. *The Baggara Arabs: Power and Lineage in a Sudanese Nomadic Tribe*. London: Oxford University Press, 1966. The book discusses the force and power of the nomadic Bedouin in the history of Sudan while illustrating it with Baggara tribes.

Paul, Andrew. *A History of the Beja Tribes of the Sudan*. Cambridge: Cambridge University Press, 2012. The book discusses the social, cultural, and political history of the Beja tribes in Sudan.

Sorbo, Gunnar. *Tenants and Nomads in Eastern Sudan*. Khartoum: Khartoum University Press, 1985. The book discusses the history of the nomadic tribes in eastern Sudan.

Syria

Chatty, Dawn. "The Bedouin in Contemporary Syria: The Persistence of Tribal Authority and Control." *Middle East Journal* 64, no. 1 (Winter 2010): 29–49. The article discusses conservatism by contrast to modernism among the Bedouins in contemporary Syria.

Tunisia

Idris, Hady Roger. *La Berberie Orientale sous les Zirides*. Paris: Adrien-Maisonneuve, 1962. This book covers the area of Tunisia in the time of the Zirid dynasty, which was placed in control of Tunisia, Eastern Algeria, and Granada in Spain by the Fatimid dynasty in Egypt in the 10th century (AD 972). (The book is in French.)

Turkey

Bruinessen, Martin van. *Agha, Shaikh and State: The Social and Political Structures of Kurdistan*. London: Zed Books, 1992. The book discusses the social and political structure of the Kurdistan region.

Lindner, Rudi Paul. *Nomads and Ottomans in Medieval Anatolia*. Bloomington: Indiana University Press, 1983. The book discusses the nomadic population in central Anatolia.

United Arab Emirates

Gareeb Edmund, and Ibrahim Al Abed, eds. *Perspectives on the United Arab Emirates*. London: Trident Press, 1999. The book is built from a number of articles that discuss various angles of the United Arab Emirates, including reference to the tribal element.

Yemen

Al-Dawsari, Nadwa. *Tribal Governance and Stability in Yemen*. Washington, DC: Carnegie Endowment for International Peace, 2012. This book discusses the place of the tribes in the political life of Yemen.

Zahiri, Marzuki Maulud. *The Political Role of the Tribes in Yemen, 1962–1990*. Cairo: Madbuli Bookstore, 1996. This book discusses the place of the tribes in the political life of Yemen.

BEDOUIN CULTURE

Abu-Lughod, Lila. *Veiled Sentiments: Honor and Poetry in a Bedouin Society*. Berkeley: University of California Press, 1999.

———. *Writing Women's Worlds: Bedouin Stories*. Berkeley: University of California Press, 1993.

Abu-Rabia, Aref. "The Evil Eye and Cultural Beliefs among the Bedouin Tribes of the Negev, Middle East." *Folklore* 116, no. 3 (2005): 241–54.

———. *Folk Medicine among the Bedouin Tribes in the Negev*. Beer Sheva: Ben-Gurion University of the Negev, 1983.

Al-Aref, Aref. *Bedouin Love Law and Legend: Dealing Exclusively with the Badu of Beersheva*. New York: AMS Press, 1974.

Al-Krenawi, Alean, and John R. Graham. "Social Work and Blood Vengeance: The Bedouin-Arab Case." *British Journal of Social Work* 27, no. 4 (1997): 515–28.

———. "The Story of Bedouin-Arab Polygamous Marriage." *Women's Studies International Forum* 22, no. 5 (September–October 1999): 497–508.

Chelhod, Joseph. *Le Droit dans la Société Bédouine, Recherches Chronologiques sur the 'orf ou Droit Coutumier des Bédouins*. Paris: Marcel Rizière, 1971.

Denis, Pierre. *La Justice Chez les Nomades Algériens avant 1960*. Paris: Harmattan, 2001.

Fernea, Robert A. *Shaykh and Effendi*. Cambridge, MA: Harvard University Press, 1970.

Ginat, Joseph. *Blood Revenge: Family Honor, Mediation and Outcasting*. Brighton: Sussex Academic Press, 1997.

———. *Women in Muslim rural Society: Status and Role in Family and Community*. New Brunswick, NJ: Transaction, 1982.

Hobbs, Joseph J. *Bedouin Life in the Egyptian Wilderness*. Austin: Texas University Press, 1992.

Jettmar, Karfl. *Art of the Steppes*. New York: Crown Publishers, 1967.

Kenneth, Austin. *Bedouin Justice: Laws and Customs among the Egyptian Bedouin*. London: Kegan Paul, 2000.

Kressel, Gideon. *Ascendancy Through Aggression: the Anatomy of a Blood Feud among Urbanized Bedouins*. Wiesbaden: Harrassowitz, 1996.

Lavie, Smadar. "Sinai for the Coffee Table: Birds, Bedouins and Desert Wanderlust." *Middle East Report* 150 (January–February 1988): 40–44.

Losleben, Elizabeth. *The Bedouin of the Middle East*. Minneapolis, MN: Lerner Publications, 2003.

Simms, Steven R. "The archaeological structure of a Bedouin camp." *Journal of Archaeological Science* 15, no. 2 (March 1988): 197–211.

Stewart, Frank H. "Tribal Law in the Arab World: A Review of the Literature." *International Journal of Middle East Studies* 19, no. 4 (November 1987): 473–90. The book discusses Bedouin tribal law.

General

Akbar, Ahmed S., and David Montgomery Hart. *Islam in Tribal Societies: From the Atlas to the Indus*. London: Routledge, 2013.

Allan, William. *The African Husbandman*. Edinburgh, Scotland: Oliver and Boyd, 1976.

Al-Rasheed, Madawi. *Politics in an Arabian Oasis: The Rashidi Tribal Dynasty.* London: I.B. Taurus, 1991.

Awad, Mohamed. "Nomadism in the Arab Lands of the Middle East." In *Problems of the Arid Zone*, 325–39. Paris: UNESCO, 1962.

———. "Settlement of Nomadic and Semi-Nomadic Tribal Groups in the Middle East." *International Labor Review* 79, no. 1 (1959): 25–56.

Barfield, Thomas J. *The Nomadic Alternative.* Englewood Cliffs, NJ: Prentice Hall, 1993.

Berque, Jacques. "Du nouveau sur les Bani Hilal?" *Studia Islamica* 36 (1972): 99–111.

Biebuyck, Daniel P. "On the Concept of the Tribe." *Civilisations* 16, no. 4 (1966): 500–515.

Bishai, Wilson B. *Islamic History of the Middle East: Background, Development, and the Fall of the Arab Empire.* Boston: Allyn and Bacon, 1968.

Bulliet, Richard W. *The Camel and the Wheel.* Cambridge: Harvard University Press, 1975.

Chatty, Dawn. "Animal Reintroduction Projects in the Middle East: Conservation Without a Human Face." In D. Chatty and M. Colchester, eds., *Conservation and Mobile Indigenous Peoples: Displacement, Forced Settlement and Sustainable Development*, 227–43. Oxford: Berghahn Books, 2002.

———. *From Camel to Truck: The Bedouin in the Modern World.* New York: Vantage Press, 1986.

———, ed. *Nomadic Societies in the Middle East and North Africa: Entering the 21st Century*. Leiden, Netherlands: Brill, 2006.

Colchester, Marcus. "Indigenous Peoples and Protected Areas: Rights, Principles and Practice." *Nomadic Peoples* 7, no. 1 (2003): 33–51.

Cole, Donald Powell. "Where Have the Bedouin Gone?" *Anthropological Quarterly* 76, no. 2 (Spring 2003): 235–67.

Cribb, Roger. *Nomads in Archaeology*. Cambridge: Cambridge University Press, 2004.

Crone, Patricia. *Slaves on Horses: The Evolution of the Islamic Polity.* Cambridge: Cambridge University Press, 1980.

———. "The Tribe and the State." In John A. Hall, ed., *States in History*, 48–77. Oxford: Basil Blackwell, 1986.

Dostal, Walter. "The Evolution of Bedouin Life." In F. Gabrieli, ed., *L'antica Societa Beduina*, 11–34. Rome: Universita de Roma, 1959.

Doughty, Charles. *Travel in Arabia Desert*. London: Jonathan Cape, 1888.

Eickelman, Dale F. *The Middle East: An Anthropological Approach*. Englewood Cliffs, NJ: Prentice Hall, 1989.

Galaty, John G., and D. Johnson, eds. *The World of Pastoralism*. London: Guilford Press, 1990.

Galaty, John G., and Philip Carl Salzman, eds. *Change and Development in Nomadic and Pastoral Societies*. Leiden, Netherlands: Brill, 1981.

Ginat, Joseph, and Anatoly Khasanov. *Changing Nomads in a Changing World.* Brighton, England: Sussex Academic Press, 1998.

Goitein, Shlomo Dov. *Jews and Arabs. Their Contacts through the Ages*. New York: Schocken Books, 1955.

Helm, June, ed. *Essays on the Problem of Tribe*. Seattle, WA: American Anthropological Society, 1968.

Hitti, Philip. *The History of the Arabs*. 5th ed. London: Macmillan, 1951.

Horner, Deborah. "Planning for Bedouin." *Third World Planning Review* 4, no. 2 (1982): 159–76.

Ibn Khaldun, 'Abd al-Rahman. *The Muqaddimah*. Translated by Franz Rosenthal. Princeton, NJ: Princeton University Press, 1957.

Jabar, Faleh, and Dowad Hocham, eds. *Tribes and Power: Nationalism and Ethnicity in the Middle East*. London: Saqi Books, 2002.

Khasanov, Anatoly M. *Nomads and the Outside World*. Translated by Julia Crookenden. Cambridge: Cambridge University Press, 1984.

Khasanov, Anatoly M., and Andre Wink, eds. *Nomads in the Sedentary World*. London: Routledge, 2001.

Khoury, Philip, and Joseph Kostiner. *Tribes and State Formation in the Middle East*. Berkeley: University of California Press, 1990.

Lerner, Daniel. *The Passing of Traditional Society: Modernizing the Middle East.* Glencoe, NY: Free Press, 1958.

Lindner, Rudi Paul. "What Was a Nomadic Tribe?" *Comparative Studies in Society and History* 24, no. 4 (October 1982): 689–711.

Marx, Emanuel. "The Tribe as a Unit of Subsistence: Nomadic Pastoralism in the Middle East." *American Anthropologist* 79, no. 1 (June 1977): 343–63.

Montagne, Robert. *La Civilisation du Désert: Nomades d'Orient et d'Afrique.* Paris: Hachette, 1947.

Mundy, Martha, and Basim Musallam, eds. *The Transformation of Nomadic Society in the Arab East*. Cambridge: Cambridge University Press, 2000.

Salzman, Philip Carl, ed. *When Nomads Settle: Processes of Sedentarization as Adaptation and Response.* New York: Praeger, 1980.

Thomas, Martin. "Bedouin Tribes and the Imperial Intelligence Services in Syria, Iraq and Transjordan in the 1920s." *Journal of Contemporary History* 38, no. 4 (October 2003): 539–61.

Ancient Period (Pre-Islamic Era)

Ali, Juwad. *Al-mufassal fi tarikh al-'Arab qabl al-Islam*. Beirut: Dar al-Iim Iil Malayeen, 1968. (Arabic.)

Aqil, Nabih. *Ta'rikh al-'Arab al-qadim wa'asr al-rasul.* Damascus, Syria, 1972. (Arabic.)

Bamyeh, Mohammed. *The Social Origins of Islam: Mind, Economy, Discourse*. Minneapolis: University of Minnesota Press, 1999.

Berkey, Jonathan Porter. *The Formation of Islam.* Cambridge: Cambridge University Press, 2003.

Bienkowski, Piotr, and Eveline van der Steen. "Tribes, Trade, and Towns: A New Framework for the Late Iron Age in Southern Jordan and the Negev." *Bulletin of the American Schools of Oriental Research* 323 (August 2001): 21–47.

Bulliet, Richard W. *The Camel and the Wheel.* Cambridge: Harvard University Press, 1975.

Crone, Patricia. *Meccan Trade and the Rise of Islam*. London: Blackwell; Edinburgh, Scotland: Gorgias Press, 2004.

Donner, Fred. *The Early Islamic Conquests*. Princeton, NJ: Princeton University Press, 1981.

Eph'al, Israel. *The Ancient Arabs: Nomads on the Borders of the Fertile Crescent 9th to 5th Centuries B.C.* Jerusalem: Magnes Press; Leiden, Netherlands: Brill, 1982.

Hawting, Gerald R. *The Idea of Idolatry and the Emergence of Islam: From Polemic to History*. Cambridge: Cambridge University Press, 1999.

Hoyland, Robert G. *Arabia and the Arabs: From the Bronze Age to the Coming of Islam*. London: Routledge, 2001.

Ibrahim, Mahmood. *Merchant Capital and Islam*. Austin: University of Texas Press, 1990.

Julien, Charles-André. *Histoire de l'Afrique du Nord. Tunisie-Algérie-Maroc. Des origines à la conquête arabe (647 A.D.).* Paris: Payot, 1956.

Korotayev, Andrey. *Ancient Yemen.* Oxford: Oxford University Press, 1995.

———. *Pre-Islamic Yemen.* Wiesbaden, Germany: Harrassowitz Verlag, 1996.

O'Leary, De Lacy Evans. *Arabia Before Mohammed.* New York: E.P. Dunson, 1972.

Rice, Michael. *The Archaeology of the Arabian Gulf.* London: Routledge, 1994.

Yule, Paul A. *Himyar—Die Spätantike im Jemen/Himyar Late Antique Yemen*. Aichwald, Germany: Linden, 2007.

Zaidan, Georgie. *Al-'Arab qabl al-Islam*. Cairo, 1961. (Arabic.)

Medieval and Early Modern Period

Abou El-Lail, Khalid. "The History of Bani Hilal between Written Texts and Oral Performances." *Journal of American Science* 8, no. 6 (June 2012): 84–90.

Agoston, Gabor, and Bruce Alan Masters. *Encyclopedia of the Ottoman Empire*. New York: Infobase, 2009.

Anscombe, Frederick F. *The Ottoman Gulf: The Creation of Kuwait, Saudi Arabia, and Qatar.* New York: Columbia University Press, 1997.

Armstrong, Karen. *Islam: A Short History*. New York: Modern Library, 2000.

Atiyeh, George N., and John R. Hayes. *The Genius of Arab Civilization*. New York: New York University Press, 1992.

Burckhardt, John Lewis. *Notes on the Bedouins and the Wahabys.* 2 vols. London: Henry Colburn and Richard Bentley, 1831.

Cohen, Amnon. *Palestine in the 18th Century: Patterns of Governments and Administration*. Jerusalem: Magnes Press, Hebrew University, 1973.

Davison, Roderick H. *Reform in the Ottoman Empire, 1856–1876*. New York: Gordian Press, 1973.

Deringil, Selim. "They Live in a State of Nomadism and Savagery: The Late Ottoman Empire and the Post-Colonial Debate." *Comparative Studies in Society and History* 45, no. 2 (April 2003): 311–42.

Douwes, Richard. *The Ottomans in Syria and Lebanon: A History of Justice and Oppression.* London: Tauris Academic Studies, 1995.

Falah, Ghazi. "The Evolution of Semi-Nomadism in Non-Desert Environment: The Case of Galilee in the 19th Century." *GeoJournal* 21, no. 4 (August 1990): 397–410.

Findley, Carter V. *Bureaucratic Reform in the Ottoman Empire: The Sublime Porte, 1789–1922*. Princeton, NJ: Princeton University Press, 1980.

Galley, Micheline. "Retracing the Path of the Sons of Hilal." *Diogenes* 56, no. 4 (November 2009): 61–78.

Gerber, Haim. "Palestine and Other Territorial Concepts in the 17th Century." *International Journal of Middle East Studies* 30, no. 4 (November 1998): 563–72.

Gibb, Sir Hamilton Alexander Rosskeen. *Studies on the Civilization of Islam*. Princeton, NJ: Princeton University Press, 1982.

Gil, Moshe. *A History of Palestine, 634–1099*. Cambridge: Cambridge University Press, 1997.

Goodwin, Stefan. *Africa's Legacies Of Urbanization: Unfolding Saga of a Continent*. Lanham, MD: Rowman & Littlefield, 2006.

Gordon, Murray. *Slavery in the Arab World*. New York: New Amsterdam Books, 1987.

Hart, Michael. *The 100: Ranking of the Most Influential Persons in History.* New York: Carol, 1978.

Hasan, Naji. *The Role of the Arab Tribes in the East during the Period of the Umayyads*. Baghdad, Iraq: Al-Jamea's Press, 1978.

Hawting, Gerald R. *The First Dynasty of Islam: The Umayyad Caliphate, AD 661–750*. London: Routledge, 2000.

Hourani, Albert, and Malise Ruthven. *A History of the Arab Peoples*. Cambridge, MA: Belknap Press, 2003.

Imber, Colin. *The Ottoman Empire, 1300–1650: The Structure of Power*. Basingstoke, England: Palgrave Macmillan, 2002.

Itzkowitz, Norman. *Ottoman Empire and Islamic Tradition*. Chicago: University of Chicago Press, 1980.

Julien, Charles-André. *Histoire de l'Afrique du Nord. Tunisie-Algérie-Maroc. De la conquête arabe à 1830*. Paris: Payot, 1956.

Kark, Ruth, and Seth J. Frantzman. "Empire, State and the Bedouin of the Middle East, Past and Present: A Comparative Study of Land and Settlement Policies." *Middle Eastern Studies* 48, no. 4 (July 2012): 487–510.

———. "The Negev: Land, Settlement, the Bedouin and Ottoman and British Policy 1871–1948." *British Journal of Middle Eastern Studies* 39, no. 1 (April 2012): 53–77.

Kushner, David. *Palestine in the Late Ottoman Period: Political, Social, and Economic Transformation*. Leiden, Netherlands: Brill, 1986.

Landau, Rom. *Islam and the Arabs*. London: Routledge, 2013.

Lapidus, Ira M. *A History of Islamic Societies*. Cambridge: Cambridge University Press, 2002.

Lewis, Bernard. *The Arabs in History*. London: Oxford University Press, 1993.

Lombard, Maurice. *The Golden Age of Islam*. New York: American Elsevier, 1975.

Meri, Josef W. *Medieval Islamic Civilization: An Encyclopedia*. London: Routledge, 2005.

Murray, George William. *Sons of Ishmael: A Study of the Egyptian Bedouin*. London: Routledge, 2012.

Nasr, Seyyed Hossein. *Islam: Religion, History and Civilization*. New York: HarperCollins Publishers, 2003.

Naylor, Philip C. *North Africa: A History from Antiquity to the Present*. Austin: Texas University Press, 2009.

Norris, Harry T. "The Rediscovery of the Ancient Sagas of the Banū Hilāl." *Bulletin of the School of Oriental and African Studies* 51, no. 3 (October 1988): 462–81.

Oppenheim, Max F. *Die Beduinen*. 4 vols. Leipzig, Germany: Otto Harrassowitz, 1939.

Rafeq, Abdul Karim. *The Ottoman Province of Damascus, 1723–1783.* Beirut, Lebanon: Khayata, 1966. (Arabic.)

Rogan, Eugene L. *Frontiers of the State in the Late Ottoman Empire: Transjordan, 1850–1921.* Cambridge: Cambridge University Press, 2002.

Saunders, John Joseph. *A History of Medieval Islam.* London: Routledge, 2002.

Schölch, Alexander. "The Decline of Local Power in Palestine after 1856: The Case of 'Aqīl Aġā." *Die Welt des Islams* 23/24 (1984): 458–75.

Sharon, Moshe. "The Political Role of the Bedouins in Palestine in the 16th and 17th Centuries." In Moshe Ma'oz, ed., *Studies on Palestine in the Ottoman Period,* 11–30. Jerusalem, 1975.

Suwaed, Muhammad. *Al-Budo Fi Falastin Al-Hakba Al-Otmaniya: 1516–1914.* Amman, Jordan: Dar Zahran, 2008. (Arabic.)

———. *Relations between the Bedouins and the Jewish Settlement in Palestine during the British Mandate: 1918–1948.* New York: Edwin Mellen Press, 2014.

Touati, Houari. *Islam and Travel in the Middle Ages.* Chicago: University of Chicago Press, 2010.

Volney, M. Constantin-François. *Voyage en Egypt et en Syrie.* The Hague: Mouton Press, 1787.

Wellhausen, Julius. *The Arab Kingdom and Its Fall.* London: Routledge, 2000.

Winter, Michael. *Egyptian Society Under Ottoman Rule: 1517–1798.* London: Routledge, 1992.

Wintle, Justin. *History of Islam.* London: Rough Guides, 2003.

Ze'evi, Dror. *An Ottoman Century: The District of Jerusalem in the 1600s.* New York: Albany Press, 1996.

Algeria

Barth, Mustafa. "Sand Castles in the Sahara: US Military Basing in Algeria." *Review of African Political Economy* 30, no. 98 (December 2003): 679–85.

Boyer, Pierre. *La vie quotidienne à Alger.* Paris: Hachette, 1964.

———. *L'évolution de l'Algérie Médiane.* Paris: Librairie de l'Amérique et de l'Orient, 1960.

Despois, Jean. *L'Afrique du Nord.* Paris: Presses Universitaires de France, 1949.

Duveyrier, Henri. *Les Touareg du Nord.* Paris: Challamel, 1864.

Fanon, Frantz. *L'an de la Révolution Algérienne.* Paris: François Maspero, 1962.

Galisson, Robert. *L'Algérie pré-coloniale: Classes sociales en système pré-capitaliste.* Paris: C.E.R.M., 1968.

Keenan, Jeremy. "From Tit (1902) to Tahilahi (2002): A Reconsideration of the Impact of and Resistance to French Pacification and Colonial Rule by the Tuareg of Algeria (the Northern Tuareg)." *Journal of North African Studies* 8, no. 3–4 (Autumn–Winter 2003): 27–66.

———. *The Lesser Gods of the Sahara: Social Change and Contested Terrain amongst the Tuareg of Algeria.* London: Routledge, 2004.

Laroui, Abdallah. *L'histoire du Maghreb: Un essai de synthèse.* Paris: François Maspero, 1970.

Nicolaisen, Johannes. *Ecology and Culture of the Pastoral Tuareg.* Copenhagen: University of Copenhagen, 1963.

Pandolfi, Paul. *Les Touareg de l'Alhaggar.* Paris: Karthala, 1998.

Bahrain

Fuccaro, Nelida. "Understanding the Urban History of Bahrain, Critique." *Critical Middle Eastern Studies* 9, no. 17 (Fall 2000): 49–81.

Khuri, Fuad I. *Tribe and State in Bahrain: The Transformation of Social and Political Authority in an Arab State.* Chicago: University of Chicago Press, 1980.

Qubain, Fahim Issa. "Social Classes and Tensions in Bahrain." *Middle East Journal* 9, no. 3 (Summer 1955): 269–80.

Radhi, Hassan Ali. *Judiciary and Arbitration in Bahrain: A Historical and Analytical Study.* Leiden, Netherlands: Brill, 2003.

Egypt

Abou-Zeid, Ahmed. *A Preliminary Report on the Western Desert.* Alexandria: Alexandria University, n.d.

Abu-Lughod, Lila. *Veiled Sentiments: Honor and Poetry in a Bedouin Society.* Berkeley: University of California Press, 1999.

Aharoni, Reuven. *The Pasha's Bedouin: Tribes and State in the Egypt of Mehemet Ali, 1805–1848.* London: Routledge, 2007.

Baer, Gabriel. *Studies of the Social History of Modern Egypt.* Chicago: University of Chicago Press, 1969.

Cole, Donald, and Soraya Altorki. *Bedouin, Settlers and Holiday Makers: Egypt's Changing Northern Coast.* Cairo: American University Press, 1998.

Hobbs, Joseph. *Bedouin Life in the Egyptian Wilderness.* Austin: University of Texas Press, 1992.

Jarvis, Claude Scudamore. *Yesterday and Today in Sinai*. Edinburgh, Scotland: Blackwood, 1931.

Lavie, Smadar. *The Politics of Military Occupation: Mzeina Allegories of Bedouin Identity under Israeli and Egyptian Rule*. Berkeley: University of California Press, 1990.

Marx, Emanuel. *Bedouin of Mount Sinai: An Anthropological Study of Their Political Economy*. Oxford: Berghahn Books, 2013.

Murray, George William. *Sons of Ishmael: A Study of the Egyptian Bedouin*. London: George Routledge and Sons, 1935.

Stewart, Frank Henderson. *Texts in Sinai Bedouin Law*. 2 vols. Wiesbaden, Germany: Harrassowitz, 1988–1990.

Iran

Barth, Fredrick. *Nomads of South Persia: The Basseri Tribe of the Khamseh Confederacy*. New York: Humanities Press, 1964.

———. *Principles of Social Organization in Southern Kurdistan*. Oslo, Norway: Universitetes Ethnografiske Museum Bulletin, no. 7, 1953.

Beck, Lois. *Nomad: A Year in the Life of a Qashqa'i Tribesman in Iran*. Berkeley: University of California Press, 1991.

———. *The Qashqa'i of Iran*. New Haven, CT: Yale University Press, 1986.

Digard, Jean-Pierre. *Techniques des Nomades Baxtiyari d'Iran*. Cambridge: Cambridge University Press, 1981.

Garthwaite, Gene R. *Khans and Shahs: A Documentary Analysis of the Bakhtiyari in Iran*. Cambridge: Cambridge University Press, 1983.

Ghirshman, Roman. *Iran: From the Earliest Times to the Islamic Conquest*. Harmondsworth, England: Penguin Books, 1954.

Lockhart, Laurence. *The Fall of the Safavi Dynasty and the Afghan Occupation of Persia*. Cambridge: Cambridge University Press, 1958.

Oberling, Pierre. *The Qashqa'i Nomads of Fars*. The Hague: Mouton, 1975.

Salzman, Philip Carl. *Black Tents of Baluchistan*. Washington, DC: Smithsonian Institution Press, 2000.

———. "Pastoral Nomads: Some General Observations Based on Research in Iran." *Journal of Anthropological Research* 58, no. 2 (Summer 2002): 245–64.

Tapper, Richard. *Frontier Nomads of Iran: A Political and Social History of the Shahsevan*. Cambridge: Cambridge University Press, 1997.

———. *Pasture and Politics: Economics, Conflict and Ritual among Shahsevan Nomads of Northwestern Iran*. London: Academic Press, 1979.

Tapper, Richard, and Jon Thompson, eds. *The Nomadic Peoples of Iran*. London: Azimuth Press, 2002.

Iraq

Al-Mohammad, Hayder. "Relying on One's Tribe: A Snippet of Life in Basra since the 2003 Invasion." *Anthropology Today* 26, no. 6 (2010): 23–26.

Baram, Amatzia. "Neo-Tribalism in Iraq: Saddam Hussein's Tribal Policies 1991–96." *International Journal of Middle East Studies* 29, no. 1 (February 1997): 1–31.

Blunt, Anne. *Bedouin Tribes of the Euphrates*. London: John Murray, 1879.

Carroll, Katherine Blue. "Tribal Law and Reconciliation in the New Iraq." *Middle East Journal* 65, no. 1 (Winter 2011): 11–29.

Eisenstadt, Michael. "Tribal Engagement Lessons Learned." *Military Review* (August 2008): 161–76.

Glubb, John C. "The Bedouins of Northern Iraq." *Journal of the Royal Central Asian Society* 22, no. 1 (1935): 13–31.

González, R. J. "On 'Tribes' and Bribes: 'Iraq Tribal Study,' al-Anbar's Awakening, and Social Science." *Focaal* 53 (2009): 105–16.

Haj, Samira. *The Making of Iraq, 1900–1963: Capital, Power, and Ideology*. New York: SUNY Press, 1997.

———. "The Problems of Tribalism: The Case of Nineteenth-Century Iraqi History." *Social History* 16, no. 1 (January 1991): 45–58.

Jamil, Maki. *Al-Bdou Walkbaa'l al-Ruhalah fi Al-A'raq*. Baghdad, Iraq: Dar al-Rafdein, 2005.

Nakash, Yitzhak. "The Conversion of Iraq's Tribes to Shiism." *International Journal of Middle East Studies* 26, no. 3 (August 1994): 443–63.

———. *The Shi'is of Iraq*. Princeton: Princeton University Press, 1994.

Silverman, Michael E. *Awakening Victory: How Iraqi Tribes and American Troops Reclaimed Al Anbar and Defeated Al Qaeda in Iraq*. Oxford: Casemate, 2011.

Stevens, Ethel Stefana. *Folk Tales of Iraq*. Oxford: Oxford University Press, 1931.

Toth, Anthony B. "Conflict and a Pastoral Economy: The Costs of Akhwan Attacks on Tribes in Iraq, 1922–29." *Critique: Critical Middle Eastern Studies* 11, no. 2 (September 2002): 201–27.

———. "Tribes and Tribulations: Bedouin Losses in the Saudi and Iraqi Struggles Over Kuwait's Frontiers, 1921–1943." *British Journal of Middle Eastern Studies* 32, no. 2 (November 2005): 145–67.

Ucko, David. "Militias, Tribes and Insurgents: The Challenge of Political Reintegration in Iraq." *Conflict, Security & Development* 8, no. 3 (September 2008): 341–73.

Israel

Abu Rabi'a, Aref. *A Bedouin Century: Education and Development among the Negev Tribes in the 20th Century*. Oxford: Berghahn Books, 2001.

———. *Bedouin Justice*. Jerusalem: Beit Al Maqdas, 2001. (Arabic.)

———. *The Negev Bedouin and Livestock Rearing*. Oxford: Berg, 1994.

Abu Rabia, Aref, and D. Barnes. *Statistical Data about Bedouin Schools*. Research Report to the Ministry of Education. Beersheba: Ministry of Education, 1998.

Ashkenazi, Tuvia. *Tribus Semi Nomades de la Palestine du Nord*. Paris: Geuthner, 1939.

Bailey, Clinton. "The Negev in the Nineteenth Century: Reconstructing History from Bedouin Oral Traditions." *Asian and African Studies* 14 (1980): 35–80.

Burckhardt, John. *Travels in Syria and the Holy Land*. London: John Murray, 1822.

Dinero, Steven C. "Resettlement and Modernization in Post-Nomadic Bedouin Society: The Case of Segev Shalom, Israel." *Journal of Planning Education and Research* 15, no. 2 (January 1996): 105–16.

Dyer, Caroline, ed. *The Education of Nomadic Peoples: Issues, Provisions and Prospects*. Oxford: Berghahn, 2005.

Falah, Ghazi. *The Role of the British Administration in the Sedenterization of the Bedouin Tribes in Northern Palestine 1918–1948*. Durham: Center for Middle Eastern and Islamic Studies, University of Durham, 1983.

Gerber, Haim. *Ottoman Rule in Jerusalem, 1890–1914*. Berlin: Klaus Schwarz Verlag, 1985.

Ma'oz, Moshe, ed. *Studies on Palestine during the Ottoman Period*. Jerusalem: Magnes Press, the Hebrew University, Institute of Asian and African Studies, and Yad Itzhak Ben-Zvi, 1975.

Marx, Emanuel. *Bedouin of the Negev*. Manchester: Manchester University Press, 1967.

Meir, Avinoam. *As Nomadism Ends: The Israeli Bedouin of the Negev*. Boulder, CO: Westview Press, 1997.

Meir, Avinoam, and Yosef Ben-David. "Welfare Support for Israeli Negev Bedouin Elderly Men: Adaptation during Spatioecological Transformation." *The Gerontologist* 33, no. 3 (June 1993): 308–14.

Muhsam, Helmut Victor. *Bedouin of the Negev: Eight Demographic Studies*. Jerusalem: Jerusalem Academic Press, 1966.

Suwaed, Muhammad. *Al-Budo Fi Falastin Al-Hakba Al-Otmaniya: 1516–1914*. Amman, Jordan: Dar Zahran, 2008. (Arabic.)

———. *Relations between the Bedouins and the Jewish Settlement in Palestine during the British Mandate: 1918–1948*. New York: Edwin Mellen Press, 2014.

Jordan

Alon, Yoav. "The Balqa' revolt: Tribes and Early State-Building in Transjordan." *Die Welt des Islams* 46, no. 1 (2006): 7–42.

———. *The Making of Jordan: Tribes, Colonialism and the Modern State*. London: Tauris, 2007.

———. "Tribes and State-Formation in Mandatory Transjordan," *Civil Wars* 8, no. 1 (2006): 66–82.

Antoun, R. T. "Civil Society, Tribal Process, and Change in Jordan: An Anthropological View." *International Journal of Middle East Studies* 32 (2000): 441–63.

Helms, Svend. *Early Islamic Architecture of the Desert: A Bedouin Station in Eastern Jordan*. Edinburgh, Scotland: Edinburgh University Press, 1990.

Jureidini, Paul A., and R. D. McLaurin. *Jordan: The Impact of Social Change on the Role of the Tribes*. New York: Praeger, 1984.

Layne, Louise Linda. *Home and Home Land: The Dialogics of Tribal and National Identities in Jordan*. Princeton, NJ: Princeton University Press, 2001.

———. "Tribalism: National Representations of Tribal Life in Jordan." *Urban Anthropology and Studies of Cultural Systems and World Economic Development* 16, no. 2 (1987): 183–203.

Lewis, Norman N. *Nomads and Settlers in Syria and Jordan, 1800–1980*. Cambridge: Cambridge University Press, 1987.

Nabulsi, Abdalla. "Mating Patterns of the Abbad Tribe in Jordan." *Biodemography and Social Biology* 42, nos. 3–4 (1995): 162–74.

Rowe, A. "The Exploitation of an Arid Landscape by a Pastoral Society—the Contemporary *Badiya* of Jordan." *Applied Geography* 19, no. 4 (1999): 345–61.

Shryock, Andrew J. "Bedouin in Suburbia: Redrawing the Boundaries of Urbanity and Tribalism in Amman, Jordan." *Arab Studies Journal* 5, no. 1 (1997): 40–56.

———. *Nomadism and the Genealogical Imagination: Oral History and Textual Authority in Tribal Jordan*. Berkeley: University of California Press, 1997.

———. "Popular Genealogical Nationalism: History Writing and Identity among the Balga Tribes of Jordan." *Comparative Studies in Society and History* 37, no. 2 (1995): 325–57.

Weir, Shelagh. *The Bedouin: Aspects of the Material Culture of the Bedouin of Jordan*. London: World of Islam Festival, 1976.

Yom, Sean L. "Tribal Politics in Contemporary Jordan: The Case of the Hirak Movement." *The Middle East Journal* 68, no. 2 (Spring 2014): 229–47.

Kuwait

Al-Kandari, Yagoub Yousif, and Ibrahim Naji Al-Hadben. "Tribalism, Sectarianism and Democracy in Kuwaiti Culture." *Digest of Middle Eastern Studies* 19, no. 2 (2010): 268–85.

Casey, Michael S. *The History of Kuwait.* Westport, CT: Greenwood, 2007.

Dickson, Harold Richard Patrick. *The Arab of the Desert: A Glimpse into Badawin Life in Kuwait and Sa'udi Arabia*. London: George Allen and Unwin, 1951.

———. *Kuwait and Her Neighbors*. London: George Allen and Unwin, 1968.

Toth, Anthony B. "Tribes and Tribulations: Bedouin Losses in the Saudi and Iraqi Struggles over Kuwait's Frontiers, 1921–1943." *British Journal of Middle Eastern Studies* 32, no. 2 (November 2005): 145–67.

Lebanon

Bhattacharya, A. N., and M. Harb. "Sheep Production on Natural Pasture by Roaming Bedouins in Lebanon." *Journal of Range Management* 26, no. 4 (July 1973): 266–69.

Chatty, Dawn. "Bedouins in Lebanon: The Transformation of Life or an Attitude?" *International Journal of Migration, Health and Social Care* 6, no. 3 (2010): 21–30.

———. "Introduction: Bedouin in Lebanon: Migration, Settlement, Health Care and Policy." *International Journal of Migration, Health and Social Care* 6, no. 3 (2010): 19–20.

Chatty, Dawn, Nisrine Mansour, and Nasser Yassin. "Bedouin in Lebanon: Social Discrimination, Political Exclusion, and Compromised Health Care." *Social Science & Medicine* 82 (April 2013): 43–50.

Harris, William. *Lebanon: A History, 600–2011*. Oxford: Oxford University Press, 2012.

Libya

Ahmida, Ali A. "From Tribe to Class: The Origins and the Politics of Resistance in Colonial Libya." *Africa* 63, no. 2 (2008): 297–310.

Bates, Oric. *The Eastern Libyans: An Essay*. London: Frank Cass, 1970.

Behnke, Roy H. *The Herders of Cyrenaica: Ecology, Economy and Kinship among the Bedouin of Eastern Libya*. Urbana: University of Illinois Press, 1980.

Evans-Pritchard, Edward Evan, *The Sanusi of Cyrenaica.* Oxford: Clarendon Press, 1949.

Faraj, Najem. Tribe, Islam and State in Libya: Analytical Study of the Roots of the Libyan Tribal Society and Interaction up to the Qaramanli Rule (1711–1835). PhD dissertation, University of Westminster, School of Social Sciences, Humanities and Languages, London, England, 2004.

First, Ruth. *Libya: The Elusive Revolution*. New York: Penguin Books, 1974.

Hweio, Haalo. "Tribes in Libya: From Social Organization to Political Power." *African Conflict & Peacebuilding Review* 2, no. 1 (Spring 2012): 111–21.

Khadduri, Majid. *Modern Libya: A Study in Political Development*. Baltimore, MD: Johns Hopkins University Press, 1963.

Lacher, Wolfram. "Families, Tribes and Cities in the Libyan Revolution." *Middle East Policy* 18, no. 4 (Winter 2011): 140–54.

Toktamış, Kumru. "Tribes and Democratization/De-democratization in Libya." *Challenges to Democratic Governance in Developing Countries* 11 (2014): 121–36.

Mauritania

Bousquet, Georges-Henri. *Les Berbères*. Paris: Presses Universitaires de France, 1957.

Bovill, Edward William. *The Golden Trade of the Moors*. London: Oxford University Press, 1958.

Chappelle, Jean. *Nomades Noirs du Sahara*. Paris: Plon, 1958.

Klein, Martin. *Slavery and Colonial Rule in French West Africa*. Cambridge: Cambridge University Press, 1998.

Kowalska-Lewicka, Anna. *Mauretania*. Warsaw, Poland: Wiedza Powszechna, 1976.

Marchesin, Phillippe. *Tribus, Ethnies et Pouvoir en Mauritanie*. Paris: Karthala, 1992.

Marty, Paul. *Les Tribus de la Haute Mauritanie*. Paris: Comité de l'Afrique Française, 1945.

Office National de la Statistique. *Mauritanie: Enquête Démographique et de la Santé. 2000–2001*. Nouakchott, Mauritania: Office National de la Statistique, 2001.

Ould Cheikh, Abdel Wedoud. *Eléments d'Histoire de la Mauritanie*. Nouakchott, Mauritania: Centre Culturel Français Antoine St. Exupéry, 1991.

Sigman, Marlene C. "The Romans and the Indigenous Tribes of Mauritania Tingitana." *Historia* 26, no. 4 (1977): 415–39.

Taylor, Raymond. Of Disciples and Sultans: Power, Authority and Society in the Nineteenth Century Mauritanian Gebla. PhD dissertation, University of Illinois at Urbana-Champaign, 1996.

Morocco

Abu-Nasr, Jamil M. *A History of the Maghreb*. Cambridge: Cambridge University Press, 1971.

Ait Hamza, M. *Mobilité Socio-Spatiale et Développement Local au Sud de L'Atlas Marocain (Dadès-Todgha)*. Passau, Germany: Verlag GmbH, 2002.

Amahan, Ali. *Mutations Sociales dans le Haut Atlas: Les Ghoujdama*. Rabat, Morocco: Editions La Porte, 1998.

Azam, Paul. *Sédentaires et Nomades dans le Sud Marocain: le Coude de Dra*. Paris: CHEAM no. 1009, 1946.

Berque, Jacques, and Paul Pascon. *Structures Sociales du Haut-Atlas suivi de Retour aux Seksawa*. Paris: Presses Universitaires de France, 1978.

Boughdadi, Mohamed. *Le Passé et le Présent Marocains du Sahara*. Casablanca: Editions Maroc-Soir, 1998.

Capot-Rey, Robert. *Le Sahara Français*. Paris: Presses Universitaires de France, 1953.

Drague, Georges. *Esquisse d'Histoire Religieuse du Maroc*. Paris: Peyronnet, 1951.

Ensel, Remco. *Saints and Servants: Hierarchical Interdependence between Shurfa and Haratin in the Moroccan Deep South*. Amsterdam, Netherlands: Universiteit van Amsterdam, 1998.

Gellner, Ernest. *The Saints of the Atlas*. Chicago: University of Chicago Press, 1969.

Gellner, Ernest, and Charles Micaud, eds. *Arabs and Berbers: From Tribe to Nation in North Africa*. London: Allen & Unwin, 1972.

Hart, David M. *The Ait Atta of Southern Morocco: Daily Life and Recent History*. Cambridge: Middle East and North African Studies Press, 1984.

Jacques-Meunié, Djamila. "Hiérarchie Sociale au Maroc Présaharien." *Hesperis* 45, nos. 3–4 (1958): 137–50.

Kenbib, Mohammed, ed. *La Grande Encyclopédie du Maroc: Histoire*. Rabat, Morocco: GEM, 1987.

Montagne, Robert. *Les Berbères et les Makhzen dans le sud du Maroc*. Paris: Alcan, 1930.

Norris, Harry T. *The Arab Conquest of the Western Sahara*. Harlow, England: Longman; Beirut, Lebanon: Librairie du Liban, 1986.

Seddon, David. *Moroccan Peasants: A Century of Change in the Eastern Rif 1870–1970*. Folkestone, England: Dawson, 1981.

Vinogradov, Andrey R. *The Ait Nahir of Morocco: A Study of the Social Transformation of a Berber Tribe*. Ann Arbor: University of Michigan Museum of Anthropology Papers, 1974.

Oman

Chatty, Dawn. "The Bedouin of Central Oman." *Journal of Oman Studies* 6, no. 1 (1984): 149–63.

———. *Mobile Pastoralists: Development Planning and Social Change in Oman*. New York: Columbia University Press, 1996.

Janzen, Jorg. *Nomads in the Sultanate of Oman*. Boulder, CO: Westview Press, 1986.

Wikan, Unni. *Behind the Veil in Arabia: Women in Oman*. Baltimore, MD: Johns Hopkins University Press, 1982.

Wilkinson, John C. *The Imamate Tradition of Oman*. Cambridge: Cambridge University Press, 1987.

Saudi Arabia

Ageili, Mahmoud. The Settlement of the Nomadic Tribes in the Northern Province. PhD dissertation, University of Manchester, England, 1986.

Alabbadi, Abdullah. *Nomadic Settlement in Saudi Arabia: A Semi-Historical and Analytical Case Study*. Lansing: Michigan State University, 1981.

Al-Rasheed, Madawi. *A History of Saudi Arabia*. Cambridge: Cambridge University Press, 2002.

Al-Rasheed, Madawi, and R. Vitalis. *Counter-Narratives: History, Contemporary Society, and Politics in Saudi Arabia and Yemen*. London: Palgrave Macmillan, 2004.

Blunt, Lady Anne. *A Pilgrimage to Nejd*. London: John Murray, 1881.

Doumato, Eleanor. *Getting God's Ear: Women, Islam and Healing in Saudi Arabia and the Gulf*. New York: Columbia University Press, 2000.

Ebrahim, Mohammed Hossein S. *Problems of Nomad Settlement in the Middle East with Special Reference to Saudi Arabia and the Haradh Project*. Ithaca, NY: Cornell University Press, 1981.

Fabietti, Ugo. "Control and Alienation of Territory among the Bedouin of Saudi Arabia." *Nomadic Peoples* 20 (1986): 33–40.

Farra, Osman Taha. The Effects of Detribalizing the Bedouin on the Internal Cohesion of an Emerging State: The Kingdom of Saudi Arabia. PhD dissertation, University of Pittsburgh, PA, 1973.

Fattah, Hala. *The Politics of Regional Trade in Iraq, Arabia, and the Gulf, 1745–1900*. Albany: State University of New York, 1997.

Garba, Shaibu Bala. "Managing Urban Growth and Development in the Riyadh Metropolitan Area, Saudi Arabia." *Habitat International* 28, no. 4 (December 2004): 593–608.

Gardner, Andrew. "The New Calculus of Bedouin Pastoralism in the Kingdom of Saudi Arabia." *Society for Applied Anthropology* 62, no. 3 (2003): 267–76.

Goldrup, Lawrence Paul. *Saudi Arabia, 1902–1932: The Development of a Wahhabi Society*. Berkeley: University of California Press, 1971.

Habib, John S. *Ibn Saud's Warriors of Islam.* Leiden, Netherlands: Brill, 1978.

Hajrah, Hassan Hamza. *Public Land Distribution in Saudi Arabia*. London: Longman, 1982.

Helms, Christine Moss. *The Cohesion of Saudi Arabia*. Baltimore, MD: Johns Hopkins University Press, 1981.

Ibrahim, Saad Eddin, and Donald Powell Cole. *Saudi Arabian Bedouin: An Assessment of Their Needs*. Cairo: American University of Cairo Press, 1978.

Jaussen, Antonin P. *Coutumes des Arabes au pays de Moab*. Paris: Victor Lecoffre, 1908.

Katakura, Motoko. *Bedouin Village: A Study of a Saudi Arabian People in Transition*. Tokyo: University of Tokyo Press, 1977.

Kostiner, Joseph. *The Making of Saudi Arabia, 1916–1936*. New York: Oxford University Press, 1993.

Kupershock, P. M. *Oral Poetry and Narratives from Central Arabia: Bedouin Poets of the Dawasir Tribe. Between Nomadism and Settlement in Southern Najd*. Leiden, Netherlands: Brill, 1999.

Lacey, Robert. *The Kingdom: Arabia and the House of Saud*. New York: Avon Books, 1981.

Lancaster, William. *The Rwala Bedouin Today.* Prospect Heights, IL: Waveland Press, 1997.

Meeker, Michael E. *Literature and Violence in North Arabia.* Cambridge: Cambridge University Press, 1979.

Montagne, Robert. "Notes sur la vie sociale et politique des Chammar du Nejd." *Revue des Etudes Islamiques* 6 (1932): 61–79.

Musil, Alois. *The Manners and Customs of the Rwala Bedouins.* New York: American Geographical Society, 1928.

Nawaq, Alhamzi. *The Shararat Tribe*. Beirut, Lebanon: Risala, 1993. (Arabic.)

Philby, Harry St. John. *The Heart of Arabia. A Record of Travel and Exploration.* London: Constable, 1922.

Raswan, Carl R. *The Black Tents of Arabia.* London: Paternoster Library, 1936.

Sowayan, Sa'd Abdullah. *Nabati Poetry: The Oral Poetry of Arabia*. Berkeley: University of California Press, 1985.

Sweet, Louise E. "Camel Raiding of North Arabian Bedouin." *American Anthropologist* 67, no. 5 (October 1965): 1132–50.

Tamisier, Maurice. *Voyage en Arabie.* Paris: Louis des Essarts, 1840.

Vassiliev, Alexei. *The History of Saudi Arabia.* New York: New York University Press, 2000.

Sudan

Abd el-Ghaffer, Mohammed A. *Shaykhs and Followers: Political Struggle in the Rafa'a Al-Hoi Nazirate in the Sudan*. Khartoum, Sudan: Khartoum University Press, 1973.

Arkell, A. John. *A History of the Sudan, from the Earliest Times to 1821*. London: University of London, 1961.

Cunnison, Ian. *The Baggara Arabs: Power and Lineage in a Sudanese Nomadic Tribe*. London: Oxford University Press, 1966.

Dahl, Gudrun, and Hjort Anders. *Responsible Man: The Atmaan Beja of North-Eastern Sudan*. Uppsala, Sweden: Nordiska Afrikaninstituet, 1991.

Grandin, Nicole. *Le Soudan Nilotique et l'Administration Britannique (1898–1956)*. Leiden, Netherlands: Brill, 1989.

Hasan, Yusuf Fadl. *The Arabs and the Sudan*. Edinburgh, Scotland: Edinburgh University Press, 1967.

MacMichael, Harold Alfred. *A History of the Arabs in the Sudan*. Cambridge: Cambridge University Press, 2011.

Paul, Andrew. *A History of the Beja Tribes of the Sudan*. Cambridge: Cambridge University Press, 2012.

Sanchez, Nicolas. "The Local Variability of Rainfall and Tribal Institutions: The Case of Sudan." *Journal of Economic Behavior & Organization* 39, no. 3 (July 1999): 263–91.

Sorbo, Gunnar. *Tenants and Nomads in Eastern Sudan*. Khartoum, Sudan: Khartoum University Press, 1985.

Teraifi, Al-Agab Ahmed, ed. *Decentralization in Sudan*. London: Oxford University Press, 1987.

Syria

Ashkenazi, Touvia. "The 'Anazah Tribes." *Southwestern Journal of Anthropology* 4, no. 2 (Summer 1948): 222–39.

Aurenche, Olivier, ed. *Nomades et Sédentaires Perspectives Ethnoarchéologiques*. Paris: Editions Recherche sur les civilisations, 1984.

Barbir, Karl. *Ottoman Rule in Damascus*. Princeton, NJ: Princeton University Press, 1980.

Batatu, Hanna. *Syria's Peasantry, the Descendants of Its Lesser Rural Notables, and Their Politics*. Princeton, NJ: Princeton University Press, 1999.

Bell, Gertrude. *Syria, the Desert and the Sown*. London: W. Hernman, 1907.

Boucheman, Albert de. *Matériel de la Vie Bédouine Recueilli dans le Désert de Syria.* Damascus, Syria: Institut Français de Damas, 1953.

Chatty, Dawn. "The Bedouin in Contemporary Syria: The Persistence of Tribal Authority and Control." *Middle East Journal* 64, no. 1 (Winter 2010): 29–49.

D'Hont, O. "Sédentarisation et Passage Récent au Nomadisme en Mésopotamie Syrienne." *Les Cahiers du Carnac* 1 (1991): 197–208.

Khoury, Philip S. "The Tribal Shaykh, French Tribal Policy, and the Nationalist Movement in Syria between Two World Wars." *Middle Eastern Studies* 18, no. 2 (April 1982): 180–93.

Meyer, Günter. "Promotional Measures and Present State of Development in the Field of Nomadism in Syria." *Applied Geography and Development* 19 (1982): 97–106.

Muller, Victor. *En Syrie avec les Bédouins. Les Tribus du Désert.* Paris: Leroux, 1931.

Perthes, Volker. *The Political Economy of Syria under Asad.* London: I.B. Tauris, 1995.

Teitton, A. S. "The Tribes of Syria in the Fourteenth and Fifteenth Centuries." *Bulletin of the School of Oriental and African Studies* 12, nos. 3–4 (1948): 567–73.

Thoumin, Richard. *Géographie Humaine de la Syrie Centrale.* Paris: Ernest Leroux, 1936.

Wachholtz, Rolf. Socio-economics of Bedouin Farming Systems in Dry Areas of Northern Syria. PhD dissertation, Universitat Hohenheim-Germany, 1996.

Tunisia

Anderson, Lisa. *The State and Social Transformation in Tunisia and Libya, 1830–1980.* Princeton, NJ: Princeton University Press, 1986.

Auclair, Laurent, and Mohamed Sghaier Zaafouri. "The Sedentarisation of the Nomads in Tunisia: Energetic Behaviour and Desertification." *Secheresse* 7, no. 1 (1996): 17–24.

Fozzard, Adrian. Tribesmen and the Colonial Encounter: Southern Tunisia during the French Protectorate 1882 to 1940. PhD dissertation, Durham University, England, 1987.

Idris, Hady Roger. *La Berberie Orientale sous les Zirides.* Paris: Adrien-Maisonneuve, 1962.

Turkey

Bruinessen, Martin Van. *Agha, Shaikh and State: The Social and Political Structures of Kurdistan*. London: Zed Books, 1992.

Finkel, Andrew, and Nukhet Sirman, eds. *Turkish State, Turkish Society*. London: Routledge, 1990.

Hammer, Emily Louise. Local Landscapes of Pastoral Nomads in Southeastern Turkey. PhD dissertation, Harvard University, Cambridge, MA, 2012.

Inalcık, Halil. *An Economic and Social History of the Ottoman Empire, 1300–1914*. Cambridge: Cambridge University Press, 1994.

Kasaba, Resat. *A Moveable Empire: Ottoman Nomads, Migrants, and Refugees*. Seattle: University of Washington Press, 2009.

Lindner, Rudi Paul. *Nomads and Ottomans in Medieval Anatolia*. Bloomington: Indiana University Press, 1983.

United Arab Emirates

Abdulla Muhammad Morsy. *The United Arab Emirates: A Modern History*. New York: Harper & Row, 1978.

Gareeb Edmund, Ibrahim Al Abed, eds. *Perspectives on the United Arab Emirates*. London: Trident Press, 1999.

Hawker, Ronald W. "Tribe, House Style, and the Town Layout of Jazirat al-Hamra, Ras al-Khaimah, UAE." *Proceedings of the Seminar for Arabian Studies* 36 (2006): 189–98.

Hull, Daniel. *Perceptions of the Past: The Role of Archaeology in the United Arab Emirates*. London: University of London, 2000.

King, David C. *United Arab Emirates*. Tarrytown, NY: Marshall Cavendish, 2008.

Rabi, Uzi. "Oil Politics and Tribal Rulers in Eastern Arabia: The Reign of Shakhbut (1928–1966)." *British Journal of Middle Eastern Studies* 33, no. 1 (May 2006): 37–50.

Scholz, Fred, and Rainer Cordes. *Bedouins, Wealth, and Change: A Study of Rural Development in the United Arab Emirates and the Sultanate of Oman*. Tokyo: United Nations University Press, 1980.

Yemen

Abu Ghanim, Fadil Ali Ahmad. *The Tribal Structure in Yemen between Continuity and Change*. Damascus: Arab Writer Press, 1985.

Al-Abdali, Samir. *The Culture of Democracy in the Political Life of the Tribes of Yemen*. Beirut, Lebanon: Centre for Arab Unity Studies, 2007.

Al-Dawsari, Nadwa. *Tribal Governance and Stability in Yemen*. Washington, DC: Carnegie Endowment for International Peace, 2012.

Bakr, Busheer. *The War in Yemen: Tribe Triumphs over Nation*. Beirut, Lebanon: Arab Institute for Studies, 1995.

Dresch, Paul K. *Tribes, Government, and History in Yemen*. Oxford: Clarendon Press, 1989.

Fattah, Khaled. "Yemen: A Social Intifada In a Republic of Sheikhs." *Middle East Policy* 18, no. 3 (Fall 2011): 79–85.

Jones, Clive. "A Tribal Order: Politics and Law in the Mountains of Yemen." *Middle Eastern Studies* 47, no. 2 (March 2011): 902–16.

———. "The Tribes That Bind: Yemen and the Paradox of Political Violence." *Studies in Conflict & Terrorism* 34, no. 12 (November 2011): 902–16.

Petersen, John E. *Yemen: The Search for a Modern State*. Baltimore, MD: Johns Hopkins University Press, 1982.

Weir, Shelagh. *A Tribal Order: Politics and Law in the Mountains of Yemen*. Austin: University of Texas Press, 2007.

Zahiri, Marzuki Maulud. *The Political Role of the Tribes in Yemen, 1962–1990*. Cairo, Egypt: Madbuli Bookstore, 1996.

About the Author

Muhammad Suwaed is a senior lecturer in the Department of Social Sciences in Western Galilee College and Kinneret College in Israel. He received his PhD from Bar-Ilan University, Israel. Dr. Suwaed specializes in the society, culture, and politics of the Middle East. He won the first prize of the prime minister of the state of Israel for his studies on the subject of the Bedouins in 1994. He was a laureate of the Research and Creation Prize of the Ministry of Science and Culture of the state of Israel in 2008. He has participated in dozens of international conferences. He published several scholarly articles and books on subjects related to culture and politics in the Middle East. They include *Relations between the Bedouins and the Jewish Settlement in Palestine during the British Mandate: 1918–1948* and *The Bedouins in Palestine in the Ottoman Era: 1516–1914*.

Lightning Source UK Ltd.
Milton Keynes UK
UKHW041511210223
417388UK00003B/7

9 781442 254503